Capability Britain - for a country that works

Will Podmore

ISBN: 978-1-8383868-8-7

Published By: -

i2i
PUBLISHING

i2i Publishing. Manchester.
www.i2ipublishing.co.uk

Acknowledgements
Contents page

Acknowledgements

This book is, more than most, the product of collective activity and thought.

I would very much like to thank all the following:

Steve Dodd and Phil Thompson for reading, commenting on and improving the typescript.

Tony and Muriel Coughlan.

Gill Wrobel and Kate Brown, Nick and Val Bateson, Anna McKeown, Keith Turner, Dave Blundell, Bob Davies, Rahim, Tony Strong and Eddie McGuire, for continual inspiration.

Especially to Pete Wrobel, for suggesting the cover photo, for his exemplary political and journalistic integrity, and for the chapter on the environment, which owes everything to his research and understanding of the science of climate change.

My (now) ex-colleagues at the University College of Osteopathy, especially James Barclay, Adele Sharp, Claire O'Donovan, Karl Holder, Husaina Waliji, Cormac O'Dalaigh, Myles King, and Ugo Ejionye, for their moral, intellectual and practical support.

Alistair McConnachie of A Force For Good.

My wonderful publisher, i2i's Lionel Ross, and i2i's brilliant editor Jasmine Carver.

None of the above is in any way responsible for any errors of fact or interpretation: any mistakes are all my own.

The library staffs of Redbridge, Southwark, University College London, and the School of Slavonic and East European Studies, especially for their invaluable Click-and-collect services during the lockdown.

For up-to-date news and views on these and other matters, please refer to the website cpbml.org.uk and to the magazine *Workers*.

Chapter 1
The long rise of democracy in Britain

'A topsy-turvy order'

Anglo-Saxon England had a form of collective decision-making; the 'king and his witans', his advisers. England took shape between the eleventh and fourteenth centuries, when the country's territory, government and law were unified. English government achieved unity across the realm by 1200 through its common law. A vigorous monarchy weakened feudalism. The territorial baronage disappeared at an early date. This cleared the way for the establishment of a centralised, unified state under the rule of law. Of all the countries that had been part of the Roman Empire, England had escaped most thoroughly from Roman imperial traditions, helping it to set up durable local units of government and political representation.

The Provisions of Oxford of 1258 were forced upon King Henry III (1216-72) by his barons, who were angered by the King's war in Sicily and its huge costs. The Provisions limited the King's power. A council of 15 barons appointed and replaced high officials. A parliament, consisting of the 27 most powerful barons, was to assemble three times a year to discuss with representatives of the realm the most important affairs of state. But in 1261, divisions among the barons enabled Henry to get the pope to release him from his oath to observe the Provisions. In 1264 the French King Louis IX, acting as an arbitrator, decided in favour of abrogating the Provisions. In the Barons' War of 1263–67, the barons were not supported by the knights and burghers so were defeated by the king. The clauses

1

of the Provisions that limited monarchical authority were then annulled.

The first English parliament was convened in 1265. *The Melrose Chronicle* of 1270 commented,

"England has sanctioned a topsy-turvy order.

It is astonishing, even in the telling; who has heard of such a thing?

For the body has aspired to be preeminent over the head;

The people have sought to rule their king!"[1]

In England, as the jurist Henry de Bracton asserted, "the law maketh the king."[2] As Winston Churchill observed, "law flows from the people, and is not given by the king."[3] Significantly for the development of democracy this was not Roman law. Churchill noted, "Digests and codes imposed in the Roman manner by an omnipotent state on a subject people were alien to the spirit and tradition of England."[4] As Blandine Kriegel observed, "Roman law privileged royal interest, returned a freedman back to slavery for ingratitude, did not allow a woman to plead for another person or bear witness to a will, prohibited a son from acquiring property without the consent of the paterfamilias. English law, on the other hand, protected the national interest, forbade the return to slavery of freedmen, allowed women to plead, and permitted sons freely to acquire property."[5] Roman law was patriarchal, giving great powers to fathers over all family matters. Common law by contrast stressed the rights of other family members. It emphasised the consensual and contractual nature of marriage, very much to the benefit of women and children.

Donald Kelley pointed out, "Corresponding to Roman imperialism in public law was the notion of property (*dominium*)

in the private sphere, and this, too, was a dehumanizing expression of power and a threat to liberty in the sense (which the Romans never knew) of subjective rights. Personal liberty, which is the first of all rights, has been threatened from two quarters. One is private property, which allows human beings to be treated as things and which is the premise of slavery in all its forms. […] The other threat is associated with the natural-law worship of the contract, which allows the alienation of human liberty. But freedom of contract to the contrary notwithstanding, human beings are not things; their humanity is not for sale or contract except in a speciously 'free' market; and only the sovereign state can ensure this first inalienable right."[6] Common law traditions, in which judges referred among competing lawyers and layman juries, was democratic. By contrast, the Roman law tradition of courts run by expert judges generally enhanced top-down control by the central state. Habeas corpus, a key element of the rule of law, was early seen as an implication of the idea of liberty espoused in the Magna Carta of 1215. In France, by contrast, habeas corpus was a late arrival: secret prisons and lettres de cachet survived until 1789.

The revolt of 1381 changed the country. The historian David Rollison noted, "The *comuynes* of 1381 were the first to raise the banner of popular sovereignty. It would prove a tenacious cause."[7] He continued, "1381 marks an obvious turning-point. It was the first time that common people rose in rebellion without the leadership and encouragement of magnates. In the period from *Magna Carta* to the deposition of Edward II, magnates led and commons followed. After 1381 the commons led and the governing ranks reacted."[8] This was a key step forward in the country's long social revolution achieved by the rising working class – the 'communes' or 'commonalty'. The first statute of *praemunire* came in 1392-3 under Richard II. Its purpose was to prevent anybody aiding and abetting any foreign jurisdiction, papal included, from interfering in the exercise of royal administration and justice. Over the centuries the crucial elements of life of production and reproduction - making the goods needed for life and for passing on that life through the family - increasingly dominated and eventually routed older aristocratic ways of life. This affirmation of the values of ordinary life was a form of social levelling which upset the previous social hierarchy. It led to ideas of the commonweal as a better form of society.

The Reformation

Century after century, successive Popes tried to assert their dominion over Britain. Finally, in response, the people of Britain launched the Reformation; a revolution breaking with a thousand years of the papacy, a struggle to liberate people's minds from the ties of Rome. They largely rejected mysteries, signs and wonders, obsessions with Dooms and Last Days, pardons, the Latin Mass and the cult of intercession on behalf of the dead in purgatory. They opposed healing shrines, sacred places and devotional and penitential pilgrimages. They rejected the corrupt practice of indulgences (remissions of punishment for sins). They opposed the monastic ideal, which neglected the service of widows, children and the poor in the selfish quest for personal salvation.

The people moved against the 600 religious corporations, the Pope's fortresses, which ran vast estates and made huge profits.

In 1535 the monasteries' total net income was £140,000, when the Crown's was £100,000. The monasteries were rentiers for two-thirds of their income, from whole estates put out to farm, from rents taken from smallholders, from tenements and from woods. Even their historian, Dom David Knowles, admitted, "monks and canons of England [...] had been living on a scale of personal comfort and corporate magnificence [...] which were neither necessary for, nor consistent with, the fashion of life indicated by their rule and early institutions." The people opposed the hierarchical, compulsorily celibate priesthood that assumed the right of sole mediation between man and God. People opposed a church hierarchy that claimed proprietorial rights over what people should think and believe. They opposed canon law, which had been the basis of the Western Church's international organisation for the past four centuries. They forbade appeals to the Pope and payments such as annates and 'Peter's pence'.

By the Act of Supremacy of 1534, the monarch became the head of the Church of England, able to decide its doctrine and appoint its leading officials. The Church would no longer be part of an international organisation, it would be part of the state, tamed and subordinate. Henry VIII's break from papal Rome made England a pioneer in creating a national church. Henry ended the study of canon law in England's universities. Unsurprisingly, some still defended the doctrines and trappings of traditional religion. Sir Thomas More, for one, upheld papal rule. His *Dialogue Concerning Heresies* of 1529 had a chapter 'concerning the burning of heretics, and that it is lawful, necessary well done'. In 1536 the 'Pilgrimage of Grace' in parts of the north of England was an attempt to throw back the

Reformation.

A series of laws between 1532 and 1540 destroyed monastic life in England and Wales and in half of Ireland too. In 1535 Henry ordered visits to the smaller monastic houses to ensure that they "shall not show no reliques, or feyned miracles, for increase of lucre." The Act of Suppression of 1536 ended 376 of the smaller houses. In 1538 Henry dissolved all the friaries, which gave fealty to the Pope. He dissolved the gilds, voluntary organisations where clergy prayed for the gild's membership. In 1538 Royal Injunctions ordered that the Bible in English be availabie to all, cementing the division between the Church of England and the Church of Rome. This stimulating reading and the use of the English language, ending the priestly monopoly of learning. Reformers urged people to go 'ad fontes', back to the sources.

The Reformation stimulated people to think for themselves, to compare and assess rather than contemplate and acquiesce. Some people developed a systematic and self-confident confrontation with all religious tradition, against all orthodoxy. Henry banned the selling of indulgences and had shrines dismantled. The Royal Injunctions of 1538 opposed "wandering to pilgrimages, offering of money, candles or tapers to images or relics, or kissing or licking the same, saying over a number of beads, not understood or minded on." In 1539 Henry suppressed the rest of the monastic houses. Henry kept Britain independent. He used some of the proceeds from the dissolution of the monasteries to build a strong navy and a string of forts along the south coast to deter French or Spanish invasion. These proved their worth in the 1545 Battle of the Solent, when his naval forces stopped an attempted French invasion.

The Injunction of 1547, Edward VI's first year, was to "destroy all shrines, covering of shrines, all tables, candlesticks, trindles or rolls of wax, pictures, paintings and all other monuments of feigned miracles, pilgrimages, idolatry and superstition." The state finally dissolved the chantries - chapels where priests sang masses for the founder's soul - and abolished the laws against heresy. The Reformation enabled the development of science, industry, history and archaeology. It promoted the investigation of material evidence rather than the study of texts and authorities. Amid the complexities and divisions of the Protestant world, there was far more room to manoeuvre, to question and innovate. 1547-48 saw the end of Henrician censorship. In 1549 and 1552 two successive editions of the Book of Common Prayer were issued, in English.

In the parishes of England, all that sustained the old devotion was attacked. The church furniture and images came down, the Mass was abolished, Mass-books and breviaries surrendered. The altars, veils, vestments, chalices, chests and hangings all were gone, the niches were empty and the walls were whitened. These were cultural losses accompanying the cultural gains. Land and properties were seized and sold to landowners and the bigger farmers, making the settlement impossible to reverse. Queen Mary tried to re-establish Catholicism, but few monasteries were restored, few new chantries were founded, few shrines were retrieved and few gilds revived. Purgatory was not preached and the Pope was still unpopular. Without the support of the religious orders, Mary's effort was doomed. Her failure proved that there was no going back. Monasticism, a major force in the world ever since the fall of the Roman Empire was over.

The great historian of the Reformation, Peter Marshall, summed it up: "the Reformation was not a mysterious, faceless force, obtruding upon individuals and their communities from somewhere beyond their reckoning. Rather, it was a transformative historical moment enacted by the calculations and decisions, sometimes heroic and sometimes shameful, of innumerable men and women, both great and small, at the centres of high policy-making and in myriad localities where ordinary people lived."[9] As he pointed out, "for thirty years and more, the English people had been party to, and participants in, an unrelenting series of arguments, concocted in print and pulpit, and continued in homes and taverns, about what God's laws actually were. The difficulties of identifying God's laws accurately shook to the core any residual assumption that kings, Parliaments or bishops could automatically be relied on to implement them correctly."[10]

He concluded, "The real significance of the English Reformation, I would suggest, lies not in the achievement, but in the struggle itself. Though never anything like an exercise in proto-democracy, the Reformation was nonetheless, from first to last, a vocal, vibrant national conversation, about issues of uttermost importance, and one from which few voices were ever entirely excluded."[11] Finally, the Reformation asserted the sovereignty and independence of Britain, a nation free from foreign ownership and control, "a noble and puissant nation rousing herself like a strong man after sleep, and shaking her invincible locks" in John Milton's magnificent words.

'The Happy Revolution' – 1688

In the seventeenth century the Stuart monarchs tried to roll back all these achievements. But the people did not want kingly absolute rule. Charles I's tyranny provoked a series of popular efforts to defend themselves. In the process they created practices and theories of society and government. The Commonwealth was an attempt to do without a monarch. It laid the foundation for the 1688 revolution, which would not have been possible without it, and it led to all the further steps towards democracy in the 1680s and 1690s. Steve Pincus, the leading historian of the 1688 revolution, noted, "unlike James and his advisers, the revolutionaries imagined that England would be most powerful if it encouraged political participation rather than absolutism, if it were religiously tolerant rather than Catholicizing, and if it were devoted to promoting English manufactures rather than maintaining a landed empire."[12]

Karl Marx wrote that the Glorious Revolution was 'the first decisive victory of the bourgeoisie over the feudal aristocracy'. The great eighteenth century jurist Sir William Blackstone agreed, writing that 'the happy revolution' marked the decline of feudalism and the full establishment of Britain's 'civil and political liberties'.[13] The historian of England's common law, Sir William Holdsworth, agreed, writing that in 1688, "the people, through their representatives, had assumed the right to make and unmake kings."[14] Historian Sir David Lindsay Keir agreed, "Sovereignty in 1688 was for practical purposes grasped by the people."[15]

William III's manifesto, the *Declaration of Reason*, went through 21 editions in 1688. Three printing houses each printed

20,000 copies. He gave supporters 3,000 copies each for putting into 'the hands of the generality of the nation'. Hundreds of pamphlets were written and distributed. People widely welcomed them. Pincus observed, "Popular uprisings, then, spread throughout England, Wales, Scotland, Ireland, and North America with bewildering rapidity in the autumn of 1688 and winter of 1689. In some cases, townspeople rose up against their governors; in others, aristocrats and gentry coordinated with their tenants and local yeomen to defy loyalist elements. An outpouring of popular support transformed William's Anglo-Dutch expeditionary force into a massive army."[16] Almost half of William's force was British.

Pincus noted, "By the late seventeenth century, most observers agreed, the English were extremely well informed about foreign affairs. [...] What news about foreign affairs did patrons of coffeehouse and country taverns, readers of newspapers and highbrow pamphlets, frequenters of the London exchange and country markets collect so eagerly? How did they understand the developments about which they so viciously gossiped? Instead of reacting with a visceral xenophobic reaction to all things foreign, Restoration English men and women placed the news they received within sophisticated ideological frameworks. They were eager to gather information about European power politics because they understood it and thought it vitally affected their lives. [...] This deep nationalist sensibility that was so profoundly challenged by the policies and actions of James II led the English to insist that ultimate political authority lay in the nation – though they disagreed whether the nation meant Parliament or the people more broadly defined. They claimed that their allegiance was to

English liberty, English religion, and English law rather than to a particular king. And the English of all social classes took political action based on those beliefs."[17] Pincus summed up, "The Revolution of 1688-89 was neither a *coup d'état* nor a foreign invasion but a popular revolution. Just as in the French and Russian Revolutions, there was extensive and violent crowd activity. And just as in other modern revolutions, the revolutionary events resulted not in consensus and compromise but in deep ideological cleavages."[18] He concluded, "the Revolution of 1688-89 represented the victory of those who supported manufacturing, urban culture, and the possibilities of unlimited economic growth based on the creative potential of human labor."[19] The industrial revolution has been called the industrial enlightenment, as industry and enlightenment advanced hand in hand.

The Revolution fostered revolutionary thinking about society and economics. Thinkers of the time developed the labour theory of value. Richard Blome wrote that it was the 'labour' of the lower orders "that improves countries, and to encourage them is to promote the real benefit of the public." John Locke wrote, "if we rightly estimate things as they come to our use, and cast up the several expenses about them, what in them is purely owing to nature, and what to labour, we shall find that in most of them 99/100 are wholly to be put on the account of labour."[20] Daniel Defoe wrote that it is 'manufactories' that "[are] the treasure of this nation, and keeps our exports to a balance with our imports; otherwise this kingdom would have been as poor as Spain, and as effeminate as Italy." James Whiston wrote that 'industrious inhabitants', not land, were the "original riches, as well as strength of the nation." John Cary wrote that it was 'the great interest of England to advance its manufactures'. Through manufactures "we not only employ our poor, and so take off that burden which must otherwise lie heavy on our lands, but also grow rich in our commerce with foreign nations, to whom we thereby sell our product at greater prices than it would otherwise yield, and return them their own materials when wrought up here, and increased in their value by the labor of our people."[21]

John Locke applied revolutionary thinking to political matters. He wrote, "the Legislative being only a fiduciary power to act for certain ends, there remains still in the people a supreme power to remove or alter the Legislative, when they shall find the Legislative act contrary to the trust reposed in them [...] the trust must necessarily be forfeited, and the power devolve into the hands of those that gave it, who may place it anew where they shall think it best for their safety and security. And thus the community perpetually retains a supreme power of saving themselves from the attempts and designs of any body, even of their legislators, whenever they shall be so foolish, or so wicked, as to lay and carry on designs against the liberties and properties of the subject. [...] the *Community* may be said [...] to be *always the Supream Power*."[22] Locke argued that in 1689 political power had reverted to the people and "when it is so reverted, the Community may dispose of it again anew into what hands they please, and so constitute a new form of government."[23] He wrote that absolute monarchy 'can be no form of Civil Government at all'.[24] He refuted the charge that the people cannot be trusted with the power of deciding when to revolt because they may be deceived by 'ill affected and factious men.' He asserted that even "where the welfare of millions is

12

concerned", it was still the case that *every man is judge* for himself [...] whether another hath put himself into a state of war with him."[25] Supporters of King Charles II, by contrast, denounced 'the sovereignty of the rabble', 'the dregs of mankind', 'a headless, a disordered multitude'.

The British people fought for a law-governed society, rightly seeing the rule of law as a weapon against royal absolutism. Law was not, in practice or in theory, a mere reflection of the interests of the rulers. People used the law, with its norms of equity and universality, as a defence against all forms of arbitrary power. In earlier centuries, before the Reformation, religion had been the guiding ideology, but had proved to be no defence against arbitrary and absolute powers. In the seventeenth and eighteenth centuries, the rule of law proved to be a better defence of British liberties. Many writers of the time backed the relatively new idea of making decisions by majority vote. The Dutch philosopher Hugo Grotius wrote, in the midst of the Dutch people's revolution for independence from Spain, "it is altogether unreasonable, that a greater Number should be governed by a less [...] the Majority would naturally have the Right and Authority of the Whole."[26]

Thomas Hobbes wrote, "the wish of the majority shall be taken as the will of all [...] they are bound by the decisions made by agreement of the majority. And that is a *Democracy* [...]"[27] Adding, "every one, as well as he that *Voted for it*, as he that *Voted against it*, shall *Authorise* all the Actions and Judgements, of that Man, or Assembly of men, in the same manner, as if they were his own."[28] Jean-Jacques Rousseau later agreed: "the vote of the majority always binds the rest."[29]

Chapter 2
The struggles for American independence, against secession and against slavery

American Revolution

In 1776, the American people acted to create a society based on these great democratic principles. Their revolution was an assertion of the American people's interests, sovereignty and independence against imperial rule. It was a revolution led by conservatives. It defeated the most powerful empire of its day. Any contribution to the advance of liberty elsewhere depended on the successful defence of liberty in America. 1776 helped to inspire the 1789 French revolution which destroyed the eighteenth century's worst absolute monarchy, then the world's greatest power. George III's supporters claimed that independence for America would bring 'inevitable ruin'. It would be 'ruinous, delusive, and impracticable'. The early American patriot James Otis defined democracy in its purest and simplest form as 'a government of all over all', in which 'the votes of the majority shall be taken as the will of the whole' and where the rulers were the ruled.

James Wilson, one of the founders of the USA, said in 1787, "The majority of people wherever found ought in all questions to govern the minority."[30] And in May 1778 the state of Massachusetts followed this advice and submitted its constitution to the people in the first general referendum ever held. President Thomas Jefferson wrote, "the will of the majority […] ought to be the law." New York's *Evening Post* wrote of the 'democratic theory […] that the people's voice is the supreme law." As President James Madison said, "the censorial power is in the people over the Government, and not in the Government over the people." Part of democracy was the free-for-all uproar of popular debate. Jefferson acknowledged the rancour of the 1801 election but called it the normal to-and-fro of a people able 'to think freely and to speak and to write what they think'. After the people had voted they would all 'of course, arrange themselves under the will of the law, and unite in common efforts for the common good'. According to the USA's Declaration of Independence, 'the Creator' is the source of rights. The Declaration refers to 'Nature's God' as the source of natural rights. But God, nature, kings, parliaments, bills of right, constitutions, laws, did not give and do not defend or guarantee our rights. The American Noah Webster noted in 1788 that written constitutions and bills of right could never guarantee freedom: "Liberty is never secured by such paper declarations; nor lost for want of them."[31] Only the people defended our common rights.

Majority Rule

The American people had to struggle to keep their new nation united. The slave-owners of the South constantly threatened to secede. President Andrew Jackson denied the right of any minority to break away from the United States of America. He said in his first message to Congress in 1829, "the majority is to govern." When in 1832 he faced the threat of separatism from the leaders of South Carolina, he said, "the crisis must be now met with firmness, our citizens protected, and the modern doctrine of nullification and secession put down forever."

Senator Daniel Webster agreed: "those who espouse the doctrines of nullification reject [...] the first great principle of all republican liberty: that is, that the majority must govern." Secession is anarchy. In the early nineteenth century, Supreme Court justice Joseph Story wrote, "in a conflict of opinion the majority must have a right to accomplish that object by the means, which they deem adequate for the end. The majority may, indeed, decide, how far they will respect the rights and claims of the minority [...] But this is a matter on which it decides for itself, according to its own notions of justice or convenience. In a general sense the will of the majority of the people is absolute and sovereign, limited only by its means and power to make its will effectual."[32] Some opposed majority rule, calling it 'mob rule', claiming that majority rule would destroy minority rights. This was class prejudice. Democracy as the sovereignty of the people did not in itself guarantee the protection of individual or minority rights, but it did not necessarily threaten them. It has almost always safeguarded these rights. Democrats trust the people.

The fight to end slavery

In the period from the 1650s to 1860s the key issue abroad was ending slavery and the slave trade. 9-12 million Africans were forced across the Atlantic, 3-4 million on British ships. In 1772, Lord Mansfield, the Lord Chief Justice, decided that no person, slave or otherwise, could be removed from England against his will. He declared that chattel slavery – the idea of people as property – was not supported by English law: 'on English soil, no man is a slave'. Joseph Knight, who had been a slave, was brought back to Perthshire from the West Indies. He wanted to leave the person who had brought him back. When the case went to the highest Civil Court in Scotland in 1778, Henry Dundas, the Lord Advocate in Scotland and the Chief Legal Officer for the Crown in Scotland, made and won the case for Knight. This case established that slavery was illegal in Scotland.[33]

The British Empire (including the slave trade) was built and run by and for the capitalist class. As Robert Tombs observed, "The truly 'imperialist' group in English society were those who ruled the empire, often inter-related families with a tradition of colonial service. They were few: those with direct experience of the empire, including soldiers, missionaries and families, were around 1.5 per cent of the English population, considerably more in Scotland and Ireland."[34] No British worker gained from empire. No British worker gained from slavery or from the slave trade. No British worker owned a slave - many did not even own a roof over their heads. British workers were not privileged. Only the members of the tiny minority ruling class were privileged.

British workers were not complicit in slavery or the slave trade. Only members of the tiny minority ruling class were complicit in slavery and the slave trade. The working class suffered enormously under the British Empire. The period that saw Britain become the 'workshop of the world' saw a sustained and brutal attack on British workers. In the early industrial revolution, children as young as four or five were put to work in the mines. Working hours shot up, so much so that the Cotton Mills and Factories Act of 1819 had to limit working hours to 12 a day – but only for children between 9 and 16! In 1840, 57 per cent of all working class children in Manchester died before their fifth birthday. Life expectancy at birth in Liverpool was just 15 years.

The vast profits from slavery and the slave trade went to the slave-owners and the traders and were hardly ever invested in Britain or in industry. Most was spent on creating beautiful country houses, estates and gardens. Oppression abroad bred oppression at home. Workers looked at the slavers and saw the same enemy they faced in the factories and in the countryside. The advanced section of the British working class - the trade unions and the Chartists - recognised the unity of purpose of black slaves and British workers organised for the emancipation of the whole working class. In the eighteenth century, San Domingo became the most successful colony in the Caribbean. By 1789 it was exporting sugar, coffee, cocoa, wood, indigo and hides. French ships would take slaves from the coast of Guinea to French ports to be loaded with goods to be sold to the colonists along with the slaves. By 1787, San Domingo was buying 40,000 slaves annually. Britain and France were rival empires.

The British government could see that San Domingo was buying slaves from British traders as well as French traders. Britain had enough slaves in the West Indies. If Britain could stop San Domingo from buying slaves, it could destroy San Domingo, which would do serious damage to France. The British Prime Minister, Pitt the Younger, asked his friend William Wilberforce to lead a campaign to abolish the slave trade. They may well have had heartfelt concern about the welfare of African slaves, but destroying French commerce in the Caribbean was also a motive. This is not to say that harming the main imperial rival was the real motive and that concerns about slaves' welfare were just hypocrisy. Popular opposition to slavery enabled them to seize the moral high ground and made their government look good. It was a policy of genuine moral worth, which should be applauded – Marxists do not reduce other people's motives just to selfishness. We are not cynics who deny all virtues to others.

Once launched, the struggle against the slave trade took on a logic of its own, going far beyond Pitt's original intentions. In 1792, Henry Dundas stated in Parliament, "That the slave trade ought to be abolished, I have already declared." He wanted to convince the powerful 'West India interest' that it was in their interests to abolish slavery. That was the only way he could get the Bill through the House of Lords. Dundas inserted the word 'gradual' into the Act to ensure that it speeded up the end of slavery. Those who now wax indignant should note that if the MPs then had followed their advice, the Act abolishing slavery would not have been passed that year, thus condemning slaves to yet more years of slavery. Some might call this being wise after the event. It is better than being unwise after the event.

Similarly, that the British government financially compensated the owners of slaves but made no reparation to the slaves for the appalling injustices they had suffered appears hugely unjust. This was, on the face of it, compounding the injustice, but if that was necessary to get slavery abolished throughout the British Empire, was it not a cost worth paying? The abolitionists who got the Act passed thought that the compensation scheme was necessary to ensure its passage.

On 25 March 1807 Parliament passed the Act for the Abolition of the Slave Trade. The Act abolished the trading of slaves in the British Empire. Although it did not abolish the practice of slavery, it did encourage British action to press other nations to abolish their own slave trades. Britain committed itself to stamping out the slave trade. In 1810 Britain signed a treaty with Portugal which insisted on a ban in the 'vile traffic'. Similar treaties followed with Spain, France, the Netherlands, and Sweden.[35] But when the war against France ended in 1815, it freed shipping across the world, enabling the reinvigoration of the slave trade. The treaties were routinely broken, ignored or abandoned and soon more slaves than ever before were forced across the Atlantic. In 1819, the British government created the Royal Naval 'Protection Squadron' to try to enforce the treaties.[36] In 1833 the Slavery Abolition Act was passed ending the practice of slavery in the whole British Empire. Who abolished slavery? Not a leader. Not William Wilberforce. Abolitionism was a mass movement, that is, a working class movement. The British working class abolished slavery. The Royal Navy played a key part in the worldwide struggle against the slave trade.

The Slave Trade Consolidation Act 1822, the Spanish Equipment Clause of 1835 and Palmerston's Portuguese Act (Act for the Suppression of the Slave Trade) 1839 allowed the Royal Navy to act far more effectively against the illegal slave trade. Implementing the 1839 Act brought Brazilian imports down from 45,000 slaves in 1838 to 10,000 in 1842. In 1849 the Navy finished off the Brazilian slave trade by seizing Brazilian ships in Brazilian waters and bombarding Brazilian slave ports. Historian Sian Rees summed up, "Over the sixty years of its existence, the Preventive Squadron freed about a hundred and sixty thousand slaves and lost seventeen thousand British seamen to death by disease, battle or accident. In 1869, the Preventive and Cape Squadrons merged. The slave trade was suppressed on the West African coast. Slavery was abolished in North America and Cuba."[37]

The Royal Navy played a progressive role in other struggles. As its historian Ben Wilson wrote, "During Latin America's struggle for liberation from Spain and Portugal the Royal Navy's South America Squadron was a potent force. It did not actively intervene, but it prevented Spanish and Portuguese ships from operating freely." 'Only England, mistress of the seas, can protect us against the united force of European reaction', said Simon Bolivar, the liberator of Latin America. In 1825 British warships in the Tagus helped persuade Portugal to recognize Brazilian independence. The gains in trade were considerable. They also allowed Britain to take the moral high ground: the country favoured liberal constitutional governments against dictatorships and decrepit empires. The reason was straightforward. States governed by the rule of law and the consent of the people made good trading partners; illiberal absolutist regimes were unstable and risky for business. Britain, herself a constitutional monarchy, made herself the champion of freedom – when it suited her."[38]

The Royal Navy assisted the liberation struggles of Greece and Chile. In 1860 its ships gave cover to Garibaldi's Red Shirts when they crossed from Genoa to Sicily and again when they crossed from Sicily to Naples in their struggle to unify an independent Italy.[39] The struggle against slavery continued across the Atlantic where President Abraham Lincoln stood against slavery and for national unity. Under his leadership, the forces for union and democracy defeated the forces for secession and slavery. He pointed out that the Southern rebellion was 'largely, if not exclusively, a war upon the first principle of popular government – the rights of the people'.[40]

Thomas Jefferson wrote, "Because Sir Isaac Newton was superior to others in understanding, he was not therefore lord of the person or property of others."[41] Greater talents do not justify granting anyone greater legal or civil rights. There is of course no difference of natural talents between different races, or between the sexes.[42] Nothing could ever justify slavery. In his first inaugural address, of 4 March 1861, Lincoln said, "Plainly, the central idea of secession, is the essence of anarchy. A majority, held in restraint by constitutional checks, and limitations, and always changing easily, with deliberate changes of popular opinion and sentiments, is the only true sovereign of a free people. Whoever rejects it, does, of necessity, fly to anarchy or to despotism. Unanimity is impossible; the rule of a minority, as a permanent arrangement, is wholly inadmissible; so that, rejecting the majority principle, anarchy or despotism in some form, is all that is left [...]".

American historian Sean Wilentz commented, "As in all constitutional disputes, either the majority would acquiesce to the will of the minority or vice versa. [...] Permit a minority to secede and it would only be a matter of time before a minority within that minority would secede – a formula for chaos. [...] Secession flouted the bonds of nationality, but even more important, it repudiated democracy."[43] In the USA too, the struggle for democracy aroused revolutionary thinking. Lincoln said, "As labor is prior to and independent of capital" and as "capital is only the fruit of labor", then "labor is the superior of capital, and deserves much the higher consideration."[44] He said that members of his Republican party "are for both the *man* and the *dollar*; but in cases of conflict, the man *before* the dollar" - devoted, as they were, "to the *personal* rights of men, holding the rights of *property* to be secondary only, and greatly inferior."

In the American Civil War, the British working class consistently opposed the ruling class schemes to intervene on the slave-owners' side. Karl Marx wrote, "It was not the wisdom of the ruling classes, but the heroic resistance to their criminal folly by the working classes of England, that saved the west of Europe from plunging headlong into an infamous crusade for the perpetuation and propagation of slavery on the other side of the Atlantic [...] The fight for such a foreign policy forms part of the general struggle for the emancipation of the working classes." A Union victory would inevitably lead to the end of slavery.

Marx knew that the working class could influence public policy even when it had no parliamentary representation. Its mass demonstrations helped to achieve the end of slavery, Catholic emancipation, electoral reform and the ten hour day. Despite the dire consequences of the Union blockade on employment and despite the unremitting pro-slaveholder propaganda of the British press, British workers backed Lincoln and the Union. In the first three months of 1863 the working class held some 56 rallies calling for an end to slavery.

But all too many liberals backed the ruling class, arguing that the American South was an oppressed people rebelling against centralised, imperial tyranny. These liberals ignored the fact that the South was built on slavery. For Marx, democracy - however flawed – was better for workers, allowing them to organise for change. Marx and Engels called on the proletarian party of their 'backward' German fatherland to focus all efforts on creating a democratic, unified nation-state.

Chapter 3
Revolution and counter-revolutions

Russia's revolution

When World War One began, just 18 per cent of Britain's population had the vote, only slightly more than in Russia under the Tsar's absolute rule – 15 per cent. The British Empire had 350 million colonial subjects, none of whom were allowed a vote. World War One was a war between rival empires - Russia, France and Britain against Germany, Austria-Hungary and the Ottoman Empire - in which democracy scarcely figured. Russia excluded 85 per cent of the people from any say. Its parliament (the Imperial Duma) only existed from 1906, set up after the failed 1905 revolution. From 1907 noblemen, landowners and businessmen dominated. More than half the members of the 1912-17 Duma were nobles.

Wikipedia notes, "The war made the political parties more cooperative and practically formed into one party." This called itself the Progressive Bloc.[45] The government that the people overthrew in October 1917 was a relic of tsarism, not a democratically elected government. After three years of unnecessary and murderous war, opposition to its continuance was growing in all the combatant empires. In Russia, the Bolsheviks opposed the systemic injustices of both Tsarist despotism and of the war. Their programme of peace, land and bread became more and more popular. But the Russian government was determined to fight on and determined to crush the calls for peace. The rival empires could not rely on appeals to imperial ideals to win support for their war efforts. They were forced to appeal to popular ideas of nation and democracy. Indeed one of the Allies' key propaganda claims was that they were fighting for the rights of small nations, especially for 'plucky little Belgium'. The result of the war was supposed to be a victory for peoples' rights to democracy and national freedom. US President Woodrow Wilson promised to make the world safe for democracy, which included the democratic right of national self-determination.

At the war's end, peoples across the world demanded national independence and democracy. Wilson promised self-determination but then backed the British, French and Japanese governments as they reimposed their imperial rule over subject peoples. This proved the bankruptcy of liberal anti-colonialism. The war discredited the claims of the rival empires to be agents of peace, progress, superior civilisation and national freedom, especially when the Bolsheviks exposed the Allies' secret treaties in which they had promised other people's lands to Tsarist Russia, Italy and Japan. This in turn stimulated the peoples of the colonies to take action to escape from the world of empires into a world of self-governing, democratic nation-states with equal rights to respect, a community of equals. In late 1917 the Bolsheviks won majorities in all the Soviets, bodies that were far more representative of the people than the Duma. At the 2nd All-Russian Congress of Soviets in October 1917, the Bolsheviks had 60 per cent of the delegates. They won 90 per cent majorities in the elections to the workers' Soviets, 60-70 per cent majorities in the Soldiers' Soviets, majorities in the Peasants' Soviets and majorities in the Soviets of Moscow, Petrograd and many other cities.

They had the majority of delegates to the First All-Russian

Conference of Factory Committees. The Constituent Assembly elected in 1917 was 78 per cent socialist. The Bolsheviks and their allies, the Left Socialist-Revolutionaries, had won majority support throughout the country. But Britain's Ambassador to the Tsar, Sir George Buchanan, did all he could to get the Tsar to beat down the democratic majority. In July 1917 he urged the Tsar to "crush the Bolsheviks once and for all."[46] He told the Lloyd George government, "normal conditions cannot be restored without bloodshed and the sooner we get it over the better."[47] The Russian government had appointed General Lavr Kornilov commander-in-chief of the Russian army. He launched a *coup d'état* and attacked Petrograd in August. The British and French governments at once backed the attempted coup but an army of workers and soldiers defended Petrograd, defeated the coup and arrested Kornilov.

Robert Bruce Lockhart, a British government agent in Moscow, kept Foreign Secretary Lord Curzon informed about his plot with Boris Savinkov: "Savinkov's proposals for counter-revolution. Plan is how, on Allied intervention, Bolshevik barons will be murdered and military dictatorship formed."[48] Curzon replied, "Savinkoff's methods are drastic, though if successful probably effective, but we cannot say or do anything until intervention has been definitely decided upon." The people foiled all these plots and propelled the Bolsheviks into power. The Russian working class had to seize power to save the people of the country from the Tsar's war and counter-revolution.

They knew that the Duma would not deliver peace or democracy. Historian Ronald Suny noted, "the Bolsheviks came to power in 1917 with considerable popular support in the largest cities of the empire – a case, as Terence Emmons puts it, that is 'incontrovertible'."[49] Suny explained, "The Bolsheviks came to power not because they were superior manipulators or cynical opportunists but because their policies as formulated by Lenin in April and shaped by the events of the following months placed them at the head of a genuinely popular movement."[50]

The Russian Revolution was an act of self-defence against violent counter-revolution. In the revolutionary days of 24-26 October [Old Style dates], fewer than 15 people were killed. As Robert Gerwarth pointed out, "this was an almost peaceful revolution. [...] compared to other revolutions the initial seizure of power by the Bolsheviks was remarkably non-violent."[51] The revolution was a democratic act, not the work of a minority. It was not a coup, the only coup was General Kornilov's failed attempt. On 28 October, there was a massacre, when counter-revolutionary Cadet Forces killed 500 unarmed soldiers of the captured Kremlin garrison. Russia would not have developed into a parliamentary democracy if the Bolsheviks had not taken power. The class forces that backed Kornilov and the other counter-revolutionary generals, the 'Whites', would have restored despotism. In the regions that the White generals later briefly governed, power moved fast from non-Bolshevik Soviets to anti-Soviet socialist regimes, then to socialist-liberal coalitions, then to the forces of counter-revolution. If the White generals had won, they would have enforced a dictatorship, just as General Francisco Franco did after the 1936-39 war in Spain.

By late 1917, the two alliances of rival empires had killed at least 10 million people and wounded 20 million. When the Bolsheviks led Russia out of the war a year early, they saved millions of lives and helped to end the war. Even so, Russia had lost two million killed, five million wounded and 2.5 million

POWs – more than any other belligerent and more than the other Allies' total losses. After the revolution, fourteen governments, led by the British, sent armies into Russia to back the Whites and restore the Tsarist autocracy. Their War of Intervention (1918-22), although hugely destructive, ultimately failed. Japan deployed 70,000 troops to occupy Russia's Maritime Provinces. In June 1922, Japan finally withdrew its forces from Russia's territory except for northern Sakhalin Island, which it occupied until May 1925. The Whites hated Jewish people as much as they hated the Bolsheviks. General Denikin's Volunteer Army murdered 100,000 Jewish people between June and December 1918.[52] Admiral Kolchak's men executed an estimated 25,000 people in the Yekaterinburg region alone.[53] The US commander-in-chief in Siberia said, "I am well on the side of safety when I say that the anti-Bolsheviks killed a hundred people in eastern Siberia to every one killed by the Bolsheviks."[54]

The aggressive intervention failed because, as General Edmund Ironside, chief of the general staff of the Allied forces, later acknowledged, "the majority of the population is in sympathy with the Bolsheviki."[55] Historian Clifford Kinvig later noted, "the Reds also enjoyed more popular support than their opponents."[56] Modern historians have acknowledged that the Soviet Union was defending itself against Western aggression, not vice versa. After its revolution, it was subjected to decades of a comprehensive blockade imposed by the Western powers.

This brutal blockade regime enforced on the Soviet Union throughout its existence (except during the years of World War Two) stopped it gaining from trading freely with other countries. Gabriel Gorodetsky pointed out, "Given the reality of capitalist encirclement and fears of renewed intervention, defence against the external threat was a prerequisite for the achievement of 'Socialism in One Country'.[57] Stephen Dorril observed that the British and US governments were "guilty of all the sins of subversion and interference, disregard for national sovereignty and war-mongering, of which they always accused their Cold War enemy, the Soviet Union."[58] Dorril noted that the NKVD was "an essentially defensive 'vigilant' organisation, primarily concerned with security and threats, both external and internal, against the USSR."[59]

Counter-revolutions in Europe

Subsequently, reactionary forces seized power in all too many European countries. In 1919 the Entente powers sent a mission to Hungary, led by British diplomat George Clerk. In November Clerk signed an agreement with Admiral Miklós Horthy under which Hungary's National Army would take over all the territory previously occupied by the withdrawing Rumanian Army and the Army would place itself under the command of a new government to be formed under Clerk's supervision. In November 1919, Horthy entered Budapest at the head of the Army and in 1920 he became the regent of Hungary. He ruled as a dictator until October 1944. In 1940 Hungary joined the Axis of Germany, Italy and Japan and in 1941 Hungarian forces joined in the attack on the Soviet Union.By 1942, tens of thousands of Hungarians were fighting on the eastern front in the Royal Hungarian Army. In 1917, Samuel Hoare, acting on behalf of the British government, paid British Intelligence funds to Mussolini.

As Conservative MP Henry Channon wrote in his diary, "[he] raised the money to form the Fascist party and finance the march on Rome. So English Government funds did much to create the Fascist revolution. This is very secret."[60] As Anthony Eden later wrote, "We built Mussolini into a great power."[61] In Italy's May 1921 general election, Mussolini's Fascist Party campaigned as part of Giovanni Giolitti's National Blocs, which won 105 seats, of which Mussolini's fascists won just 33. The Blocs came third behind the Socialist Party (123 seats) and the People's Party (108 seats). After the fascist march on Rome, Mussolini seized power in October 1922, overthrowing the elected government. He had the blessing of King Victor Emmanuel III and the support of the army and the business class. The British government supported Mussolini's coup. In May 1923, King George V and Queen Mary went to Rome to present Mussolini with the Knight Grand Cross of the Order of the Bath. In May 1926 General Pilsudski overthrew Poland's democratically elected government. In the same month, General Gomes da Costa overthrew Portugal's republican government after marching on Lisbon with 15,000 men. This coup installed a military dictatorship known as Ditadura Nacional, followed by António Salazar's Estado Novo, which lasted until the revolution of 1974.

The Soviet Union in the 1930s

In 1932 appalling weather wrecked the harvest in the Soviet Union. Some kulaks used the crisis to sabotage the collectivisation of agriculture. Isaac Mazepa, former president of the Nationalist 'government' in Ukraine in 1917-18, boasted that much of the crop shortfall was due to this sabotage: "At first there were disturbances in the kolkhosi [collective farms] or else the communist officials and their agents were killed, but later a system of passive resistance was favored which aimed at the systematic frustration of the Bolsheviks' plans for the sowing and gathering of the harvest."[62]

American historian Frederick Schuman wrote of the Ukrainian kulaks, "Some murdered officials, set the torch to the property of the collectives, and even burned their own crops and seed grain. More refused to sow or reap."[63] These kamikaze tactics, not the government's actions, worsened the famine. All through this tragic period, the Western powers maintained their ruthless blockade, preventing the Soviet government from buying food from other countries. The American historian Mark Tauger wrote, "New Soviet archival data show that the 1932 harvest was much smaller than has been assumed and call for revision of the genocide interpretation. […] the leadership […] did try to alleviate the famine. […] The harvest of 1932 essentially made a famine inevitable."[64]

Tauger explained, "The evidence that I have published and other evidence, including recent Ukrainian document collections, show that the famine developed out of a shortage and pervaded the Soviet Union, and that the regime organized a massive program of rationing and relief in towns and in villages, including in Ukraine, but simply did not have enough food."[65] He summed up, "Ukraine received more in food supplies during the famine crisis than it exported to other republics. […] Soviet authorities made substantial concessions to Ukraine in response to an undeniable natural disaster and transferred resources from Russia to Ukraine for food relief and agricultural recovery."[66]

Leading scholars of Russian history challenged the claim that the famine was a genocide. Adam Ulam wrote, "Stalin and his closest collaborators had not willed the famine."[67] "There is no evidence it was intentionally directed against Ukrainians," said Alexander Dallin of Stanford, the father of modern Sovietology. "That would be totally out of keeping with what we know - it makes no sense." During and after the Second World War, Ukrainian fascists tried to justify their collaboration with Hitler by claiming that collectivisation in the Soviet Union had killed seven million people. How did they arrive at this number? Not by research, but simply because they wanted to be able to claim falsely that the Soviets had killed more Ukrainian people than the Nazis had killed Jewish people. In World War One, the feudal countryside had failed to feed the cities and the army, but in World War Two the collective farms fed the cities and the Red Army. The American magazine *Life* observed on 29 March 1943, "[...] these large farm units [...] made possible the use of machinery [...] which doubled output [...] and released millions of workers for industry. Without them [...] Russia could not have built the industry that turned out the munitions that stopped the German army."

More recently, Matthew Klein and Michael Pettis confirmed, "Had the Soviet Union remained a primitive agrarian society, it could not have defeated the Germans, who had outmatched Russia in World War 1."[68] Without collectivisation the Soviet Union could not have industrialised. Without industrialisation the Soviet Union could not have created a modern army. Without a modern army it could not have beaten the Nazis. Capitalist forces, inside and outside the Soviet Union, fought to prevent these working class achievements. The Soviet Union had to fight a war of self-defence against internal fascism, supported from outside.

As those Russian archives opened in the 1990s show, during

the 1930s approximately 300,000 people were killed in this war. Anti-communists like Robert Conquest publicised hugely inflated figures for deaths in the Soviet Union in the 1930s. Richard Evans, Professor of Modern History at Cambridge University, explained how Conquest reached his figures: "Robert Conquest's *The Harvest of Sorrow: Soviet Collectivization and the Terror Famine* (New York, 1986) argues that the 'dekulakization' of the early 1930s led to the deaths of 6,500,000 people. But this estimate is arrived at by extremely dubious methods, ranging from reliance on hearsay evidence through double counting to the consistent employment of the highest possible figures in estimates made by other historians."[69] Professor Richard Overy, Professor of History at King's College London, agreed, "For years the figures circulating in the West for Soviet repression were greatly inflated. […] The archive shows a very different picture."[70]

More and worse counter-revolutions

In Germany's November 1932 election, the Nazis won 33 per cent of the votes, 11,737,395, which was two million fewer than in the July election. The Social Democrat vote was 7,251,690 and the Communist Party's vote 5,980,614. The anti-Hitler forces had the support of the majority of those who voted – over 13 million as against under 12 million for the Nazis. In the Reichstag the largest party was the Nazi Party with 196 members. Added together, the Social Democrats with 121 members and the Communists with 100, had more – 221. Tragically and disastrously, the Communist Party absurdly treated the Social Democrats as the main enemy, preventing the formation of any possible anti-Hitler alliance. Then in January 1933 Germany's President, Field Marshal Paul von Hindenburg, appointed Hitler as Chancellor. This forced on the German people a politician who had won the votes of only a third of those Germans who had voted. In February the Nazis burned down the Reichstag and blamed the communists. The American journalist William Shirer wrote, "There is enough evidence to establish beyond a reasonable doubt that the Nazis planned the arson and carried it out for their own political ends."[71]

In March the Reichstag passed the Enabling Act, which gave Hitler dictatorial powers. In 1935, Goebbels told the Nuremberg Rally, "National socialism confines itself to Germany and is not a product for export." He accused the Soviet Union of 'arming at a fantastic rate in preparation for a war of aggression'. He accused the Soviet Union of putting out false "stories of war preparations in the interests of German imperialism, preparations for a revanche against France, annexations, in Denmark and Holland and Switzerland, in the Baltic States and the Ukraine, etc. and a German crusade against the Soviet Union [...]."[72]

From 1933 onwards, most countries were still struggling to recover from the depression and with Hitler's coming to power, the great new issue facing the world's countries was whether to resist Nazi conquest or to accept it. With Hitler in power, the Soviet Union was under threat from Germany in the West and from Japan in the East. In 1931 Japanese forces attacked China and threatened the Soviet Union, which repeatedly tried to get Japan to sign a non-aggression pact. It refused. Conservative forces in Japan openly urged an attack on the Soviet Union.

Trapped in a fascist pincer, the Soviet Union sought allies to prevent the war they saw coming. But the British and French governments both thought that the Soviet Union was a greater enemy than Nazism. Conservative leaders in the 1930s believed that the survival of the British Empire was the supreme need: it was hardly surprising that they were quite happy to nudge Hitler into going east. Prime Minister Stanley Baldwin said in July 1936, "if there is any fighting to be done I should like to see the Bolshies and the Nazis doing it."[73]

Conservative MP Robert Boothby warned the House of Commons that some people were advocating unlimited concessions to Germany hoping that "a day will come when we shall get the Germans and the Russians fighting each other and everybody else can stand back; and then somehow or other, these two great menaces will 'do in' each other and we shall be free from Communism and Socialism and everything of that kind."[74] The drive to war accelerated when Neville Chamberlain replaced Baldwin as Prime Minister in May 1937. He firmly believed that the Soviet Union, not Hitler Germany, was the real danger to peace and civilisation. Nevile Henderson, the British Ambassador in Berlin, told the German government that "he entirely agreed with the Fuhrer that the first and greatest danger to the existence of Europe was Bolshevism, and that all other viewpoints had to be subordinated to this view."[75] Henry Channon MP, a loyal Chamberlain follower, said, "we should let gallant little Germany glut her fill of the reds in the East."[76]

John Simon, when Foreign Secretary under Baldwin, said that if Germany had to act "it is surely better that she act to the East."[77] Sir Alexander Cadogan, the Permanent Under-Secretary of State for Foreign Affairs, expressed the government's preference: "If the problem could be so simplified as to be put in the form of a question - Italy or Russia? - I would unhesitatingly plump for the former."[78] Chamberlain supporter Sir Arnold Wilson MP said on 11 June 1938, "unity is essential and the real danger in the world today does not come from Germany or Italy … but from Russia."

The British government and its supporters persistently worked to get Hitler to attack the Soviet Union.[79] In May 1936, Winston Churchill suggested a Western pact to deter German aggression in the West and to turn Germany to the East: "we should have to expect that the Germans would soon begin a war of conquest east and south and that at the same time Japan would attack Russia in the Far East. But Britain and France would maintain a heavily-armed neutrality."[80] As the Marquis of Zetland pointed out, Hitler would be deterred from fighting Britain and France by "a western pact [...] that would permit him to attack Russia while [...] prohibiting France from coming to Russia's aid."[81] This was the aim behind all the efforts in 1938 and 1939 to destroy France's alliances with the Soviet Union and Czechoslovakia. The trade union movement alone consistently and vigorously opposed the policy of collaboration with Nazi aggression. Allan Findlay expressed this in his Presidential address to the 1936 Trades Union Congress: "I would warn both the British Government and the German Government that British labour will never acquiesce in, but will fight strenuously against, any policy which secures temporary peace in Western Europe, whilst giving Hitler a free hand in Eastern Europe and against the Soviet Union."

Hitler and Mussolini intervene in Spain

In July 1936 General Franco launched his coup against the elected Spanish Republic. The Republic's Popular Front government was a broad coalition whose largest member was the Spanish Socialist Workers' Party, a social democratic party. MI5 sent a plane from Croydon Airport to the Canaries to pick up Franco and take him to Spanish Morocco.[82] Fascists like Franco had no scruples about seizing power when defeated in elections. Peaceful parliamentary methods had not been able to prevent fascist coups. Could the anti-Hitler forces in Germany have defeated Hitler using only peaceful methods? Any efforts to defeat murderous counter-revolutionary forces could not limit themselves to peaceful methods of resistance. So strong was popular opposition to the coup that by the end of the first week of the rebellion Franco was in danger of defeat.[83]

Germany and Italy at once began to ship in large numbers of troops and huge amounts of war materials, rightly convinced that Franco would lose without their aid.[84] The British government admitted - in private, "Help for the rebels was immediately forthcoming from Italy."[85] In public, it claimed not to know about the Italian intervention. From July to October, Germany flew 13,523 Spanish and Moroccan infantrymen across the Straits of Gibraltar to Seville. Known as 'Operation Feuerzauber' it was the first successful large-scale airlift in history. Franco could not have won without the forces that Hitler and Mussolini sent to Spain, the 30,000 German and 80,000 Italian troops. This well-armed and powerful fascist intervention defeated the Republic. As Hitler boasted to Mussolini's foreign minister (and son-in-law) Count Galeazzo Ciano, "Without the help of both our countries, there would be no Franco today."[86] Chamberlain agreed, writing in his diary of "Franco winning in Spain by the aid of German guns and Italian planes."[87] As a rule, generals' military coups do not win and hold power without the help of outside forces. Hitler and Mussolini helped Franco, US governments helped the generals of Greece, Brazil, Indonesia, Chile, etc.

The Cabinet Foreign Policy Committee admitted that the British and Italian governments had the same aim - to defeat the Republic: "The Italian Government have repeatedly made it plain that their principal desire in this Spanish business is to secure that Spain should not fall under the domination of a Bolshevist regime. His Majesty's Government are at one with the Italian Government in their anxiety that no such issue should result from the Spanish conflict."[88] Oliver Harvey in the Foreign Office recorded that "the Government are praying for Franco's victory ."[89] A Foreign Office Memo noted that "We had perhaps pinned our faith on the early victory of Franco."[90] On 1 June 1938, Chamberlain suggested to the Cabinet that Britain seize Minorca from the Republican government. The Cabinet decided not to do so, because "it would not do much to help General Franco."[91]

The British government began the policy it called Non-Intervention and kept it going to the end. This policy supposedly banned countries from sending arms and military forces to Spain. In practice it meant that the British government prevented countries from aiding the legitimate, elected Spanish government, while allowing Germany, Italy and Portugal to intervene to defeat the Republic. The British government chaired and led the Committee which organised the implementation of the policy. Germany and Italy, the intervening powers, were members of the 'Non-Intervention' Committee. As Claude Bowers, the US Ambassador to Spain, later summed up, "Each movement of the Non-Intervention Committee has been made to serve the cause of the Rebellion [...] this Committee was the most cynical and lamentably dishonest group that history has known." Alvarez del Vayo, the Spanish Republic's Minister for Foreign Affairs, later wrote of Non-Intervention that "It was the finest example of the art of handing victims over to the aggressor States, while preserving the perfect manners of a gentleman and at the same time giving the impression that peace is the one objective and consideration."[92]

The Labour Party supported Non-Intervention. It fiercely and successfully resisted trade union and popular pressure to end the farce of Non-Intervention. It opposed the Spanish government's legal right to buy arms to defend itself from attack. It opposed the call to send 'Arms to Spain.' Baldwin and Chamberlain rigged the fight while claiming to hold the ring. Non-Intervention blockaded only the Republic, enabling the fascist aggression to succeed. As Pedro Sainz Rodriguez, Minister of Education in Franco's first government, wrote, "the fundamental reason for our winning the war was the English diplomatic position opposing intervention in Spain."[93]

The British government always intended to leave the Spanish Republic alone and at the mercy of Nazi Germany and fascist Italy. Henry Stimson, a former American Secretary of State, wrote that the main responsibility for the Republic's defeat lay, not with the governments enabled to intervene, but with the British government which had prevented other nations intervening on behalf of the Republic. Stimson wrote that "If this loyalist Government is overthrown, it is evident now that its

40

defeat will be solely due to the fact that it had been deprived of its rights to buy from us and from other friendly nations the munitions necessary for its defence."[94] The British government's policy towards the war helped Mussolini and Hitler to achieve their aims, of crushing Spanish independence and democracy, of strengthening fascism and the Axis, and of weakening and separating Britain and France.

The British government's fanatical anti-communism led to the Republic's defeat and to victory for the most dangerous and anti-British forces in the world. Fascist aggression could have been checked and thrown back. Instead the Axis powers isolated and then attacked Austria, Czechoslovakia, Albania, France and the Soviet Union in turn. British policy made fascism confident enough to start the Second World War just six months after the end of the war in Spain. Anti-communism had endangered Britain's very survival: it had been in effect anti-Britain. Only the Soviet Union spoke out clearly and consistently for Spain and opposed Non-Intervention when its dishonesty was plain. The Soviet Union aided the Spanish Republic more than any other country did, until British-Italian naval collaboration cut off its supply routes to Spain. The Communist Party of Spain saw clearly that the overriding aim was to beat Franco and his Axis allies. Of all the Spanish parties, it fought longest and hardest, right to the end, for Spain's independence. The Republic tried to defend Spain by uniting it against the attack of the two major fascist powers. For Spain, this strategy ended in failure, but not because the strategy was wrong. After all, Spain's Popular Front government fought on against fascist aggression for three years. France's anti-Popular Front government fought for less than three months in 1940 before capitulating to Hitler.

41

The strategy of uniting the nation against foreign aggression worked for China against Japan, for the Soviet Union against Hitler Germany and for Vietnam against the USA. In each country, a Communist Party led the nation to victory over the invaders, to national liberation from the foreign occupier.

The Axis intervention in Spain had a lasting effect. A vicious fascist state, lasting until 1975, was imposed, over the dead bodies of nearly a million Spanish men, women and children. The immediate, but no less terrible, effect was to strengthen the Axis powers and the forces for war, while weakening those working for peace. The Axis powers benefited through military agreements with Franco, through their battle-hardening experience of war and through weakening Britain and France's strategic positions. All with the enthusiastic support of the British and French governments. Franco had stitched up the British government.

He proceeded to aid the Axis in the Second World War. His government seized Tangier from France in 1940. He gave the Axis the use of Spain's ports and bases and assisted it with secret police and espionage liaison. 40 per cent of Spain's exports went to Germany, including the vital war materials of ammonia, nitrogen, glycerine, iron ore, lead, nickel, zinc and tungsten. In 1941, Franco sent 100,000 Spaniards to work in Germany and 47,000 troops to fight for Hitler against the Soviet Union.

But the Spanish Republic in its defeat had still struck two vital blows for freedom, to the ultimate benefit of Britain and France. The resistance of the Spanish people had taken such a toll of Franco's forces that he was unable to open a front against France in the Second World War, not even in 1940. The Spanish Republic damaged the Italian forces and drained the Italian war-treasury so much that Mussolini could not join Hitler's onslaught until June 1940. When he did, his economic and military resources were so weakened that he was more hindrance than help to Hitler.

Chapter 4
Peace in danger

Attempted counter-revolution in the Soviet Union

In the Soviet Union, some generals and political figures tried to copy the Spanish generals and carry out a *coup d'état* in alliance with the fascist powers. One opposition conspiracy involved Marshal Mikhail Tukhachevsky, the Red Army's commander in chief. French journalist Genevieve Tabouis related that on 29 January 1936, "Tukhachevsky [...] had just returned from a trip to Germany and was heaping glowing praise upon the Nazis. Seated at my right, he said over and over again, as he discussed an air pact between the great powers and Hitler's country: 'They are already invincible, Madame Tabouis!'"[95] Should the Soviet Union have allowed a known defeatist to stay as its army's commander-in-chief? Later in 1936, Tukhachevsky held secret talks with Czechoslovakia's President Edvard Beneš and its Commander-in-Chief General Jan Sirový. There were no secretaries at these talks and no minutes were kept. Tukhachevsky then left Prague for talks in Berlin. Later, the Czech secret service told Beneš that the Nazis knew all the details of the Prague meeting. Beneš had to conclude that only Tukhachevsky could have given the Nazis these details. Should the Soviet government not have punished a commander-in-chief who gave confidential state and military information to the leaders of a power determined to destroy the Soviet Union?

Churchill affirmed, "communications were passing through the Soviet Embassy in Prague between important personages in Russia and the German Government. This was a part of the so-called military and old-guard Communist conspiracy to overthrow Stalin and introduce a new regime based on a pro-German policy. President Beneš lost no time in communicating all he could find out to Stalin. Thereafter there followed the merciless, but perhaps not needless, military and political purge in Soviet Russia, and the series of trials in January 1937, in which Vyshinsky, the Public Prosecutor, played so masterful a part."[96] There is documentary evidence of Tukhachevsky's collaboration with the Japanese – a report by Arao, a Japanese military attaché, on his secret contact with a representative of Tukhachevsky. Three of the nine senior officers accused in the 1937 trial of Tukhachevsky – Primakov, Putna and Tukhachevsky himself – had direct contact with the Nazis.[97] A German government document of 9 February 1937 showed that it believed that "there was a growing probability of a sudden turn of events very soon, the fall of Stalin and Litvinov, and the imposition of a military dictatorship."[98] Documents from the German Foreign Ministry showed that Germany's General Staff showed great interest in Tukhachevsky at this time, strong corroboration that Tukhachevsky was indeed planning a coup, as he confessed at his trial.

Josef Goebbels, Hitler's Minister of Propaganda, wrote later, "The Führer recalled the case of Tukhachevskii and expressed the opinion that we were entirely wrong then in believing that Stalin would ruin the Red Army by the way he handled it. The opposite was true: Stalin got rid of all opposition in the Red Army and thereby brought an end to defeatism."[99] The existence of an Opposition bloc and its treasonous contacts with the governments of Germany and Japan were the major allegations in the 1936-38 Moscow Trials. Leon Trotsky and his son Leon

Sedov always denied that any bloc existed and claimed that it was a fiction invented by Stalin. When the Harvard Trotsky Archive was opened to researchers on 2 January 1980, Pierre Broué and his team found documents that proved that the bloc had indeed existed.[100] In a letter of 1932, Sedov had written that the bloc "has been organised. In it have entered the Zinovievists, the Sten-Lominadze group and the Trotskyists (former 'capitulators')."[101] Trotsky always claimed that there had been no communication with Karl Radek and Gyorgy Piatakov, two of those accused of anti-Soviet activity. That was untrue. The Trotskyists had communicated with them. On 22 January 1937, Sedov said in an interview with the Dutch newspaper *Het Volk*, "The defendants in the first trial [...] had been exiled or arrested years before the start of the trial for their criticism and political activity: Smirnov three and a half years earlier, Zinoviev and Kamenev one and a half years before. Radek and Piatakov were two of the last supporters of Stalin and were totally committed to his ideas. The Trotskyists have had much less contact with them than with the others."[102]

As for the charge of treasonous contacts with Germany and Japan, the American historian Grover Furr wrote, "of the defendants at the three public Moscow trials eight men claimed to have heard directly from either Trotsky or his son Sedov about contacts between Trotsky and German or Japanese officials: Ol'berg, Piatakov, Radek, Shestov, Rakovsky, Krestinskii, Bessonov, and Rozengol'ts. One man, Sokol'nikov, heard of Trotsky's collaboration with Japan from a Japanese diplomat."[103] The conspirators intended, as American historian Alvin Coox concluded, "to conduct a putsch in the Far East and to reach agreement with the Japanese for help and for combined operations against the Soviet Union."[104] On 2 June 1937, Nikolai Bukharin admitted straight after his arrest with no protest, that he had been "a participant in the organization of the Rights up to the present, that he was a member of the centre of the organization together with Rykov and Tomsky, that this organization had set as its goal the forcible overthrow of Soviet power (uprising, *coup d'état*, terror), that it had entered into a bloc with the Trotskyite/Zinovievite organization." He confirmed these statements at the close of the investigation and then again at his 1938 trial.[105]

Every country's legal system treats as valid any admissions made by a suspect during investigation and repeated at trial. At his trial, Bukharin admitted, "If my programme conception were to be formulated practically, it would be in the economic sphere, state capitalism, the prosperous muzhik individual, the curtailment of the collective farms, foreign concessions, surrender of the monopoly of foreign trade, and, as a result - the restoration of capitalism in the country."[106] Furr stated that "There is no reason whatever to doubt that Bukharin was telling the truth in his pre-trial and trial confessions and in his post-trial appeal. Bukharin was very clear and explicit that Radek had told him more than once about Trotsky's involvement with the Germans and Japanese. This is corroborative evidence. Bukharin's first confession corroborates Radek's confession at the January 1937 trial – Bukharin confirms what Radek said, meanwhile adding a bit more detail. [...] Radek, Sokol'nikov, and Iakovlev testified that they were approached by German and Japanese officials who told them about Trotsky's collaboration with their countries."[107]

NKVD General Genrikh Liushkov defected to the Japanese in

June 1938. He told his Japanese handlers that Aleksei Rykov, one of the chief defendants in the March 1938 Moscow trial, really had been conspiring with military men against the Soviet regime. He told them that the conspiracy included General Yakov Gamarnik, a member of Tukhachevsky's group. In the last Moscow trial, Prosecutor Andrei Vyshinsky asked Bukharin, "Were Tukhachevsky and the military group of conspirators members of your bloc?" Bukharin answered, "They were."[108] Furr wrote, "There is not now, nor has there ever been, any evidence that any of the Moscow trials defendants were tortured. On the contrary: there is good evidence that they were not. Zinoviev stated in a pre-trial letter that he was being well treated. Even Stephen Cohen, a world authority on Bukharin and staunchly anti-Stalin, concluded in 2003 that Bukharin was not tortured.[109]

In 1956 Anastas Mikoyan told American writer Louis Fischer that 'Bukharin and the other Moscow trial defendants were not tortured.' Mikoyan had no reason to lie about this. He believed that they were innocent and he supported Khrushchev's attempt to 'rehabilitate' them as 'victims of Stalin'."[110] Radek told Bukharin, "No one forced me to say what I did. No one threatened me before I gave my testimony. I was not told that I would be shot if I refused."[111] Furr summed up, "there is not now, nor has there ever been any evidence that the Moscow Trials defendants were in reality innocent, compelled or persuaded by some means (threats to them or against their families, loyalty to the Party, etc.) to testify falsely."[112] Furr noted, "None of the rehabilitation reports yet published disproves the guilt of the person 'rehabilitated'. Khrushchev and later Gorbachev, had access to all the investigation and trial materials.

The fact that their researchers could not find any evidence to exculpate any of the defendants at any of the Moscow trials means that they could not find any such evidence."[113]

Historian Robert Thurston affirmed that Bukharin, Grigory Zinoviev, Lev Kamenev and others had "engaged in opposition, had had contacts with Trotsky and leaked secret documents to the West, and had wanted to remove Stalin, all of which they had lied about, while proclaiming their complete loyalty."[114] Sarah Davies and James Harris recently concluded, "It would appear that Stalin believed, and had good reason to believe, the essence of the prosecution case as it was presented at the Moscow trials."[115] How likely would it have been that the one place that the forces of reaction did not attempt a counter-revolution was the Soviet Union? Trotsky believed that the future of humanity depended on the correct, that is Trotskyist, leadership. As he wrote in 1938, "the historical crisis of mankind is reduced to the crisis of revolutionary leadership."[116] It was hardly surprising that the Trotskyists would do anything, even ally with Hitler, to ensure their success.

Trotskyists call World War Two an imperialist war and they believe that the correct, Leninist policy to adopt in an inter-imperialist war is to call for the defeat of one's own ruling class. Trotskyists in the Soviet Union called for Stalin to be overthrown, in Britain they called for the Churchill government to be ousted and in the USA they called for President Roosevelt to be kicked out. Who gained? In the Soviet Union, the Trotskyist opposition; in Britain, the appeasers; in the USA, the isolationists. Of course, the greatest beneficiaries would have been Hitler, Mussolini and Tojo. Furr summed up, "consider for a moment what WW2 would have been like if Tukhachevsky and his co-conspirators had been successful. The industrial and military might of the Soviet Union, plus its resources of raw material and manpower, would have been teamed up with those of Hitler's Germany. [...] One could conclude that in uncovering and stopping this conspiracy the Soviet leadership – 'Stalin' – saved European civilization from Nazism."[117]

The struggle for peace

Throughout the late 1930s the British government blocked the collective security pact between Britain, France and the Soviet Union that alone could have prevented war. Hitler's actions had not convinced Chamberlain and his colleagues that Nazi Germany was a greater threat to Britain than the Soviet Union was. Churchill and his allies now realised that Hitler was the main enemy, so they struggled to achieve this Triple Alliance. Churchill's ally Boothby wrote in the *Daily Telegraph* of 13 September 1938, "The Soviet government has on many occasions during the last ten years proved that it has no aggressive intentions of any kind. Russia has always been an exemplary member of the League of Nations, and there is no reason to believe that she would not have fulfilled both her obligations [to France and to Czechoslovakia.]"

Archibald Sinclair, the leader of the Liberals, said that the Soviet Union had been 'true to all her international obligations', had been a 'loyal member of the League' and had 'actually befriended the victims of aggression' throughout the 1930s. The Soviet government was fully intent on defending Czechoslovakia together with Britain and France. Chamberlain had a very different policy, which earned him the nickname in

France of *Monsieur J'aime Berlin*. He told the Italian Ambassador Count Dino Grandi on 28 February 1938, "my immediate aim is a strong and permanent treaty with the Duce [Mussolini] and Fascist Italy, my long range and no less important aim is a permanent and as strong as possible a treaty with the Fuhrer and National Socialist Germany. I consider the treaty with Italy an indispensable step toward the subsequent conclusion of a treaty with the second power of the Rome-Berlin Axis, namely Germany."[118] This encouraged Hitler to invade Austria on 12 March. In May, Chamberlain suggested that Hitler annex the Sudetenland from Czechoslovakia.[119] The Nazis in this region had long been pressing for it to secede it from Czechoslovakia, knowing that this would weaken Czechoslovakia and strengthen Germany. From now on, the British government worked for the Hitler government.[120] Only the Soviet Union worked for Czechoslovakia.[121]

The British government signed three pacts with Hitler: the Four-Power Treaty of 1933, the Anglo-German Naval Agreement of 1935 and the Munich Agreement of 1938. None was a non-aggression pact. Each was a pro-aggression pact, encouraging and rewarding Hitler's aggressions. The Munich Agreement proved not the futility of negotiation but the bankruptcy of the anti-Soviet, pro-Hitler policy. The anti-Soviet agreement produced war. After the Munich Agreement, Chamberlain schemed with the Nazi and French governments to use calls for an 'independent' Ukraine to destroy the Soviet Union, just as they had used calls for an 'independent' Sudetenland to destroy Czechoslovakia. The Nazis wanted Ukraine as a base for their planned attack on the Soviet Union.

All the Ukrainian organisations that wanted to secede from

the Soviet Union were pro-Nazi. In talks with the French government, on 24 November 1938, Chamberlain said, "there might be in the minds of the German Government an idea that they could begin the disruption of Russia by the encouragement of agitation for an independent Ukraine."[122] He asked Georges Bonnet, the French Foreign Minister, "What the position would be if Russia were to ask France for assistance on the grounds that a separatist movement in the Ukraine was provoked by Germany. Bonnet explained that French obligations towards Russia only came into force if there were a direct attack by Germany on Russian territory. Chamberlain said that he considered Bonnet's reply "entirely satisfactory."[123] In January 1939 Chamberlain assured Mussolini that a war in Eastern Europe would "not necessarily involve the Western powers."[124]

Hitler called for a Ukraine separate from the Soviet Union.[125] The British and French governments secretly backed Ukrainians based in Germany who wanted to break Ukraine away from the Soviet Union.[126] In 1939 Trotsky published four articles urging the Ukraine to secede from the Soviet Union.[127] These articles were a message to the Nazis that Trotsky would concede Ukraine to Germany as a base for war. Chamberlain saw the Munich Agreement as a further step towards a general European agreement and refused to see that Nazi Germany was the main threat to peace. On 6 October 1938, he defended Germany against the charge that it sought to dominate Europe.[128] Samuel Hoare told the German government that Chamberlain's "objective of an Anglo-German rapprochement was simultaneously dictated by the head and the heart."[129] He said, "after a further rapprochement between the Four European Great Powers, the acceptance of certain defence obligations, or even a guarantee by them against Soviet Russia, was conceivable in the event of an attack by Soviet Russia."[130]

This promised the Nazis a possible renewal of the 1918-1922 war against the Soviet Union, should she respect her Treaty and League obligations and go to the defence of Czechoslovakia. With all this encouragement from Chamberlain, Hitler stepped up his plans of attack. Hitler regularly signed non-aggression treaties with countries he intended to attack. He signed a non-aggression pact with Poland in 1934 and the Polish government used this pact to seize Czech territory in 1938. Hitler broke that pact. On 31 May 1939 he signed a non-aggression treaty with Denmark. He sent troops to occupy Denmark on 9 April 1940. In June 1939 Germany and Latvia signed a non-aggression pact. In late June 1941, Hitler's forces occupied Latvia, as part of Operation Barbarossa, completing the occupation by 10 July.

The Soviet government, knowing full well that Hitler intended war, did what it could to prevent war. Its non-aggression pact with Germany was an agreement that neither government would start a war. Like other such pacts this was, as historian Geoffrey Roberts pointed out, an 'instrument of defence, not aggression'. Yet there are apologists for Nazi Germany who still try to blame the Soviet Union for starting the Second World War. On 19 September 2019, the eightieth anniversary of the start of the Second World War, the EU's parliament voted for a resolution that blamed the Soviet Union equally with Nazi Germany for starting the war. It alleged that "the most devastating war in Europe's history was caused by the notorious Nazi-Soviet Treaty of Non-Aggression of 23 August 1939 [...] which allowed two totalitarian regimes that shared the goal of world conquest to divide Europe into two zones of influence." It alleged that the Soviet Union was 'an ally and partner of Nazi Germany that contributed politically and financially to Hitler's conquest of Western Europe'. Niall Ferguson declared that Stalin was 'as much an aggressor as Hitler'. Orlando Figes wrote that the non-aggression pact was 'the licence for the Holocaust'.[131]

The claim that the pact triggered the war is, as historian Mark Mazower wrote, 'too tainted by present day political concerns to be taken seriously'. Hitler gave the order to attack and occupy Poland well before he signed the pact. The Nazis claimed that all their wars were defensive. In the autumn of 1939, Goebbels wrote an article, 'England's guilt', in which he claimed, "We did not want war. England inflicted it on us. English plutocracy forced it on us. England is responsible for the war and it will have to pay for it." Hitler claimed that his attack on the Soviet Union was an act of 'preventive defense'. Historian Paul Hanebrink commented, "Of course, this was a lie. The invasion of the Soviet Union was a premeditated war of choice not a necessary pre-emptive strike."[132]

In Britain, the Communist Party of Great Britain failed its big test when it accepted the notion that the war that started with Hitler's attack on Poland was a war between rival imperialisms, like World War One. The Soviet Union, confined by the need to save the general peace, could not at that point support Britain's fight for independence. As late as May 1939 the Chamberlain government was negotiating a £1 billion loan to Hitler. Finance capital sought profit regardless of national interests. The City of London helped to fund Hitler's arms programme. The British people wanted the negotiations for an alliance with the Soviet Union to succeed. A Gallup poll of May 1939 showed that 92 per

55

cent wanted an alliance with the Soviet Union. Cadogan noted on 20 May 1939: "P.M. says he will resign rather than sign alliance with Soviet."[133] General Sir Edmund Ironside, Chief of the Imperial General Staff from September 1939 to May 1940, wrote that Chamberlain asked him whether he thought an understanding with the Soviet Union was the right course of action. "I told him that though it was very much against the grain, it was the only thing we could do. Chamberlain ejaculated that it was 'the only thing we cannot do.'"[134]

Conservative historian Maurice Cowling wrote that Chamberlain "was actively hoping that the Anglo-Russian negotiations would break down."[135] Historian Lewis Namier explained the failure of the negotiations: "Behind it all was a deep, insuperable aversion to Bolshevist Russia, such as was not shown in dealings with Hitler or Mussolini."[136] As Alvin Finkel and Clement Leibovitz wrote of Chamberlain and his allies, "the ruling group before May 10, 1940 were bloody-minded protectors of privilege whose fixation with destroying communists and communism led them to make common cause with fascists. They were not honest idiotic patriots; they were liars and traitors who would sacrifice human lives in their defence of property and privilege."[137] The British government's class hatred of the Soviet Union overrode all considerations of Britain's national interest.

The Soviet Union prepares its defences

In 1939, the Soviet Union was the only country willing to admit Jewish people fleeing the Nazis.[138] As the American historian Stephen Cohen pointed out, "the Soviet Union saved more

European Jews from Nazism than any other country, first by providing sanctuary for hundreds of thousands of Jews fleeing eastward after the German invasion of Poland, in 1939, and then by destroying the Nazi war machine and liberating the death camps in Eastern Europe."[139] Brian Fugate and Lev Dvoretsky wrote, "It is an enduring myth of the twentieth century that the German invasion of the Soviet Union in June 1941 caught Stalin and the Red Army totally by surprise. [...] Stalin and the Soviet High Command were not caught off guard by the invasion but in fact had developed a skilful, innovative, and highly secret plan to oppose it. [...] This strategy would ensure the nation's ability not only to survive the biggest and most violent invasion in history but indeed to prevail over it."[140]

They developed the strategy's key elements in three war games held in January and February 1941, probably the most important war games ever played. The Red Army has always considered war games the best way to test alternative strategies. Two strategies were proposed. General Pavlov, Commander of the Western Front, advocated a forward strategy of defending Bialystok, which jutted 150 miles into the Nazi-controlled part of Poland, following with a counterattack into Germany. This strategy meant placing the Red Army's main forces near the border. Alternatively, Marshal Timoshenko, commissar for defence and General Zhukov, head of the Kiev Special Military District, proposed placing their main forces deep in Soviet territory for an active strategic defence. This would create the conditions for a counterattack by the strategic reserve that would sweep the invader out of the Soviet Union and destroy the core of his army. The general staff put the military situation on the map board, then launched the Nazi attack and played out the moves, testing the two strategies. The first game tested Pavlov's strategy. Zhukov led the German forces and broke through Pavlov's defences, surrounding and annihilating them. The second game tested the Zhukov-Timoshenko strategy. Zhukov led the Red Army against Pavlov's German forces which had advanced deep into the Soviet Union. Zhukov counterattacked, outflanked and defeated Pavlov's forces. The day after the Politburo received the reports of these games, it appointed Zhukov chief of the general staff. The third game tested a more developed version of the second, in-depth strategy, with a defence zoned in three echelons. The first, tactical, echelon was behind the border. The first strategic echelon was 200 to 300 miles behind the first, on the upper Dnepr. This launched a powerful counterattack against the southern flank of Army Group Centre as it crossed to the north of the Pripyat Marshes. The second strategic echelon was a mobile reserve, massed around Moscow, ready to attack the flanks of the enemy as he advanced towards Moscow. The plan worked in the game: the Red Army's forces were placed accordingly and it carried out this strategy in July and August 1941.

Evan Mawdsley, one of the best historians of World War Two, wrote, "It is unfair, however, to charge Stalin and his government with not preparing the USSR for war."[141] Richard Overy agreed: "The absence of preparation is a myth. The Soviet political and military leadership began to prepare the country from the autumn of 1940 for the possibility of a war with Germany."[142] The military historian Albert Axell agreed: the Soviet Union was not caught off guard by the invasion.[143] On the day of the invasion, 22 June 1941, Stalin had meetings with nineteen political and military leaders, as the logbook of his appointments showed. This disproved Khrushchev's claim, repeated by all too many, that panic immobilised Stalin after the invasion.

Chapter 5
World War Two and its consequences

Hitler's war of annihilation

Hitler, while preparing his attack, always claimed that 'Judeo-Bolsheviks' were responsible for starting the war. He told the Reichstag on 30 January 1939, "if international Jewry within Europe and abroad should succeed once more in plunging the peoples into a world war, then the consequence will be not the Bolshevization of the world and there with a victory of Jewry, but on the contrary, the annihilation of the Jewish race in Europe."[144] On 12 December 1941 he reminded a mass meeting of his Gauleiter (the regional Nazi leaders) of his earlier threat, "He had prophesied to the Jews that if they once again brought about a world war they would experience their own extermination. This was not just an empty phrase. The World War is there, the extermination of Jewry must be the necessary consequence."[145] He talked of extermination on 1 and 30 January 1942, and on 14, 22 and 24 February 1942.[146] His invasion forces inflicted extermination on a scale without precedent or repetition. The Holocaust started on the Soviet Union with the Nazi killings of a million Soviet Jewish people. The Nazis' aim was predatory. Nazi Germany was never self-reliant. Its economy increasingly depended for food and raw materials on imports and on foreign labour.

Mazower wrote, "The rising power in the Agriculture and Food Ministry, Herbert Backe, was a long-time advocate of de-industrializing Russia. His goal was to weaken the urban working class which Stalin had built up and turn the country back into the wheat supplier for Western Europe that it had been before the Bolsheviks seized power."[147] Hitler said in 1942, "Russia is our Africa, and the Russians are our niggers."[148] Goering told all the Reich Commissioners and Military Commanders of occupied territories, "I could not care less when you say that people under your administration are dying of hunger. Let them perish so long as no German starves."[149] In one Soviet village the invaders erected a sign – "The Russians must die, so that we can live."[150] The Nazis had the racist notion that the Soviets, like 'Asians', were indifferent to human life. This, again, was projection: the Nazis were indifferent to all non-German life. Unforgivable arrogance, to invade someone else's country, kill twenty million of their people and then accuse them of being indifferent to human life. But the Soviet Union did not collapse under the onslaught. The first three months of Nazi Germany's war against the Soviet Union were by far the bloodiest three months of Hitler's war until then: 185,000 Germans were killed and 366,000 wounded.

David Stahel wrote, "Far from waging a seamless blitzkrieg wreaking havoc on the Red Army, the German panzer groups in the conduct of their advance suffered debilitating losses, which, in the first three months of the campaign, had already undercut Germany's whole war effort. [...] Operation Barbarossa [...] was a strategic failure with disastrous implication for Nazi Germany's war effort. [...] Clearly, Hitler and the Army General Staff had dramatically underestimated the Soviet Union."[151] In line with its strategy, the Red Army successfully counterattacked the southern flank of Army Group Centre as it moved along the upper Dnepr, delaying its advance on Moscow. This delay enabled the forces in the second strategic echelon virtually to destroy Army Group Centre at Moscow in December. By adopting this strategy, the Soviet Union survived the greatest onslaught in history. Hitler's forces waged a war of extermination against Soviet soldiers and civilians alike, as they had done in their onslaught on Poland. Hitler had said, "I have ordered my Totenkopf units to the east with the order to kill without pity or mercy all men, women and children of Polish race or language."[152] He had said on 30 March 1941, "Bolshevism is anti-social criminality."[153] But this was projection: the criminality was Hitler's programme of a 'war of annihilation' against the USSR. His Barbarossa Jurisdiction Decree of May 1941 exempted German soldiers from prosecution for crimes committed in the Soviet Union. This Decree purported to legitimise the Wehrmacht's mass criminal behaviour, including the mass rape and murder of female Soviet civilians.[154]

As Richard Overy pointed out, "When the Soviet government tried in the first weeks of the conflict to reach agreement through the International Red Cross on mutual respect for prisoners' rights, the German government refused to comply."[155] The first mass gassings at Auschwitz, in August and September 1941, were of Soviet prisoners of war. 3.5 million Soviet POWs died in the Nazi camps. The Wehrmacht's 707th Infantry Division reported taking 10,940 prisoners in anti-partisan operations in just four weeks starting on 11 October 1941. Of these prisoners, 10,431 were shot, although only 90 rifles had been found. Army Group Centre alone recorded killing around 80,000 'partisans' between July 1941 and May 1942. Field Marshal Walter von Reichenau, commander of Sixth Army until early 1942, ordered in October

1941, "the soldier must have full understanding for the necessity of a severe but just revenge on Jewish subhumans. [...] Soldiers must fulfil two tasks: 1. Complete annihilation of the false Bolshevist doctrine of the Soviet State and its armed forces. 2. The pitiless extermination of foreign treachery and cruelty and thus the protection of the lives of military personnel in Russia. This is the only way to fulfil our historic task to liberate the German people once and for all from the Asiatic-Jewish danger."[156] Historian Prit Buttar wrote, "Although he later denied being aware of this order, Field Marshal Gerd von Rundstedt, commander of Army Group South at the time, expressed complete agreement with Reichenau's order and advised other army commanders to issue similar instructions."[157] He said he was 'completely in agreement' with the order, and the Army High Command passed it on to all army groups and armies in the east, telling them 'to issue appropriate instructions along the same lines'.[158] Buttar noted that Field Marshal Erich von Manstein, commander of Army Group Don, "was later successfully prosecuted during the Nuremberg Tribunals, where it was shown that units under his command killed hundreds of commissars and were involved in mass killings of Jews; critically, the prosecution produced an order with his signature that effectively repeated the order that Reichenau had sent out the previous month."[159]

Hew Strachan wrote, "The Wehrmacht was complicit in war crimes and particularly so on the Eastern Front. [...] Guderian was a committed Nazi and Manstein ordered the extermination of Jews and Bolsheviks."[160] Buttar summed up, "there is no doubt that from the beginning, the Wehrmacht played a full role in the barbarous conduct of German forces in the Soviet Union."[161]

After the Wehrmacht's Sixth Army surrendered at Stalingrad, nearly 91,000 soldiers were taken prisoner. Buttar observed that "Typhus ravaged the camps to which the exhausted, emaciated prisoners were taken, leading to tens of thousands of deaths. Only 5,000 survived to return to Germany after the war. This was not – as claimed by many, including Manstein – evidence that Hitler had been correct in his statement that the Russians would not look after prisoners; the number of captives was simply overwhelming, and they were in such a debilitated condition that even had plentiful supplies of food and medicine been available, many would still have died. The Russians struggled to feed their own army and civilian population during the war, and had no capacity to cope with having to take responsibility for such a large number of sick, emaciated prisoners."[162] Buttar remarked, "Soviet power grew as the commanders of the Red Army became increasingly skilled at the operational art. An important difference between German and Soviet developments during the war is the manner in which the Soviet general staff rigorously analysed each campaign and tried to learn whatever lessons it could from its experiences; by contrast, Hitler retreated increasingly into a world in which his personal domination and the power of the 'will to win' were of greater importance than practical matters relating to battlefield experiences."[163]

Manstein wrote after the war, "This brings me to the factor which probably did more than anything else to determine the character of Hitler's leadership – his overestimation of the *power of the will*. This *will*, as he saw it, had only to be translated into *faith* down to the youngest private soldier for the correctness of his decisions to be confirmed and the success of his orders ensured. [...] Such a belief inevitably makes a man impervious to reason and leads him to think that his own will can operate even beyond the limits of hard reality – whether these consist in the presence of far superior enemy forces, in the conditions of space and time, or merely in the fact that the enemy also happens to have a will of his own."[164]

Churchill: "the Red Army [...] has torn the guts out of the filthy Nazis."[165]

In World War Two, the Eastern front was the most important front. From its entry into the war the Soviet Union never faced less than three quarters of all Axis forces. The Soviet Union, under Stalin's leadership, played the leading role in defeating the Nazi menace to the peoples of the world. Roosevelt noted, "the Russian armies are killing more Axis personnel and destroying more Axis material than all the other twenty-five United Nations put together."[166] Churchill said, "I have left the obvious, essential fact to this point, namely, that it is the Russian Armies who have done the main work in tearing the guts out of the German army. In the air and on the oceans we could maintain our place, but there was no force in the world which could have been called into being, except after several more years, that would have been able to maul and break the German army unless it had been subjected to the terrible slaughter and manhandling that has fallen to it through the strength of the Russian Soviet Armies."[167]

Field Marshal Bernard Montgomery pointed out, "Russia had to bear, almost unaided, the full onslaught of Germany on land; we British would never forget what Russia went through."[168] US Chief of Staff General George C. Marshall stated in his final report on the war, "It is certain that the refusal of the British and Russian peoples to accept what appeared to be inevitable defeat was the great factor in the salvage of our civilization."[169] The Soviet Union's astonishing achievement of defeating the massive Nazi-led onslaught aroused great admiration among the peoples of the world, especially of Britain. The Prime Minister's wife Clementine Churchill was Chairman of the Red Cross Aid to Russia Fund, launched in October 1941. It held auctions, flag days, galas, concerts and home nation football matches to raise money. The Fund raised £8 million during the war (£300 million in today's money), an impressive amount from a people suffering shortages. The money went towards clothing, blankets, first aid kits, medicines and hundreds of thousands of tons of medical supplies. In tribute to her work, the Soviet government awarded her the Order of the Red Banner of Labour.

An under-emphasised aspect of the Soviet Union's war effort was the role played by women. Anne Eliot Griesse and Richard Stites summarise their study of Soviet women's contribution: "The evidence assembled here should be sufficient to convince anyone that [Soviet] women played an important role in World War II, far in excess of all of the belligerent nations."[170] Roger Reese commented, "This is too modest an assessment. Women, by their sheer numbers and demonstrated competence, were a *vital* part of the Soviet success in the war."[171] As Reese affirmed, "The ideology of the women's liberation movement was an integral part of the revolutionary socialist movement adopted in the Bolshevik program."[172] During the siege of Leningrad, the women of the coal and steel towns of Airdrie and Coatbridge created and sent a book 'Greetings to the women of Leningrad', saying, "Your fight is our fight and we shall fight with you. [...] We realise humanity's debt of gratitude to the women of Russia. [...] Women of Leningrad, your Scottish sisters salute you!"

As Philip Bell wrote, "Between late 1941 and early 1943, admiration for the toughness and fighting power of the Soviet Union, expressed by the press and in popular opinion (as revealed by public opinion polls and Home Intelligence reports) was so strong that it was virtually impossible for any public figure to express any doubt about Soviet policies, intentions or virtues. Stalin was described as the benevolent 'Uncle Joe'; though he was also regarded as being merciless towards the Germans, which earned him great respect. The British government was worried lest this admiration for Soviet fighting power and for Stalin should extend to support for the Soviet regime and so for Communism in Britain. A systematic propaganda policy was devised to try to guide public opinion, which was far too strong to be inhibited or changed, in 'safe' directions. The height of admiration for the Soviet Union came during the battle of Stalingrad in the winter of 1942-43 and one aspect of the government attempt channel it was the official celebration of Red Army Day on 21 February 1943. In the event, despite the best endeavours of ministers and officials, the celebrations quite outstripped government intentions and the whole occasion was very 'Red' indeed."[173]

Churchill admitted that Britain's central planning of production in both world wars 'constitute the greatest argument for State Socialism that has ever been produced'.[174] Historian Chris Bellamy observed, "The socialist victory in the 1945 general election owed something to the upsurge of pro-Russian, and therefore, at that time, pro-communist – certainly socialist – feeling among the British people during the war. After all, the British people had faced the Germans alone for a year in 1940-41 and the Russians had held them and knocked them back, pretty well alone, apart from the limited support the Western Allies could send, in 1941-2."[175]

"Let Germany and Russia bleed each other white"

But, after the Battle of Stalingrad had proved that the Soviet Union was not going to be defeated, the British ruling class changed tack. They now hoped to see their signed-up ally the Soviet Union bled to death. Lord Brabazon, the Minister for Aircraft Production, let the cat out of the bag when he said, "Let Hitler and Russia devour each other." The Chair of the Joint Intelligence Committee, Victor Cavendish-Bentinck, agreed, writing in February 1943, "Since Stalingrad our immediate strategic objectives had changed. Until then it had been in our interest to do all we could to take pressure off Russia. Now that the tide had turned it was in our interest to let Germany and Russia bleed each other white."[176] Cavendish-Bentinck had earlier described eye-witness reports of the Nazi massacre of 33,771 Jewish people at Babi Yar near Kiev on 29-30 September 1941 as 'products of the Slavic imagination'.[177] Every dirty trick was used to try to discredit the Soviet Union and the Red Army. One story was that only government terrorism made Soviet soldiers fight. American historian Roger Reese refuted this allegation; "the death penalty [...] was not widely used, and soldiers knew it. The idea that soldiers were machine-gunned by blocking detachments and arbitrarily executed by officers and NKVD men en masse – and thus kept in the line by fear of such treatment – is essentially a myth."[178]

Another key project was the attempt to blame Soviet forces for Nazi atrocities, a propaganda effort that focused on the massacre at Katyn near Smolensk in the Soviet Union. In April 1943, Joseph Goebbels accused 'Jewish commissars' of killing 10,000 Polish officers in 1940. Unhappily for Goebbels, the German government report of 1943, *Amtliches Material zum Massenmord von Katyn*, acknowledged that all the spent shells found at Katyn were German. Goebbels wrote in his private diary, "Unfortunately German munitions were found in the graves of Katyn [...] it is essential that this incident be kept top secret. If it were to come to the knowledge of the enemy the whole Katyn affair would have to be dropped."[179] How could 'Jewish commissars' have got hold of German ammunition in 1940? The execution method was typical of the German mass murder team led by SS Obergruppenführer Friedrich Jeckeln. German troops, aided by Ukrainian nationalist units, carried out similar mass killings at Volodymyr-Volyns'kiy in Ukraine soon after the invasion. Some in the British government were looking forward to working with the Nazis. In November 1943 a member of Britain's Military Mission, with the knowledge of the Middle East commander of the Special Operations Executive, held secret talks with the head of the German Secret Police in Athens on possible joint action against the Soviet Union.[180]

Reactionaries in the British government, parliament and the press next seized on the Red Army's halt outside Warsaw in August 1944 and claimed that it had deliberately held back in order to enable the Nazis to crush Warsaw's people. This was to ignore all the material factors governing the Red Army's advance and instead to impute, with no evidence, malevolent intention. Historian Andrew Roberts wrote, "They stopped on the Vistula, outside Warsaw, because [German Field Marshall] Model managed to check Rokossovsky's 1st Belorussian Front [Army Group] to the east of the Polish capital. It is often assumed that the Russians stopped on the Vistula for entirely political reasons, in order to allow the Germans to crush the Warsaw Uprising, but they had a good excuse to do so, for their 450-mile advance since 22 June had stretched their supplies and lines of communication to the limits."[181] Robin Edmonds wrote, "Subsequent research suggests that the Red Army's need for a pause of months - not just weeks - on the Vistula, after an advance of four hundred miles, was genuine, as indeed Stalin assured Churchill in Moscow (an assurance accepted absolutely by Churchill at the time)."[182] American historian Timothy Snyder, no friend of the Soviet Union, concluded, "There is no reason to believe that Stalin deliberately halted military operations at Warsaw."[183] The Red Army did not liberate Warsaw until January 1945.

As Soviet forces drove towards Berlin in the winter of 1944-45, Goebbels claimed that the leading Soviet journalist Ilya Ehrenburg was encouraging Red Army soldiers to rape German women and that a flyer was circulating among Red Army units saying "Break the racial arrogance of German women with violence! Take her as a rightful prize!"[184] Paul Hanebrink commented, "In the years that followed, various people claimed to have seen the flyer and some works even cite it. Teams of professional historians have been charged with looking for a physical copy. None has found evidence that it

71

ever existed."[185] Buttar summed up, "Ehrenburg has – wrongly – been accused of inciting Soviet soldiers to rape German women [...]"[186] The atrocity of mass rape was not Soviet government or Red Army policy. The government repeatedly tried to promote responsible and appropriate behaviour outside the Soviet Union. In 1944, Red Army soldiers were told that they were entering Poland as 'liberators' and that looting and rape would not be tolerated. The Red Army's Front Military Councils issued Orders of the Day reminding the troops that they were entering Germany as liberators and called on them all maintain the highest discipline and uphold the honour of the Soviet soldier. Troops were required to take an oath swearing to conduct themselves 'properly' and to 'obey the authorities' at all times. There were severe punishments for rape and looting. Any atrocities were individual criminal acts, carried out against the orders of Soviet authorities. This was the opposite of Hitler Germany, where the atrocity of mass extermination was official policy, as ordered by Hitler himself and by the Wehrmacht's leaders. German soldiers who raped, murdered and looted were following Hitler's orders. Mao Tse-tung had spelt out communist policy on treatment of civilians in liberated areas. The Eight Points for Attention are as follows:

1. Speak politely.
2. Pay fairly for what you buy.
3. Return everything you borrow.
4. Pay for anything you damage.
5. Do not hit or swear at people.
6. Do not damage crops.

7.   Do not take liberties with women.

8.   Do not ill-treat captives.[187]

Nazi propagandists, echoed by some in British government circles, warned that the Soviet Union wanted to seize all of Europe's countries. Foreign Secretary Anthony Eden spoke out against the idea that the Soviet Union was "dreaming of European domination. This of course is the constant theme of German propaganda. It is poured out, day by day and night after night and it comes to us in all sorts of unexpected forms and guises. It was their theme before the war. It was then the Bolshevik bogey and how well Hitler used it. Can anyone doubt that this theme before the war was an element in making it difficult for us to establish an understanding of Soviet Russia. Can anyone doubt that if we had had unity in 1939, the unity between Russia, this country and the United States that we cemented at Yalta there would not have been the present war?"[188] Hanebrink pointed out, "Some people did welcome Soviet forces as liberators without qualification. The Red Army victory saved the lives of Jews trapped in the Budapest ghetto, allowed Jews to emerge from hiding places in basements and haylofts across Poland, freed those still alive in Majdanek (July 1944) and Auschwitz (end of January 1945) and toppled anti-Semitic regimes in Hungary and Romania.

Working-class activists and labor leaders were released from prison or were free to return from exile. Soviet victory also raised hopes for sweeping social reform."[189] Queen Elizabeth II said on VE Day, 8 May 2020: "we kept belief that the cause was right and this belief carried us through. [...] Never give up, never despair – that was the message of VE Day. [...] When I look at our country today and see what we are willing to do to protect and support one another, I say with pride that we are still a nation that those brave soldiers, sailors and airmen would recognise and admire." Historian Paul Hehn pointed out, "If one considers that World War I also occurred as a quarrel within capitalism with the United States coming in later as in World War II, the first Great War having caused an estimated 35 million casualties and the Second World War about 55 million, totalling 90 million, then capitalism may be credited with generating one of the greatest slaughters in history."[190]

The Labour governments of 1945-51

At home, the war had brought security of employment, a greatly strengthened trade union movement and rising wage levels. The National government pledged in 1944 to maintain a high, stable level of employment after the war ended, a promise which none of its successors dared to repudiate for almost a generation. In 1945, the British working class, determined to rebuild Britain, swept out the Conservative Party. The Labour Party had vast public support and a huge parliamentary majority. This was the supreme test of social democracy, of its claims that there was a parliamentary road to socialism and that the working class could win socialism just by voting for a social democratic party. Although the people achieved great things, especially creating the NHS, nobody would claim that the Labour government delivered socialism.

At workplaces across the country, workers fought for better wages and conditions, none more than the engineers. The Amalgamated Engineers Union demanded 'equal pay for equal work'. The Labour Research Department urged, "the money the capitalists have in the bank must be utilised for rebuilding Britain. The 'ups and downs' of the past must give place to a

74

plan, and the freedom of capitalists to do as they like with their profits must be checked where the Nation's interest requires it." Post-war union organisation made great headway and the militancy of the shop floor in conditions of 'full employment' became a problem for employers used to holding the whip. Incomes policies, rising unemployment and anti-union laws were intended to deflate and destroy the confidence of workers. From the start the Labour government took the employer's side in disputes. It kept the wartime ban on strikes. In 1945, within its first month of office, it sent troops to the Surrey Docks in London to break the dockers when they struck against the employers' arbitrary system of punishments and penalties. In April 1947, the government set up an emergencies committee to break strikes and arranged for the secret services to spy on strike leaders. It continued the practice of misusing state benefits to break strikes.[191]

Justin Davis Smith noted, "The peculiarly hostile policy adopted by the Attlee Governments towards strikes. […] Never before or since has a government intervened on such a massive scale during industrial disputes."[192] In 1948, the government introduced a pay freeze. It rejected the miners' call for higher wages and better conditions to attract workers to the industry. It rejected the National Engineering Joint Trades Movement's proposals for a national plan for engineering, geared into an overall economic plan to rebuild Britain. The result of Labour's capitalist offensive was that between 1946 and 1951 prices rose by 34 per cent and wages by 29 per cent. Production rose by 43 per cent and profits by 100 per cent. So workers were producing half as much again as they had during the war, for lower wages, while employers doubled their profits. Under Labour, the working class was more exploited than it had been during the war. It was a similar story in international economic affairs. In 1946, the government chose to accept a loan from the US government. Its unacceptably high price was the convertibility of the pound. The American historian Thomas McCormick noted that convertibility "literally implied the demise of British economic management at home [...] Free convertibility [...] left the Labour Party government with no alternative save the ironic and deflationary one of cutting government spending and pro-labor programs."[193] Without control of the currency, the government had no control of the economy.

The loan was not used to rebuild Britain. The economist John Maynard Keynes wrote in 1946, "It comes out in the wash that the American loan is primarily required to meet the political and military expenditure overseas."[194] The government used Marshall Plan aid to help pay the costs of empire, instead of investing the funds in industry. The government spent 28 per cent of its budget on war preparations and the Empire. This huge unnecessary overseas spending starved Britain's industry and welfare services of necessary investment. The government failed to stem the huge outflow of private capital abroad - £1650 million between 1945 and 1951. Between 1947 and 1949, the capitalist class invested only £320 million in manufacturing industry, £262 million in transport and communications, £160 million in the energy industries and £85 million in agriculture and fisheries. The machine tool industry, the barometer of British industry, was not rebuilt. Machine tools in Britain were acquired through the Marshall Plan, so there was no rebuilding of domestic industrial strength. Only 9 per cent of Gross National Product was invested in industry. Private appropriation prevented adequate productive investment. Reactionary at home, the Labour government was also reactionary abroad. From the start it was hostile to the Soviet

Union, our recent war ally. Ernest Bevin, the new Foreign Secretary, boasted that the government followed Churchill's anti-Soviet policy. It worked closely with the US administration, together opposing every Soviet proposal for peace, disarmament and cooperation. Culturally, economically, politically and militarily, the USA and Labour collaborated to strengthen capitalism and destroy socialism.

In 1947, the British and US governments signed the UK-USA Security Agreement. Britain's intelligence, espionage and covert action services would collaborate with the CIA and the FBI. This meant cooperating in US covert military action abroad: in August 1948, the US government for the first time officially authorised terrorist operations against the socialist countries. In July 1948, the government agreed to allow American bases and nuclear bombers in Britain, putting Britain in the front line of any future attack on the Soviet Union.[195] Parliament was not informed. Chancellor Cripps said, "Britain must be regarded as the main base for the deployment of American power, and the chief offensive against Russia must be by air." In 1949, Labour helped to found the North Atlantic Treaty Organisation. The government refused to respect the wartime agreements that Britain had signed. The Potsdam Agreement, if implemented, would have maintained cooperation with the Soviet Union, preventing the Cold War and guaranteeing European security. But the British and US governments together agreed, "Where there is any inconsistency between the principles contained in the Potsdam Agreement and the principles contained in the present statement, the latter shall prevail." The British government had agreed at Potsdam to break up Germany's giant corporations. Instead it protected the private property of those who had funded, and profited from, the Nazi party. In 1942, the Labour Party had promised to nationalise

Germany's key industries after the war. Yet in 1945 Labour instructed its military government in Germany to veto nationalisation. In other parts of Europe too, Labour tried to restore conservative rule. It opposed Stalin's efforts to oust General Franco, despite the Spanish dictator's wartime support for the Axis.

As the historian David Pike wrote, "Official British documents released in March 1975 show that Stalin tried at Potsdam to get British and US support in a bid to overthrow Franco, and that the move against Franco was cautiously welcomed by Truman, resisted by Churchill, and finally rejected by Attlee and his Foreign Secretary, Ernest Bevin."[196] Labour continued Churchill's policy of waging a dirty war in Greece to reimpose a fascist government. Labour used the Yugoslav leader Tito to destroy the Greek people's struggle for independence. As Bevin said of Tito, "He's a bastard, but he's our bastard."[197] Tito betrayed the Greek people's struggle by closing Yugoslavia's borders to Soviet military supplies, and by trapping half the Greek Liberation Army inside Yugoslavia, then letting the Greek army in to attack them. As a reward, he received aid from Britain and the USA.

By 1947, Britain's armed forces were overextended worldwide, trying to fight too many colonial wars at once. Bevin announced that the British government could no longer pay for troops in Greece and asked the US government to occupy the country. US forces stayed until 1954, propping up the unpopular regime. In Eastern Europe, the British and US governments tried to roll back the social and economic gains that the new democracies had made after the war. At the Yalta Conference in

1945, the British, US and Soviet governments had agreed that the peoples of Eastern Europe had the right to build their own societies in peace. But the British government ordered its Secret Intelligence Service to assist pro-Western forces there to overthrow the governments; Labour organised a counter-revolution in Albania, which was a fiasco.[198]

In the rest of the world too, Labour did what it could to thwart nations seeking self-government. At the war's end, the British Empire was still the leading power in South and South-East Asia. Two-thirds of the region and three-quarters of the people were under direct British rule. British capital still dominated India, Ceylon, Burma, Malaya and Siam. It controlled sectors of production in Indonesia (especially oil), the Philippines, Singapore, North Borneo, Brunei and Sarawak. The Labour government fought against India's independence as long as it could and tried to partition the country. This caused massive popular protest and revolts by the Indian Army and Navy. No longer able to use the armed forces to crush the national movement, Labour was forced, reluctantly, to quit India. As it admitted, it could not rule India "when we had not the power." India's independence was the key event in unravelling the British Empire in Asia because it deprived the British government of control over the Indian Army, a huge reserve of manpower and it stimulated other independence struggles. Labour tried to keep the Empire by forcibly repressing movements for national liberation. It used troops against the people of Burma. In Indonesia, it rearmed Japanese troops to fight alongside British soldiers against Indonesian nationalists, helping to reimpose Dutch colonial rule. In Malaya, where British investments yielded £460 million profit between 1946 and 1951, and tin companies paid dividends of up to 65 per cent, it secretly agreed with the country's feudal rulers to renew imperial control, breaking earlier promises of self-government.[199] When the people rebelled, Labour launched a vicious colonial war, using terror-bombing, collective punishments, concentration camps and death squads.

Rebuilding the Soviet Union

After the war, the Soviet Union focused on the huge task of rebuilding its shattered economy. The Soviet economy grew by 7.3 per cent a year between 1947 and 1958, and by 4.9 per cent a year between 1959 and 1973.[200] Girsh Khanin summed up the Soviet achievements in the 1950s, "at the beginning of the decade the level of consumption of basic foods was characteristic rather of a developing country, as a result of the rise in per capita consumption of high-quality goods like meat, milk, sugar, vegetables and pulses by 1.5-2 and more times, it reached the level of a number of developed countries. [...] Completion of housing rose two and a half times, reaching the level of highly developed countries per head of population. [...] the enormous increase in life expectancy, to 69 – the level of the most developed countries in the world at the time. [...] These immense economic and social achievements, in my opinion, permit us to call the 1950s the decade of the 'Soviet economic miracle'. [...] a unique social and economic achievement. [...] The command economy in this period demonstrated its viability and macroeconomic efficiency. The Soviet economy, being in essence the largest corporation in the world, made skilful use of the strengths of any large corporation: preparing and implementing long-range plans, using colossal financial resources for development in priority directions, carrying out major capital investments in a short period of time, spending large sums on scientific research and so on. The achievements of the 1950s were based on the powerful heavy industrial and transport potential created in the 1930s-1940s [...] The USSR skilfully used its limited resources for the development of sectors which determine long term economic progress: education – including higher education – healthcare and science."[201]

In 1956 US Secretary of State John Foster Dulles acknowledged "the phenomenon of Russia's rapid industrialization. Its transformation from an agrarian to a modern industrialized state was an historical event of absolutely first-class importance." In Eastern Europe, the growth rate was 5.1 per cent a year in the 1950s, as against Western Europe's 4.9 per cent. It was 4.3 per cent a year in the 1960s, as against Western Europe's 4.8 per cent. Life expectancy nearly caught up with Western Europe's and infant mortality rates dropped more quickly. 6 per cent of homes in East Germany had a fridge in 1965, 56 per cent in 1970. Homes with a TV rose from 16 per cent to 69. The socialist countries achieved this progress despite the brutal blockade which the Western powers, led by the USA, enforced on them. In 1948, the USA had begun a campaign of economic sanctions against the Soviet Union that would last for forty years. In March 1948, the Department of Commerce announced restrictions on exports to the Soviet Union and its European allies. Congress formalized these restrictions in the Export Control Act of 1949. The blockade prevented the socialist countries from improving the quality of their products through trading freely with other countries. But the counter-revolutions of 1989-90 rolled back all this social progress.

The UN Human Settlements Programme concluded in 2003, "The region where the increase in extreme poverty was the most pronounced comprised the former socialist countries of Eastern Europe and Central Asia. Poverty rates moved to over 50 per cent in half of the transitional countries in the transition period of 1988 to 1995; and persons in poverty increased from 14 million to 168 million in the region, as a whole. The number of people in poverty in Russia rose from 2 million to 74 million, in the Ukraine from 2 million to 33 million and in Romania from 1.3 million to 13.5 million."[202]

Except for Belarus. In 2004, the World Bank reported, "Belarus has some of the best education and health indicators in the region and an extensive coverage of basic services that are mostly subsidized. [...] overall health expenditures are progressive, in the sense that the poor benefit relatively more than the better off. [...] The poverty reduction and inequality performance of Belarus is impressive [...] Over the last five years, poverty has fallen substantially in Belarus. [...] Belarus has made tremendous achievements in reducing national poverty without triggering sharp increases in income inequality. [...] Belarus can be justly proud of the elaborate system of social services it provides to its population. The ability of households to access quality education, health and social protection services makes a large difference to their living standards in the present, and their prospects for the future."[203]

Ending colonialism post-1945

The war against the Nazi attempt at empire-building gave a huge impetus to peoples struggling to free themselves from colonial rule. There were sixty nations in 1945. In the decades after 1945, the five-hundred year era of European imperial expansion came to an end. In the late 1940s and 1950s, the USA backed the crumbling British, French and Dutch empires against the rising nations; Britain against Egypt and Iran, France against Indochina, Algeria, Tunisia and Morocco, and the Netherlands against Indonesia. All to no avail. A key event in the demise of the British Empire was India's independence in 1947. China's declaration of independence in 1949 was an even more radical act of national liberation from colonial chains. After 1945 many African and Asian nations won their independence. Since 1945 we have been in an era of new nations. By 2020 there were more than 200 independent nations. This period of decolonisation since 1945, when empires were forced to give way to nations, was more peaceful than the period of 1914-1945, admittedly not a high standard.

On 14 December 1960, the General Assembly of the United Nations adopted, on the Soviet Union's initiative, its famous Declaration on Granting Independence to Colonial Countries and Peoples, 1514 (XV), by 89 votes to none. Nine governments abstained - the USA, Britain, South Africa, Portugal, France, Spain, Belgium, Australia and the Dominican Republic. This Resolution made colonialism unlawful and made opposition to national liberation movements a crime under international law. On 27 November 1961, the General Assembly passed its famous Resolution, The situation with regard to the implementation of the Declaration on Granting Independence to Colonial Countries and Peoples, 1654 (XVI), by 97 votes to none. There were four abstentions; the British, South African, French and Spanish governments. This called "upon States concerned to take action without further delay with a view to the faithful application and implementation of the Declaration."

On 20 December 1965, the UN adopted a Resolution on Implementing the Declaration on Granting Independence to Colonial Countries and Peoples, 2105 (XX), that "recognizes the legitimacy of the struggle by the peoples under colonial rule to exercise their right to self-determination and independence and invites all States to provide material and moral assistance to the national liberation movements in colonial Territories." Six governments voted against; the British, US, South African, Portuguese, Australian and New Zealand.

On 24 October 1970, the General Assembly adopted, without a vote, Resolution 2625 (XXV), the Declaration on Principles of International Law concerning Friendly Relations and Cooperation among States. This outlawed all 'forcible actions' depriving peoples of their right to freedom and independence and proclaimed that colonised peoples had the right to seek and receive outside support when exercising their right to defend themselves. These principles were and are binding on all states and peoples. Thus, the UN's overriding prohibition on the use of force in international relations does not prohibit nations from exercising their right to defend themselves when their independence is attacked. Nor does it prohibit other nations from supporting such a struggle. The NATO powers, having abstained on the Resolution, replied to their defeat by secretly agreeing to consult 'in the event of a threat in any part of the world, including a threat to their overseas territories.' Britain's rulers had no intention of giving up their colonies.

Capitalist wars of aggression

The US and British government worked together to try to roll back the gains made by peoples struggling to free themselves from colonial rule. Between 1945 and 1990, US-backed anti-communist regimes carried out mass murders of innocent civilians in these 22 countries; Argentina, Bolivia, Brazil, Chile, Paraguay and Uruguay (the Operation Condor member countries) in the 1970s-1980s: 80,000, Colombia 1985-1995: 5,000, Timor 1975-99: 300,000, El Salvador 1979-92: 75,000, Guatemala 1954-96: 200,000, Honduras 1980-93: 200, Indonesia 1965-66: 1,000,000, Iraq 1963 and 1978: 5,000, Mexico 1965-82: 1,300, Nicaragua 1979-89: 50,000, the Philippines 1972-86: 3,250, South Korea 1948-50: 200,000, Sudan 1971: more than 100, Taiwan 1947: 10,000, Thailand 1973: 3,000, Venezuela 1959-70: 1,500 and Vietnam (Operation Phoenix) 1968-72: 50,000. In total, just under two million people killed. These numbers do not include deaths from regular war.[204]

American historian John Coatsworth wrote that "Between 1960 [...] and the Soviet collapse in 1990, the numbers of political prisoners, torture victims, and executions of nonviolent political dissenters in Latin America vastly exceeded those in the Soviet Union and its East European satellites. In other words, from 1960 to 1990, the Soviet bloc as a whole was less repressive, measured in terms of human victims, than many individual Latin American countries."[205] We should note that the common phrase Cold War, used to describe the post-war period, is a misleading piece of

85

propaganda. The relationship between the USA and the Soviet Union conventionally described as the Cold War was not any kind of war. It was peaceful; it was precisely, thankfully, the absence of war. The anti-communist propagandist Eric Blair, known as George Orwell, coined the phrase in 1945 to describe what he called 'a peace that is no peace'. But there never was a war between the USA and the Soviet Union. There was peace between them.

The notion that there was a 'Cold War era' reduced everything in the world to the conflict between the USA and the Soviet Union, relegating to insignificance every other country and every other aspect of human life. Today, some reactionaries want to call our time one of a New Cold War, against Russia and/or China and then want to focus all attention on waging this new conflict. Clyde Prestowitz, who worked for President Reagan and has advised more recent Presidents, wrote in 2021 that 'the China challenge' is 'the most difficult and dangerous external challenge that the United States and the free world have ever faced.'

Chapter 6
National liberation struggles in China and Korea

China shakes the world

During World War Two, the Chinese people fought against the Japanese occupying forces, so they were our allies in the historic struggle against the worst threat the peoples of the world have ever faced, the Nazi tyranny and its Axis allies Japan and Italy. How did the Labour government in Britain and the Democrat government in the USA repay the Chinese people's sacrifices? By treating them as if they were a replica of the Nazi enemy. This was slanderously untrue. Genuine common principles united all those fighting Hitler. The alliance against the Axis was not based solely on realpolitik.

In 1945, the USA, Britain and the Soviet Union together 'reaffirmed their adherence to the policy of non-interference in the internal affairs of China'. The US government then sent 50,000 marines to support Chiang Kai-Shek's dictatorial regime. US General Wedemeyer declared his 'determination to keep the fifty-three thousand marines operating on behalf of the Nationalists in North China'.[206] These US troops controlled Beijing, Tianjin and other major cities. US and Kuomintang forces even used Japanese troops, still under arms, to try to help Chiang restore his brutal, corrupt and incompetent rule. The US 7th Fleet ferried KMT troops to North China. The United States Air Force, in the largest airlift in history, transported KMT troops to Shanghai, Nanking and Peiping. This military intervention against the Chinese people's war of liberation prolonged the war, adding to the suffering of the people. The US government supported Chiang Kai-Shek's regime to the end, to no avail.

Despite the US state's huge intervention, the Chinese people freed their country from imperial and feudal oppression, in an epic struggle for freedom.[207] In April 1949, People's Liberation Army forces crossed the Yangtze River, to free Shanghai. American journalist Jack Belden wrote, "The crossing of the Yangtze – like the crossing of so many other river barriers in history, from the Rubicon to the Rappahannock or the Rhine – may stand as a decisive date in world history. [...] the day which sounded the death knell of imperialism in Asia. The crossing of the Yangtze rang down the curtain on an era of history. [...] Gone was the era of gunboat diplomacy, gone the treaty port concessions, gone the specially conceded naval bases, the military missions, the ill-disguised interference in Chinese affairs."[208]

The US government had to admit, in its China White Paper, that the revolution in 1949 "was the product of internal Chinese forces." The "unfortunate but inescapable fact is that the ominous result of the civil war in China was beyond the control of the government of the United States." Almost immediately after China's revolution, the US government endangered the country's independence with a war in Korea that constantly threatened to develop into a US war against China. The Chinese people's revolution restored unity and independence to China. British economic historian Angus Maddison summed up, "The establishment of the People's Republic in 1949 marked a sharp break with the past. It provided a new mode of governance, a new kind of elite and a marked improvement on past economic performance."[209] Once 'the sick man of Asia', China now awakened as a modern nation-state with full national independence.

War against Korea

The people of Korea have long seen themselves as one nation. The Japanese occupation of 1905 stimulated a national struggle for independence. World War One ended with the victorious powers talking of self-government. Popular national movements across the world wanted the talk translated into action. On 1 March 1919, Korean nationalists signed Korea's Declaration of independence and launched a great popular movement to end Japanese imperial rule. During World War Two, the people of Korea fought against the Japanese occupying forces, so they were in effect an ally of Britain, the USA and the Soviet Union. Their struggle was a success. At the war's end, popular forces ran most of the country. Their reward for their long struggle against our common enemy was that the British and US governments split their country. In 1945, the Allies agreed temporarily to divide Korea, but people on both sides of the temporary border were keen to reunite their country. South Korea's dictatorial leader Syngman Rhee always aimed to attack North Korea in order to reunify the country, saying, "We will achieve victory in a hot war."

General Roberts, Head of the US Military Mission to Korea, said in January 1950, "The campaign against the north has been decided upon, and the date for carrying it through is not very far off." US Secretary of State John Foster Dulles boasted on 21 June, "My talks with General MacArthur will be followed by positive action." On 25 June 1950, Rhee's forces attacked. He later admitted, "We started the fight."[210] The US government claimed that North Korea started the war by attacking South Korea, but even if it had been that way round, what was that to do with any other country? In international law, no other country has the right, still less the duty, to interfere in the internal affairs of another country. The US government won UN backing by lying that the Soviet Union started the war, but when a State Department team later combed North Korea's captured archives, it found no evidence of Soviet complicity.[211]

Labour Prime Minister Clement Attlee at once backed the US assault. He put Britain's naval forces in the Far East at President Truman's disposal and raised military spending from £3.6 billion a year to £6 billion to fund Britain's contribution to the war. On 7 October 1950, US troops first invaded North Korea, clearly threatening North Korea's existence and China's security. The next day, Chinese forces acted to defend its own North-eastern border and the fraternal country of North Korea. At the UN, the US and British representatives branded China the aggressor. In 1961, a Rand Corporation report concluded, "China neither participated in planning the initial North Korean aggression nor intervened later as the result of Russian pressure, but was 'rationally motivated' when it moved its armies into Korea after apparently ignoring the first three months of war there. [...] China intervened because it assumed from belligerent statements issuing from General MacArthur's headquarters in Tokyo that he intended to invade China. [...] General MacArthur this week reaffirmed that this was his intention and that it remains an unfulfilled ambition."[212] Typically, it took until 1961 to admit that China's motivation was defensive. In this genocidal US war of aggression, the US and allied forces killed 2.5 million Korean and Chinese soldiers and more than two million Korean civilians. MacArthur ordered his air forces "to destroy every means of communication and every installation and factories and cities and villages."[213]

The USAF dropped more bombs on Korea than on all Europe in World War Two and dropped 7.8 million gallons of napalm. General Curtis LeMay, who directed the bombing, later observed, "We burned down just about every city in North

Korea and South Korea *both*."[214] The US government prolonged the war by deadlocking the peace talks over the issue of repatriating prisoners of war.[215] The 1949 Geneva Convention called for the return of all POWs at the end of hostilities, but the US government refused to abide by the Convention, insisting that Korean and Chinese POWs had the right to refuse repatriation. It did not repeat this policy at the end of its war against Vietnam. Instead it demanded that both sides promptly 'return all captured persons' with no delays for 'any reason'.[216] A rare case of the US government learning from experience.

The Chinese and Korean forces together defeated the US government's efforts to occupy all Korea and to invade China. In 1953 President Eisenhower finally accepted the North Korean peace proposal that President Truman had rejected. Morton Halperin, a deputy assistant secretary of defense in President Johnson's administration, said of President Richard Nixon's plan to end the war against Vietnam, "When Nixon said he had a secret plan to end the war it really was a repeat of what he thought Eisenhower had done – that he had threatened the North Koreans with nuclear weapons through the Chinese and that's why they agreed to a settlement. A major flaw in that reasoning is that Eisenhower accepted the deal that Truman had refused to accept so the war ended because we switched our position, not because the North Koreans switched."[217]

China stands up

From 1949 to 1974, China's economy tripled in size. Faced with the huge task of rebuilding China in 1949, no government could have left the job to market forces. Every country which has industrialised, including Britain and the USA, has used the state to protect industry, because infant industries are unprofitable in the short and perhaps even medium term. The

91

new Chinese government chose to develop a wide range of industries and rejected the World Bank's advice to put textiles first. This industrial development included as key the steel industry, which was vital to building the railways, dams, power stations and other infrastructure that were needed. The resulting energy and transport networks connected the whole of the vast country, helping to build national unity. The government tried to balance the need to develop heavy industry with due attention to light industry and farming.

Consumer goods output rose by 29 per cent a year in 1950-52 and by 13 per cent a year in 1953-57. Food grain output grew by 7 per cent in 1950-52. Both outputs grew faster than the population. In 1953-57, national income grew by 8.9 per cent a year, farm output by 3.8 per cent a year and industrial output by 18.7 per cent a year. Wages rose 30 per cent in real terms, peasant income by 20 per cent. In 1950-55 China's infant mortality was 195 per 1,000 live births as against India's 163.7. By 1970-75, China's infant mortality was 61.1 per 1,000 live births as against India's 119.7. Otto Kolbl concluded in his article, *The evolution of infant mortality in China since 1950*, that "the Chinese communist regime is the most efficient baby-life-saving machine ever."[218] Life expectancy rose from 36 in 1950 to 57 in 1957, as against poor countries' average of 42. China cut its death rate from 38/1,000 in 1949 to 12/1,000 in 1957, which saved tens of millions of lives, the largest mortality reduction in history. In the same years, India reduced mortality only from 28 to 24/1,000 and Indonesia only from 26 to 23/1,000. By 1970-75 China's life expectancy was 63.2 years as against India's 50.4.

In China, as in Russia, the small scale of private farming, based on individual household work, prevented the use of farm machinery and investment in irrigation, conservation and infrastructure. The people had to end this ownership structure to modernise farming. They created mutual aid teams, working collectively and set up producers' cooperatives, where land, implements and cattle were pooled, then they created socialised cooperatives, with collective land ownership. There was some success in industrial rural projects with benefits of scale and planning achieved at commune levels and improvements in local governance. Michael Dillon commented, "The People's Communes did have positive aspects, notably economies of scale when compared with small family farms and the ability to engage in the long-term planning of agricultural production."

As historian Chun Lin observed, "[T]he lack of thoroughgoing land reform is a major developmental obstacle in large parts of the postcolonial world. The fact that China has done a great deal better – in meeting basic needs, alleviating poverty, raising the general standard of living, and giving political recognition to the social standing of labor and the common people (as in the Maoist legacy) – is an awesome testimony. It carries a universal implication: By transforming 'feudal' structures and relations, land reform, broadly defined to also include cooperative farming, eradicates backward and reactionary social power while empowering hitherto subjugated and marginalized classes. In so doing it can be a decisive promoter of economic growth and social development. [...] historical evidence has amply vindicated the superiority of revolutionary paths in transforming large, poor, agrarian, illiterate, and patriarchal societies."[219]

But in 1957-58, China was hit by an El Nino event, whose after-effects lasted for years. In July 1959 the Yellow River flooded, killing two million people. In 1960, no rain fell on 60 percent of the country's agricultural land. There were floods in South China and drought in North China. The government did all it could to make up for the shortfall in food. It organised strict food rationing, rather than letting the worst-hit areas starve, as had always happened before the 1949 revolution. It launched a massive programme of buying food from abroad. Between 1961 and 1965, it bought 30 million tons of grain from Australia, France, Sudan, Burma and Canada at a cost of $2 billion.[220] Robert North judged, "Undoubtedly the Communist regime was unique among Chinese governments of the nineteenth and twentieth centuries with respect to the efforts it made toward alleviating the inevitable mass suffering that accompanied these catastrophes."[221] But the US government continued to enforce the punitive blockade that it had imposed ever since the revolution. As Henry Liu pointed out, "More would have been imported except that US pressure on Canada and Australia to limit sales to China and US interference with shipping prevented China from importing more."[222]

In March 1962 the US government stopped the International Trading Corporation of Seattle from selling 10.5 million tons of wheat and barley to China.[223] In addition, the Soviet Union imposed sanctions on China from 1960 to 1970. Tragically, the death rate rose to 25 per thousand in 1960. This figure was close to India's usual annual death rate, 24/1,000, Indonesia's 23/1,000 and Pakistan's 23/1,000. The Chinese people worked hard to improve agriculture, to prevent famine ever happening again. By 1978 they irrigated half the land, up from a fifth in 1952. This expansion, combined with the increased productivity achieved by large collective farms, allowed for big increases in double cropping. The communes spread the use of improved technology, made greater use of fertilisers and planted high-yield semi-dwarf rice on 80 per cent of China's rice land. Between 1949 and 1978, food production rose by 169.6 per cent, while the population grew by 77.7 per cent. Food production per person grew from 204 kilograms to 328 kilograms. Grain output increased by 2.4 per cent a year from 1952 to 1978. By 1977, China was growing 40 per cent more food per person than India, on 14 per cent less arable land and distributing it more equitably to a population which was 50 per cent larger.[224] China had become self-sufficient in food.[225] As Y. Y. Kueh pointed out, "by the close of Mao's period China's historic food problem was basically solved."[226]

The World Bank's 1981 development report said, "China's most remarkable achievement during the past three decades has been to make the low-income groups far better off in terms of basic needs than their counterparts in most other poor countries. They all have work; their food supply is guaranteed through a mixture of state rationing and collective self-insurance; most of their children are not only at school but are also comparatively well taught; and the great majority have access to basic health care and family planning services. Life expectancy – whose dependence on many other economic and social variables makes it probably the best single indicator of the extent of real poverty in a country – is outstandingly high for a country at China's per capita income level."[227] The Bank pointed out in 1983, "The poorest people in China are far better off than their counterparts in most other developing countries."[228]

From 1965 to 1985, China's GDP grew by 7.49 per cent a year, more than India's 1.7 per cent, the USA's 1.34 per cent, Britain's 1.6 per cent, Japan's 4.7 per cent, South Korea's 6.6 per cent and West Germany's 2.7 per cent. Modern scholars pointed to the Chinese people's great achievements during the Mao era. Y. Y. Kueh judged, "what Mao did as an economic strategist was absolutely necessary [...] the economic heritage of Mao has to be assessed in its entirety to include the massive material foundation in both agriculture and industry, that he helped to create with the particular economic strategy practised."[229] Amartya Sen stated, "The Maoist policies of land reform, expansion of literacy, enlargement of public health care and so

95

on had a very favourable effect on economic growth in post-reform China. The extent to which post-reform China draws on the results achieved in pre-reform China needs greater recognition."[230]

Maurice Meisner concluded that China's progress resulting from the revolution 'must be seen as one of the greatest achievements of the twentieth century'. He summed up, "few events in world history have done more to better the lives of more people."[231] By 1986, China's death rate was down to 7 per 1,000. India's was 12 per 1,000. India's population was 781 million in 1986, so its excess mortality was 3.9 million in that year.[232] As economists Jean Drèze and Amartya Sen observed of India and China, "the similarities were quite striking" in 1949, but by 1989 "there is little doubt that as far as morbidity, mortality and longevity are concerned, China has a large and decisive lead over India."[233]

After Mao's death China changed direction. Between 1978 and 2005, labour's share of GDP was cut from 57 per cent to 37 per cent. Yet 800 million people moved out of poverty. Inequality grew to new highs. Economic policy in the Mao period had sought development across all regions and hinterlands, but more recently millions of people moved south to coastal areas, depopulating much of the countryside and overcrowding the cities. There were growing divides between rich and poor, between city and countryside and between the east and the west of the country. China became the world's second largest economy, its largest exporter and second largest importer. It has been one of the five largest global investors since 2010. China kept its own currency and kept control of its exchange rate. It kept a large state sector and public ownership of agricultural land. The central government kept control of enterprises in strategic sectors like energy, communications, railways, finance and national defence.

Chapter 7
The wars against Vietnam

The Vietnamese people defeat French colonialism

During World War Two, the people of Vietnam, led by their communist party, fought against the Japanese occupier. Like the people of Korea, they were in effect an ally of Britain, the USA and the Soviet Union. Their struggle succeeded. At the war's end, popular forces ran most of the country. What was their reward for their long struggle against our common enemy? The British and US governments split their country and tried to reimpose France's colonial rule. The people of Vietnam wanted a united and independent country. Joseph Buttinger, a former advisor and supporter of the US-backed Diem regime in South Vietnam, wrote, "There can be no doubt that, had it not been for outside military interference, Vietnam, independent and again unified, would have become a Communist-controlled state in the fall of 1945. [...] the Vietnamese Communists were capable of gaining power without the presence of a single soldier of a foreign Communist army in their country."[234]

The free, all-Vietnam general election of 6 January 1946 resulted in the overwhelming victory of the Viet Minh. Any outside intervention against this independent state, whether France's attempt to re-establish its colonial rule, or the British military intervention to support this French intervention, or setting up a separate regime in the South, was an act of aggression against an independent and sovereign nation. From 1945 to 1954 the people of Vietnam fought for their freedom from French colonialism. President Eisenhower wrote later, "I have never talked or corresponded with a person knowledgeable in Indochinese affairs who did not agree that, had elections been held at the time of the fighting [against France], possibly 80 per cent of the population would have voted for the Communist Ho Chi Minh as their leader."

The Vietnamese finally defeated the French forces in the battle of Dien Bien Phu. The governments of France, the Democratic Republic of Vietnam, the Bao Dai regime in the south, the United Kingdom, the United States of America, the Soviet Union and the People's Republic of China all endorsed the Final Declaration of the 1954 Geneva Peace Conference. Its Article 12 read, "In their relations with Cambodia, Laos and Vietnam, each member of the Geneva Conference undertakes to respect the sovereignty, the independence, the unity and the territorial integrity of the above-mentioned states and to refrain from any interference in their internal affairs." They all pledged to support 'general elections which will bring about the unification of Vietnam', to be held under UN supervision before August 1956. The Final Act of the Accords defined Vietnam as one state and nation. Part 6 stated, "the military demarcation line is provisional and should not in any way be interpreted as constituting a political or territorial boundary." The US delegate assured the Conference that the USA 'would refrain from the threat or use of force to disturb the agreement.'

The USA breaks the Geneva Agreements

But successive US governments were determined to prevent the people of Vietnam from having an election to decide their future, because they knew that the forces of national liberation led by the communist party would win. Leo Cherne, a founder of American Friends of Vietnam, warned in 1955 that "if elections were held today, the overwhelming majority of Vietnamese would vote Communist."[235] Historians agreed. John Spanier and Steven Hook wrote, "Ho's popularity was the reason that neither the US nor the new government in the South favoured the election."[236] The US government and its ally Ngo Dinh Diem, not the communists, prevented the promised all-Vietnam election. Instead, Diem with US backing, organised a separate poll in the south, which the US Ambassador called 'a travesty of democratic procedures'.[237] In Saigon, with 450,000 registered voters, Diem got 605,025 votes.[238]

Historian George Kahin wrote, "In mid-1955 […] Diem – with U.S. encouragement – announced that the elections would not be held. […] Having chosen not to carry out the heart of the Geneva Agreements, Diem made civil war inevitable. For when a military struggle […] ends on the agreed condition that the competition will be returned to the political level, the side which repudiates the agreed conditions can hardly expect that the military struggle will not be resumed."[239] Secretary of State Dean Rusk cabled the US embassy, "No admission should be made that [Geneva] Accords are not being observed."[240]

From 1954 on, the USA and the Diem regime imposed sanctions on the North. In June 1956, Diem used his army to attack regions of the South controlled by his opponents the Viet Minh, contrary to the Geneva Agreements. The Agreements specifically forbade any reprisals against former resistance fighters, but as Jeffrey Race, a former US Army advisor in South Vietnam, wrote, Diem "employed every means to track them down and arrest them. […] After arrest, the cadres would be liquidated."[241] Joseph Buttinger, the Diem supporter, admitted that in these illegal assaults, "there can be no doubt […] that innumerable crimes and absolutely senseless acts of repression […] were committed."[242] Buttinger added, "thousands of Communists as well as non-Communist sympathizers of the Vietminh were killed and many more thrown into prison and concentration camps […] all of this happened more than two years before the Communists began to commit acts of terror against local government officials."[243] The Pentagon Papers revealed that US intelligence knew that "the war began largely as a rebellion in the South against the increasingly oppressive and corrupt regime of Ngo Dinh Diem." The people "who took up arms were South Vietnamese and the causes for which they fought were by no means contrived in the North."[244] The American historian Paul Chamberlin explained, "as had been the case in China and Korea, the United States opted to back a repressive anti-communist regime with a narrow base of popular support [...]."[245]

Supporters of Diem's regime tried to win public support by inventing stories of communist atrocities. US missionary Tom Dooley published lurid stories of Viet Minh atrocities against Catholic children. In 1956, the U.S. Information Agency investigated Dooley's stories and found no evidence to support them. William Lederer, who helped Dooley write and publish his book, later admitted that the stories were fake: the "atrocities [...] never took place or were committed by the French. I travelled all over the country and never saw anything like them."[246] Others falsely accused the government of North Vietnam of mass murder. President Nixon later claimed that "a half a million, by conservative estimates [...] were murdered or otherwise exterminated by the North Vietnamese."[247] American historian Edwin Moïse, in his study of land reform in the North, wrote, "Various people in Saigon had been manufacturing counterfeit North Vietnamese documents, and falsified translations of genuine documents, in order to support the idea that large numbers of people had been killed in the land reform. The documentary evidence for the bloodbath theory seems to have been a fabrication almost in its entirety."[248] Moïse concluded that "the slaughter of tens of thousands of innocent victims, often described in anti-communist propaganda, never took place."[249]

On 11 May 1961 President Kennedy approved National Security Action Memorandum 52 ordering an increase in covert military operations against North Vietnam and an expansion in the forces available for these operations. By the time of his death, he had sent more than 16,000 military 'advisors' to Vietnam, far more than permitted under the Geneva Accords. But Diem started to act against US government wishes. He stated in late September 1963 that he had agreed with Ho Chi Minh the outlines of a peace settlement including a cease-fire, the departure of US forces, accepting National Liberation Front representatives into the government and an election in which the Communists could participate. Kennedy and his officials worked with South Vietnamese generals to oust Diem, an act that resulted in Diem's murder. The Pentagon Papers stated that 'the U.S. must accept its full share of responsibility' for the coup against Diem and for his murder, because beginning in August 1963 Washington 'authorized, sanctioned and encouraged the coup efforts.'[250]

Pretext for aggression

In August 1964 President Johnson used the 'Tonkin Gulf incidents' to justify launching the US war of aggression. The US government falsely alleged that North Vietnamese patrol boats had attacked two US destroyers in the Gulf. The destroyers were there to assist covert US raids into North Vietnam under Operational Plan 34A, also known as OPLAN 34A, which was a secret programme of agent team insertions, aerial reconnaissance missions and naval sabotage operations. The US destroyers were assisting commando attacks on North Vietnamese installations in the area. The USA controlled the missions, using boats procured and maintained by the US Navy, attacking targets which the CIA selected, in an operation for which the USA paid.[251] The USA was the aggressor. Edward Moïse wrote, in the leading study of the incidents, "The initial government announcements on the first Tonkin Gulf incident had given the impression that the North Vietnamese PT boats had gotten in the first shots – that until the PT boats had opened fire, the *Maddox* either had not fired at all or had fired nothing but warning shots.

The initial press accounts reflected this version of events. The Defense Department quickly released a more detailed chronology reflecting the reality that the destroyer had fired first."[252] Moïse wrote of the alleged attack on USS *Turner Joy* on 4 August, "the weight of the evidence against an attack becomes overwhelming."[253] Secretary of Defense Robert McNamara gave the Senate Foreign Relations and Armed Services Committee what Moïse called "a simple picture of unprovoked attack against U.S. ships on the high seas. [...] This picture was false in almost every detail. [...] McNamara denied, even long afterward, that there had been any dishonesty in his testimony. [...] He denies having said in 1964 that the *Maddox* did not know anything about the raids. Thirty years later, in his memoirs, he admitted that his statement had been 'totally incorrect' because Captain Herrick [of the *Maddox*] *did* know about OPLAN 34A, but he continued to claim that 'our Navy [...] was not aware of any South Vietnamese actions.' Was Captain Herrick not part of the U.S. Navy? McNamara continued to claim that 'the U.S. Navy did not administer 34A operations.'"[254]

The US government claimed that cynical, exploitative foreign powers started the war for their own expansionist purposes. Ironically, this was true – but only of the US government, not of any other government. US leaders saw the Vietnamese people as gullible and misled. As so often, the US government falsely accused a national liberation movement of working for a foreign power, of being run from Moscow. Ironically, it was the USA's allies, the counter-revolutionaries led by Diem, who were working for a foreign power, run from abroad – from Washington. In the same way, some pro-EU politicians falsely accused Brexiteers of working for a foreign power, of being run from Moscow or Washington. In the same way, some pro-EU politicians falsely accused Brexiteers of working for a foreign power, of being run from Moscow or Washington. It was reaction's allies, the pro-EU politicians, who were working for a foreign power, run from abroad – from Brussels. Johnson absurdly warned, "If you start running from the Communists, they may just chase you right into your own kitchen."[255] He claimed, "If we don't fight them over there, we fight them on our doorstep." He said, "We will defend our kitchens." The National Rifle Association took adverts showing a man with a rifle defending his kitchen against straw hat-wearing Vietnamese. But the public knew that the Vietnamese could not swim across the Pacific Ocean and knew that they did not have Higgins Boats or Coast Guardsmen to drive them. On the day Vietnamese troops liberated Saigon, a colleague of mine joked uneasily, "we'll all be eating rice now." He seemed to have believed Johnson's ludicrous claim. Decades later, President Reagan, equally absurdly, warned that the Sandinistas were 'just two days' driving time from Harlingen, Texas'.[256]

Kissinger: kill 'anything that moves'[257]

What kind of war did the US government wage? From December 1968 to May 1969, the US Ninth Infantry launched a major attack – 'Operation Speedy Express' - to gain control of a large and heavily populated region of the Mekong Delta. It achieved a reported enemy body count of 10,889. Yet they found just 748 enemy weapons. Clearly, most of those killed were unarmed civilians. An American officer defended the bombing of Ben Tre by saying, "it became necessary to destroy the town in order to save it." Kissinger said in July 1969, "I refuse to believe that a little fourth-rate power like North Vietnam doesn't have a breaking-point." This approach – make them suffer, they will have a breaking point – is the torturer's mindset. Between 1962 and 1973, US forces dropped eight million tons of bombs on Vietnam, Laos and Cambodia, more than three times the amount it dropped in World War Two. US forces dropped four million tons of bombs on South Vietnam, the supposed victim of aggression and one million tons on the north, the supposed aggressor. The bombing killed about 55,000 civilians in the North. By the war's end, half the villages in the South had been destroyed. US forces sprayed about nineteen million gallons of defoliants on South Vietnam, destroying twelve million acres of forest.

A 2008 study of wartime mortality in Vietnam by researchers from Harvard Medical School and the Institute for Health Metrics and Evaluation at the University of Washington concluded that there had been 3,800,000 violent war deaths, combat and civilian, mostly civilian. That is about 8 per cent of the country's 35,000,000 population in 1975. The equivalent death toll in the USA would be about 17,500,000 people. The USA, a country of 200 million, lost about 58,000 troops. Further, the Vietnamese government has estimated that unexploded ordnance has killed 40,000 people and maimed 65,000 since the war's end. By 1971, 71 per cent of Americans told pollsters they believed that intervening in Vietnam had been a 'mistake' and 58 per cent regarded the war as 'immoral'.

In April 1974, a Harris poll on whether the USA should continue its military aid to Vietnam found 74 per cent against, 17 per cent for, and 9 per cent not sure. US reactionaries echoed the Nazi myth that the German army was never defeated but was stabbed in the back by civilians when they claimed that the US army was never defeated but that cowardly civilian politicians did not allow it to win. But all these unrealistic, arrogant absurdities are not accidental intellectual or moral failures, coincidentally repeated time and again. They are systemic. They flow from the bourgeois idealist conception of history, born of a reactionary ruling class. In 1949 Mao Tse-tung brilliantly exposed this conception when he demolished the claims of the US State Department's White Paper on US-China relations.[258] The White Paper was an attempt to answer the question, why did we lose China? But China, like Korea, like Vietnam, was never the USA's to lose. Mao showed that it was not that western ideas of democracy stirred up ferment and unrest in other countries, but that US imperialist aggression provoked justified resistance.

Opposing the war

In Britain, by September 1965, the Foreign Office was 'increasingly concerned about the state of public opinion on Vietnam'. Gallup polls showed that most people in Britain disapproved of American actions in Vietnam and that most believed that Britain's role should be to start peace talks. The anti-war movement in Britain grew. Many trade unions passed resolutions attacking the 'subservience of the British government to American policy'. Several pre-existing groups – like the Movement for Colonial Freedom and the Campaign for Nuclear Disarmament – were joined by new single-issue groups in protesting against the US attack on Vietnam and against the Labour government's support of the aggression. In May 1965, the British Council for Peace in Vietnam (BCPV) co-ordinated political, religious and trade union organisations to

105

press the Labour government to 'dissociate itself from America's military intervention in Vietnam'. It organised a 100,000-signature petition of British citizens who were 'gravely disturbed by the mounting cruelty and destruction of the war in Vietnam'. In January 1966 more radical activists formed a higher profile anti-war group, the Vietnam Solidarity Campaign (VSC) which backed the Viet Minh. Student unions provided a base for much of the British opposition to the war. As elsewhere, university campuses became the scene of anti-war demonstrations and 'teach-ins', with notable actions at the LSE, Oxford and Warwick. This popular pressure forced Prime Minister Harold Wilson to place limits on British support.

In June 1966, Wilson dissociated Britain from the American bombing of oil depots in Hanoi and Haiphong, despite desperate pleas from Washington not to do so. In July 1967, 7,000 people marched to the US embassy with placards accusing the US of war crimes. VSC organised two major demonstrations in Grosvenor Square. The first, on 17 March 1968, attracted 25,000 marchers. The second, on 27 October 1968, attracted more than 100,000 people. The American historian William Appleman Williams responded to criticisms of the anti-war movement: "that some critics are Communists. This is true as fact. It is also true that some extreme reactionaries are also critics of American policy in Vietnam. Both facts are incidental to the substantive issues. Criticism is properly judged by its relevance, by its evidence, and by its internal coherence and logic."[259] A CIA study of the peace movement found "pacifists and fighters, idealists and materialists, internationalists and isolationists, democrats and totalitarians, conservatives and revolutionaries, capitalists and socialists, patriots and subversives, lawyers and anarchists, Stalinists and Trotskyites, Muscovites and Pekingese, racists and universalists, zealots and nonbelievers, puritans and hippies, do-gooders and evildoers, nonviolent and very violent." What brought them all together was not outside money or manipulation but 'their opposition to US actions in Vietnam.'[260]

The war undermined the central tenet of American national identity, the faith that the USA is a unique force for good in the world, with a uniquely moral governmental system and a uniquely admirable way of life. Americans saw that their own government could wage a war of aggression and try to justify it with unfounded claims and that their government could support antidemocratic governments abroad. The American historian Henry Steele Commager wrote in 1972, "Some wars are so deeply immoral that they must be lost, that the war in Vietnam is one of those wars, and that those who resist it are the true patriots."[261] It was always a canard that those who opposed the war were 'anti-American'.

The American historian Christian Appy concluded his brilliant account of the war, "the public is not blameless. As long as we continue to be seduced by the myth of American exceptionalism, we will too easily acquiesce to the misuse of power, all too readily trust that our force is used only with the best of intentions for the greatest good. If so, a future of further militarism and war is virtually guaranteed. Perhaps the only basis to begin real change is to seek the fuller reckoning of our role in the world that the Vietnam War so powerfully awakened – to confront the evidence of what we have done. It is our record; it is who we are."[262] After the war against Vietnam, the USA never again saw broad public support for lengthy military interventions. The war's failure made US governments reluctant to send troops overseas. Fewer than eight hundred American troops were killed in the many US military interventions of the 1980s and 1990s. The American historian John Marciano concluded, "During the American war, those who controlled this nation's foreign policy were, in the words of the late historian Gabriel Kolko, 'devious, incorrigible, and beyond the pale of human values'. They revealed themselves in Vietnam, and since then in Latin America, Africa, the Middle East, and Central Asia, for what they are: international terrorists."[263]

Chapter 8
Working class advance in Britain, and the Thatcher counter-attack

The struggle for equal pay

Women workers have long struggled to achieve equal pay. Women in the textile industry fought to achieve the rate for the job well before the TUC adopted its first policy on equal pay, in 1888. The engineers' union consistently fought for equal pay. During the Second World War many women joined their male colleagues in the engineering factories and the AEU began to recruit these women workers. In 1954, when a fifth of engineering workers were women, they earned £11.50 a week less than their male equivalents, so the union put forward a claim for women to receive no less than the average male worker's rate. Women moved towards equal pay through strong workplace collective bargaining, against the employers' unremitting hostility. In 1956, the union won a major improvement. By 1959, women's hourly pay in the engineering industry was 77.4 per cent of men's; by 1967 it was 85 per cent, compared to 66 per cent in other industries.

On 29 May 1968, all 187 women employed as sewing machinists at Ford's Dagenham River plant struck for an upgrading of their jobs and for better pay. Reg Birch, the Secretary of the trade union side of the Ford National Joint Negotiating Committee (NJNC) and the AUEW executive member for London North, put it to the AUEW Executive that the strike was not about grading, but over equal pay. He said, "It was our job as officials to get the company to pay equal rates. The conditions weren't our concern. We didn't have to agree to anything. We just had to get the equal pay. And then, on the shop floor, the women could set about blocking the company's demands. But we had to get them the equal pay in the first place."[264] On 7 June, the women unanimously voted for an all-out strike. By 1 July, the women won an increase of 7 pence an hour, a 12 per cent increase that took their rate up from 85 per cent to 92 per cent of the men's equivalent for each grade. After another three years of struggle, they brought women's pay up to equality with the average male rate. At last, in 1970, the union forced the employer to agree to an equal pay clause, an important precedent for the struggle of women throughout industry. The long struggle bore fruit in the Equal Pay Act of 1970, which however did not come into effect until 29 December 1975.

Barbara Castle, Labour's Secretary of State for Employment, who introduced the Act, typified social democracy by claiming all the credit and slandering the trade unions, writing, "left to themselves the unions would never do anything serious about equal pay."[265] Sander Meredeen, in his study of industrial disputes, judged more accurately and more generously that "this handful of women won themselves an honoured place in labour history by securing equal pay for the women of Britain. [...] From small beginnings, it became the biggest and most important strike by any group of British women since the Bryant & May Matchgirls' strike in 1888."[266] Many people thought the Act would finally secure equal pay as a right. Not so. It took more than an Act in parliament to change reality. Trico-Folbert, a US multinational company, had a factory in Brentford, West London, which produced windscreen wiper systems. It ignored the 1970 Act. In the summer of 1976 the women workers at Trico struck for equal pay. The company did all it could to break the strike – US-style picket-busting, strike-breaking lorry convoys aided by the police, bussing in of scab labour, threats of redundancy.

Sally Groves and Vernon Merritt, the historians of the strike, explained how the women won: "there were some critical points during the strike when official support was on a knife-edge. [...] They were the result of the political complexion of the AUEW Executive Council, which at the time was almost entirely right-wing in complexion, apart from the lone figure of Reg Birch, the strikers' EC man. How important this was for the women has only become publicly known recently. The continuation of official support for the strike was crucial, but it was never a foregone conclusion. Without strike pay, which only came with continuing official endorsement of the strike, the women and their male supporters would not only have been demoralised and delegitimised in the eyes of the trade union movement: they would also have been starved back to work."[267] The "lack of support from the Labour and TUC leadership meant that all the negotiations with company were kept firmly under the control of the local AUEW officials, as well as the region's AUEW Executive Committee member Reg Birch. It was Reg Birch who ensured that the EEF [Engineering Employers' Federation] did not ultimately take over and negotiate directly with the AUEW Executive Council, which would have taken the final settlement out of the hands of the strikers' representatives."[268]

On 14 October 1976, the company conceded the women's demands and agreed to introduce a common operational rate throughout the payment-by-results areas, regardless of sex. The women would now get an average £6.50 more a week. It was the most successful strike for equal pay in British history. The AUEW's Roger Butler said, "This is a lesson to the movement on how equal pay can be achieved. It won't be brought about by tribunals. It's only through trade union unity and working-class struggle that justice for women workers will be won."[269] Reg Birch said later that this was "one of the best struggles that workers have ever joined together in, based on a

111

principle, the Trico women's battle for equal pay. Black and white together, only wanting to know: are you with us or against us? Straight, simple, classic thinking, indomitable, unbeatable." Bob Singh, a press setter at the factory, said that the strike "galvanized a lot of people's ideas about the rights of trade unionists and workers. But everything has its opposite, and the opposite to all that was the growth of Thatcherism. The ruling class – the upper classes and employers – realized that they needed something else to destroy the power of the trade unions, and Thatcher became that person, and that's why she became the leader of the Conservative Party."[270]

In the late 1970s many workers took industrial action to improve their wages and conditions. As Groves and Merritt pointed out, "the media significantly exaggerated the impact of the strikes of winter 1979-80, in order to discredit Labour and assist Thatcher. In contrast to genuine catastrophes such as the collapse of UK manufacturing in the 1980s under Thatcher, or the banking crisis of 2008, it had very little economic impact. Despite this, the legend of the 'winter of discontent' is now set in stone, impervious even to the admission of Derek Jameson, editor of the *Daily Express* in 1979, who said, 'We pulled every dirty trick in the book. We made it look like it was general, universal and eternal, whereas it was in reality scattered, here and there, and no great problem.'"[271]

Thatcher

Thatcher ushered in the age of neoliberalism. Her first act in October 1979 was to end capital controls. In 1979, Britain's capitalists held £199 billion in overseas assets, by 1990, £950 billion. Finance capital flourished at the expense of industry. British manufacturing industry's gross capital stock rose only from £253 billion to £278 billion between1979 and 1990, the worst record of any industrial country. The big lie was that Thatcherism was necessary to save the economy. Philip Johnston wrote in the *Daily Telegraph* of 7 July 2020 that all through the 1950s, 1960s and 1970s 'the economy crashed and burned'. Actually, it grew faster in each of those decades than in the 1980s under Thatcher. Thatcher promised that her tax cuts would lift wages and investment, and reduce government deficits. They did not. American historian Sean Wilentz wrote, "supply-side economics were a delusion. The promise of increased investments and revenues accruing as a direct result of lower taxes could never be a reality."[272]

In Thatcher's first eighteen months, Britain's manufacturing output fell by a record 16 per cent. (Between 1929 and 1930 it had fallen by 6.9 per cent.) 1.5 million jobs in industry were destroyed. Manufacturing jobs fell from 31 per cent of all jobs in 1980 to 22.5 per cent in 1990. Our share of the world market in manufactured goods fell from 9.1 per cent in 1979 to 7 per cent in the late 1980s and to 4.7 per cent in 1995. Our share of the world's high-technology exports fell from 11.2 per cent to 9.2 per cent. Engineering output was lower in 1992 than in 1980, at constant prices. Imports as a proportion of GDP rose from 29 per cent in 1981 to 37 per cent in 1988. In 1982-83 we had our first-ever deficit in trade in manufactured goods. Between 1979 and 1993 the British economy grew 1.6 per cent a year, the lowest rate of any industrialised country in the world for any comparable period since 1945.[273] The American economist Joseph Stiglitz summed up, "The results are now unambiguous. Growth slowed relative to the years after World War II, and what growth occurred went largely to upper-income individuals."[274]

Thatcher claimed that her policies were needed to fight the greatest danger of all – inflation. But her remedy was worse than the problem. Her policies did not even succeed on her own terms – inflation was higher when she left office in 1990, at 10.9 per cent, than when she came in, 10.1 per cent.[275] Thatcher's deflationary policies failed and were, eventually, abandoned. As Stiglitz pointed out, "No economy in a recession has recovered through contractionary policies."[276] Deflation always produces depression: deflationary policies, not protectionism, had caused and lengthened the Great Depression of the 1930s. Thatcher backed up her destruction of industry with the fiercest anti-trade union laws in Europe. As Robert Taylor, the *Financial Times'* industrial correspondent, wrote, "By 1993 Britain had the most restrictive industrial relations laws of any western European market economy."[277] Labour Prime Minister Tony Blair retained most of these repressive laws.

'Thatcherism in Europe'

Thatcher signed us up to the 1986 Single European Act (SEA), the biggest step towards a single European state since the 1957 Treaty of Rome. EU-supporter Michael Heseltine wrote that the Act "was as comprehensive a redefinition of national sovereignty as we have ever known."[278] The Act's intention and effect was to Thatcherise the EU. The Act introduced the Single European Market (SEM), adopted Thatcher's policy of scrapping exchange controls, made protectionism illegal, created the legal basis for a single EU foreign policy, greatly extended the practice of qualified majority voting (QMV) and included a commitment in principle to Economic and Monetary Union.[279] The European Roundtable of Industrialists wanted the SEM because it added to employers' powers. The head of the Bundesbank approved: "The single market means not stability but more flexibility in the labour market." The European Commission saw the SEM as 'the most ambitious and comprehensive supply-side programme ever launched'.[280]

The Act's Article 43 stated that all the EU's existing treaties were sacrosanct and could not be renegotiated. The Conservative Party policy of seeking to renegotiate those treaties that it did not like was pointless. There was no room for flexibility or revision: the EU train can only move one way. Article 13 read, "The internal market shall comprise an area without internal frontiers in which the free movement of goods, persons, services and capital is ensured." For businesses, getting rid, in one swoop, of exchange controls, tariff barriers and barriers to migration between member countries was a great EU achievement. Free movement of goods meant strike-breaking: in September 2000, when French workers blockaded Channel ports to cut fuel costs, the EU threatened to invoke the clause about the free movement of goods to help to break the blockade. Free movement of persons meant forced emigration, more job insecurity, and more unemployment. Free movement of capital meant closures.

The Single Market helped to shape liberalisation across the world, and in turn liberalisation shaped the Single Market.[281] The SEM increased EU interference in states' welfare, social and health programmes. The EU's drive towards market integration eroded national welfare state autonomy.[282] Its 'harmonisation' of social and labour market policies led to cutting trade union powers and integrating workers into company structures to get them to accept job losses, worse conditions and wage cuts.[283] The European Commission admitted - or boasted - in 1993, "The single market programme has done more for business than it has for workers."[284] Lord Young, Thatcher's Trade and Industry Minister, said, "The Single Market meant 'Thatcherism in Europe'."[285] The EU wrote Thatcherism into its treaties. Richard Tuck noted, "The EU enshrines in near-perpetuity the capitalism of the 1980s."[286]

In 1990 Thatcher took us into the Exchange Rate Mechanism [ERM], the EU's rehearsal for the euro. The entire establishment, including the Labour party, forecast doom if we did not join. Two years later, the entire establishment forecast doom if we left. Economist Roger Bootle pointed out, "Before the exit, the Treasury had proclaimed that if we left the ERM, inflation and interest rates would rise and the economy would fall back. In fact, interest rates and inflation fell and the economy surged ahead."[287] Doom did not follow, at least, not for the economy. Ironically, entry doomed Thatcher. Exit doomed her chosen successor John Major. Thatcher later claimed that creating Tony Blair and New Labour was her greatest achievement. She could have claimed that getting the EU to adopt Thatcherism was her greatest achievement.

Chapter 9
The European Union and its euro

Ever closer union, ever less growth

The EU's Stability and Growth Pact, adopted in 1997, requires member states to keep their budget deficits below 3 per cent of their GDP. This pushed governments into seeking to raise money from the private money markets, and took infrastructure investment off the government's books, while loading future generations with the burdens of repayment. These Private Finance Initiatives were far dearer than the cheaper method of government borrowing and gave huge profits to privateers. Nobody pushed PFIs more enthusiastically than Labour's Gordon Brown. Outside the EU, we will no longer be required to use these costly, damaging PFIs. The EU introduced the euro in 1999. Up to 2018, Germany's GDP grew by 32 per cent, France's by 32 per cent, Italy's by just 9 per cent, Greece's by just 1.3 per cent. These figures proved that the EU was no 'level playing field'. The field tilts to favour German and French interests.

The EU called itself cooperative, but its policies did not foster partnership, they fostered antagonism between member nations, particularly between those in the north and those in the south. People who voted to stay in the EU were right to want international cooperation and peaceful relations with our European partners, but unfortunately the EU instead fostered divisions. Between 1999 and 2018, eurozone GDP grew by 26 per cent, By contrast, outside the eurozone, Britain's GDP grew by 43 per cent. Between 1999 and 2018, eurozone GDP grew by26 per cent. By contrast, outside the eurozone, Britain's GDP grew by 43 per cent. Between 2009 and 2017 the eurozone's

GDP grew by just 4.5 per cent, while GDP grew 139 per cent in China, 96 per cent in India, and 34 per cent in the USA, according to the World Bank. Commonwealth markets have expanded faster than the EU since 1973. Eurozone unemployment averaged 9.8 per cent between 2009 and 2017. Eurozone members' average GDP growth was 2.7 per cent in 1973-79, 2.5 per cent in 1984-94, 2.3 per cent in 1994-98, 2.1 per cent in 1999-2003, 1.8 per cent in 2004-08, and 1.2 per cent in 2012-19. Ever closer union, ever less growth.

Since the 1980s, the average incomes of 90 per cent of the populations of EU members have not risen, while the richest one per cent have nearly doubled their incomes. The American economist Joseph Stiglitz observed in general, "There is no plausible moral or economic argument for a market economy whose growth benefits only a small number of people while excluding the great majority from its fruits."[288] Bojan Bugarič, Professor of Law at Sheffield University, observed, "For the first time in the EU history we see an emergence of a new economic constitution which explicitly entrenches one economic paradigm at the expense of other alternatives, with simultaneously dismantling the remaining protections of social policy autonomy of member states. This approach is not only constitutionally problematic, but also economically questionable. It threatens the very existence of the EU as we have known it".

The [2012] Fiscal Treaty, for example, basically entrenches a certain economic theory at the level of constitutional law requiring the signatories of the Treaty to change their constitutions, preferably, with new provisions of binding force and permanent character. In other words, the signatories of the compact are asked to introduce into their constitutions provisions which can't be changed through regular amendment procedures. As a consequence, the austerity policy of Angela Merkel thus achieves binding and eternal legal validity. While it elevates the austerity paradigm of the German Chancellor Angela Merkel to the status of 'unbreakable law', it basically outlaws Keynesianism and its counter-cyclical economic policies. No surprise then that in the editorial, one of the leading constitutional journals in Europe [*European Constitutional Law Review*, 2012, 8, 5] concluded that the Fiscal compact 'strikes at the heart of the institutions of parliamentary democracy by dislocating as a matter of constitutional principle the budgetary autonomy of the member states."[289]

Stiglitz pointed out that "Neoliberalism played a more conscious and more important role in the design of the economic framework for the Eurozone than it did in the earlier ideas of Reagan and Thatcher, and ordinary Europeans paid a heavy price."[290] Some people who voted to stay in the EU did so because they opposed the neoliberalism that some in the leave camp backed. They were right to oppose it, but they should have noticed that the EU was essentially just such a neoliberal project. Staying in the EU was the reactionary, the neoliberal policy.

Roger Eatwell and Matthew Goodwin observed, "Financiers in the City of London *did* line up to fund anti-Brexit campaigns and issued dubious economic forecasts about the short-term impact of the vote for Brexit, many of which were wide of the mark."[291] The bastions of neoliberal orthodoxy all told us that independence would be a disaster, leading to a slump and the destruction of workers' rights, consumer protections, and the environment. Roger Bootle noted, "Before the referendum in June 2016, the international forecasting community was pretty united in asserting that a vote to leave would produce an immediate sharp downturn in the UK economy. This august group included HM Treasury, the Bank of England, the IMF, the OECD and umpteen private sector organizations."[292] The

Treasury forecast that by 2018 "GDP would be around 3.6 per cent lower" and "unemployment would increase by around 500,000." In reality, from end June 2016 to end December 2018, GDP rose from £490,502 million to £511,175 million, a rise of £20,673 million, 4.1 per cent higher. Unemployment fell by around 250,000. These forecasts were wrong, and always erred in the same direction. The Bank of England forecast in August 2016 that our exports would fall by 0.5 per cent in 2017. They increased by nearly 8 per cent. It forecast that business investment would fall by 2 per cent. It increased by 2 per cent. It forecast that housing investment in 2017 would fall by 4.75 per cent. It increased by 5 per cent. It was no surprise that all its forecasts were that things would get worse: its anti-Brexit mindset, not reality, determined its forecasts. These were forecasts not facts, and were, like all human affairs, subject to human corrective action. These forecasts revealed not future events but the forecaster's wishes. All this experience made more and more people reject deflationary policies.

As the 2017 British Social Attitudes survey found, "After seven years of government austerity programmes by the Conservative-Liberal Democrat coalition and then Conservative majority government, the public is turning against spending less. For the first time since the financial crash of 2007-8, more people (48%) want taxation increased to allow greater spending, than want tax and spend levels to stay as they are (44%). More people (42%) agree than disagree (28%) that government should redistribute income from the better off to those who are less well-off. Shortly before the financial crisis fewer people supported redistribution than opposed it (34% and 38% respectively in 2006)."[293] Many people rightly opposed 'Tory austerity', but some then voted to stay in the EU whose treaties required austerity. Staying in the EU would have guaranteed that we would get austerity policies imposed by whatever government we elected, because the EU imposed austerity policies across the EU. Syriza in Greece in 2015 won an election by talking tough about fighting the EU's austerity policies, then, when the election was won, being committed to the EU, at once surrendered and imposed the EU's mandatory austerity policies. It was 'talk left then act right'. The EU inflicted on the people of Greece what *Forbes* magazine called 'the worst peacetime depression experienced by any advanced economy in recorded history'.[294] Deaths in Greece rose from 70,830 in 2013 to 124,832 in 2017 and 121,349 in 2019.

The EU banned progressive policies like those that Bernie Sanders put forward in the USA. As Tuck pointed out, "The three proposals which Sanders put at the heart of his movement were: pull out of or radically modify NAFTA and do not enter the TPP; greatly increase the tax on the big Wall Street banks; and introduce free state college and university tuition paid for largely by the Wall Street tax. The British version of these proposals obviously resonate with Labour's newly energised electorate, but - and I want to stress this – *none of them would have been feasible for a British government within the EU.*"[295] A Labour government committed to staying in the EU would not have been allowed to deliver its programme. If people who supported Labour want progress, they should welcome our leaving the EU. They should demand an end to the neoliberal policy of Bank of England 'independence'. Without public control of the Bank, none of Labour's policies could be implemented. Our history showed that if a country did not own the keys to all the banks but talked of an investment bank in a 'mixed economy', it would fail. People of all political persuasions and none increasingly realised, as Stiglitz pointed out, that "It was the excesses of the financial sector [...] not the welfare state that brought on the crisis."[296]

Private finance capital not public spending caused the crash. Anatol Lieven noted, "Over the past 200 years, it has been proved, and beyond reasonable doubt, that capitalism is incapable of regulating and limiting itself. The nation state has to play a central role, based on the wider interests of the state and people. Unregulated financial speculation inevitably leads to crashes like those of 1929 and 2008. Even more important, without state and social controls, the capitalist search for increased profit tends inevitably to the immiseration of large parts of the population, the destruction of the environment, and the disintegration of society."[297] Stiglitz again: "The evidence is that many of our society's ills, from air and water pollution to excesses of inequality, stem from markets."[298] Stiglitz acknowledged that capitalism did not even do well what some claimed was its key advantage over socialism: "the market is inefficient in the production of knowledge and the translation of that knowledge into advances in productivity, as embodied in new products and new production processes."[299]

John Mills summed up, "monetarism and neoliberalism [...] managed to get their grip on the European Union, leading to the determination, exemplified in the provisions of the 1992 Maastricht Treaty, to put monetary stability before prosperity."[300] Professor John Weeks acknowledged, "For three decades the European Union has moved away from Christian and social democracy towards neoliberalism. The dominant consequence of the Treaties of Maastricht [1992], Amsterdam [1999] and Lisbon [2009] has been to constrain policy at the national and EU level to conform to the ideologies of 'free' trade, fiscal austerity and a deregulated labour market. The

2012 Treaty on Stability, Coordination and Governance consolidated in draconian language what the other treaties might have missed."[301] Stiglitz wrote, "There was no increase in growth rates in the Eurozone after the creation of the euro. In fact, even before the onset of the financial crisis, growth was lower than in prior decades. Moreover, Eurozone countries responded to the crisis less effectively than the non-Eurozone countries. [...] the structure of the Eurozone weakened crisis countries by facilitating capital flight. We must admit that the policy of austerity, and the refusal to consider sufficiently large debt restructuring, and the so-called structural reforms imposed on the crisis countries that were neither well-timed nor well-chosen, combined to deepen the downturns."[302]

Paul Krugman concluded that the EU's leaders "have spent a quarter-century trying to run Europe on the basis of fantasy economics. [...] When the predicted and predictable strains on the euro began, Europe's policy response was to impose draconian austerity on debtor nations - and to deny the simple logic and historical evidence indicating that such policies would inflict terrible economic damage while failing to achieve the promised debt reduction. [...] trying to deal with large debts through austerity alone - in particular, while simultaneously pursuing a hard-money policy - has never worked. It didn't work for Britain after World War I, despite immense sacrifices; why would anyone expect it to work for Greece?"[303]

Workers' rights

Unlikely friends of workers like Cameron and Osborne assured us that the EU protected workers' rights. But, as Dani Rodrik pointed out, "in practice the EU subordinates its concern with workers' rights to its concern to maintain the freedom of companies to shop around within the EU for the weakest regimes of labour protection."[304] The EU adopted the neoliberal idea that capitalism could generate full employment if only there were no strong trade unions to limit or prevent money-wage deflation. By contrast, Keynes always insisted that free-market capitalism, not unions, caused high unemployment.

How did the EU treat workers' rights in practice? The crisis of 2008 hit Romania hard. When it asked the EU for 20 billion euros to keep it afloat, the European Commission obliged – on condition that Romania cut workers' rights, individual and collective, made it easier to fire workers, introduced new 'flexible' employment contracts, outlawed cross-sectoral collective bargaining, cut down sectoral collective agreements (their number fell by 60 per cent), slashed public sector salaries by a quarter, and cut benefits. In 2011 the ECB demanded wage reductions and deregulation from Spain in 2011 in exchange for financial assistance. It bullied the Greek government to cut wages, cut public spending and cut trade union rights. This was the true face of the EU, which some told us safeguarded our trade union rights. In Britain, did EU protections stop one zero-hours contract? One privatisation? One pay cut? Did the EU protect British workers' hard-won pension rights? No - its Directive on Pensions wrecked Britain's unique system of negotiated final-salary pensions. The Institute for Employment Rights states that the EU's neoliberal policies "have disempowered workers across the bloc." Stiglitz summed up the EU's approach to trade union rights: "The Troika's economic strategy for recovery [...] was one of internal devaluation, an approach that required wages to fall. Companies and governments came under pressure to weaken unions.

Unfortunately, while these abrupt changes generally lowered labor incomes, they did not lead to the promised improvements in dynamic competitiveness, growth, and employment."[305] When one effect – lower wages - is achieved, and other effects - more competitiveness, growth and jobs - are promised but not achieved, this is not due to misfortune, but to intent. The employing class attacked workers' rights before we joined the EEC. It carried on attacking workers' rights after we joined. We do not need and should not seek some mother hen to protect us from capitalism. Workers needed to organise at work to advance their interests and protect their wages and conditions. Only organised workers ever have and ever will defend workers' rights.

Chapter 10
British foreign policy since 2003

War on Iraq

On 18 March 2003, the House of Commons voted by 412 to 149 to approve the US-British attack on Iraq, with 94 abstentions. 254 Labour MPs voted for the war, 84 voted against and 69 abstained. The EEC backed the illegal attack. Its resolution of February 2003 was an ultimatum demanding Iraq's 'unconditional cooperation', which opened the way to war. The 2016 Chilcot inquiry into this war "concluded that the UK chose to join the invasion of Iraq before the peaceful options for disarmament had been exhausted. Military action at that time was not a last resort."[306] There was no 'imminent threat from Saddam Hussein'. The inquiry concluded that the intelligence "had not established beyond doubt that Saddam Hussein had continued to produce chemical and biological weapons." "The judgements about the severity of the threat posed by Iraq's weapons of mass destruction - WMD - were presented with a certainty that was not justified." It was not a war of self-defence, it was a war of aggression, a crime in international law.

Blair told the inquiry that the outcome in Iraq could not have been foreseen. Chilcot said, "We do not agree that hindsight is required. The risks of internal strife in Iraq, active Iranian pursuit of its interests, regional instability and Al Qaida activity in Iraq, were each explicitly identified before the invasion." Blair and President George W. Bush ignored warnings that war would increase the threat from al-Qaida and might lead to Iraq's weapons being transferred into the hands of terrorists. Chilcot stated, "Despite explicit warnings, the consequences of the invasion were underestimated. The planning and preparations for Iraq after Saddam Hussein were wholly inadequate." British government ministers knew of the 'inadequacy' of the American plans. From August 2006 until December 2011, polls consistently showed that most of the British people and most Americans opposed the war. Yet the war went on. Where was any respect for public opinion? Where was the democracy?

Attack on Libya

In 2011 British and French forces attacked Libya. On 21 March, 557 MPs backed Britain's participation in the attack. 13 MPs opposed: one Conservative, just nine Labour, one Green Party, and two SDLP. Not one MP from the LibDems, the SNP or Plaid Cymru. The EU supported the attack. In 2016 the House of Commons Foreign Affairs Committee produced a report into this war.[307] It was a stunning indictment of the British state. The Committee pointed out, "When the then Prime Minister David Cameron sought and received parliamentary approval for military intervention in Libya on 21 March 2011, he assured the House of Commons that the object of the intervention was not regime change. In April 2011, however, he signed a joint letter with United States President Barack Obama and French President Nicolas Sarkozy setting out their collective pursuit of 'a future without Gaddafi'.

The report's summary read, "In March 2011, the United Kingdom and France, with the support of the United States, led the international community to support an intervention in Libya to protect civilians from attacks by forces loyal to Muammar Gaddafi. This policy was not informed by accurate intelligence. In particular, the Government failed to identify that the threat to civilians was overstated and that the rebels included a significant Islamist element. By the summer of 2011, the limited intervention to protect civilians had drifted into an opportunist policy of regime change. That policy was not underpinned by a strategy to support and shape post-Gaddafi Libya. The result was political and economic collapse, inter-militia and inter-tribal warfare, humanitarian and migrant crises, widespread human rights violations, the spread of Gaddafi regime weapons across the region and the growth of ISIL in North Africa. Through his decision making in the National Security Council, former Prime Minister David Cameron was ultimately responsible for the failure to develop a coherent Libya strategy."

NATO evoked its 'Responsibility to Protect' (R2P) doctrine and began its military intervention supposedly to 'protect civilians'. Far from protecting civilians, NATO provided air support, intelligence and special operations assistance to the rebels, targeting Gaddafi's inner circle, bombing the homes of his family and killing some of his children and grandchildren. The Committee noted, "Despite his rhetoric, the proposition that Muammar Gaddafi would have ordered the massacre of civilians in Benghazi was not supported by the available evidence. The Gaddafi regime had retaken towns from the rebels without attacking civilians in early February 2011." Amnesty International agreed: "much Western media coverage has from the outset presented a very one-sided view of the logic of events, portraying the protest movement as entirely peaceful and repeatedly suggesting that the regime's security forces were unaccountably massacring unarmed demonstrators who presented no security challenge."

The Committee pointed out, "The possibility that militant extremist groups would attempt to benefit from the rebellion should not have been the preserve of hindsight. Libyan connections with transnational militant extremist groups were known before 2011, because many Libyans had participated in the Iraq insurgency and in Afghanistan with al-Qaeda. [...] militant Islamist militias played a critical role in the rebellion from February 2011 onwards." After the war ended, UN Secretary-General Ban Ki-moon confirmed that the NATO-backed rebels had illegally detained and systematically abused 7,000 people, including women and children, in private jails. The rebel militias were 'out of control', committing rape, torture and murder. They smuggled thousands of weapons out of Libya into the hands of their Al Qaeda allies across North Africa.

The war caused major migration. The Committee commented on the EU's incompetent response: "In 2013 a migrant crisis had developed in Libya, Italy implemented border patrols and a search and rescue service under a national programme called Operation Mare Nostrum. This scheme was withdrawn in 2014. The European Union border control Operation Triton was initially less well-resourced than Operation Mare Nostrum. Between October 2014 and April 2015, Operation Triton involved the expenditure of 3 million euros a month on an operation which extended 30 miles from the Italian coastline; Operation Mare Nostrum had involved the expenditure of 9 million euros a month on an operation that covered 27,000 square miles of the Mediterranean. The International Organization for Migration (IOM) calculated that

30 times as many migrant deaths occurred between January and April 2015 under Operation Triton compared with the same period in 2014 under Operation Mare Nostrum."

UN Security Council Resolution 1970 imposed an embargo on the supply of military equipment to Libya. Resolution 1973 and the Arms Trade Treaty explicitly banned arming groups such as the rebels. But the US, British and French governments all armed and supplied the rebels, breaching these legally binding agreements. US government officials admitted that President Obama had authorised the CIA to provide the rebels with arms and other support. The Committee concluded that Cameron had taken the country to war against Libya on a series of 'erroneous assumptions' and that the attack 'had led to the rise of Islamic State in North Africa'. This report was wise five years after the event. In April 2016 outgoing President Obama said that intervening in Libya was the worst mistake of his presidency. In a cowardly evasion of responsibility, he blamed the advice he got from the British and French governments. Of course, Cameron and Sarkozy gave him bad advice, but he did not have to take it.

The imperialism of free trade

Just as in the nineteenth century the British Empire enforced free trade and unequal treaties as far as it could, so in the twentieth and twenty-first centuries the USA and its associates tried to enforce the rule of the IMF, the World Bank and the World Trade Organisation. The British Empire imposed what it called Pax Britannica through some one hundred colonial wars. Now NATO wages wars claiming the right of 'humanitarian intervention' and the 'right to protect'. James Crawford observed, in the leading textbook of international law, "It remains clear that the 'responsibility to protect' cannot be used within the framework of Articles 2(4) and 50 to justify the unilateral use of force. [...] the prohibition of the use of force as established in the post war period was designed to prevent precisely this kind of adventure, and the overall record of high-minded intervention is dismal."[308]

Capitalism wants global militarism, interventions wherever it chooses, interventions always called 'humanitarian' nowadays to draw liberals' applause. It means NATO's expeditionary warfare, no longer directed against the Soviet Union, no longer restricted to Europe, but across Africa, Asia and Latin America. The EU and NATO seem to assume they have a standing right to intervene in other countries' affairs to promote capitalism and democracy, with the first being deemed a necessary condition of the second. They use government bodies like the National Endowment for Democracy and all too many non-governmental organisations. In practice, the results are always the imposition of capitalism, almost always under oligarchic rule, covered by a façade of democracy.

The French government, under various presidents, intervened – often in the name of the EU but more often without prior consent – in Libya, Syria, Iran, Lebanon, the eastern Mediterranean, Belarus and Nagorno-Karabakh. In 2020 there were six military EU Common Security and Defence Policy operations and ten civilian missions, involving some 5,000 troops deployed internationally. Joseph Borrell, the High Representative of the EU for Foreign Affairs and Security

Policy, set the goal of expanding this to an EU-flagged force of 60,000. The EU draft budget for the 2012-2027 period included 34 billion euros for establishing this force. Borrell told MEPs, "We have the instruments to play power politics. The EU has to learn to use the language of power." The EU's military capabilities are slowly but inexorably growing, its intent is clear, its direction is as ever, towards a single federal EU state. Under the UK-EU Political Declaration of 17 October 2019, we could be pulled into EU foreign policy interventions and into defence industry schemes which are not in our interest and which we have no legal obligation to accept. We must not enter military interoperability with the EU.

Senior MEP, former Belgian Prime Minister and the European Parliament's Brexit Coordinator Guy Verhofstadt told *IB Times* on 29 November 2016, "Let's create a European defence union, let's take on our responsibilities [...] Let's become an empire, an empire of the good and not of the bad." Verhofstadt told the LibDem conference on 15 September 2019, "In the world order of tomorrow, the world order of tomorrow is not a world order based on nation states or countries, it's a world order that is based on Empires. [...] The world of tomorrow is a world of Empires, in which we Europeans and you British can only defend your interests, your way of life, by doing it together in a European framework and a European Union." The LibDem members present rapturously applauded this call for a European empire.

Provocative actions by the EU and NATO bear much of the responsibility for the Ukraine crisis. They engineered a coup in the Ukraine which toppled a democratically elected President and set off a civil war. In 2004 President George W. Bush signed the Belarus Democracy Act which gave millions of dollars to opposition groups through the National Endowment for Democracy. In August 2020's general election President Aleksandr Lukashenko was re-elected with 80 per cent of the votes. His opponent the pro-EU Svetlana Tikhanovskaya, with ten per cent of the votes, claimed that she had won. The US-Saudi-British alliance has caused carnage across the Middle East, especially in Libya, Syria and Yemen. A key priority for an independent Britain will be to develop a foreign policy not entangled in alliances that produce only wars and aggression. To oppose wars of aggression is not to support, or sympathise with, the government of the country under attack.

On the democratic principle of non-intervention in the internal affairs of other countries, there is no obligation to comment on that country's internal affairs. We should mind our own business. Wars abroad helped to hold back democratic advances at home. The notion that the nation needed to solve problems abroad weakened the focus needed to make political progress at home. All talk about 'global' this or that, a global economy, a global community, globalisation, is just cover for capitalism. Some in government want a 'Global Britain'. This supranationalist vision means turning away from our vote for an independent Britain. Our vote for independence was an assertion of democracy and national self-determination against globalisation. Only nation states protect people against exploitation and the uncontrolled movements of transnational finance.

When our ruling class cheated us into joining the EEC, it wanted the EEC as a substitute for its vanishing empire, it wanted a new leading role, 'a seat at the top table'. We voted for independence as a vote against empire and its delusions of grandeur. We voted to take control here, not abroad. Respect for sovereignty must be extended to other nations. We have no truck with empire. The British overseas territories, remnants of the British Empire, are not part of the UK. They were seized by force and maintained by imposing on other nations' sovereignties. We have no responsibilities towards them. We do not need overseas territories and overseas bases. We should reject all claims based on alleged imperial obligations. We have no overseas territories. We make no claims to the Rock of Gibraltar, to the Falkland Islands, to Hong Kong or to Northern Ireland. We have no special responsibilities to the people who live there. They will have to come to their own agreements with their neighbours. The Johnson government has even proposed to interfere in ex-colonies by posturing as defenders of their rights, even by enticing all their citizens to come here, as in the case of Hong Kong. More mass migration would increase tensions between and within nations. What defence policy do we need? Coastal defence, defence of our fishing grounds, defence of our territorial waters, controlling our borders, deterring the criminal gangs of people-smugglers.

Torture: a crime

One of the key signs of a country's level of democracy, indeed of its civilisation, is a refusal to tolerate torture. Torture is never justified. Torture is a crime under international law, with no exceptions allowed. As President Abraham Lincoln said in 1863, "military necessity does not admit of cruelty [...] nor of torture to extract confessions." The Geneva Convention, which the USA signed, says "No exceptional circumstances whatsoever, whether a state of war or a threat of war, internal political instability or any other public emergency, may be invoked as a justification for torture."[309] It is a crime under every country's domestic law. Torture is vile, immoral and illegal. That should be enough. Aggressive interrogation techniques are counter-productive because they discredit the user, undermine the user side's war effort and increase the risks to the user side's POWs. Torture does not achieve what its advocates claim. The Senate Select Committee on Intelligence's Report on Torture, after five years of study of six million documents, demonstrated that claims that torture was critical to getting essential, life-saving intelligence were unfounded. Torture did not help to find Osama bin Laden. The Committee concluded that the "CIA's use of its enhanced interrogation techniques was not an effective means of acquiring intelligence."[310] The FBI acknowledged that "the scientific community has never established that coercive interrogation methods are an effective means of obtaining reliable intelligence information."[311]

Yet the George W. Bush administration in its 'war on terror' adopted a policy of torturing prisoners. In counter-insurgency wars, the people do not want to cooperate with the occupiers. The occupiers, unable to get volunteered information about the resistance, resort to mass torture. Our responses to terrorism must be lawful, not mimic terrorists' actions. In February 2002, President Bush ruled that none of the Guantanamo detainees could rely on the Geneva Conventions. This ruling removed all constraints on interrogation. Torture was authorised from the top and therefore became widespread and systematic. On 2

December 2002 Defense Secretary Donald Rumsfeld signed an 'Action Memo' one of whose four attachments authorised the use of eighteen interrogation techniques.

These all contravened US Army Field Manual 34-52, the rule book for military interrogation and broke Common Article 3 of the Conventions, which prohibits cruel or inhumane treatment and 'outrages upon personal dignity', without exceptions for 'necessity' or national security. The Bush administration's definition of where torture started was where the Spanish Inquisition had ruled that it must stop.[312] The International Committee of the Red Cross stated that the "enhanced interrogation techniques [...] amounted to torture and/or cruel, inhuman or degrading treatment" and that "the ill-treatment to which [the detainees] were subject while held in the CIA program, either singly or in combination, constituted torture."[313] In May 2003, the Committee told Blair and Bush that their troops were torturing Iraqi prisoners. Blair and Bush did nothing, until the pictures from Abu Ghraib horrified the world, a year later.

In June 2006, the US Supreme Court ruled that Bush's 2002 decision was unlawful and that Common Article 3 applied to all Guantanamo detainees. As Justice Anthony Kennedy said, "violations of Common Article 3 are considered 'war crimes'." All acts of torture and all acts of complicity or participation in torture were criminal offences. But late in 2006, Congress passed and President Bush signed, a bill allowing the CIA to continue harsh interrogation – torture – of suspected terrorists in secret CIA prisons abroad. This bill ended the right of habeas corpus for anyone, including US citizens, whom the President or the Secretary of Defense designated as an 'unlawful enemy combatant'.

American journalist Mark Danner pointed out, "the notion that our president has the power to prohibit it [torture] follows insidiously from the pretense that his predecessor had the power to order it [...] before the war on terror, official torture was illegal and anathema; today it is a policy choice."[314] But whatever the revelation – atrocities in the field, torture in secret prisons, government sanction of abuses of rights – the US government mantra was, and is, the same: we are not guilty, we did nothing wrong, only our enemies do anything wrong. As President Obama said of US government involvement in torture, "It's not who we are." Hillary Clinton said, "This is not who we are." Defense Secretary Leon Panetta said, "This is not who we are, and what we represent." This is a dogmatic denial of reality.

In Britain, we are not defending democracy unless we assert its values here, including habeas corpus and the right to a fair trial. Blair's Labour government assisted the US state's 'extraordinary renditions' by secretly incarcerating people without trial and conniving at kidnapping, torture and other human rights abuses. MI6 officers were 'embedded within' the US interrogation unit at Abu Ghraib, as the Intelligence and Security Committee admitted in its March 2005 report.[315] British officials participated in coercive interrogations. The government lied that our laws did not apply to UK forces operating abroad. The governments of Britain, France and Germany all cooperated with the foreign intelligence services of countries that routinely used torture. The three governments used the resulting foreign torture information for intelligence and policing purposes. The director-general of MI5, Eliza

Manningham-Buller, told Britain's highest court in 2005 that foreign governments often refused to identify sources of information, but that Britain needed to rely on such sources to save lives. The government argued that inquiring too closely might antagonise countries on which it relied for intelligence to combat terrorism.

Britain's most senior law lord, Lord Bingham, replied that he was "not impressed by the argument based on the practical undesirability of upsetting foreign regimes which may resort to torture."[316] Britain's highest court, the House of Lords judicial committee, unanimously ruled on 8 December 2005 that intelligence extracted by torture was not admissible in any British court. The law lords unanimously overturned an appeal court judgment of August 2004 that such evidence could be used if it was obtained abroad from third parties and if the British government had not condoned or connived in the torture. The appeal court had ruled that the government need not inquire into whether evidence supplied by foreign countries had been obtained by torture. Lord Bingham said, "The issue is one of constitutional principle, whether evidence obtained by torturing another human being may lawfully be admitted against a party to proceedings in a British court, irrespective of where, or by whom, or on whose authority the torture was inflicted. To that question I would give a very clear negative answer."[317] Article 4 of the UN Convention against Torture, which the UK ratified in 1988, expressly prohibits complicity in torture. Lord Bingham wrote later, "it cannot be said that the UK has shown that implacable opposition to torture and its fruits which might have been expected of the state whose courts led the world in rejecting them both."[318]

We could do nothing about past cases of torture, but if our opposition were genuine, we should oppose it when it is practised now. What we say or do now can make a difference. Those genuinely concerned about abuses should focus on those committed by people we are responsible for, our elected representatives. It is not right to tie ourselves as a country to another country that uses such profoundly immoral means. Time and again, the British people have shown that they back peace, while our supposed representatives preferred to vote for war. But if we want peace, we must take control of our country's affairs. Without control, we cannot have peace. We should not delegate powers over the vital matters of war and peace to those who oppose our commitment to peace.

Chapter 11
Cuba: The Pursuit of Freedom

By contrast, Cuba's foreign policy was in line with the norms of international law, as expressed in the UN's Declaration on Granting Independence to Colonial Countries and Peoples, Resolution 1514 (XV) and its Declaration on Principles of International Law concerning Friendly Relations and Cooperation among States, Resolution 2625 (XXV). These outlawed all forms of colonialism and stated that in law all colonised peoples had the right to seek and receive outside support when exercising their right to self-determination and independence. Cuba upheld the basic principle of international law: that countries must not interfere in each other's internal affairs – other countries must not threaten, never mind attack, the lives and liberties of any of our citizens or of those under our protection. Cuba respects the sovereignty and territorial integrity of all other states and promotes peaceful relations between countries.

Cuba's fight for freedom

President Kennedy said "there is no country in the world, including all the African regions, including any and all the countries under colonial domination, where economic colonization, humiliation and exploitation were worse than in Cuba, in part owing to my country's policies during the Batista regime.[319] He pointed out that "Fulgencio Batista murdered 20,000 Cubans in seven years [...]."[320] CIA director Allen Dulles acknowledged that "in some cases, especially in South

America, a dictator has later taken over an internal security service previously trained to combat Communism and has diverted it into a kind of Gestapo to hunt down his local political opponents. This happened in Cuba under Batista."[321] On 6 April 1960, Lester Mallory, Deputy Assistant Secretary of State for Inter-American Affairs, wrote in an internal memorandum: "The majority of Cubans support Castro [...] The only foreseeable means of alienating internal support is through disenchantment and disaffection based on economic dissatisfaction and hardship. [...] every possible means should be undertaken promptly to weaken the economic life of Cuba."

Mallory urged 'a line of action which, while as adroit and inconspicuous as possible, makes the greatest inroads in denying money and supplies to Cuba, to decrease monetary and real wages, to bring about hunger, desperation and overthrow of government'.[322] The US government admitted, "The embargo on Cuba is the most comprehensive set of American sanctions ever imposed upon a country."[323] The blockade cut Cubans' access to medicines and medical goods. In 1990, Cuba imported $55 millions' worth and in 1996, just $18 million. WHO officials noted, "In the health sector, the consequences of the embargo have a negative multiplier effect on the cost of basic everyday health products, on the difficulties in acquiring health products, on the availability of basic services and, therefore, on the overall living conditions of the population [...] The embargo affects the individual health care of all people, regardless of age or gender, through its impact on Cuba's unified health system institutions, research facilities, epidemiological surveillance institutions and disease control agencies."[324]

Successive US governments have attacked, blockaded and bombed Cuba for 60 years. The US government funded the Cuban American National Foundation, a former board member of which publicly admitted that its leaders had created a paramilitary group to destabilise Cuba and to kill Fidel Castro.[325] Laura Pollan, the spokeswoman of the *damas en blanco* (the Ladies in White) admitted on camera that the Rescate Juridico, a US-based opposition group, paid the Ladies. The EU backed the US blockade. It refused to sign any cooperation agreement with Cuba, the only Latin American country with which it had no such agreement. Helen Yaffe summed up, "For six decades, the Caribbean island has withstood manifold and unrelenting aggression from the world's dominant economic and political power: overt and covert military actions; sabotage and terrorism by US authorities and allied exiles; imposition of the blockade to asphyxiate the Cuban economy and its people; obstruction of third parties' trade with Cuba; pressure on regional and international governments to isolate and ostracise Cuba; encouragement of illegal and dangerous emigration, including of unaccompanied Cuban children (Operation Peter Pan, 1960-1962) and Cuban doctors (Cuban Medical Parole Programme, 2006-2017); the obstruction of remittances and family visits and refusal to issue visas to Cubans; and lucrative funding for regime change programmes."[326]

Despite the blockade, Cuba has achieved great things. A 1972 report for the Joint Economic Committee of the US Congress said, "The genuine socio-economic and political accomplishments of the Cuban revolution have attracted international attention. These accomplishments include: A highly egalitarian redistribution of income that has eliminated almost all malnutrition, particularly among children; Establishment of a national health care program that is superior in the Third World and rivals that of numerous developed countries; Near total elimination of illiteracy and a highly developed multi-level educational system; and Development of a relatively well-disciplined and motivated population with a strong sense of national identification."[327] In November 2019, the UN, for the 28th year in a row, called for an end to the blockade. 187 countries voted to end the blockade; the USA, Brazil and Israel voted against. Ukraine and Colombia abstained. The UN's regional economic body for Latin America said in 2018 that the 'unjust' blockade had cost Cuba an estimated $130 billion.[328]

The Special Period

When the Soviet Union and Eastern Europe collapsed, Cuba lost 80 per cent of its trade and over 40 per cent of its GDP. It suffered power cuts and hunger, with shortages of everything. The US government tightened its blockade to try to make Cuba collapse too. The Torricelli-Graham Act of 1992 and the Helms-Burton Act of 1996 banned US companies from trading with Cuba and made it illegal for foreign companies to do so. The sanctions blocked Cuba's access to US markets and to loans and aid, restricting investment and growth. With the Soviet Union gone and the US government intensifying its assault, Cuba faced unprecedented difficulties. So the Cuban government declared a 'Special Period not in time of war'. This put Cuba on a footing like Britain's during World War Two. Despite severe hardship, there was a strong sense of working class unity.

Cuba's other assets included the welfare state, price controls, the monopoly of international exchange, national ownership of the means of production, a capacity for a state-led, collective response and a tradition of winning voluntary support through mass mobilisations after public participation and debate.

The Special Period, for all its pain, was the first time since colonisation that Cuba was a fully free and independent country, no longer dependent on a major power.[329] The Committees for the Defence of the Revolution took care of their local communities and made sure that no one fell through the safety net. Trade union farms were opened to grow food. The health workers' union looked after the health of the people and the health system's infrastructure. The transport union looked after the transport system. The government distributed half a million bicycles to workers and students. The education and science union maintained educational standards despite lack of equipment and supported world-leading developments in biotechnology and genetics. Workers created the Institute of Innovators and Rationalisers to help other workers to solve the problems caused by the blockade.

In 1998, in response to the US/EU blockade, the Cuban TUC and the Cuban Health Union asked London Ambulance Service UNISON if it could add an ambulance to a shipment of aid from British trade unions. The contributions for Salud International included fire engines and buses from Scotland, hospital beds and medical equipment from Wales and England, making it an all-British effort. In the end, with the help of generous union and individual donations, organised British workers sent 97 ambulances, 20 buses (including one for the Cuban national football team), four cars and hundreds of tons of medical and hospital equipment. Cuba maintained basic food security. The state distribution body used the food-rationing system and networks like the *vías sociales* which provided free or subsidised meals at workplaces, schools and health centres. Thanks to the ration system's fixed prices, the cost of meeting basic food needs, around 40 pesos a month per person, was kept below the minimum social-security allowance of 85 pesos a month. The monthly ration basket, for which the average Cuban family paid about $4.70 in 2009, actually cost $61. Similarly, the average family quarterly electricity bill was 32.22 pesos, while the actual cost of the energy supplied was 708.84 pesos.[330]

The government introduced a Food Programme which encouraged local self-provisioning and small-scale experimentation including using animal traction, organic fertilisers, biological pest control, sustainable farming and renewable energy sources.[331] Foreign investment was sought to develop tourism which was the only short-term way to get hard currency to buy the goods needed to survive. Tourism brought with it the new problem of a dual currency, which meant that those with access to hard currency were better off than others and this had to be managed. In 2000, Cuba launched its Battle of Ideas, a nationwide campaign to reassert humanitarian, working class morals. They took this campaign into schools, youth organisations, trade unions and all the other mass organisations. Social workers visited every household, learned the specific problems facing different groups – families, single mothers, unemployed, children, pensioners – and tried to find solutions for them. They especially sought out disaffected young people, tried to befriend them, win their trust and help them to find a rewarding life-project that chimed with the larger collective project of the Cuban revolution.

Internationalism

As part of its survival strategy, Cuba developed more links with countries around the world, especially with its neighbours in Latin America. In 1991, the US government proposed the Free Trade Area of the Americas (FTAA) – an agreement to eliminate or reduce the trade barriers among all countries in the Americas, excluding Cuba. Latin America's countries opposed it because of the unfair competitive advantage that US federal subsidies gave to American agricultural exports. On May Day 2001 the Cuban government launched a slogan, '*Annexion no, plebiscito sí*', which proposed a continental plebiscite about the FTAA. This proposal helped to prevent the FTAA ever being achieved. In 2004, Cuba and Venezuela founded the Bolivarian Alliance for the Peoples of Our America.[332] In 2011, all 33 countries south of the USA founded the Community of Latin-American and Caribbean States.[333] Cuba launched a programme of international medical aid. Giving medical aid has been a basic principle of the Cuban Revolution from the first, flowing from its belief that medicine is not a business but the right of every citizen and the duty of every doctor.

By 2020, Cuban medical staff had cared for over seventy million people in the world and had saved more lives – one and a half million – more than all the G8 countries, the World Health Organisation, and *Médicins Sans Frontières* put together. Surgeons working on Cuba's Operation Milagro, founded in 2004, had performed free eye surgery on over four million people. Ban Ki-moon, the UN secretary-general, wrote that

Cuba "has given us a new vision of the world – one of generosity and solidarity: we are all one, human beings who are all brothers and sisters. Healthcare has to cease being a privilege for a few, and should become the right of the majority."

Since 1959, Cuba has provided free medical education for thousands of Cubans (it now has seventy thousand doctors) and for fifty-two thousand people from one hundred and thirty other countries. Cuba educated more health workers from other countries than did all the G8 member countries combined. Cuban medical schools are government run and free to attend. Study includes primary care, public health, preventive medicine and the social determinants of health. Health promotion is prioritised over sickness control. In 1999, Cuba set up the world's largest medical school, with more than eight thousand students from countries in Asia, Africa and Latin America, for people who could not afford medical school in their own country. Most were from working class and peasant families and half were women.[334]

Cuba was the only country in the world's history to create a WHO-validated, six-year course of medical education, with no fees and with full food and board. The graduates' only commitment was to return to their home countries and provide medical care to those who could least afford it. Ban Ki-moon called it 'the most advanced medical school in the world'. It blends evidence-based medical education, an understanding of health as a right for all and compassionate care, guided by need not by the patient's ability to pay. Students get monthly pocket money and free housing, food and toiletries. The World Health Organization estimates that the world needs another 2.4 million health workers. Poorer countries are in particular need. Cuba has been addressing this problem, as a sovereign country can and should do. Countries like Britain should do far more to meet the world need for health workers. An independent Britain can follow Cuba's excellent example.

Disaster preparedness

Cuba had the world's best programme of community-based disaster preparedness.[335] Four years after the 1959 Revolution, Hurricane Flora caused 1,157 deaths in Cuba, leading Fidel Castro to declare "Never again [...] a Revolution is a force more powerful than Nature!" The real experience of risk and disaster in Cuba led to a building of resilience within society itself, built on local and national risk reduction structures, annual simulation exercises and on strong continuing education in schools and communities among a highly literate population. The Cubans used this experience to assist other peoples facing natural disasters. The following is from an account by the late Phil Lenton, UNISON National Secretary, the founder of Salud International, the first foreigner invited to visit and meet the Cuban Medical Brigade in Haiti.

"The Brigade had been in Haiti since the devastation caused by Hurricane Georges in September 1998. Because most of the higher ground has been deforested over decades, Haiti is particularly prone to mudslides and flooding by hurricanes. Nearly three hundred people had been killed and there was no medical support for the survivors until the Cubans sent doctors and specialists immediately after the hurricane. Cuba appealed to the richer countries to provide technical and pharmaceutical aid whilst Cuba would provide the skilled medical staff. This appeal fell on deaf ears although one small French NGO did work directly with the Cubans in the north of the country. No diplomatic relations existed between Haiti and Cuba at the time. However, Cuba offered to build a free health system in the country offering to send doctors and nurses whilst simultaneously providing free medical training for young Haitians from poor areas of the country. The training would take place in Cuba and Haiti. This would obviously take some time as the students would need at least five years to graduate. At the beginning of 1999, the full Cuban Medical Brigade arrived to start this work. The Brigade we were with was a continuation of that task, comprised of nearly six hundred Cuban doctors and, at the time of our visit, the Cuban Medical Brigade worked with *Médicins sans Frontières*, a number of church based charities, the Pan American Health Organisation, a Canadian NGO and a Japanese NGO. But only the Cubans visited Haitians in their homes because of the risks and hazards involved."

"It was these visits that provided the basis for the development of a Primary Health Care system based on the Cuban domestic model. After learning the local Creole language, visits would be made to homes and all potential health risks identified and tackled. For example high blood pressure was often the result of the salty porridge, which was the staple food, so the diets were altered. Latrines were dug to improve sanitation. 'Circles' or groups of pregnant women were used to educate them to ensure safe and healthy births and also for the elderly, which included exercising and circles for the youth would include sexual health education. Provision of clean drinking water was a priority. Eventually a Cuban doctor would get to know every family they were responsible for and work on a programme for each family, as in Cuba. They would tackle the high rates of infant and maternal mortality recording everything. They had already vaccinated three hundred thousand Haitian kids against Polio, Chicken Pox and Tetanus. The Brigade covered nearly eighty per cent of Haiti's population. For most Haitians, meeting Cuban doctors was their first ever encounter with a doctor. Health education and prevention of disease was the first part of the programme, but if Haitians needed specialist treatment, they would be flown to Cuba free of charge and be treated."

"What impressed me most was the fact that most of the Cuban doctors were so young, mostly in their early to mid-twenties, many having trained at the same medical school in Cuba. There were also some older experienced specialists. But perhaps most significantly, we discovered that Cuba was implementing the same programme in sixty other poor countries around the world! What other country on the planet would or could do likewise? Answer – None!"

Community officers visit residents to establish and list who are most vulnerable. When disaster strikes, people know exactly what to do and they do it. As in health, the people of Cuba are its greatest resource in difficult times. That this works is shown by the very low fatality levels experienced in Cuba in recent years even in the fiercest hurricanes. Between 1996 and 2005, during the period of dire economic difficulties for the island, only seventeen people died during eight major hurricanes. During Hurricane Wilma, in October 2005, which caused massive floods along the Cuban coastline, six hundred and forty thousand people were successfully evacuated, with just one death. During the three devastating hurricanes Fay, Gustav and Ike that hit Cuba in 2008, causing eight billion dollars' worth of damage, the working class worked selflessly and collectively to repair the damage and to care for those who lost homes and property, under the slogan 'every human life is sacred'. In Cuba seven people died. When the same three hurricanes hit neighbouring Haiti, over one thousand people were killed. Cuba is a world leader in disaster response and has responded to international natural disasters more than any other country. When the 2005 earthquake in Pakistan killed eighty thousand people, Cuba at once sent two thousand and five hundred members of the newly formed Henry Reeve contingent with thirty-two field hospitals (all given to the people of Pakistan) and provided one thousand medical scholarships to local students. The Cubans stayed for seven months, treating 1,743,000 patients, three quarters of those medically assisted in Pakistan after the earthquake. By contrast, the USA and the EU sent one base camp each and stayed for a month. In 2017, the Henry Reeve contingent received the WHO's Public Health Prize for its work in nineteen countries. After Haiti's 2010 earthquake, the Cubans treated 227,443 patients and performed 6,499 operations.[336] The US Navy treated 871 patients and performed 843 surgical operations.

In 2010, the organisation 'Project Censored' maintained 'Cuba Provided the Greatest Medical Aid to Haiti after the Earthquake' and asserted that it was one of the year's 'outstanding stories ignored by the US corporate media'. In 2014, when Ban Ki-moon and Margaret Chan, director general of the World Health Organization, appealed to the world to

152

help the West African countries afflicted by Ebola, Cuba was first to offer help. It sent one hundred and three nurses and sixty-two doctors, all volunteers. Ban Ki-moon said, "They are always the first to arrive and the last to leave – and they always remain after the crisis. Cuba has a lot to show the entire world with its health system, a model for many countries." Dr Chan said, "Cuba has shown that it is possible to have health and well-being for all."

Working class democracy

The Cuban working class was still in control. The dictatorship of the proletariat still meant democracy for the workers and the direct application of power and control by Cuban workers. Cuba is, constitutionally, a 'socialist state of workers'. There were no capitalists apart from a few foreign entrepreneurs in mixed companies and a few clandestine workshop owners.[337] As the 19th Congress of the Cuban trade union, the *Central de Trabajadores de Cuba* (CTC), stated "the principal conquests of the Revolution have been preserved, first of all, the political power of the workers."[338] This meant that workers as the ruling class were not to be treated as just labour power. Cuba decided not to compete with other countries in a race to the bottom by offering low-wage workers to foreign companies. Instead it would invest in its people's skills, especially in health care, education, biotechnology, medications and other high-value goods. The saving of material resources and a more productive workforce were the key sources of this investment. As workers improved their skills, they increased productivity, so fewer were needed to carry out particular jobs. Workers could then

153

redeploy to other areas of work to develop new lines of production and to upgrade their skills. This would again raise productivity and workers' skill and educational levels in a virtuous circle.

Yamil Eduardo Martinez, a young trade unionist, said "Sections of the western, hostile, media are claiming that these changes are a retreat from socialism. In fact, they are about making our economy more efficient so that we can develop further in health and education – with the public sector not having to directly manage everything. One thing we really want to do is to raise agricultural production, so in a world of uncertain food security we can be as close to being self-sufficient as possible."[339] At all stages, workers were in control. Unions initiated laws and trade unionists sat in the National Assembly and participated in ministerial decision-making. Legislative proposals affecting workers were always referred to the unions.

In 1995, the unions rejected a draft law to allow foreign companies to directly employ Cuban workers on their own terms. The unions insisted that those workers must be employed through a state agency and under Cuban labour laws. In the 1990s, the unions defeated a proposal to raise the retirement age. *Resolución No.8/2005* provided that no worker could be dismissed through redundancy, redeployment or temporary lay-off. Any such had to be negotiated with the unions and management had to pay the worker one hundred per cent of his or her salary for a month, then sixty per cent until an alternative was agreed. This would be either another job, with training if necessary, or 'study as a form of work', with workers keeping their salaries and employment rights.

Cuba held competitive elections for delegates to its municipal assemblies, in which the people, not the Communist Party, proposed the candidates.[340] There were usually four to seven candidates, never fewer than two. There was no campaigning for or against any candidate; negative campaigning was not allowed. There were no electoral promises or bribes or funding. There were no lobbyists to promote private interests over the general good.[341] Delegates were unpaid and their work was on top of their regular work, so Cuba had no caste of professional politicians. The delegates did not represent themselves or parties; they had to act in the interests of the whole people. Delegates had to live in their electoral districts and had to account to their constituents at all times. The constituents formally instructed the delegates and had the right to recall them at once at any time. The delegates held weekly and six-monthly meetings to report back to their constituents, who held them to account. Cuba's one hundred and sixty-nine municipal and fourteen provincial assemblies met at least twice a year. There are direct elections to the provincial assemblies and the National Assembly.[342] US governments, Cuban exiles and 'dissidents' always told the Cuban people to abstain or to spoil their ballot papers in elections, without great success.

In the 1993 National Assembly elections, 7.67 per cent abstained or spoilt their ballot papers, in 1995, 11.3 per cent, in 1998, 6.65 per cent, in 2003, 6.25 per cent, in 2007, 7.01 per cent, in 2010, 8.89 per cent and in 2012, 9.42 per cent. In 2011, in preparing for the 2011 Party Congress, 8.9 million people attended 163,000 meetings and came up with over three million suggestions. This was democratic centralism in action, where

155

the Cuban people consulted together, then decided policy. Cuba persistently sought to keep high standards of behaviour. All those in leading positions and their families were expected to live in a manner no different from other people. Those found guilty of corruption were punished severely. Cuba did well on the World Bank and Transparency International scores of corruption. A thorough US-sourced study which set out to show the extent of corruption in Cuba ended by confirming the extent of the efforts to contain it.[343] Cuba's 1992 Constitution banned all discrimination based on race, skin colour or sex. Its Article 44 said, "Men and women have equal rights in the economic, political, cultural and social realms and in the family." Women held sixty-six per cent of professional and technical jobs, were forty-seven per cent of the members of the Supreme Court and forty-nine per cent of judges.

In 1994, the *Federación de Mujeres Cubanas* [FMC] had 3.6 million members, eighty-two per cent of the adult female population. It was the largest organisation in Cuba and the largest women's organisation in Latin America. It helped to improve women's health, education, legal rights and rights at work. National control of the economy and the government's policy of encouraging women's work brought women more independence, professional opportunities and social mobility.[344] The FMC's 1985 Congress successfully called for more childcare centres, more provision of contraception, better sex education and more emphasis on the need to share housework, in line with the 1975 Family Code which required men and women to share household duties and child care.

In 2008, thirty-six per cent of members of the National Assembly were between eighteen and thirty. After February

156

2013's general election, 37.9 per cent of the Assembly's members were people of colour. The average age of members was forty-eight. In 2015, 48.9 per cent of members were women, the sixth highest proportion in the world. Britain came sixtieth, with 22.6 per cent. In April 2011, Cubans elected a new Central Committee of the Communist Party. Forty-eight of the one hundred and fifteen members were women, 41.7 per cent, triple the proportion elected at the previous Congress. There were thirty-six black and mestizo members, 31.3 per cent, the highest ever, ten per cent more than on the previous Central Committee.

In 2016 the party congress elected a new Central Committee. Cuba was the only country in the world where black people and mestizos had the state and the government as their ally. They still needed to make more use of the state and the government as their allies to achieve full equality. The government and the party were not racist but there was still some discrimination by some individuals. The black and mestizo population in Cuba was the healthiest and best-educated mass of Afro-descendants in the hemisphere. No other country has done as much as Cuba to end racial discrimination and injustice.

Social progress

As President Jimmy Carter said, "Of all the so-called developing nations, Cuba has by far the best health system. And their outreach program to other countries is unequalled anywhere." Edward Campion and Stephen Morrissey wrote in the *New England Journal of Medicine*, "The Cuban healthcare system seems unreal. There are too many doctors. Everybody has a family physician. Everything is free, totally free [...] It is tightly organized, and the first priority is prevention. Although Cuba has limited economic resources, its health care system has solved some problems that [the US system] has not yet managed to address."[345] In 1990, Cuba spent a fifth of its GDP on social services (education, social security and health care all provided free of charge to all), as against other Latin American countries' tenth. By 1998, Cuba had raised this spending by sixty per cent (against a Latin American average rise of thirty per cent) to thirty-two per cent, again the highest proportion in Latin America. Cuba maintained its comprehensive early childhood support programmes.[346] In 2010, Save the Children ranked Cuba the best place to be a mother of all the eighty-one less developed countries.[347] In the 1950s, the maternal mortality rate was 120 per 100,000 live births, by 2017, it was 36. In 1958, Cuban life expectancy was fifty-five years. By 2020, it was 78.89, the same as in the USA. On World Bank figures, Cuba's infant mortality rate in 2020 was a record low of 4.337 per 1,000 live births. The USA's was 5.6 in 2018, the latest figure available at the time of writing.

At first, Cuba did not respond well to the AIDS epidemic of the 1980s, but it adapted fast. It was one of the first countries in the region to rollout an HIV prevention and treatment programme, which now provides antiretroviral therapy to all people with HIV. On 30 June 2015, Cuba became the first country in the world to receive official recognition from the World Health Organization for having eliminated mother-to-child transmission of HIV and syphilis as public health problems. The WHO said that this was "a major victory in our long fight against HIV and sexually transmitted infections, and an important step towards having an AIDS-free generation." "Eliminating transmission of a virus is one of the greatest public health achievements possible," WHO Director-General Dr. Margaret Chan said. The United Nations stated that Cuba's AIDS programme was 'among the most effective in the world'.[348] In the past, hardly anyone contemplated openly coming out on the island.

Until the 1990s, gay people were socially excluded: they got disapproving looks around the neighbourhood and even lost their jobs. In 2010, Fidel Castro expressed regret for the government's earlier attitude towards gay people. Now the Cuban government rejects all discrimination against gay people. Cuba has laws and policies prohibiting discrimination against men who have sex with men and against transgender people. Since 2008 sex reassignment surgery and hormone replacement therapy are offered free of charge. In 2012, as part of the International Day Against Homophobia, Cubans marched through the city of Cienfuegos. On 17 May 2013, Cuba held lectures and workshops to mark the International Day Against Homophobia and Transphobia. Mariela Castro Espin, the daughter of Cuban President Raul Castro, heads the National Centre for Sex Education. She has campaigned for years for gay rights and called for same-sex marriage to be allowed. The Communist Party stated that it favoured allowing same-sex marriage. In May 2019 the government said that the Union of Jurists was working on producing a new family code which would address same-sex marriage.

Cuba made great strides in education. By 2012, its illiteracy rate was two per cent (the USA's was twelve per cent.) Its literacy programme *'Yo, sí puedo'* helped six million adults in twenty-nine countries to read and write. It became a model for developing countries.[349] In 2006, UNESCO awarded Cuba its Literacy Award for its contribution to literacy campaigns. Cuba devoted seven per cent of its GDP to education. Education was free at all levels, including university and postgraduate. It had one teacher for every forty-two people, one of the highest ratios in the world. Primary school classes were twenty-five at most. There were 300,000 enrolled in secondary technical schools in 1983-84. 13,600 teachers taught in 425 special schools across the country. Women made up nearly half of all students attending high schools, half of those at technical schools and more than half of all university students. Emulation, not competition, was the ethic. Racial and gender inequalities vanished as educational opportunities grew. Cuba had sixty universities, all public and sixteen medical schools. In 2015/16 there were 547,555 university students, sixteen times as many in the late 1950s. Cuba focused on providing higher education courses in technology, medical sciences, pure sciences, agricultural sciences, economics and teaching to meet people's needs. Cuba had one of the largest numbers of scientists per head of any country in Asia, Africa and Latin America.

Social workers prioritise the prevention of criminal activities and promote a comprehensive social work programme. Helen Yaffe noted, "Having identified the link between criminality and lack of education, there was a huge expansion of educational provision within Cuba's prisons, including university-level courses. Sentencing policy leaned towards community punishments or part-time prison which enabled offenders to maintain family relations and community integration."[350]

Resilience

Cubans developed their economy in a way that cared for the environment. They achieved the world's largest conversion from conventional farming to organic, environmentally sustainable farming. People stopped using costly, harmful petroleum-based pesticides. They adopted a soil management programme that helped to preserve the natural environment. They reintroduced traditional peasant practices where appropriate. They reduced tillage and rehabilitated the soil. They used green manures, bio-fertilisers and organic fertilisers rather than chemical ones. They used integrated pest-management methods, biological control and bio-pesticides. They used crop diversity, crop rotations and intercropping. They recycled waste. Cuba's farming became the most organic in the world. Cuba's urban farming movement employed 326,000 people. They reared small animals in kitchen gardens. From home gardens in the cities they sold fruit, vegetables, meat, herbs, plants and flowers in farmers' markets. Havana grew ninety per cent of its fruit and vegetables on seven thousand *organopónicos* – kitchen gardens - covering eighty thousand acres. There was no need for costly refrigerated transport, which saved energy, time and spoilage.

Monty Don, the presenter of the BBC's *Gardeners' World*, judged that Cuba had organised its food production through gardens better than any other country in the world. He was hugely inspired by this and full of admiration for the intelligence and dignity of the Cuban people.[351] In 2006 the World Wildlife Fund said that Cuba was the only country in the world to achieve sustainable development - improving quality of life within the carrying capacity of its ecosystem. The Fund said that Cuba led the world in reducing its ecological footprint.[352] Yaffe wrote "By 2006, when Cuba was recognised as the only nation in the world living sustainably, 80 per cent of the island's agricultural production was organic and the annual use of chemical pesticides had fallen from 21,000 tonnes in the 1980s to 1,000 tonnes (a 95 per cent reduction) [...] Cuba had become the only country in the world to produce most of its food locally, employing agro-ecological techniques for production. Urban agriculture accounted for nearly 15 per cent of national agriculture, occupied 87,000 acres of land and was meeting over 50 per cent of the total vegetable needs of Havana's population of 2.2 million inhabitants.

"Monty Don concluded 'The Cubans have created a working model for the future we all face. In the middle of a large city, with practically no money and no resources, they are producing fresh, organic fruit and vegetables by and for local communities, not industrially, but in the garden.'"[353] Cubans protected their environment through environmental education at all stages of schooling to encourage people to take part in making decisions on the environment.[354] Cubans understood the need for environmental ethics and aesthetics. They knew they had a duty to protect Cuba's unusually rich biological diversity. They worked hard to reforest Cuba – forest covered 15 per cent of the island in 1970 and 31.49 per cent in 2019. Cuba was the only country in the Caribbean and Central America region to reforest.

The blockade forced the Cuban people to husband their energy sources. They had to achieve self-reliance and sustainability in one country. They had to develop and use a variety of energy sources. Enrico Turrino, founding member of *Eurosolar* and honorary member of *CubaSolar*, said that the island was a model of good use of clean sources of energy. He highlighted the solarisation projects where thermal, photoelectric, wind, water and biomass sources were used to develop communities sustainably. Yaffe observed "In Cuba's centrally planned economy the profit motive does not determine production and reproduction, meaning that environmental as well as social costs can be factored into economic decisions. It is not enough, for example, for electricity to be within physical reach: it must also be affordable for all Cubans. That does not mean, however, that socialism is synonymous with environmental respect; environmental disasters occurred in the socialist bloc. A leading environmental policy-maker in Cuba pointed out that the process 'is not automatic, you have to try to create a socialist system where the environmental agenda is driven well, otherwise you will still have environmental problems. Nothing is given, it has to be achieved."[355]

Yaffe concluded, "Cuba's achievements in sustainability and its long-term plan to protect the population from the devastating impact of global warming serve as an inspiration, countering attempts to ostracise the island. The fact that Cuba is socialist introduces to the environmentalist table a discussion about alternative development models. It strengthens the argument that the profit-driven capitalist system is incapable of redressing the environmental damage caused by the process of accumulation (through exploitation) integral to capitalism. [...] Revolutionary Cuba, it appears, wrote the rule-book on resilience. However, its best form of resistance has been not just the assertion of national sovereignty, but the creation of an alternative model of development that places human welfare and environmental concerns at its core. That this poor, blockaded island has achieved world-leading human development indicators, that it mobilises the world's largest international humanitarian assistance, that it has contributed to global innovations in medical science, that its contributions in culture and the arts are admired throughout the world, is an achievement to be examined and respected. We are left to ask, what could the revolutionary people of Cuba achieve if they were left in peace – if they were finally given the chance to prosper, and not just survive."[356]

Controlling Covid-19

In 2020, socialist Cuba showed the strength of its society through its capacity to bring a rise in Covid-19 infections under control – while continuing to innovate and resist the attacks on it from the USA. Covid-19 has been almost eliminated by aggressive anti-virus measures and 'shoe leather epidemiology' across the country. This painstaking method of inquiry into the origin of an infection by walking door to door to ask direct questions was famously used, successfully, by John Snow in 1850s London to investigate the spread of cholera in Soho. In Cuba, over ninety per cent of all cases have been traced through following up the contacts of spreaders. Medical students have knocked door to door to screen for virus symptoms in homes and to check on quarantine compliance.

By early September 2020, the population of around eleven million had suffered about four thousand confirmed cases and fewer than one hundred deaths, among the lowest in the region, so the strategy was working well. But during August, the rise in Havana from a few cases to dozens daily meant decisive action was needed. From early September, a 7:00 PM to 5:00 AM curfew was put in place, with people racing home in the evenings to make sure they were not breaking the curfew. By the time it started, the normally crowded streets were deserted. Police were posted at road junctions around the city, stopping all traffic to check whether drivers had the necessary special travel permits which were only issued in extraordinary situations. Most shops were forbidden to sell to people from outside the immediate neighbourhood, to reduce as much as possible the incentive for anyone to move around the city. The usual requirements from people in many countries across the world in the period of Covid were strictly enforced – mask-wearing, avoiding large gatherings and maintaining social distancing. Breaking these and other Covid measures brought large fines and even prison for serious violations. These measures were eased as the situation improved, with the daily Covid news reporting a handful of new confirmed cases and almost no deaths. The government has announced a 'period of new normality'.

The global pandemic has not caused any let-up in the US government's blockade. During the 2020 election period President Trump increased the regime of sanctions to ramp up the pressure on the Cuban economy. If the US blockade already makes life in general harder in Cuba, how are the Cuban people managing in the Covid period? There are the usual grumbles about the difficulties in everyday life caused by the restrictions, but there is a high level of compliance. Some western commentators put this down to heavy-handed authoritarianism on the part of the government, but this is to misunderstand how government works in Cuba. The high level of 'buy in' shown by the populace has been hard won, by democratic structures built over decades since the Cuban revolution. There is a robust system of community-based medical and mental health services with coverage for all citizens, including in the most remote rural areas. This system is based on local polyclinics and family medical offices which serve specific residential areas, so nobody is missed. These provide basic primary care services in both the local offices and on home visits.

Health promotion is an essential part of the role of medical staff, including screening, education and an understanding of family and social circumstances. In treating patients, doctors consider all factors in health, including education, housing, environment, nutrition and employment. This system means that in a health emergency such as Covid the strong relationships between professionals and the people enable swift decisions to be made at both government and local levels and the decisions can be quickly put into practice due to the trust built up by strong health education.

What are the lessons for us in Britain? Of course, we have a capitalist, profit-led society, but the example of Cuba can teach us a great deal about how we could do better in dealing with the pandemic. A *Daily Mail* headline on 17 October 2020 proclaimed, "Why the UK should have followed the example of Cuba"! Cuba has a public health system staffed by appropriate numbers of its own doctors and nurses, instead of stealing them from other countries who desperately need them.

Cuba sends its medical staff abroad to assist in crises, as they did for Italy when Covid attacked in March. The country is largely self-reliant in medicines and medical equipment, unlike in Britain when our 'free market' system left government scrambling to buy in PPE from across the world.

Cuba's crisis preparedness puts to shame the short-sighted penny-pinching here, where the 'Pandemic Preparedness Strategy' published in 2011 was subsequently largely ignored while austerity reigned supreme. The creation of the NHS was a huge achievement by the British working class. But faced with a health emergency, our government has largely mobilised the private sector. In Cuba, the people are in charge and they have mobilised to manage Covid through a collective approach across society. None of this is to say that we must copy Cuba or any other country. The British people are not in the habit of copying anybody, which is one of the reasons why we voted to leave the EU's model of politics and economics.

The Cuban people's revolution was against poverty, torture, gangsterism, corruption, prostitution, racism, violence and control from the USA. It was for liberty, equality and fraternity, for thriving through their own efforts, for education, social awareness, organisation and public service, for clear thinking, intelligence and realism, for modesty, altruism, courage and for never lying or violating ethical principles. Cubans have a profound conviction that no power can crush the power of truth and ideas. The revolution meant unity, independence, patriotism, socialism and internationalism. In its struggle for national unity and sovereignty and in its efforts to develop its Communist morals and ideas, the Cuban working class is taking responsibility for its future.

Chapter 12
Referendums and democracy

The EEC and the 1975 referendum

In 1955 the six member states of the European Coal and Steel Community; France, Germany, Italy, Belgium, the Netherlands and Luxembourg, met at Messina to advance European integration. Britain's relationship with the EEC became the overriding question facing the country. Anthony Eden's Conservative government expressed no interest. Pro-integration forces in European and the US governments were seriously displeased at Eden's lack of enthusiasm. In 1956 Eden launched the disastrous attack on Egypt, expecting the usual support from the US as Britain's key NATO ally. Instead, President Eisenhower stabbed Eden in the back by refusing to support the pound when it came under attack on the international money markets. The attack failed, Eden was ousted and the enthusiastically pro-EEC Harold Macmillan became Prime Minister. He put in an application for Britain to join the EEC, but General de Gaulle rejected the bid. After de Gaulle was ousted, following the events in May 1968, the way to entry opened.

The Conservative Party under Edward Heath won the June 1970 election, promising, "Our sole commitment is to negotiate: no more, no less." Heath immediately opened new talks on joining, claiming on 24 May 1971; "Joining the community does not entail a loss of national identity or an erosion of essential national sovereignty." In 1971 the Heath government told its legal advisors to prepare a White Paper on the country's proposed entry into the EEC. The advisors' counsel which was never published, marked 'Confidential' and held in the National Archive at Kew, made some interesting points about sovereignty. The advisors wrote, "[...] we do not want to give future community partners the idea that we are frightened to commit ourselves to giving up our sovereignty." Adding, "it will be in British interests after entry that the Community should develop towards an effectively harmonized economic, fiscal and monetary system together with a fairly closely coordinated foreign and defence policy [...] it could only take place if there were a strengthening of the institutions of the Community with consequential weakening of national institutions including Parliament." They acknowledged 'the inevitable loss of sovereignty'.[357] Of course, this was all behind closed doors and 'not before the children' - the British people.

In 1973, Heath took Britain into the EEC, despite having won the election on a mandate only to negotiate. He never won a democratic mandate to take this decision. After the event, Britain was allowed a referendum. We joined the EEC on Heath's false promise that accession would accelerate growth. Yet our GDP per head grew 2.4 per cent a year from 1950-1973 and by just 2 per cent a year from 1973-2007. We had joined the EEC just as its post-war catch-up ended. The October 1974 Labour election manifesto pledged that "within twelve months of this election we will give the British people the final say, which will be binding on the government – through the ballot box – on whether we accept the terms and stay in or reject the terms and come out." Some EEC leaders strongly disapproved. Jean Rey, ex-President of the European Commission, said in 1974 about Britain's forthcoming referendum on EEC membership; "A referendum on this matter consists of consulting people who don't know the problems instead of consulting people who know them. I would deplore a situation in which the policy of this great country should be left to housewives. It should be decided instead by trained and informed people."[358]

Before the 2016 referendum, the EU's Donald Tusk echoed this, scolding Cameron; "Why did you decide on this referendum? This, it's so dangerous, even stupid, you know." Harold Wilson's Labour government spent £4.5 million on propaganda. Every household got two leaflets for entry and one against. Big business backed 'Britain into Europe', which spent £2.1 million campaigning for us to stay in the EEC. The Conservative Party, the Liberal Party and the Labour Committee for Europe (funded by the European Movement) all campaigned for us to stay in. The National Referendum Campaign had only £133,000 to campaign for leaving. The government said it would recommend that the British people vote to stay in and stated "The Government will accept their verdict."[359] That is, it saw the referendum as binding, not advisory. Exaggerated claims are nothing new. Before the 1975 referendum, Prime Minister Heath warned that "A vote against the Market could lead to a Soviet invasion of Europe." A Conservative MP warned that "a No vote [...] would mean the closing of schools and hospitals and the stopping of roads, railways and mines."[360] Politicians on both sides lied during the campaign. That did not lead to calls to overturn the result, perhaps because the then government liked the result. After the anti-EEC side lost, many of its members continued to campaign to change people's minds. Unlike the SNP before the 2014 referendum, the anti-EEC campaign leaders did not sign a pledge to respect the result of the forthcoming referendum, so they were free to keep on campaigning. They did not try to use the state machine to try to overrule what the majority had voted for, as many pro-EU politicians did after the 2016 referendum.

Referendums binding in Britain but not in the EU

The most reliable test of opinion was not when a few thousand people were asked their opinion, but when the whole population was asked to decide their country's future. Referendums and general elections were not opinion polls. Opinion polls were the views of a few, they are not even advisory. General elections and referendums were decisions by the people. The UK held twelve referendums between 1973 and 2014. After each one, the government calmly carried out the policy that won the larger number of votes. Nobody said that any of these referendums was constitutionally improper or said that they were only advisory. Our constitutional convention was that the government carried out the referendum decisions reached by the majority. Politicians did not get to choose which public votes they respected.

As Professor Adam Tomkins observed, "A constitutional convention is a non-legal, but nonetheless binding, rule of constitutional behaviour."[361] The government was duty-bound to carry out referendum decisions. The power of the 2016 vote created a mandate for Parliament, even though in strict law it was only advisory. Similarly, no law said that general elections were binding not advisory, but governments would be wise not to treat them as advisory. These are significant conventions. Governments took referendum decisions as binding. As Professor Richard Tuck wrote, "Characteristically this has

172

happened without a formal or legal acknowledgment of their fundamental role, and technically they are merely consultative; but the idea that they could be disregarded seems to most people about as fanciful as the idea that the Queen could actually use the power, still technically in her hands, to veto a Parliamentary statute."[362] Author John Lloyd argued later that "the referendum vote for leaving the EU must, however, be respected: it was advertised as binding, and both the ruling Conservatives and the opposition Labour Party committed themselves to carrying the decision of the people through. [...] No democracy can remain undamaged if it cancels out such commitments [...]."[363]

All this gave rise to the not unreasonable expectation in 2016 that if we voted to stay in the EU, we would stay in and if we voted to leave, we would leave. British people expected people to play by the rules, we respected fair play, we liked to back a winner and we did not like sore losers. By contrast, the EU convention was that the EU carried out only those majority decisions it agreed with and tried to overturn those majority decisions it disagreed with. The side that the EU backed lost nine referendums since 1992 and the EU did not respect any of them. Every time, it demanded a rerun.

In 1992, Denmark became the first member state to turn down a new EEC treaty when a majority of 50.7 per cent rejected the Maastricht Treaty. In 2001, 54 per cent of Irish voters rejected the Treaty of Nice. The EU told them both to vote again. Denmark voted against adopting the euro in 2000 – 53.2 per cent to 46.8 on a huge 87.6 per cent turnout. Sweden did likewise in 2003 – 56 per cent to 44 on an 81.2 per cent turnout. Consequently none of the 19 EU member governments that adopted the euro dared to put the decision to a referendum. Blair promised a vote on joining the euro when the time was right, but apparently it never was. A *Eurobarometer* poll of 2004 found that 61 per cent of Britons opposed adopting the euro. In 1998, polls showed that 62 per cent of the German public opposed abolishing the Deutschmark, yet the German parliament voted to do so by 575 votes to 35. Jean-Claude Juncker, at that time Luxembourg's Prime Minister, said before the 2005 French vote on the EU Constitution; "If it's a Yes vote we will say on we go, and if it's a No vote we will say we continue." The French voted against by 55 per cent to 45. The Dutch voted against by 61 per cent to 39. Neil Kinnock, the ex-leader of the Labour party, called the results 'a triumph of ignorance'. The UK, the Czech Republic, Denmark, Ireland, Poland and Portugal then cancelled their planned referendums on the Constitution. Following Juncker's advice, the EU continued regardless. It renamed the Constitution, calling it the Treaty of Lisbon. The Constitution's lead author, Giscard d'Estaing, admitted it was the same thing. Ireland then voted against the Treaty in 2008 by 53.4 per cent to 46.6, but the EU adopted it anyway. Margot Wallström, vice-president of the European Commission, said that EU officials needed to 'work out what the Irish people had really been voting against'. It was clearly inconceivable that they could have been voting against the Treaty. In his 2005 election manifesto Cameron had promised a referendum on any new EU treaty, but he broke that pledge. This linked the EU's lack of democracy to a lack of democratic control in Britain.

EU against democracy

In EU-world, referendums and general elections cannot be allowed to change anything. EU leaders were quite open about this: "Elections cannot be allowed to change economic policy", said German finance minister Wolfgang Schäuble in 2015, echoing a previous Commission President, José Manuel Barroso; "the EU is an antidote to democratic governments." President Juncker said in 2015, "There can be no democratic choice against the European treaties." Angela Merkel said "The debt brakes will be binding and valid forever. Never will you be able to change them through a parliamentary majority." The EU Commissioner for Employment, Social Affairs and Inclusion commented, "Eurozone membership and democracy are no longer compatible." The EU is by intent hostile to national democratic control of power. Richard Tuck summed it up; "Popular politics is precisely what the EU was designed to obstruct."[364]

If the British people had voted against Johnson on 12 December 2019, he would have left Downing Street the next morning. At the next election we can, if we choose, vote the rascal out. How do we vote the European Commission out? We voted the European Commission out in 2016 and it took four and a half years to get rid of the rascals. Nothing and nobody was ever to be allowed to infringe the EU's sacred Four Freedoms, as set out in the 1957 Treaty of Rome and buttressed by the ever more far-reaching case law of the European Court of Justice. The Treaty of Lisbon mandated Free Movement of Goods (Title Ia) and Free Movement of Persons, Services, and Capital (Title III). The EU's Four Freedoms expressed a single freedom – the freedom of the market. This was the EU's foundational flaw from which all else flowed. Capitalism was built in.

Stiglitz commented, "The 2009 Lisbon Treaty […] aimed to make the policymaking process more democratic. […] Unfortunately, the reality of Lisbon falls short of this lofty goal. […] Lisbon actually creates new opportunities for powerful business lobbies in Brussels to influence Europe's trade agenda." If the authors of the Treaty aimed to make the EU more democratic, why did they fail? Misfortune was no explanation. Only one other polity had a similar constitution to the EU's – Chile, where General Pinochet had in 1980 imposed the 'Constitution of Liberty' – the title of one of Friedrich von Hayek's books. Hayek, Thatcher's favourite guru, had written "So long as the present form of democracy persists decent government cannot exist." Pinochet's constitution removed all important matters from democratic influence. The EU gave itself a pro-capitalist written constitution embodied in treaties which were virtually impossible to change. Only the unanimous agreement of all the member states could make any amendment. This was bolstered by the rulings of the Court of Justice of the European Union, which only the Court itself could revise. The EU's creators intended its neoliberal core to be eternal and irreversible. This was also shown by the EU's hard opposition to a British exit and its intention to make that exit as painful as possible.

Martin Wolf of *The Financial Times* observed, "Within the Eurozone, power is now concentrated in the hands of the governments of the creditor countries, principally Germany, and a trio of unelected bureaucracies – the European

Commission, the European Central Bank and the International Monetary Fund. The peoples of adversely affected countries have no influence upon them. The politicians notionally accountable to them are powerless. This divorce between accountability and power strikes at the heart of democratic governance."[365] The EU called itself democratic, but its practice proved otherwise. In 2019, 28 politicians in the European Council appointed the new President, Ursula von der Leyen, after three days of secret talks. The European Parliament had proposed other nominees, but the Council rejected all the MEPs' nominees. The European Parliament was then required to ratify her appointment, in an 'election' with only one candidate. It was as if Boris Johnson, Nicola Sturgeon, Arlene Foster and Mark Drakeford huddled together in secret talks for three days and then appointed Tony Blair as our head of state.

Some judge the EU by what it says about itself – that it is cooperative, democratic, etc. - and then assume that those who oppose it are against those good things. We should not accept that what organisations or people say about themselves is true. Fine words butter no parsnips. Some claimed that we could have reformed the EU and made it a force for progress. Which EU body would have imposed these progressive policies? The unelected Commission? The powerless Parliament? The Council of the leaders of EU member governments? The austerity-enforcing European Central Bank? The anti-trade union European Court of Justice? The EU itself was run more by the prerogative of its Commission than by its Parliament. In no other administration were elected representatives expressly excluded from proposing laws. The EU was uniquely anti-democratic.

In Britain: sovereignty of the people

No constitution or act of Parliament originally granted us our rights to life, liberty and property, to the rule of law and our freedoms of speech, conscience, communication and association. The people won the rights we enjoy. It took centuries of struggle to make the ruling class accept that every adult should have the right to vote. The Chartists and other working class organisations worked throughout the nineteenth century to get the vote for all. Votes for all women were only won in 1928. No government or Parliament had the right to override our rights. Only the eternal vigilance of the people safeguarded those rights. Laws exist to protect these rights from interference by other individuals. A state exists to pass and enforce laws that protect our freedoms. In Britain, the people do not govern, or legislate, or interpret the law, but they are the source of the authority of those who do. Government, Parliament, the courts, all got their authority only from the sovereign people. As Lord Cranborne said in October 1945, "First, there is the Government: over them comes the authority of Parliament: and over Parliament the authority of the British people. That is the structure of the British Constitution."[366]

Parliament had no sovereignty over the people. As Vernon Bogdanor put it, "The sovereignty of the people trumps the sovereignty of Parliament."[367] Democracy is a system where elected representatives do what the people tell them to do. The legitimacy of representative democracy depended on popular sovereignty. No sovereignty, no democracy. In our democracy the people are the sovereign power. Parliament's job is to give effect to the will of the political sovereign, the nation.[368] When parliament passes a law authorising a referendum, it is accepting that the people have sovereignty. After a referendum, Parliament's job is to enact the will of the nation. In the 2016 referendum, we voted for national sovereignty, not for parliamentary sovereignty. When a pro-EU Parliament, under Theresa May, tried to assert its sovereignty over the expressed will of the people, the people asserted their sovereignty over Parliament. By contrast, the EU's principle of subsidiarity is a frank denial of sovereignty. The subsidiary nations of the EU only have the powers that the EU decides to let them have.

Private, minority, rule

The right to security of property should not extend to cover corporations' property. As John Maynard Keynes noted, "I know of no more extraordinary confusion than that which identifies the right to own the fruits of one's own labour in pre-industrial society with the right of Mr Rockefeller or the Duke of Westminster to own the labour and control the conditions of life of thousands of other people. Surely the monopoly ownership of our day is one of the great enemies of liberty. But I agree that the right of personal property is inseparable from the conception of liberty, and that this confusion between personal property, which no intelligent Socialist has ever wished to take away from anyone, and property in the sense of the right to play the money market, and employ, sack or pay what wages one likes, has had very serious results."

How democratic was it to be able to command the labour power of many people? The owners of the means of production had great power over those who owned only their labour power. The owners could decide and enforce the terms of employment. We need more democracy and control at work. How democratic was the average multinational corporation? What say did an unorganised worker have, compared to the power of a CEO? Capitalism was innately anti-democratic. The value of a person's labour power was zero if that person had no access to any means of production. A person without capital therefore had no choice about whether to put their labour power into the market or not. A person who could bring only their labour power to the market had, until their offer of their labour power was accepted, no power over those who could bring capital to the market.

The free-market economist Milton Friedman tried to prove that capitalism was innately non-coercive, but Canadian political scientist C. B. Macpherson demolished his claim.[369] Friedman argued that in a capitalist economy cooperation was voluntary provided that "individuals are effectively free to enter or not to enter into any particular exchange […]."[370] Macpherson commented, "The proviso that is required to make every transaction strictly voluntary is *not* freedom not to enter into any *particular* exchange, but freedom not to enter into any exchange *at all*." He explained, "What distinguishes the capitalist economy from the simple exchange economy is the separation of labour and capital, that is, the existence of a labour force without its own sufficient capital and therefore without a choice as to whether to put its labour in the market or not. Professor Friedman would agree that where there is no choice there is coercion. His attempted demonstration that capitalism coordinates without coercion therefore fails."[371]

Adam Smith had observed centuries before, "What are the

common wages of labour, depends everywhere upon the contract usually made between those two parties, whose interests are by no means the same. The workmen desire to get as much, the masters to give as little, as possible. The former are disposed to combine in order to raise, the latter in order to lower, the wages of labour." "It is not, however, difficult to foresee which of the two parties must, upon all ordinary occasions, have the advantage in the dispute, and force the other into a compliance with their terms. The masters, being fewer in number, can combine much more easily: and the law, besides, authorises, or at least does not prohibit, their combinations, while it prohibits those of the workmen. We have no acts of parliament against combining to lower the price of work, but many against combining to raise it. In all such disputes, the masters can hold out much longer. A landlord, a farmer, a master manufacturer, or merchant, though they did not employ a single workman, could generally live a year or two upon the stocks, which they have already acquired. Many workmen could not subsist a week, few could subsist a month, and scarce any a year, without employment. In the long run, the workman may be as necessary to his master as his master is to him; but the necessity is not so immediate."[372]

Marx wrote, "the control of the capitalist is in substance two-fold by reason of the two-fold nature of the process of production itself, - which, on the one hand, is a social process for producing use-values, on the other, a process for creating surplus-value – in form that control is despotic."[373] Capitalism was 'private', minority, ownership of the means of production. By definition, it excluded the majority, the public, the people.

Majority revolt

The claim that communism was only ever the work of an evil, violent minority was born after the First World War, when the victorious powers - who had used vast violence to impose their will on rival empires - accused the Bolsheviks of wrongly using violence to impose their will on the people of Russia to overthrow an empire ruled by an autocrat supported by the landowning minority. In 1947 President Harry Truman launched his 'Doctrine' of opposition to communism, claiming that communism was 'the will of a minority forcibly imposed upon the majority'. He claimed that communism - and communism alone - was only ever minority rule, that communist parties never won majorities. But all too often a violent reactionary minority, as in Russia, China, Korea and Vietnam, forced a civil war upon a people. These became brutal exercises in democracy, because it is hard to win a civil war against a violent ruling class without majority support. Communists are often falsely accused of having no respect for the rights to life, liberty and property.

Often this accusation comes from reactionaries trying to cover up their more flagrant abuses of people's rights. These accusations against revolutionaries have been made for centuries. The British establishment held up the guillotine as the French revolution's ultimate horror, yet the British state crushed the Irish rebellion of 1798 "with greater casualties than were visited on France by the Jacobin Terror."[374] The relative lack of liberties in many socialist countries was due to the economic and military attacks they all faced from the start rather than integral to their nature. Revolutions developed stable legality, after initial periods of chaos.

Out of capitalism emerged colonialism, imperialism, fascism, and apartheid. Capitalist competition always produces monopoly capitalism, expressed as oligarchy. Reforming it is as hopeless as trying to reform the EU - which is just another expression of monopoly capital, oligarchic and undemocratic. Socialist law aimed to end all capitalist forms of property ownership and to establish socialist economic relationships. Its laws were designed to raise social legal awareness, to promote the development of social conscience. Cuba's legal order is based on the civil law tradition. Article 3 of its 1976 Constitution said "Cuba shall never return to capitalism." As Lord Bingham, Lord Chief Justice from 1996-2008, wrote, "The rule of law requires that fundamental rights, such as that of freedom of belief and practice, should be protected, but does not require that they should be absolute."[375] This applies to all rights.

Chapter 13
The 2016 referendum

The people decide

In 2008, the Lib Dems published a pamphlet that said "It's time for a REAL referendum on Europe." It continued, "Only a real referendum on the EU will let the British people decide our country's future." Note, 'decide', not 'advise on'. In February 2008 Jo Swinson, later the Lib Dem leader, told the House of Commons, "The Liberal democrats would like to have a referendum on the major issue of whether we are in or out of Europe." The Lib Dems reaffirmed that policy in their 2010 manifesto. In the 2009 EU elections, UKIP came second with 16 per cent of the vote, behind the Conservative Party with 27.4 per cent, but ahead of Labour with 15.2 per cent. In early 2011, Parliament passed the European Union Act, making a referendum obligatory if any further treaty revision was proposed. In October 2011, 100,000 people signed a petition demanding a referendum. In 2012 the Electoral Reform Society conducted a ballot of every registered voter in the marginal constituencies of Thurrock in Essex and two in Manchester (Cheadle and Hazel Grove), asking whether they wanted a referendum. On turnouts higher than those in local elections, all three voted overwhelmingly in favour. In the 2014 EU election, UKIP came first with 26.6 per cent of the votes, the largest rise by a new party since the 1920s. Labour got 24.4 per cent of the votes, the Conservatives came third, with 23.1 per cent.

This result shocked the Conservative party into changing its policy. They promised that, if elected, they would hold a decisive in/out referendum on our EU membership. In the 2015 general election they were returned to government with more votes and MPs. Also in 2015, Prime Minister David Cameron said in a public speech, "Leave means leave […] That option of 'Let's have another go' is not on the ballot paper."[376] MPs subsequently passed the EU Referendum Act by six to one, deliberately and voluntarily giving responsibility for the final decision on our membership of the EU to the British people. A Government leaflet (costing the taxpayer over £9 million) confirmed that this 'once in a generation decision' was "[...] your decision. The Government will implement what you decide."

Cameron said on 10 November 2015, "This is a huge decision for our country, perhaps the biggest we will make in our lifetimes. And it will be the final decision [...] When the British people speak, their voice will be respected — not ignored. If we vote to leave, then we will leave. There will not be another renegotiation and another referendum." On 21 June 2016 Cameron urged older people to think of the 'hopes and dreams of your children and grandchildren'. He added, "Remember they can't undo the decision we take. If we vote out that is it. It is irreversible. We will leave Europe for good and the next generation will have to live with the consequences for far longer than the rest of us." The Leave camp also stressed that the referendum was a once-in-a-generation chance to settle the matter.

What was the question? Cameron wanted the question to be 'Should the United Kingdom remain a member of the European Union?' This would mean that he would own the Yes' vote. He did not want to repeat the mistake he had made in 2014 when his draft of the question for Scotland's referendum had gifted the SNP the question they wanted: "Should Scotland be an independent country?" In the 1975 referendum the question had been 'Do you think the United Kingdom should stay in the European Community?' That had helped to deliver the 67 per cent vote for 'Yes'. The Electoral Commission rightly ruled that Cameron's preferred question was unbalanced, because only the Remain option was offered and the 'Yes' response was for Remain. In the end, the 2016 referendum question was, "Should the United Kingdom remain a member of the European Union or leave the European Union?" The question was about whether we wanted to stay in that political body or not. The question was not "Should the United Kingdom remain a member of the European Union or leave the European Union and stay in its Single Market and in its Customs Union?" It was not "Should the United Kingdom remain a member of the European Union or leave the European Union, but leave only if the EU agrees a deal with us?"

On 8 January 2017, on BBC1, Andrew Marr said to Nicola Sturgeon, "you have made it very clear that what you mean by a 'soft' Brexit or an 'acceptable' Brexit involves staying inside the single market and the customs union. The problem is that people were told all the way through the referendum that leaving the EU meant leaving those things." Sturgeon said, "I'm not sure [...] I don't think that's the case." Marr replied, "It is the case, if I may say so. I interviewed David Cameron, George Osborne, Michael Gove, Boris Johnson and I asked all of them, and they all said yes, it means leaving the single market." The question was not about any conditions for, or results of, staying or leaving. It was not about what people might or might not believe about remaining or leaving. It was not about what else people might or might not have wanted. It did not include any other words, not nationalism, internationalism, racism; it was not about these or any other ideas. The vote was not about nationalism, or internationalism or racism, so it did not reduce to a vote for or against nationalism, internationalism or racism. Still less did it reduce to a crusade against nationalism or racism. We were not asked our opinion of any policy or party or politician. There were no names on our ballot papers, no political parties. The referendum was not about what any politician on either side said or promised. Judging from some peoples' given reasons for voting to stay in, some appear to have answered the wrong question.

The question was not, "Do you approve of the leave campaign or not?"
The question was not, "Do you like Nigel Farage or not?"
The question was not, "Do you approve of nationalism or not?"
The question was not, "Do you approve of racism or not?"

Some pro-EU MPs seemed to believe that the people must do what MPs tell them to do. Some MPs claimed independence from the people who elected them, though their legitimacy comes only from their being elected by the people. All MPs won their seats by getting more votes than any of their opponents. All too many MPs wanted the minority vote to stay in the EU to prevail over the majority vote to leave. MPs who defied the referendum result were rejecting the only legitimate basis of their own power. Some seemed to prefer that the minority wins. Perhaps we should make it a rule that in every vote, the minority wins? Or at least has the right to demand a repeat vote? Should football have a new rule that the losing team always has the right to call for a replay?

Winston Churchill, when asked what an adequate majority in a democratic vote was, replied 'One'. Labour MP Chuka Umunna acknowledged, "A majority of one is sufficient." Some other Labour MPs seemed to think that minus 1.3 million was a good majority. The late Lord Ashdown (pro-EU) said before the vote, "I will forgive no one who does not respect the sovereign voice of the British people once it has spoken. Whether it is a majority of 1 per cent or 20 per cent, when the British people have spoken, you do what they command. Either you believe in democracy or you don't." Well put. The pro-EU Conservative MP Anna Soubry said before the referendum, "We are trusting the British people. We will go to the people, and let the people decide whether or not to stay within the EU." The day after the referendum she said, "If I thought we'd lose, I wouldn't have said it, obviously." The Cameron leaflet sent to all households said, "The Government will implement what you decide." Some believed it should have said, "The Government will implement the opposite of what you decide, if you decide the wrong way", or, "The Government will implement what we decide you should have decided," or just, "The Government will implement what the Government decides."

If 52 per cent was not a mandate, then Britain had not had a legitimate government in living memory, because no party since 1945 won even 50 per cent of the votes cast. Only pressure by the people kept us out of the euro. Only pressure by the people forced parliament to agree to hold the referendum. The idea of Brexit came from the British people, when we came to understand that the EU gave all control to transnational companies and their appointed European Commissioners. Only the popular pressure that we should make decisions about our country in our country delivered the 17.4 million votes to Leave.

Not the media

Many politicians, particularly in the Labour Party and many who worked in the media believed that the media determined how people thought and thus that the media determined events. But blaming the media is shooting the messenger. As Jonathan Munro, the BBC's head of newsgathering, said "There's a truism here about all election campaigns with a democracy in a free media: the failure belongs squarely on the shoulders of the people who lost the campaign."[377] The BBC backed our EU membership. In 2005, an independent inquiry by Lord Wilson of Dinton, commissioned by the BBC, concluded "although the BBC wishes to be impartial in its news coverage of the EU, it is not succeeding." News-watch's more recent surveys of its output confirm the EU's consistently pro-EU bias.[378] But our national broadcaster failed to win the referendum for the EU.

The 2016 US election was more evidence against the notion that the media were all-powerful. Only two major newspapers backed Trump. 91 per cent of media coverage was hostile to Trump, yet *Washington Post* columnist Dana Millbank blamed the media for his election, complaining that "The problem is the media didn't show bias against Trump earlier and more often." We should not assume that propaganda is all-powerful, whether in old media or new media. People are not empty vessels, ready to be filled with the thoughts aimed at them. People chose which media they attended to; the media did not choose them. The claim that the media decided political campaigns dressed up an assault on democracy to make it look like an attack on corporate capitalism. Criticism of the media as vulgar was really aimed against the public. It was code for 'the people are stupid, the people are gullible'.

Not the politicians

Politicians often overrated their influence. They tried to tell us what to think and how to vote. They should not assume that we thought the way they wanted us to think and that we voted the way we did because of what they said and wrote. We heard and saw them but then we made up our own minds. What assorted politicians said was beside the point. No politicians came with us into the voting booths to tell us how to vote. We did not clutch a batch of their quotes and anxiously consult them, trying to count whether Cameron and Blair told more lies than Gove and Farage. We ignored the politicians or said a plague on the whole lot of them. Too much subsequent debate was just commentary on the campaign, not debate on the issue. Some still went on about this slogan or that, or some claim made by this or that politician. Many politicians and others said foolish things during the campaign. Some then assumed, not proved, that people voted as they did because we listened to one set of politicians rather than another. They were missing the point. Referendums are about what the people think about the issue at stake, not about what they think of various politicians' performances. The whole point of referendums was that they

191

were not about what political 'leaders' told us to think. Referendums were opportunities for the whole people to decide important matters.

Some EU supporters were in thrall to the discredited 'great man of history' approach, combined with conspiracy theory. Some seemed to think that history was driven by this or that man's ambition, with unnamed 'powerful interests' pulling the strings. The pro-EU campaign did all it could to promote Farage as the one and only face of the 'Out' campaign. Too many voted against independence because they did not want to be in the same camp as Farage. But Brexit was not all about Farage. It was not about his future, as events since the referendum have proved. Some had said he would become an MP, or a Lord, or Prime Minister, or our man in Washington. Where is he now? Not in the House of Commons, not in the House of Lords, not in 10 Downing Street and not in our Washington embassy. The referendum was about the country's future, not about what anyone thought or felt about any individual. One could support the cause of British independence without supporting any of its cheerleaders. It was not about the politicians. Why assume that we took any notice of any of them? Very few of us, however we voted, voted as we did because a politician told us to. We rejected all the politicians' advice. We answered the question before us. We made up our own minds.

Some continued to obsess about the lies told in the campaign. This was to assume that what politicians said had decided the result, that the vote was only procured by lies told by the leave camp and that people voted to leave because they believed the lies. Did no pro-EU politician lie during the campaign? Did their lies make pro-EU people vote the way they did? This approach obscured the simple, unbearable truth that people did their best to answer the question on the ballot paper and voted to leave. It was no lie that the vote was on the question of whether we wanted decisions affecting the UK to be made in the UK. The Electoral Reform Society reported that most people had a 'highly negative' view of both campaigns and that most people said that politicians' appeals had made 'no difference' to how they voted. An Ipsos MORI poll of May 2016 found that when people answered the question, 'Who do you trust on issues related to the referendum on EU membership?' 73 per cent said, 'Friends and immediate family', 46 per cent said, 'Work colleagues' and 46 per cent said, 'The ordinary man/woman in the street'. Only 12 per cent said, 'Politicians generally'.

Increasingly people were fed up with politicians' mirror-image false accusations – that the Conservative party would sell off the NHS, destroy workers' and consumers' rights and tear up environmental safeguards, that Brexit would destroy the economy, that the Labour party would wreck the economy, support terrorists and abolish our armed forces and the monarchy. Some Tories said that people who voted Labour were motivated by envy. Some Labour supporters said that people who voted Conservative were motivated by selfishness. These too were mirror-image simplifications, slogans not analysis. Maybe a few people were motivated as accused, but we should not take the atypical as the typical. Some EU supporters said that people who voted leave were motivated by bigotry and some Leave supporters said that people who voted Remain were motivated by elitism. 'Left behind' and

193

'liberal elite' were yet more mirror-image caricatures. Some on the left were pro-EU because they thought of themselves as 'anti-American'. Some seemed to think that anyone who was anti-EU must therefore be pro-American. Again, mirror-image simplifications. These were not the only choices: one did not have to be anti-anybody to be pro-independence. Being pro-Britain did not mean being anti any other country. One could be 'pro' all countries, friends of all countries, including Britain.

Writing in *The New Statesman* in June 2015, author John King noted: "The media tell us that the Tories are anti-EU while Labour and the Lib Dems are fighting their narrow-mindedness, and UKIP is dismissed as a far-right group bordering on the fascist. This is bubble gum politics. Little Europeans sneer 'Little Englander' at those with a different opinion, peddling stereotypes, unwilling to consider the bigger arguments [...] A lazy acceptance of establishment propaganda and a fear of being branded 'xenophobic' have silenced many liberals and left-wingers. And yet the EU is driven by big business. This is a very corporate coup." Increasingly, people rejected the descriptions some tried to impose on them. An October 2020 survey found that "When asked where they line up between left and right, only 22 per cent of Britons describe themselves as left or right, while 53 per cent of Britons position themselves in the centre (either as centre, centre-left or centre-right). At the same time, only 30 per cent believe that left and right labels are still useful in describing people's beliefs."[379]

An anti-fascist nation

Some saw Brexit as a reactionary Tory plot and denied that the principle of democracy was at stake. The Conservative Prime

Ministers Harold Macmillan (1957-63) and Edward Heath (1970-74) were pro-EEC. In 1975 Thatcher campaigned to stay in the EEC. Prime Minister John Major (1990-97) was pro-EU. Conservative prime ministers David Cameron (2010-16) and Theresa May (2016-19) were pro-EU. Some seem to think that the way to work out what is the right policy is to look at what the Conservative party does and then do the opposite. This is to let the Conservative party do your thinking for you. In the 1930s the Conservative party was – largely – pro-fascist, so it was right to oppose it. It changed its policy fundamentally when it ditched Chamberlain and chose Churchill: it became anti-fascist. Not many would say that it was right to oppose it then. The nature of populism in a country depended on the nature of the people in question, their history and their culture. Populism in a country like Britain, with its very strong anti-fascist traditions, was very different from populism in Italy or Spain. There was a rise of fascism in Spain, with Vox, accompanying growing support of the EU.

Brexit was not a far-right project, the British people would not vote for such a thing, if it were on offer. The British are a profoundly anti-fascist nation. Some said that the far right are a profoundly anti-fascist nation. Some said that the far right was on the march. The British National Party, the only authentic far right party, got just 1,667 votes across the whole country in the 2015 general election. By the 2017 election, it had surged to all of 4,642 votes across the whole country. Yet some on the left geared their whole 'strategy' to opposing this tiny insignificance? Some said that Britain in the twenty-first century was like Germany in 1933, but it was prettifying Nazism to claim that it was. In a mirror-image, some people

195

who voted to leave called the EU the Fourth Reich, which also prettified Nazism. Fascist governments destroyed democratic bodies, violently repressed workers' organisations and killed or jailed their opponents. The left all too often cried 'wolf' about fascism. A left paper in France in 1958 said, "today, without any risk of error, we can state that the regime of de Gaulle is in contemporary France the necessary step to the installation of Fascism." This was wrongly generalising from World War Two's struggle against fascist regimes. de Gaulle always championed national self-determination. The false portrayal of him as a fascist was a factor in the events of May 1968, when leftists like Daniel Cohn-Bendit played a part in ousting de Gaulle. Some were surprised when Cohn-Bendit emerged later as a passionately pro-EU MEP, but there was a consistency to his career, as an opponent of national self-determination. Similarly, some anti-communists wrongly treated the Soviet Union as if it was another version of fascism.[380]

Some on 'the left' in Britain wrongly accuse the Conservative Party of being 'far right'. This absurd misjudgement did much to explain why 'the left' did much to explain why 'the left' failed so consistently. Many on the left portrayed the EU as progressive. They were like those Chinese leftists who in the 1930s wanted to fight against Chiang Kai-Shek rather than against Japanese intervention. They assisted, wittingly or not, Japanese imperialism. The Remain cause was the conservative option, wanting to keep the status quo. By contrast, many who voted to leave did so because they saw leaving the EU as a chance to change things for the better. When a protestor harassed MP Anna Soubry in the street and called her a Nazi, liberal indignation knew no bounds. The protestor was arrested, tried and sentenced to eight weeks' imprisonment, suspended for a year. He had to do 220 hours of unpaid work, pay Ms Soubry compensation of £200 and pay court costs of £215. Labour MP David Lammy, on national television, called Conservative MP Jacob Rees-Mogg a Nazi. Lammy called the Conservative MPs of the European Research Group 'worse than neo-Nazis'. When challenged, he said, "that that wasn't strong enough'.[381] Lammy called Johnson 'an extreme hard-right fascist', which did more to discredit Lammy than Johnson. Labour leader Sir Keir Starmer promoted Lammy Shadow Minister for Justice. Lammy tweeted about 'the will of the people bollocks'. One participant in the debate about the EU had had a real link with a genuine fascist. When EU enthusiast Kenneth Clarke was a student politician at Cambridge University, he invited Oswald Mosley to speak at the University's Conservative Association. Why? Because Mosley's British Union of Fascists was the first political party in Britain to call for European Union. Mosley's theoretical journal was called *The European*. Clarke was always loyal to the EU above all, even when it meant courting a real fascist.

Some people claimed that the vote for Brexit was just like the vote for Trump and that they were both part of some worldwide reactionary movement. One key difference demolished this claim. In the US election, the richer you were, the more likely you were to vote for Trump. In our referendum, the richer you were, the more likely you were to vote to stay in the EU. A report by the Centre for Social Justice and Legatum Institute, 48:52: Healing a divided Britain, 2016, found there was a direct correlation between household income and the way people voted. "At every level of earning, there is a direct correlation between household income and your likelihood to vote for leaving the EU – 62 per cent of those with income of less than £20,000 voted to leave, but that percentage falls in steady increments until, by an income of £60,000, that percentage was just 35 per cent." The only socioeconomic group where a majority voted to Remain was the most affluent stratum of the population. Trump won in all income groups whose income was over $50,000 a year: the US rich largely voted for Trump. By contrast, the leave side won in all income groups except the richest: the British rich largely voted to stay in the EU. Demographically, the vote for Trump and the vote for Brexit were polar opposites. The vote for Remain more closely matched the vote for Trump.

'Decisions about the UK should be taken in the UK'

Leave won largely because it had a better ground campaign, with a more convincing message. It took a lot of effort by many people and organisations to get Brexit under way with a more convincing message. It took a lot of effort by many people and organisations to get Brexit under way with the referendum. Seb Handley's splendid book 'Brexit - how the nobodies beat the somebodies', showed how a brilliant local group helped to reduce the pro-EU vote in Brighton. The group 'We Voted Leave', organised by Robert and Sally Wright, maintained a consistent and dignified presence outside the Houses of Parliament. The pro-EU camp had tried to displace any discussion of the issues of democracy and sovereignty and to focus the debate on their forecasts of economic doom if we dared to vote to leave. But the majority stayed focused on the issues and voted to take control over their own lives, over our politics, laws and borders. Lord Ashcroft's poll in June 2016 found, the biggest single reason for wanting to leave the EU was 'the principle that decisions about the UK should be taken in the UK'. A post-referendum ComRes poll found that 53 per cent of people who voted Leave prioritised the 'ability of Britain to make its own laws'. 17.4 million people voted to leave the EU – more than have ever voted for any issue or party in British history. The 17.4 million majority voted, in a free, fair, legitimate, democratic referendum, to leave the EU. By voting in the referendum, however they voted, people legitimised that decision-making process. All Conservative and Labour MPs were elected on manifesto pledges to respect our referendum decision.

Lots of prejudice – against Leave voters

Some saw the 17.4 million democratic majority as witting or unwitting agents of reaction. Some in the pro-EU camp threw Leave voters the crude anti-democratic trope that people are stupid, which some Conservatives used to throw at people who voted Labour. Some EU enthusiasts sounded like the nineteenth century proto-fascist Thomas Carlyle who called democracy 'blockheadism, gullibility, bribeability, amenability to beer and balderdash'. In the nineteenth and early twentieth century, the forces of reaction resisted enfranchising the poor and women on the grounds that they were ignorant and would vote the wrong way. The Conservative party opposed the 1832 Reform Bill claiming that it would plunge the country over a cliff-edge into an abyss of chaos. The rhetoric of reaction has not changed much over the centuries. There are echoes of the same prejudice in the arguments for a second referendum:

199

'people didn't know what they were voting for', 'the issues were too complex' and 'they should never even have been asked'. Sneers at 'white van man', 'Essex man', even 'the white working class' were not exclusive to Labour's Lady Thornberry.

Polls have found that in all the long-standing Western democracies about three-quarters of those born in the 1930s believed that it was 'essential' to live in a democracy, but only a little more than a quarter of those born in the 1980s agreed. In Britain older people were more supportive of Brexit than young people. Richard Tuck commented, "it may well be true that the older and less educated voters were more supportive of Brexit, but (as other people have observed) 'less educated' is the *same* as 'older', given the staggering expansion of higher education since the 1990s. The fact that older voters are in general both keener on democracy and keener on Brexit is unlikely to be a coincidence."[382]

The great science writer Richard Dawkins called the Leave vote 'a slender majority of an ignorant and misled public'. To test this assertion, Noah Carl and his colleagues conducted a study comparing levels of knowledge about the EU among people who voted leave and people who voted Remain. They gave a 15-item EU knowledge quiz to a nationally representative sample of the British population via an online survey. They found that "there was – contrary to Dawkins' claim – no average difference in EU knowledge between the two groups." They concluded that this provided 'tentative evidence against the claim that Remain voters were substantially better informed than Leave voters.'[383]

One of the main reasons Labour has lost so many elections

was the way some of its supporters behaved. Too many of them seemed to have the old colonial mentality – we know better than these people what is good for them. Paul Mason in *The Guardian* called Johnson's election win 'a victory of the old over the young, racists over people of colour, selfishness over the planet.' Great message – we call you old, racist and selfish – so vote for us next time. Clearly, Mason's socialist values, even his liberal values, were only skin-deep. Some pro-EU people still do not get why they lost in 2016 and in 2019 - because they underestimated their opponent. You underestimate, you lose, is the iron law of politics. Calling our leaders stupid is to imply that everyone who voted for them is stupid too. From this follows 'vote for us, we're brighter than you' – a sure way to lose the next election too. It is a good rule in debate to avoid using the words stupid and intelligent. Social democracy sees workers as unthinking. Sidney and Beatrice Webb, who played key roles in founding the Labour Party, patronisingly called trade union democracy 'primitive democracy', where they found 'the most childlike faith not only that 'all men are equal' and the belief that 'what concerns all should be decided by all'.[384] This implied that workers should not make decisions for themselves: the clever Fabians would do the thinking for them. Labour's Lord Peter Mandelson told us that Members of Parliament were there to 'think for you'. The class does not need people to think for it, it can think for itself.

A YouGov poll of 2019 suggested that 37 per cent of people who had voted to stay in the EU had de-friended, on social media sites, people who had voted leave. Only 9 per cent of people who had voted to leave had de-friended people who voted to stay in. This was evidence that too many people on both sides of the debate did not believe that there were good people on the other side of the debate and evidence that more EU enthusiasts than people who voted leave adopted this intolerant attitude. Some claimed that referendums should never be called because the people were innately reactionary. Some sought to back this up by claiming that in a referendum on capital punishment, people would vote to bring back hanging. The 2015 British Social Attitudes survey found that, for the first time, fewer than half those surveyed backed the return of capital punishment, 48 per cent, down from 75 per cent in 1983.[385] Those who made this false accusation were behind the times, not the British people.

Some echoed the Tory ex-MP Matthew Parris who wrote that Brexit meant 'trusting the people' (in Churchill's words). Parris retorted "I don't. Never have and never will." He said that Parliament's job is to curb 'the instincts of the mob'.[386] Parris seemed to be channelling the eighteenth century MP Edmund Burke, who said that MPs must never be bound by the views of 'the swinish multitude'. He assumed the rationality of MPs and the irrationality of the people they represented. He wrote privately to the Duke of Portland in 1780 that the crowd 'are naturally proud, tyrannical, and ignorant, bad scholars and worse masters.'[387] 17.4 million people did not vote to leave because a clique of reactionaries duped them or because media operations procured by Russian money swayed them. Jewish people did not cause the Russian revolution. Freemasons did not cause the French revolution. Outside agitators did not induce workers to join trade unions. Demands for social change were not the product of Soviet machinations.

The referendum was legitimate

The European Commission for Democracy Through Law (Venice Commission) issued a Code of Good Practice on Referendums. These rules applied to all 47 member states of the Council of Europe, which included the UK. Section 3.1.C stated that the referendum question must be binary. Section 7.A said there should be no minimum threshold. 7.B said that it should be settled by a simple majority. Our 2016 referendum met all these standards. As in the 2014 referendums and all the previous votes, nobody demanded a recount. Everybody acknowledged the integrity of the process. We held clean referendums in this country. The Electoral Commission has never suggested that the result was in any way invalid or unsafe. The courts ruled that the 2016 vote was legitimate, not corrupt. On 21 September 2018 Mr Justice Supperstone said, "Neither of the Electoral Commission reports establish that the breaches of campaign finance or other requirements identified in the reports mean that the result of the Referendum was 'procured by fraud', or that the outcome of the Referendum was affected by any wrongdoing or unlawful conduct."[388]

On 10 December 2018 in the Queen's Bench Division Administrative Court, Mr Justice Ouseley refused permission to proceed with the judicial review of this decision on the basis of both delay and want of merit.[389] The Applicants applied for permission to appeal this Order. Lord Justice Hickinbottom and Lord Justice Haddon-Cave heard the Appeal on 21 February 2019. Lord Justice Hickinbottom said, "in my view, as Ouseley J properly said, in this case there is no evidence that gives rise to any soundly based ground for believing the outcome of the referendum result would have been different if the breaches of the rules had not occurred." He affirmed, "Thus, there is simply no evidential basis for the proposition that the breaches, or any of them, are material in the sense that, had they not occurred, the result of the referendum would have been different." He continued, "In my view, Ouseley J was right to observe that, however it was sought to present the Applicants' grounds, at the heart of their case is an attack on the democratic process, i.e. on the referendum itself and its outcome." He concluded, "In the circumstances, for the court to declare void the decision to notify withdrawal or the notification itself would clearly be a constitutionally inappropriate and unlawful interference in the due democratic process."[390]

Thus, the courts ruled that it was a valid, legal democratic process and that the Applicants were making 'an attack on the democratic process'. In September 2019, the Electoral Commission found that two pro-EU campaigns that were set up less than a month before the referendum campaign worked together, breaking electoral law: "We found that the '5 seconds campaign' was a joint campaign run by WUAV and DDB UK Limited. Spending on the campaign was 'joint' or 'common plan' spending." Wake Up And Vote (WUAV) and DDB, a marketing company, were just two of five campaigns that were set up less than a month before the referendum, sharing big donors and they funnelled £1 million to new campaigns set up in the month before the vote. The other three campaigns seem to have avoided proper scrutiny. The two bodies created unbranded videos that were shared by the official Britain Stronger in Europe campaign, as if it was their content. DDB was fined just £1,800 for failing to declare its joint spending with WUAV. This follows its £1,000 fine in March 2018 for other inaccuracies in its spending return.

Louise Edwards, the Commission's Director of Regulation, said, "Both Wake Up and Vote and DDB UK Limited had an important legal duty to accurately declare joint spending in their referendum spending returns. Both failed to do so, meaning that voters, looking at the reported spending, had no way of knowing that WUAV and DDB UK Limited had worked together on a campaign, or of how much either campaigner spent in total." It had taken well over a year for the Electoral Commission to act. In June 2018, Priti Patel handed the Commission a dossier full of evidence. At first the Commission refused to investigate. The law breaking was eventually punished more than three years after the referendum. In September 2019, the Metropolitan Police said, "It is clear that whilst some technical breaches of electoral law were committed by Leave.EU in respect of the spending return submitted for their campaign, there is insufficient evidence to justify any further criminal investigation." The Met closed its investigation with no charges. The UK's National Crime Agency said it had found no evidence of criminal activity carried out by Leave.EU or by Arron Banks. The Agency cleared Banks of any criminal wrongdoing in the referendum. It said he was legally entitled to take a loan from one of his holding companies to contribute to Leave.EU, the pro-Brexit campaign group that he founded. It added that it found no evidence that Mr Banks or his companies had received funding from 'any third party', scotching speculation that Mr Banks' contribution might have come from a foreign source, such as Russia.

On 6 November 2020, the *Guardian* and *Observer* journalist Carole Cadwalladr apologised for wrongly claiming that Banks 'had been found to have broken the law' in his role as founder of the Leave.EU campaign. In a statement on Twitter, she said: "On 22 Oct 2020, I tweeted that Arron had been found to have broken the law. I accept he has not. I regret making this false statement, which I have deleted. I undertake not to repeat it. I apologise to Arron for the upset and distress caused." There appear to be only two proven links with Russia. Since 2017, pro-EU Alex Salmond has hosted a talk show on the *Russia Today* TV channel. Evgeny Lebedev, a Russian-British businessman, owns *The Independent*, *The Evening Standard* and the TV channel *London Live*. (Lebedev's father made the family fortune from the KGB's plunder of Russia.) *The Independent* and *The Evening Standard* both consistently campaigned for Britain to stay in the EU. *The Standard's* editor is George Osborne, who was Cameron's pro-EU, pro-austerity, Chancellor of the Exchequer. In a further unholy alliance, Lebedev sold 30 per cent stakes in the two newspapers to offshore companies fronted by a Saudi businessman, Sultan Mohamed Abuljadayel, in 2017 and 2018. These investments were made through two Cayman Islands-registered companies, Scalable Inc. and International Media Company, which helped to obscure the true investor. The two companies were in turn 50 per cent owned by Abuljadayel and 50 per cent by Wondrous Investments, which is run by Saudi Arabia's state-controlled National Commercial Bank.[391]

There is no evidence that the Russian government interfered in the 2016 referendum. There is no evidence that anyone changed their mind about how to vote because of the non-existent Russian interference in the 2016 referendum. There is plenty of evidence that some pro-EU propagandists lied that there was Russian interference in the 2016 referendum. Sir Nick Clegg stated there is 'absolutely no evidence' that Russia used Facebook to influence the EU referendum. He dismissed claims that Cambridge Analytica swayed people's decision to vote leave in 2016. He said, resignedly, "The roots to British Euroscepticism go very, very deep." Alex Hern looked into similar allegations about foreign interference in the 2019 general election and concluded, "there is no evidence of any foreign interference in the election to date; no evidence of anything approaching hyper-focused ads targeting a specific subset of the population [...] Twitter is going even further: the company now shares the full details of foreign interference when it finds it, allowing journalists and researchers to download entire archives of tweets sent by Russian, Chinese and Iranian actors. Again, they've discovered nothing aimed at disrupting the UK election."[392]

The strangest myth was that Twitter influenced the 2016 vote. But just one per cent of people identify Twitter as the source they rely on for accurate news. Over 350,000 tweets are sent every minute. Studies from the universities of California, Berkeley and Swansea found that only a tiny share of tweets were sent by accounts linked to Russia and most of these were posted on 24 June 2016, the day after the vote. Some urged people to vote Remain. A study at the University of Edinburgh found Kremlin-linked accounts sent around 420 tweets about Brexit, 'mostly after the referendum had taken place'. The whole nonsense that Russian propaganda (or US money) produced the vote for independence is all too reminiscent of the old anti-communist nonsense that Bolshevism was not Russian but German or Jewish. Yet some EU enthusiasts still believe that Russian interference, not British people, decided the outcome of the 2016 referendum. The dodgiest intervention was the government's. Cameron rigged the spending limits for the referendum. Instead of allowing both sides equal amounts, he pushed through a provision that allowed the political parties to spend in proportion to the votes they had got in the previous election. This enabled the pro-EU side to spend £19.3 million against the Leave side's £13.3 million. On top of that, Cameron spent £9.3 million of public funds to send every household a pro-EU leaflet – an action that would not have been allowed in Ireland, where the government was forbidden to use public money to promote one side of a referendum proposal.

Chapter 14
The British Social Attitudes surveys of 2017, 2018 and 2019

These annual surveys are based on in-depth interviews with around 3,000 people, asking them what it is like to live in Britain and what they think about how Britain is run. They are a better guide to public opinion than the average opinion poll. In the summary chapter of British Social Attitudes 2017, Roger Harding, the Head of Public Attitudes at the National Centre for Social Research, pointed out, "the onward march of social liberalism continues with record proportions of people being comfortable with same-sex relationships, pre-marital sex and abortion, among other issues. While younger people are still more liberal on these subjects than older people, the difference is narrowing. "The EU referendum vote result led some on the left and right to speculate that this was the result of a backlash against greater social liberalism (Eagle & Baird (2017); Lawson (2016). We find no evidence that there has been a public turn against same-sex relationships, or indeed on many other personal issues. In fact, on some issues such as same-sex relationships, the long-term increase in socially liberal attitudes has actually accelerated."[393]

As the British rapper, author and poet Akala acknowledged, "Britain's inner cities – London in particular – are now some of the most successfully multi-ethnic experiments in the 'Western' world [...]."[394] The survey found that views on the EU in 2016 were: leave the EU 41 per cent, stay in but reduce its powers 35 per cent, leave things as they are 16 per cent, stay in and increase its powers 4 per cent, work for a single European government 2 per cent. As Professor John Curtice acknowledged, "Britain emerged from the referendum far more sceptical about the EU than it had ever been previously. By the time the referendum was over, as many as three in four voters (75%) felt that Britain should either leave the EU or that if it stayed the institution's powers should be reduced."[395] In the survey's chapter on the referendum, 'The vote to leave the EU - litmus test or lightning rod?' Professor Curtice speculated that "In taking on some of the attributes and characteristics of a state and creating a degree of uniformity across Europe, people may feel that their distinctive national identity and the culture that they associate with that identity are being undermined."[396]

People had many more concerns about the EU's project of becoming more of a state than just feelings about national identity. The survey had not asked any questions about other aspects of this EU project, no questions about the EU's effects on Britain, or the EU's version of democracy, or its effects on our ability to make our own decisions, or our relationship to the EU as it became more like a state. Curtice considered "two popular explanations for the vote by the British public in June 2016 to leave the EU. The first is that the vote reflects the concerns of more 'authoritarian', socially conservative voters about the social consequences of EU membership – and especially about immigration. The second is that the vote was occasioned by general public disenchantment with politics. The chapter suggests that the first of these two provides the better explanation."[397] He seems to have excluded the possibility that people might have voted to leave the EU because they wanted to leave the EU.

Curtice speculated, "However, the EU is for the most part a

relatively remote institution. Few voters have a deep appreciation of what it does, of how it operates, or of the personnel that occupy its principal political positions. In contrast, most will have at least some acquaintance with their principal domestic politicians and political institutions. So when they are asked what they think about the EU, voters might be inclined to think about how they are being governed in general, rather than about the EU in particular. And if their view is that they are not in fact being governed that well, they may decide that at least part of the blame lies with an EU they do not understand but seemingly enables its politicians and bureaucrats to enjoy a comfortable life."[398]

There was no evidence for any of these speculations about why people 'might be inclined to think'. He explicitly excluded the possibility that people might have voted 'about the EU in particular'. He gratuitously asserted that 'they do not understand' the EU, unwarranted by any evidence from the survey. The vote was neither a litmus test nor a lightning rod. The evidence from the survey did not support either conclusion. Since Curtice's two proposed explanations failed, we were left with the default position, that we voted on the question we were asked. In the next year's British Social Attitudes survey's summary chapter, Harding wrote, "Many have speculated whether the Brexit vote was driven by a resurgence of English nationalism south of the border (for example: Cockburn, 2017[399]). Here BSA data finds that although English identity is more closely associated with a leave vote, overall levels of English nationalism are down: just 13% of people in England describe themselves as 'English, not British', the lowest level since 1997. The most popular category remains

'Equally English and British', which remains stable at 41%."[400]

Journalist Patrick Cockburn had claimed on 17 March 2017 that "Brexit unleashed an English nationalism that has damaged the union with Scotland for good."[401] In the survey's chapter on Scotland, 'How Brexit has created a new divide in the Nationalist movement', Professor Curtice and Ian Montagu found that "There is little sign that English identity has become more prevalent in the wake of the Brexit referendum or that those who feel predominantly English have become particularly more antagonistic towards Scotland's current status within the UK."[402] In this survey's chapter on the EU, 'A more 'informed' public? The impact of the Brexit debate', Professor Curtice and Sarah Tipping reported that in 2017, 36 per cent of us thought that Britain should leave the EU, 33 per cent thought that we should stay in the EU but reduce its powers, 19 per cent thought that we should stay in the EU and keep powers as they are, 4 per cent thought that we should stay in the EU and increase its powers and 3 per cent thought that we should work for the formation of a single European government. 69 per cent were for a looser relationship. 33 per cent plus 19 per cent wanted options that were not actually available. (It was disappointing that, as in the previous survey, so many people chose options that were not actually on the table.) Only three per cent wanted the single European state that the EU was committed to becoming.

Curtice and Tipping summed up the surveys from 1998 to 2018, "from 1998 onwards (with the single exception of 2003) at least half of the public could be classified as 'Eurosceptic', that is, they either said Britain should leave the EU or that it should try to reduce its powers. Indeed, by 2012 as many as two-thirds were of that view, and at 69% the latest figure is, in fact, little different. Thus, scepticism about the EU is perhaps no more widespread now than it was before the EU referendum. What has changed is that it has become more likely to be expressed in the form of support for leaving the institution rather than for just trying to loosen Britain's ties with it."[403] The authors noted of the key question, 'How much do you agree or disagree that being a member of the European Union undermines Britain's right to be an independent country that makes its own laws?', "There is widespread support for this view: 57% agree while just 27% disagree (and 17% say that they neither agree nor disagree)."[404] They pointed out that "There is little sign here that the EU referendum campaign served to make Britain less tolerant towards migrants [...]."[405] The authors concluded, "Attitudes towards the EU do now appear to be more clearly structured and thus 'informed' than they were before the EU referendum campaign began in earnest."[406] The inverted commas showed that the authors did not like to admit that our great national debate about the EU had made us better informed about it.

The government had called the referendum to put an end to the debate about our membership of the EU. Our response was to lift the debate to the country's highest level of discussion since World War Two, marked by a flourishing of pamphlets and vigorous new organisations local and national. In the 2019 British Social Attitudes survey's chapter, 'The EU debate: has Brexit polarised Britain?', Professor Curtice and Ian Montagu reported that in 2018, 34 per cent of us thought that Britain should leave the EU, 33 per cent thought that we should stay in the EU but reduce its powers, 20 per cent thought that we should leave things as they are, 4 per cent thought that we should stay in the EU and increase its powers, and 3 per cent thought that we should work for a single European government. 67 per cent were for a looser relationship. 33 per cent plus 20 per cent wanted options that were not actually available. Again, only three per cent wanted the single European state that the EU aims to become. The British Social Attitudes surveys of 2008, 2012, 2013, 2015, 2016, 2017 and 2018 had all found that same three per cent.

Chapter 15
The British economy, trade, and the EU

Before the referendum, Prime Minister Cameron had ordered the Treasury to make no plans for leaving the EU. The leave camp had plans. Business for Britain published 'Change or Go' in 2015. Liam Halligan published his book 'Clean Brexit' in 2017. 'Change or Go' had a whole section on trading on WTO terms: "This section seeks to answer that question by assuming that Britain has left the EU without any 'special deal' and that its trading relationship with the Union has defaulted to World Trade Organization (WTO) terms."[407] It offered a more than adequate plan for making a success of independence trading under EU rules. We are the ninth biggest manufacturing nation, with £275 billion manufacturing exports a year and 2.7 million manufacturing jobs. Britain is the fifth largest economy in the world and the EU's largest single market – bigger than the USA, China and India.

Since the 1990s, the British economy has grown faster than the European average, according to the OECD and the Office for National Statistics. Our growth rate since 1991 has been 0.3-0.4 per cent a year higher than the eurozone countries' average. Cumulatively, since 1990 our economy grew by 78 per cent, compared with the eurozone countries' 56 per cent. The EU threat to expel us without an agreement was empty. EU members had a greater interest in achieving and maintaining a good trade agreement because without it they would suffer far more than us, simply because they sold more to us than we sold to them. By 2017 we had a £95 billion deficit in trade in goods with the EU. The EU – particularly Germany, which accounted for nearly a quarter of all EU trade to the UK – did not like the idea of failing to reach an agreement. Over a million German jobs relied on British consumers buying German goods like

BMWs. Without an agreement, the EU would have £13 billion tariffs slapped on its goods – 10 per cent on Volkswagens, 12 per cent on wine, 40 per cent on cheese. Better for everyone surely to keep on an even keel?

The UK has seen little economic benefit from the EU's Single Market. UK goods exports to the 11 fellow founding members of the Single Market grew between 1993 and 2015 by just 1 per cent a year. Over the same period, UK goods exports to the 111 countries with which we traded on WTO terms, including China, India, Russia, Brazil, Indonesia, Singapore, Canada and the USA, grew by 2.88 per cent a year, nearly three times as fast. In 2007-17 our exports to the EU increased by 40 per cent while our exports to non-EU members increased by 80 per cent. UK exports to the EU fell from 60 per cent to 44 per cent of our total exports after the Single Market was introduced. The USA and China both sold more goods to the EU's single market than we did – all under WTO rules. The USA and China were the EU's biggest markets in 2019, accounting for just under 30 per cent of total EU trade. Neither had a trade agreement with the EU, neither had aligned with the EU's 'level playing field'. Six of the EU's top ten trading partners traded under WTO rules - the USA, China, Russia, India, Brazil and Japan. We could too.

The WTO guaranteed no discrimination. The EU could not impose on us punitive tariffs or barriers to trade. The WTO guaranteed Most Favoured Nation terms: the EU and all other countries had to grant us the best terms they gave to other countries with whom they had no preferential agreement. Companies from almost every country outside the EU sold goods to and bought goods from companies based in EU member countries. People who knew about trade, and who sold goods to other countries, were not worried about selling on WTO terms because they did so already. JCB did not need an agreement to sell its brilliant machines to 140 countries across the world. Its chairman Lord Bamford said, "there is nothing to fear from WTO rules." We did not have to be in the EU's single market to buy from or sell to companies in EU member countries. We did not need trade agreements to trade. Trade agreements did not create trade. They could make trade easier but if companies or people wanted to buy something, they could do so with or without a trade agreement. To trade, you just trade. Businesses traded across borders not because politicians signed trade deals but because it made good business sense.

Under WTO rules our exports faced low or zero tariff barriers in most countries across the world. Tariffs on our exports to the EU would amount to £5-6 billion. In March 2018 – March 2019 we paid the EU £15.5 billion (£300 million a week), up by 20 per cent on 2017-2018's £12.9 billion. Paying £15.5 billion to avoid paying £5-6 billion was not a good deal. Angel Gurria, secretary general of the Organisation for Economic Co-operation and Development, said that a WTO Brexit would be manageable. Talking to Sky News at the World Economic Forum meetings at Davos, Mr Gurria said: "A no-deal, WTO rules […] the whole world is running by WTO rules these days. […] It's unfortunate that the UK is leaving the EU but that was the will of the British people so we take our bumps and we roll with it." Michael Wohlgemuth, Founding Director of the pro-EU body Open Europe Berlin, acknowledged that "one does not have to be a *member* of the single market in order to have *access* to it." Access to the single market was not granted or withheld by the EU but was available to all nations. We could still trade, even without an agreement.

Trading freely, not free trade

Free trade was not the panacea that some claimed. Stiglitz wrote, "The free-trade doctrine posits that removing barriers to trade leads to an increase in the overall well-being of all (or at least most) citizens. [...] The evidence shows that this thesis is generally not true. The advocates of free trade exaggerated its growth benefits and underestimated its distributive consequences. Even when there was growth, the losers got such a smaller share of the pie that they were worse off. [...] Too often, trade agreements have really only advanced special interests."[408] Dani Rodrik observed that economists "have overstated the magnitude of aggregate gains from trade deals, though such gains have been relatively small since at least the 1990s. They have endorsed the propaganda portraying today's trade deals as 'free trade agreements', even though Adam Smith and David Ricardo would turn over in their graves if they read the details of, say, the Trans-Pacific Partnership on intellectual property rules or investment regulations."[409]

Country-to-country free trade agreements were mini-TTIPs, designed, like TTIP, to fortify the multinational corporations' privileges. TTIP, the proposed EU/US deal, was an EU/US investors' protection racket by and for foreign investors and multinational companies. We rejected TTIP, just as we rejected the euro. We would not accept a TTIP Mark Two. We did not vote to leave one neoliberal trading bloc just to join another one. We opposed US corporations taking over parts of our NHS just as we opposed European or British corporations trying to do so. We should sign no agreement with the USA or anybody else that did not respect our sovereignty and that was not based on

218

mutual respect. TTIP had directly threatened to open our NHS to US 'health' corporations. A key part of TTIP was the 'harmonisation' of EU and US regulations, including around the healthcare sector. Cameron's Health and Social Care Act of 2012, which further opened up the sector to private involvement, was in large part intended to do this.

Richard Tuck noted, "the assumption, which seems to underlie much pro-Remain thinking on the Left, that the EU is fundamentally different from the multinational trade agreements – most recently the Transatlantic Trade and Investment Partnership (TTIP) and the TPP – that are reshaping the global economic order. While many leftists have clear and well-thought arguments against such trade partnerships, they give their unconsidered support to the EU, though it suffers from all the same failings and more."[410] As Tuck pointed out, "The EU was itself Britain's NAFTA or TPP, and it also decided all questions of trade for Britain with the rest of the world […]."[411] When the US or British governments proposed a trade deal with the EU, some saw this as evidence of their capitalist perfidy. But when the EU proposed the exact same deal, some saw this as proof of the EU's cooperative benevolence.

Stiglitz observed, "corporations have enjoyed privileged access to these trade talks, with the European Commission, in effect, seemingly negotiating on their behalf, while other key stakeholders (including labor unions, consumer protection groups, NGOs, including environmental groups, and even the EU and national parliaments) lacked similar access and influence. The concern is that these powerful agreements will work to promote and protect business interests, even when they compromise fundamental rights, protective standards, and the common good - as they often can and do. […] With American and European corporations playing such a large role in negotiations, it is not a surprise that they are unfair to workers in both developed and developing countries."[412]

Free trade was code for the free market based on the free movement of capital. In the past, free trade was all too compatible with the slave trade and the opium trade. As Benjamin Disraeli wrote in *Sybil* of James Matheson, then head of the trading company Jardine Matheson, "Oh, a dreadful man. A Scotchman richer than Croesus, one Mr Macdrug, fresh from Canton, with a million of opium in each pocket, denouncing corruption and bellowing free trade." The free movement of capital meant that when the eastern bloc disintegrated, EU companies could move production to countries in Eastern Europe where they could find enough qualified workers at significantly lower wages without having to upgrade their training systems and without having to upgrade their products through technical improvements. Free trade was not the same as trading freely. Trading freely was necessary for growth, which was why comprehensive sanctions against a country were so harmful, but the free movement of capital, far from being necessary for growth, continually threatened to wreck it. Capital controls were quite compatible with trading freely.

EU for capitalism

The EU's constitutional order was tailor-made by and for the multinational corporate giants of global capitalism. As the EU's acquis has developed, it has consistently worked against policies such as state aid to industries and nationalisation. The EU has never defended workers against the multinational corporations. It has always defended the multinational corporations against workers. As Stiglitz observed, "the

220

globalization agenda has been driven by corporate interests; the adverse effects on workers were not always accidents. [...] trade between advanced and less-developed countries lowers wages, especially unskilled wages, in the advanced country. [...] Globalization was supposed to create jobs and to quicken and sustain economic growth. It has done neither reliably and has sometimes even done the opposite. It has also weakened workers' bargaining power and created regulatory races to the bottom between countries. [...] Globalization [...] was really managed by and for large multinational corporate interests. The result has been a system with robust opportunities for tax avoidance and evasion, concentration of market power, and funnelling of gains to the top. For large multinational corporations and the world's thin layer of the ultra-wealthy, globalization has worked just fine."[413]

Capitalism in the form of globalisation was imperialist. Globalisation is finance capital's project for world domination. These corporations want no controls on their activities; they want to be out of control. They want to be freewheeling, free-range, buccaneering. Globalisation was a rich man's theory. Its main claimed benefit was that we could buy cheaper goods from other countries and that this trade somehow generated wealth, which would then trickle down to the rest of us. But trade did not generate wealth, consumption did not generate wealth, only productive labour generated wealth. Even Thatcher accepted the labour theory of value: she told the US Congress that "governments did not create wealth; people did."[414] The working class produces the goods, the wealth; the capitalist class takes the profits. Anatol Lieven noted that in post-Soviet Russia, "open borders, free-market reforms, and

221

privatisation became a license for predatory elites (comprising both old and new elements) to plunder state property and transfer the money to the West and various tax havens, with the enthusiastic help of Western banks. This was then euphemised by the Western media as 'capital flight'. Under cover of 'democracy' these elites instituted a form of kleptocratic oligarchy [...] This was the reality of the liberal internationalist dream of weakened nation states in a globalized world."[415]

Only strong independent nation-states stand in the way of this project. Especially since the 2008 crash, more people believe, in Dani Rodrik's words, that "democracy and national determination should trump hyper-globalisation. Democracies have the right to protect their social arrangements, and when this right clashes with the requirements of the global economy, it is the latter that should give way."[416] As Lieven wrote, "As in the previous great era of modern capitalist globalization between 1871 and 1914, rapid and uncontrolled economic, social and cultural change is strengthening nationalism, as people look to national identity to preserve some element of inherited culture, and to nation states to give them some protection against capitalist exploitation and uncontrolled movements of transnational finance."[417] Brexit is a blow against globalisation. Those who argue against independence and sovereignty for nation states are actually arguing for all independence and sovereignty to be put in the hands of globalised capital. Lieven noted that "Western states refused to imitate the East Asians and reshape globalization in the interests of their own populations, through economic planning, controls on financial flows, and restrictions on trade and migration."[418]

Strong, active states worked. In the nineteenth century USA, Alexander Hamilton's industrial interventionist state was an advance on Thomas Jefferson's small-state agrarian economy, just as in the twentieth century a Keynesian economy was an advance on a neo-liberal economy. The welfare state is here to stay. If reforms are good and prove to be popular, they stick. They all had to be fought for. Workers were not given them. Weekends, sick leave, equal pay, non-discrimination measures, pensions, unemployment benefits, maternity leave, paternity leave, disability rights, were all achieved in the teeth of ruling class opposition. No government that wanted to win an election would try to roll them back. This was the ratchet effect of democracy. Gains achieved would not be lightly abandoned. The 'small-state' doctrinaire, neo-liberals and libertarians were hopelessly out-of-date, bypassed by the dominant trends of the twentieth century.

Chapter 16
Migration

Britain 'one of the most racially tolerant countries in the world'

In the British Social Attitudes 2017 chapter on immigration, Robert Ford and Kitty Lymperopoulou observed that "The largest inflow of migrants in British history has not produced a general negative change in the public mood about migration's effects." They summed up, "This continues a trend identified in earlier research: the UK public has responded to high migration not by demanding migration be halted across the board, but by intensifying their demands for greater selection in immigration policy (see also Ford et al., 2012; Ford and Heath, 2014). It is migrants' skills and their commitment to a British way of life, not whether they are white or Christian or where they migrate from that chiefly matter to the public in the UK. Support for selecting migrants on ascribed criteria such as religion or race, which was already low in 2002, has declined further since."[419]

Roger Harding concluded in his summary of the survey's key findings, "there is widespread agreement that the country should be selective in who it allows to come here. Significant majorities feel the ability to speak English (87%, up from 77% in 2002), a commitment to the British 'way of life' (84%, up from 78%) and possessing needed skills (82%, up from 71%) are important criteria for selecting migrants."[420] Eleven per cent of the public saw white ethnicity as important in 2002, 7 per cent in 2014. Racial prejudice has consistently fallen since the 1980's while public concern about immigration has lessened since the 2016 referendum. A Survation poll of 17 November 2015 found that 76 per cent backed an Australian-style points-based immigration system, including 64 per cent of people who had voted to stay in the EU. Polls showed that people opposed uncontrolled immigration, that 70-80 per cent wanted immigration reduced, and that over half thought that large-scale immigration had been bad for the country. Only 3-4 per cent were avowedly racist. The 2019 British Social Attitudes survey found that "There is widespread support for ending freedom of movement with the EU."[421]

The World Values Survey found in 2013 that Britain was more racially tolerant than most European societies.[422] It rated Britain 'one of the most racially tolerant countries in the world'.[423] This did not suit the prejudice against the British people shown by *The Observer*, which misleadingly headlined an editorial citing the survey, 'Britain becoming mean and narrow-minded'.[424] The European Commission ranked British people third in Europe, narrowly behind Sweden and Denmark, 'in saying that they would be happy to have an immigrant as a neighbour, colleague, friend or family relation'.[425] The Commission's 2018 Eurobarometer survey found that British people were generally more welcoming to immigrants than the average European.[426] In Britain, over half the population opposed inter-racial relations as recently as the 1980s. Today less than one in four do. The European Union Agency for Fundamental Human Rights found in 2018 that Britain was among the least racist of EU states. 63 per cent of respondents of African descent in Finland reported that they had experienced racial harassment in the five years before the survey, but least of all in the UK – 21 per cent and Malta – 20 per cent. 14 per cent reported experiences of racial violence in Finland, but least of all in Portugal – 2 per cent and Britain 3 per cent.[427]

In 2019, Mariah Evans and Jonathan Kelley studied recent comparative surveys of prejudice against immigrants. They found that "prejudice against immigrants, other races, Muslims, Hindus, Jews, and Gypsies are all relatively low in the UK. [...] Prejudice specifically against Muslims shows a somewhat different pattern. In the UK it was already low in the 1980s when our data begin, fractionally lower than in other EU nations. It has declined slowly since then (see also Storm et al., 2017) and is now somewhat lower than in the rest of the EU - not a lot lower but clearly lower."[428] Evans said, "Prejudice against immigrant workers or minority ethnic and religious groups is rare in the UK, perhaps even slightly rarer than in equivalently developed EU countries." British people had a 'high level of tolerance for ethnic and religious diversity'. "The key message is that there are other things besides the immigrants and foreign workers issue that have made many UK folk want more autonomy from the EU." Evans and Kelley concluded their study: "All in all, prejudice and willingness to discriminate against foreign workers are relatively low. They are rising in some European nations – despite a countervailing trend of tolerance increasing with GDP – but not in others. In this, the UK is unexceptional, except perhaps that prejudice against Muslims may be a little lower than in peer countries in the EU. This strongly suggests that Brexit did not come about because the UK's population is distinctively prejudiced and that similar issues may well arise in other EU nations in future years."[429]

Roger Eatwell and Matthew Goodwin pointed out, "Wanting a tighter immigration policy or fewer immigrants is not in itself racist."[430] Even the extreme position of 'keeping everybody out' was no more racist than letting everybody in. The clue was in the word 'everybody'. Anyway, British governments have always had a default and non-racist immigration policy - if you are rich, you are in. Controlling immigration does not mean ending all immigration, any more than trading on WTO terms means no imports, or controlling your diet means eating nothing. We upheld a humane attitude to refugees, in line with the provisions of international law. We wanted other countries, especially our European neighbours, to uphold the international law governing the treatment of refugees. EU member states have been breaking the law for decades by passing refugees through their countries, instead of offering them sanctuary in the first safe country they reached.

There was a difference between opposing the policy of uncontrolled immigration and hostility to immigrants, even if some pro-EU people - along with Tommy Robinson - could not see it. Racists said and some 'anti-racists' agreed that controlling immigration meant ending immigration and even at the extreme meant expelling immigrants. Some racists and 'anti-racists' claimed – falsely - that the British people were more racist than others. Some accused millions of their fellow-citizens of racism and xenophobia. In *The Guardian* of 19 February 2019, Chitra Ramaswamy wrote of 'the racist, vengeful and weak society we are'. Was she really accusing all the black and Asian members of our society of being racist, vengeful and weak? Or didn't she count black and Asian people as members of our society? Calling the entire British population racists was an intellectually lazy and morally obtuse accusation. Some accused people of all sorts of 'hate crimes', some of which were neither crimes nor acts of hate. Incidents reported as 'hate crimes' included a man beeping his car horn 'in a racist manner', a dog barking in a racist manner, and a man saying in a library that he was campaigning to leave the EU.

The insulting claim that 'the people' were racist was deployed to try to justify opposing the people's democratic decision. Only a very small number of people who voted to leave were racist, yet some vilified the whole leave campaign as racist. Some called all people who voted leave racist. If one person who voted leave was a racist, they all were. If one person who voted leave told a lie, they were all liars. By the same false logic, because a very small number of Muslims were terrorists, all Muslims were terrorists. If a few Muslims were guilty of rape, then they were all rapists. Some on the ultra-left saw any criticism of Islam as a step on the road to Islamophobia, as contributing to Islamophobia, as playing into the hands of Islamophobes. We could see the difference between condemning people for being terrorists and condemning people for being Muslims, even if Tommy Robinson and the ultra-left could not. We opposed terrorists who were Muslims not because they were Muslims but because they were terrorists. We opposed rapists who were Muslims not because they were Muslims but because they were rapists. Similarly we opposed terrorists who were atheists and opposed rapists who were atheists.

Sir Vince Cable insultingly described people who voted leave as people who longed for a world 'where faces were white'. How did this sit with the fact that one in three of Britain's black and ethnic minority voters had voted to leave? Later, Cable accepted that the leave camp had a good case for control of immigration, writing, "I have serious doubts that EU free movement is tenable or even desirable. [...] the benefits accrue mainly to the immigrants themselves (and business owners)."[431] It was often said, in defence of a policy of open borders, that Britain is a nation of immigrants. In reality, modern research shows that "a large majority of the inhabitants of Britain today are the direct descendants of people who settled thousands of years ago [...]."[432] The facts prove "the extreme longevity of major genetic descent-lines in the contemporary populations of Britain."[433] And, "The genetic ancestors of Mesolithic immigrants have worked the landscape left by the LGM [Last Glacial Maximum] continuously, up to the present. Not alone, it must be said, but the modern data implies that they have always constituted the vast majority of people alive at any one time."[434]

The immigration market

The British government has long promoted mass immigration. Andrew Neather, a speechwriter for Blair, wrote, "the deliberate policy of ministers from late 2000 [...] was to open up the UK to mass immigration." Gus O'Donnell, then the most senior British civil servant, said in 2011, "When I was at the Treasury I argued for the most open door policy to immigration [...] I think it's my job to maximise global welfare not national welfare." Mark Thompson, then the BBC's director-general, agreed, saying that he believed that "global welfare was paramount and that therefore he had a greater obligation to someone in Burundi than to someone in Birmingham."[435] These cosmopolitans believed that by importing cheap labour for their households they were assisting the progress of mankind. In December 2018, May quietly signed us into the UN Global Migration Compact, which regularised mass migration across the world. The Compact states: "We commit to adapt options and pathways for regular migration in a manner that facilitates labour mobility [...] with a view to expanding and diversifying availability of pathways for safe, orderly and regular migration."

Immigration is a market, where entrepreneurs buy and sell workers out of and into countries. Immigration is not some free exercise of individual choice. It is a marketplace where governments and companies use their power to get what they want – labour on the cheap. As the economist George Borjas pointed out, "Just as the labor market guides the allocation of workers to firms, the immigration market guides the allocation of persons to countries."[436] The free market meant the free movement of labour, to force wages down. The Labour party talked of re-skilling workers but wanted open borders, thus removing all pressure on government and employers to re-skill workers. We needed to control immigration because this put the necessary pressure on government and firms to invest in technical education and apprenticeships. The free movement of labour blocked socialist planning. As Richard Tuck observed, "the free movement of people in the EU, as well as of goods and capital, almost necessarily entrenches markets rather than collective planning."[437]

As US presidential candidate Bernie Sanders said in 2015, a policy of open borders was "a Koch brothers' proposal. That's a right-wing proposal that says, essentially, 'There is no United States.' [...] it would make everybody in America poorer. You're doing away with the concept of the nation state. [...] What right-wing people in this country would love is an open border policy, bringing in all kinds of people working for two or three dollars an hour. That would be great for them." Employers have long known the benefits – to them – of mass immigration. Martin Daunton noted of the mass immigration from Europe to the USA before the First World War, "the large-scale movement of workers from Europe pushed up wages there and held them down in the new world."[438]

Anatol Lieven observed, "In the United States, free-market economists have long talked quite openly of using immigration to drive down wages and discipline workers; [...] the inescapable fact about US economic growth since the 1970s is precisely that it has *not* benefited unskilled and semi-skilled workers. This is in part because of the constant downward pressure on wages due to immigration, which in turn has been partially enabled by the use of migrant labor by employers to weaken the trade unions."[439] The Irish Congress of Trade Unions said, "It is an iron law of economics that an abundant supply of labour pushes down its cost. It is insulting people's intelligence to pretend otherwise." This was not to blame immigrants personally for lowering wages, any more than saying that unemployment held down wages was to blame the unemployed.

A Bank of England report of 2015 suggested that rising immigration could drive down wages for low-skilled British workers, estimating that a 10 percentage point increase in the proportion of immigrants was associated with a nearly 2 per cent reduction in pay for semi-skilled and unskilled workers in service industries such as care homes, shops and bars.[440] According to the Bank's report, the mass immigration from Eastern Europe in 2004 'drives down wages'. Lieven noted, "opposition to immigration among the less skilled (or rather very often the highly skilled in a fading occupation) is often based on rational economic calculations and not on blind 'xenophobia'. Yet among most liberals, social democrats and Greens, the response has been essentially to tell actual and potential voters for the populist parties even more loudly what illiterate chauvinist idiots they are. Then they wonder why they are losing votes among the former working classes."[441]

If Britain adopted an 'open door' policy, a 'no borders' approach, we would quickly find that millions of people would be arriving, putting even more strain on our public services. In May 2016 the Office for National Statistics revealed that between 2010 and 2015, possibly 1.4 million more migrants from the EU had settled in Britain than the one million they had registered. In 2015, 630,000 migrants had arrived, including 77,000 from the EU without a job. That summer, Angela Merkel offered Turkey visa-free access to the Schengen area. Nobody said Turkey would join the EU immediately, but Cameron was not going to exercise his veto over Turkey's accession after he had pledged to support its joining. The Conservative manifesto for the 2009 EU election stated, "Our MEPs will support the further enlargement of the EU, including to Ukraine, Belarus, Turkey, Georgia and the countries of the Balkans [...]" Vetoing Turkey's accession would have broken that election pledge.

Carrying out the pledge would have meant, given the EU's everlasting, Treaty-bound commitment to free movement of labour, that all the people of Ukraine, Belarus, Turkey, Georgia and the Balkans would have the right to move to wherever they wanted in the EU, including Britain.

Citizens' rights

The leave campaign proceeded on the basis that leaving the EU meant respecting the rights of the 3.6 million EU citizens already living and working in the UK and that controls on freedom of movement would apply only to future movement. All too many in the pro-EU camp did not scruple to claim that Brexit would tear up EU citizens' rights to continue to live and work in the UK. Channel 4's FactCheck Patrick Worrall asked on 20 May 2016 'Will Brexit lead to mass deportations?' Nobody in the Leave camp had ever suggested that it would. Worrall concluded that "Leavers are […] right to tell people not to worry too much about the prospect of being deported, either from or back to the UK." On 4 June 2016 the *Independent* ran an article, 'Will Brexit mean that Europeans have to leave the UK?' by Will Gore. He noted that the pro-EU Cameron had refused to rule out the possibility of deportations if leave won the referendum. Gore cited Tory MP Philip Davies who said, "Nobody would ever suggest that anybody who has arrived here legally should be evicted." Then Gore undermined that assurance by writing, "we cannot be absolutely sure of that."

Just before the referendum, the NHS's chief executive Simon Stevens attacked pro-Brexit Defence Minister Penny Mordaunt saying, "At her local hospital, 80 of the doctors are from the rest of the European Union, 350 nurses in her local hospital are from the EU. If only a proportion of those chose to up sticks and off on the 23 June that would create real problems in hospitals across the country."[442] He implied without any evidence or argument that EU nationals would suddenly choose to leave the UK if we voted to leave. Why would they? On the day after the vote, on 24 June 2016, a BBC reporter in Poland insinuated that mass deportation of migrants was an immediate possibility. In the House of Commons in February 2020, Labour MP David Lammy tabled an emergency question about the deportation of serious criminals back to their homeland of Jamaica. He said, "People watching will see the way the Government holds in such disrespect the contribution of West Indian, Caribbean and black people in this country," and asked, "When will black lives matter once again?"

On 30 October 2007, Gordon Brown's Labour government had passed the UK Borders Act which 'allows automatic deportation of some foreign nationals in two circumstances: if they are imprisoned for specific offences, or they are imprisoned for more than one year'. Lammy voted for this Act, which enabled the deportations that he later opposed. In 2014 Lammy had abstained on the Cameron government's Immigration Act, which enabled the Windrush scandal. Only six Labour MPs voted against it. The rest abstained. Two-thirds of the LibDem MPs voted for it. Two democratic principles were involved in the debate: the right of nations to protect their social, political and cultural collective and their labour standards in the face of uncontrolled immigration, and the right to equal treatment of all the people in a country. The two were quite compatible and both should always be respected. On the issue of EU citizens' rights, the pro-EU governments of Cameron and May adopted unjust policies. Cameron had planned to deprive new arrivals of their benefits for a period of time. This mean-spirited proposal stemmed from the pro-EU liberal line that people who wanted controls on immigration must be racist and would want the government to be mean-spirited towards the immigrants themselves.

After the referendum the May government should at once have unilaterally guaranteed the rights and tenure of all EU citizens living in Britain, so that they could continue to live and work here broadly as they had done before the referendum. The government should have told EU citizens that they would enjoy national treatment and indefinite leave to stay, with no additional rights above those of UK citizens. Then much of the rancour about EU citizens' rights and migration in general would never have arisen. Instead May tried to reach a reciprocal agreement with the EU, that we would guarantee the rights of EU citizens living in the UK and the EU would guarantee the rights of UK citizens living in EU countries. The EU was not willing to do this.[443] Instead, the EU demanded that its Court of Justice alone should have the right to make binding judgements over the rights of EU citizens in the UK. UK courts would have no equal right to adjudicate the rights of UK citizens living in EU member countries. Meanwhile May proposed to impose a £65 charge on every EU citizen who wished to continue living in the UK. Like Cameron, she was acting on the pro-EU camp's false accusation that our vote to leave was a product of hostility to immigrants as people. Only in January 2019 did she drop this proposal, but the years of unnecessary delay smeared the Leave project with hostility to immigrants. May was the Home Secretary who deported the innocent *Windrush* Jamaicans.

The lying that Brexit would mean mass deportations continued for years after the referendum. The 2019 LibDem election leaflet said, "1 in 10 NHS doctors are EU citizens, along with 13,000 teachers. Conservative and Labour Brexit plans put this at risk. By staying in the EU, we can retain these vital staff […]." This implied that leaving the EU might mean that these people could be expelled - another unscrupulous piece of scaremongering. Euronews, the European pay television news channel, claimed in December 2019 that "At least 5 million migrants, mostly from Eastern Europe, Africa, and Asian countries such as Pakistan and India, are expected to be deported from the UK post-Brexit by Boris Johnson and his right wing Conservative majority."[444] The EU had given Euronews 122 million euros between 2014 and 2018, a possible source of its bias. What was the truth? Johnson said on 25 July 2019, "And the first step is to repeat unequivocally our guarantee to the 3.2 million EU nationals now living and working among us and I say directly to you – thank you for your contribution to our society thank you for your patience and I can assure you that under this government you will get the absolute certainty of the rights to live and remain."

The UK government reached an agreement with the EU that protects the rights of EU citizens and their family members living in the UK. Most citizens from the EU needed to apply to stay in the UK. They could then continue living their lives here.[445] Over 3.3 million EU and European Economic Area citizens have been granted the right to remain in the UK permanently after Brexit, the Home Office said on 18 June 2020.

Britain granted EU nationals living here the right to stay. Spain, France, Germany and Italy published similar offers to British expats. Rules for EU visitors to the UK have not changed after Brexit, with visa-free entry for visits of up to 90 days guaranteed. The EU offered to reciprocate for UK visitors to the EU. The Johnson government guaranteed to cover the payment of awards to UK applicants for all successful Erasmus+ and European Solidarity Corps bids.[446]

End the theft of intellectual property

Too often ignored in the debate about immigration was its effects on the countries from which immigrants came. As Joseph Stiglitz pointed out, "Today some of the poorest countries in Europe are effectively subsidizing some of the richer ones, as young, well-educated people from the crisis countries migrate in search of jobs. Their education was paid for by the citizens of the country they left, but the rewards accrue to the rich country they moved to. One public official described this brain drain as the theft of his country's intellectual property, though within the European rule of law."[447] The brain drain was worst in the countries of southern and eastern Europe, where it threatened those countries' futures.[448] EU member states were quite happy to steal scarce talent from poorer countries. Haiti has lost 85 per cent of its trained people. In 2013, Ghana, a net exporter of health professionals, had only one doctor per 10,170 people. Ghana and Zimbabwe have lost nearly three quarters of their trained medical staff. This was one of the many ways in which the EEC/EU was 'discriminating against developing countries', as Sicco Mansholt, a former Commission President, said.

Devesh Kapur and John McHale insisted, "the solution should be to increase investments in domestic capabilities, rather than simply poach from poor countries."[449] As Kapur and McHale wrote, "On the rich-country side, systematic underinvestment in sectors such as health care and education (especially for public systems) had led to almost permanent skill shortages and ongoing 'crisis' recruitment from poorer countries. When such crises recur in sectors clearly being damaged by emigration, rich countries have an obligation to correct the problems with their own policies for creating human capital rather than continually relying on poor countries to fill the gaps."[450] An IMF study showed that the migration of highly skilled workers reduces income levels and long-term economic growth on the countries of origin.[451] Kapur and McHale summed up, "The idea that the migration of a significant fraction of a country's best and brightest is not particularly harmful and may even be beneficial to the country is simply unwarranted."[452]

There is a global shortage of six million nurses, predicted by the World Health Organization (WHO) to rise to nine million by 2030. Governments of wealthy countries have routinely recruited nurses from overseas to fill the gaps. Many of the richer EU member countries have relied on imported workers to staff their health services. It is unethical and in the long term unproductive. The WHO's Global Code of Practice on the International Recruitment of Health Personnel says the goal for all countries should be to have a sustainable national nursing workforce that focuses on a stable core of domestically educated nurses. Challenging international recruitment would be the first step towards workers taking responsibility for the future of the NHS.

The International Council of Nurses (ICN) represents 130 nursing associations from around the world. Writing in *Nursing Standard*, the journal of the Royal College of Nursing, Howard Catton (the ICN's chief executive) called for ethical recruitment. He said, "One answer to the nursing shortages around the world is for each country to retain the nurses it has by showing how much they are valued: pay is fundamental."[453] *One* answer? Surely it is *the* answer. The ICN's recent report *Covid-19 and The International Supply of Nurses* made the point that long-term reliance on the inflow of nurses is 'the antithesis of self-sufficiency'. Such reliance shows that a country is not investing the necessary funding and effort to training enough nurses to meet its own needs. The report recommends that all countries use the ICN self-sufficiency indicator system which highlights a country's dependence and vulnerability to overseas recruitment.

Spain's General Nursing Council reported in 2020 a shortage of 125,000 nurses. Yet in January 2020 over 5,500 Spanish nationals were working for the NHS, many of them as registered nurses. The Spanish nursing council and the Spanish unions are pleased that Brexit means more Spanish nurses returning to Spain. One of the reasons that Spanish nurses came to Britain was for longer term contracts that were not available in Spain. Over two thirds of Spanish nurses are on temporary contracts – not much evidence of wonderful EU employment rights there. Rights in the workplace are protected by workers fighting for them – whether in Britain, Spain or anywhere else. That is the key to retention of nursing staff worldwide.

Part of the reason Britain is not self-sufficient in nurses is the reliance in recent decades on EU free movement of people. That contributed to the reduction in the number of UK students from 2010. Clearly some NHS England officials are content to make the same mistake, this time relying on non-EU staff. On 25 September 2020, NHS England wrote to Directors of Nursing and Regional Chief Nurses with details of international recruitment. The letter described 'the extensive package of measures to support you with your nursing international recruitment (IR) with details on how you can apply for funding'. Our collective response should be no because it is unethical to poach other nations' staff, even more so during a global pandemic, no because international recruitment has not solved the problem in the past, indeed it made things worse and we are living with the consequences and no because the answer lies close to home.

When the *Health Services Journal* published the NHS England letter on their website, an online reader commented that the letter "proves that the NHS leadership hasn't yet got over the fact that the era of colonialism has long ended. Try attracting your home grown by improving the working conditions and you might have stumbled across the solution for your perennial staff shortage. It's not rocket science." The NHS leadership still harks back to past practices. A new NHS pan-London consortium for international recruitment was launched in 2020. Prerena Issar, NHS Chief People Officer, said at the NHS Providers conference on 8 October, "International nurses are starting to return to UK [...] with 6,500 'waiting to start'". Issar's background is in working for the United Nations and international firms like Unilever.

Chapter 17
The environment

Science tells us that we have to reduce net carbon emissions to zero within the next twenty or thirty years or the likelihood is that global warming will become, in our lifetimes at least, irreversible. The models used today to forecast climate have been tested thousands of times, refined, used on real data and real knowledge of global temperatures now and in the past, and they are the best estimate we have. So far the global projections made twenty years ago appear not to be too far out. We face problems of man-made global warming, resource depletion, environmental damage and pollution. The only way we can protect our environment is by using the institutions of effective nation states. Independence presents us with a real opportunity for environmental protection in Britain. It will only be done when we control the process.

Lord Stern stated, "Climate change is the greatest market failure the world has ever seen." The free market, monopoly capitalism, has failed the environment so we cannot look to the market to save it. Capitalist interests resist any serious effort at control. Capitalism's four freedoms in practice mean that capitalism is out of control. We cannot limit climate change without controlling the economy. It is not all about changing our patterns of consumption, or cutting down on waste. Sir David Attenborough says that the key is "Don't waste. Don't waste anything." Fine, agreed. But the necessary and difficult change is to change the relations of production in our society so that we no longer produce according solely to the dictates of profit. Nor should we do as the Soviet Union tragically did, prioritise the growth of GDP even at the expense of the environment, as virtually all countries did at the time.

To control pollution and threats to the environment, we

cannot rely on the corporations who make or sell a product to produce accurate figures about their effects on the environment. A sovereign state charged with maintaining the health and safety of its people can never outsource its responsibilities to companies or supranational bodies. We need a number of technological revolutions for sure and we need political revolution. If the peoples of the world want to save the world, they are going to have to take it over, country by country. The world's nations can cooperate through UN institutions, centrally its Intergovernmental Panel on Climate Change (IPCC). Cuba's Foreign Minister Rodriguez Parrilla said to the United Nations General Assembly on 28 September 2019 that capitalism's "irrational and unsustainable patterns of production and consumption, along with the growing and unjust concentration of wealth, are the main threat to the ecological balance of the planet. There can be no sustainable development without social justice."[454] American historian Helen Yaffe affirmed, "Driven by the profit motive, capitalist businesses are only interested in natural resources such as land, water, raw materials and hydrocarbons in so far as they can be turned into profit."[455]

Environmentalist Naomi Klein pointed out, "We often hear climate change blamed on 'human nature', on the inherent greed and shortsightedness of our species. Or we are told we have altered the earth so much and on such a planetary scale that we are now living in the Anthropocene, the age of man. These ways of explaining our current circumstances have a very specific, if unspoken meaning: that humans are a single type, that human nature can be essentialized to the traits that created this crisis. In this way, the systems that certain humans created, and other humans powerfully resisted, are completely let off the hook. Capitalism, colonialism, patriarchy – those sorts of systems."[456] She proposed, "a serious response to the climate threat involves recovering an art that has been relentlessly vilified during these decades of market fundamentalism: planning. Lots and lots of planning. Industrial planning. Land use planning. [...] bringing back the idea of planning our economies based on collective priorities rather than corporate profitability – giving laid-off employees of car plants and coal mines the tools and resources to get equally secure jobs making subway cars, installing wind turbines and cleaning up extraction sites, to cite just a few examples."[457]

Of the necessary long-term planning, policy analyst Anatol Lieven wrote, "that is not something that contemporary Western capitalism seems capable of."[458] We should enlist the positive forces of civic nationalism to support effective conservation policies and so to achieve climate security. An October 2020 survey found that "There is remarkable common ground on the need for more action to protect the environment and address climate change [...]."[459] We do not have to persuade people about climate change, people are largely already persuaded. People have to act against the multinational companies that are responsible for climate change.

Lieven observed that "The gulf between declarations of global responsibility and inability to mobilize national action has lain at the heart of the failure adequately to address the danger of climate change. Hence the argument of this book: that it is necessary to reframe the struggle against climate change in nationalist terms: the defense of nation states, their interests, and their future survival. [...] This civic nationalist program is defensive but not chauvinist. It requires strict controls on migration, but is absolutely committed to racial equality at home, to measures to increase racial equality and to strategies to assist and integrate immigrant communities."[460] One of the most predictable effects of climate change was increased migration.

We should enlist the positive forces of considerations of national security. The 2008 National Security Strategy of the United Kingdom stated that "climate change is potentially the greatest challenge to global stability and security, and therefore to national security." But, as Lieven observed, "instead, the security agenda and the attention and expenditure associated with it were frittered away on 'traditional challenges': a war in Afghanistan which by 2008 was already effectively lost and in which Britain achieved nothing; hysteria over minor post-imperial squabbles over disputed territories in the former USSR that had never been of the slightest interest to Britain [...]."[461] This unnecessary interference abroad was a key part of capitalism's 'Global Britain' project.

Was there an alternative? Oxfam's Duncan Green pointed out in his excellent book *From poverty to power*, "Cuba was the only country in the world that managed to live within its environmental footprint while achieving high levels of human development. This was probably due to its unique combination of sound environmental management, excellent health and education provision." The World Wildlife Fund said that Cuba led the world in minimising its ecological footprint. Cuba was the only country in the world that had both a quality of life above the World Wildlife Fund threshold of 0.8 on the Human Development Index and a sustainable ecological footprint. Cuba met its people's needs using reasonably low levels of natural resources.

A 2012 conference on renewable energy sources praised Cuba's use of alternative sources of energy. Enrico Turrino, founding member of Eurosolar and honorary member of CubaSolar, said that the island was a model of good use of clean sources of energy. He highlighted the solarisation projects carried out in the municipalities of Bartolome Maso and Guama in the eastern provinces of Granma and Santiago de Cuba, where thermal, photoelectric, wind, water and biomass sources were used to develop these communities sustainably. The 'greening of Cuba' was the world's most revolutionary experiment in agroecology. As Bill McKibben stated, "Cubans have created what may be the world's largest working model of a semisustainable agriculture, one that relies far less than the rest of the world does on oil, on chemicals, on shipping vast quantities of food back and forth [...] Cuba has thousands of *organopónicos* – urban gardens – more than two hundred in the Havana area alone."[462]

Britain's prospects

There was a growing national consensus that we needed to make protecting the environment a priority. Britain's 2018 *A Green Future: 25 Year Plan for the Environment* committed us to addressing the decline in public investment in managing land for conservation purposes. The Conservative party manifesto for the 2019 general election promised 'the most ambitious environmental programme of any country on earth', positioning the Conservatives as conservationist stewards of the environment and pledging billions of pounds for research into decarbonisation and environmentally friendly agriculture and fisheries. They had already published an Agriculture Bill widely hailed by environmentalists. The manifesto promised no compromise on environmental protections, food standards or animal welfare in future trade deals.

British environmental expert Ben Pontin wrote, "I argue that experience of EU membership has largely vindicated doubts about a novel supranational competence expressed by advocates of the British way on entry to the Community. [...] the responsible approach to environmental policy, law and practice in Britain (and its wider global relationships) is independent of EU institutions."[463] The EU's founders "were more willing than Britain to treat environmental law (in Ludwig Kramer's words) as 'virgin law'. Britain, by contrast, emphasised its embeddedness in national heritage. It considered relinquishing of the established crafts of environmental law shaped by centuries of experience to a new jurisdiction as unnecessary and irresponsible."[464] As a result, "Britain entered the Community believing it had the know-how, the tools, the legal craft-skills necessary to protect the environment without the help of a new, supranational jurisdiction."[465]

Britain was on track to comply with the ambitious Climate Change Act 2008. Britain has largely ended the coal power system. Our national carbon budget was to cut greenhouse gas emission by 57 per cent by 2030, against a baseline of 1990. The reduction by 2020 was 40 per cent. This was better than the EU's reduction of 23 per cent, against its relatively modest 2030 target of a 40 per reduction. We were the first major country to put big CO2 cuts into law. Concerns about the security of energy imports are encouraging investment in renewable energy. Wind is now generating a quarter of our electricity and costs have halved in the last two years. Solar power generates a tenth. The fall in the cost of renewables has been remarkable. Photovoltaic costs have dropped by 83 per cent since 2010. Offshore wind contracts are coming in at £69 (MWh) for the early 2020s, 40 per cent lower than the original estimates for 2030. LED lighting has grown from 5 per cent to 40 per cent of the world market.

All surface transport, including vans, cars, buses and lorries, will be electric or hydrogen powered. We will need 3,500 rapid and ultra-rapid charging stations near motorways and 210,000 public chargers in towns and cities. There are only 21,000 public charging points today. A move to hydrogen-based HGVs would require 800 hydrogen refuelling stations by 2050. Electrification would require 90,000 depot-based chargers for overnight electric charging. Housing needs proper insulation, double glazing, solar power, heat exchange systems, smart heating systems, heat pumps and underfloor heating. Electric boilers must replace gas boilers.

Britain handles its municipal waste better than EU member states.[466] The Royal Commission on Environmental Pollution report of 1985 said landfill was Britain's 'best practicable environmental option' for all materials other than those that are volatile or flammable. The EU's 1999 Landfill Directive made the government change its plans for the disposal of 2.2 million tonnes of waste that it could no longer landfill in its preferred way. The cost of disposing of this waste was $100 a tonne, twice that of our preferred policy. Friends of the Earth (FoE) used to believe that landfill was the best way to dispose of household waste, but now it values EU law highly for its opposition to landfill. Pontin summed up: the Landfill Directive was "a costly mistake not only for Britain but also for the EU. This is because it encapsulates the idea of rigid harmonisation and insensitivity to national sentiments that has contributed to the outcome of the 2016 Referendum."[467]

Outside the EU, we could ban the transport of live animals, which the EU allows. We banned veal crates 16 years before the EU. We are protecting elephants by introducing one of the strictest ivory bans in the world; the EU is still in the consultation stage. Our legislation to ban single-use plastics goes further and faster than anything proposed by the EU. Fewer than 10,000 hectares are reforested a year. We need to plant 30,000 hectares a year to increase the woodland cover from 13 per cent to 17 per cent. The EU had a target of a third of protected habitats being in 'favourable' or 'unfavourable but recovering' condition by 2020, but by 2012 only 16 per cent of its sites had achieved this, down from 17 per cent in 2006. By contrast, Britain had a target of 95 per cent being in these conditions for its 7,000 sites of special scientific interest. In 2020 we were at 94 per cent.[468]

In 2018, FoE paid for a 'risk analysis' of UK environmental policy post-Brexit. (Of course there was no opportunity analysis.) This concluded that under every Brexit scenario habitats and birds were at 'very high risk'. This was not because there were any plans to tear up environmental legislation, or withdraw from the intergovernmental Ramsar Convention on wild birds.[469] No, the authors claimed 'very high risk' partly because they deemed the Conservative party to be environmentally unfriendly, but mainly because the EU was not there to police our government! That was not a scientifically determined risk. It was just political prejudice plus the unwarranted assumption that the people of Britain would never demand and enforce higher environmental standards than the EU.

In another case, Britain aimed to uphold higher safety standards than the EU's. In April 2020 Britain decided to enforce stricter regulations on the importing of some plants and the banning of others. The listed plants, which included olive, rosemary and lavender, posed a serious risk of bringing in dangerous bacteria such as *Xylella fastidiosa*, which was devastating European olive groves in countries like Italy. Many ancient olive trees there have been cut down and destroyed and the infection was spreading. The European Commission judged our decision to be 'not supported by the most recent scientific justification' and 'disproportionate' – and ruled that Britain must overturn its policy. The EU's attitude was that under EU law the UK government had received its orders and must obey. But Britain did not obey the EU instruction. The government said that it had "intensified our surveillance, inspection and testing regime [in order to] make it absolutely clear that we are not changing our position". It said that it disagreed with the EU decision, that the biosecurity threat of *Xylella* had not changed and that its reasons for imposing the stronger restrictions had not changed. It said it would continue to apply the restrictions because "Protecting UK plant biosecurity and maintaining our ongoing robust approach remain our top priority."

Pontin concluded, "In none of the case studies is there evidence that the domestic environment is well protected through the EU-originated aspect of domestic law."[470] FoE called us the dirty man of Europe and claimed that only the EU cleaned up our act. Not so. Pontin proved that their "claim that Britain's environment and environmental policy and law was relatively poor environmentally [...] does not withstand scrutiny."[471] It was, like so much pro-EU advocacy, both untrue and defamatory of Britain's achievements. Pontin summed up that on the criteria of simplicity, rationality, accountability and autonomy, "given a choice between a British way independent of the EU environmental acquis on the one hand, and one tied to it on the other, my core conclusion is that each of these criteria support independence."[472] Given that after forty-five years of EU membership most of our environmental legislation had come through EU directives and regulations, was there a risk that not all of it would be transposed into or preserved in UK law and would be properly enforced? Forget that much of this legislation failed to achieve its stated objectives. Scientifically, you could not say there was no risk at all. But just talking about risk in the abstract was absurd. How great was the risk? The environmental catastrophists loved to talk about risk in the abstract, especially the risks of Brexit.

Extinction Rebellion's warnings of 'imminent' extinction, of 'biblical' apocalypses, discredited the environmentalist cause. They were signs that ER was more like a survivalist cult than an organisation able to win the mass support needed to achieve its goals. Extinction Rebellion wants the government to reduce greenhouse gas emissions to net zero by 2025.[473] NASA lists the greenhouse gases in order of abundance. First, water vapour. So never boil water again! Next, carbon dioxide, which comes from decaying and living organisms, so we must abandon fossil fuels altogether and never let anything, living or dead, decay. Third, methane, produced by (among many other things) normally functioning wetlands, using natural gas, mining coal, raising cattle and farming rice too; so drain the marshes, stop using gas and coal and eat no more beef or rice. This is an anti-growth agenda.

The Green Party calls for deindustrialisation: "The scale of industrial production worldwide must reduce if we are to live in the UK and globally within environmental limits."[474] On the other side there are the giant global monopolies, dedicated above all to the pursuit of profit. Their apologists claim that there is no climate change, or that any change is not caused by human activity. Both sides of this argument have two things in common. First they are unscientific, however much they may cherry-pick scientific findings that appear to back up their arguments. Second, they are both anti-people, anti-human.

The solutions to environmental problems will be found in science, in a material approach to reality. That does not mean that everything any scientist says is right, nor that the scientific consensus is always right – especially about the future. Science does not tell us we have to stop using fossil fuels, or revert to a pre-industrial economy. Science talks about net carbon emissions, not zero carbon emissions. It says that there was a simple equation: if an industry emits one tonne of carbon into the atmosphere, it had to find a way of taking 3.67 tonnes of carbon dioxide out of the atmosphere to achieve net zero emissions. This can be done, but it will take time, and it will cost money. Engineers will enjoy the challenge.

Dieselgate

The origins of the diesel scandal go back to the 1970s, when the European market for heavier oil products was shrinking as households turned to natural gas for heating and French nuclear power stations started coming onstream. Desperate for new markets, the oil industry started looking at the market for diesel cars. Emission-led global warming started to become a political issue in the 1980s (it had been a scientific issue for at least a century), leading to the creation of the IPCC in 1988. For the oil industry it was fortunate that all the focus at the time was on CO_2. There was no attempt to control so-called 'black carbon', sooty particles, known even then to be harmful to health but not identified as greenhouse emissions. With the climate panic in full swing, human health took a back seat. The EU duly switched to encouraging diesel in a big way. That brought us rising quantities of black carbon, which was not even listed as a climate problem in the UN's Kyoto Protocol when it was adopted in 1997. Scientists now believe that black carbon from a variety of sources is second only to carbon dioxide as a contributor to global warming. It is a killer, too.

And then there was NOx (nitric oxide and nitrogen oxide, also nitrous oxide). From 2000 to 2014, EU regulations and the standards known as Euro 3, 4 and 5 allowed diesels to emit three times as much NOx as petrol cars. Now, under Euro 6, just a third more. That had consequences for health and the environment. Nitric oxide and nitrogen oxide are serious atmospheric pollutants, leading to smog and acid rain. Nitrous oxide is a powerful greenhouse gas. Twenty years ago the EU was confidently dictating policy. Governments across the EU (though not Britain) gave diesel tax advantages and diesel car use rocketed: in Western Europe it rose from 13.8 per cent of passenger car registrations in 1990 to 53.1 per cent in 2014. Even as late as 2018, with diesel mired in scandal, it accounted for 35 per cent of new car sales in the EU.

Did the EU's shift to diesel help to reduce global warming? No, it added to the problem, because of the large number of diesels that entered the market not fitted with particulate filters and because of the higher carbon footprint involved in producing and transporting diesel. And all the while, the car manufacturers were fiddling their figures - Volkswagen and its brands Audi and Porsche, Mercedes owner Daimler and BMW. Even without the cheating devices designed to know when a car was being tested, the EU testing regime was absurdly lax. Manufacturers could even conduct the tests in their own facilities. Cars could be stationary for 24 per cent of the test time and decelerating for 16 per cent of the time. Once an authorised tester anywhere in the EU had produced a set of figures, they had to be accepted in all the other 27 countries of the EU, under single market rules.

In 2015 the USA's Environmental Protection Agency (not any EU body) conducted tests on Volkswagen vehicles that found overall emission levels 40 per cent higher than the official levels and NOx emissions 40 times the US limit. A chart in the European Court of Auditors' report on the scandal showed the divergence between test results for CO_2 emissions and real-world results for new passenger cars from 2001 to 2016. In 2001, real world CO_2 emissions were 7 per cent above the results from official testing.[475] Still, the oil companies were happy. So were the European car companies, because overwhelmingly they produced the diesel cars that were sold. Japan turned to hybrid cars instead and achieved much greater CO_2 savings, and with hybrid and electric cars being the future, they gained a march in technology development. European car manufacturers are now desperately trying to catch up.

The EU eventually banned the cheat devices in 2007, but never checked to see whether they were being used. It left that up to national governments. UK governments have never said whether they carried out any checks. Germany, Spain, Slovakia and the Czech Republic all said they had not done so. After 20-odd years of the EU's flagship environmental policy we have an avoidable increase in global warming, a growing technological gap with Japan and untold damage to human health. Cities like London fall foul of the EU's pollution standards because the streets are full of cars produced and tested under the lax EU regime. 60 per cent of the roads in Britain exceed WHO pollution standards. If you live in a town or city in Britain you are 25 times more likely to die from exposure to air pollution than in a car crash.

Meanwhile, the EU poses as an ecowarrior holding Britain to account over its pollution record. It even initiated legal action against Britain and other countries for failing to fine Volkswagen! This was a public health scandal, an environmental scandal and it was a perfect image of capitalism. Volkswagen's Michael Horn told a congressional hearing in Washington that it was wrong for companies to put profits before people. But calling on capitalism to put people before profit is like calling on gravity to push water uphill. If it did that, it would be a capitalism that did not behave like capitalism. It would not be capitalism. This all proved the folly of relying on the EU to protect our health or our environment. We need to take collective responsibility for the environment, not just individual responsibility.

The EU's Common Agricultural Policy

Pro-EU George Monbiot criticises the EU's Common Agricultural Policy (CAP): "All the good things the EU has done for nature are more than counteracted by this bureaucratic idiocy."[476] He wrote, "I'm a remainer, but there's one result of Brexit I can't wait to see: leaving the EU's common agricultural policy. This is the farm subsidy system that spends €50 bn (£44 bn) a year on achieving none of its objectives. It is among the most powerful drivers of environmental destruction in the northern hemisphere."[477] The Rivers Trust and the Countryside Alliance said that the CAP had produced "high costs to consumers, inefficient land use, subsidies for land ownership and serious environmental damage […] Many of the current subsidy payments are to compensate farmers and land managers for reducing greater levels of pollution and habitat destruction […] This is an absurdity […] in any other industry, polluters, rather than the polluted, should pay. Environmental damage should be subject to regulatory restraints and criminal penalties. Subsidies should be paid for delivery of additional services to society."[478]

EU farmers are still giving antimicrobials to their farm animals. The World Health Organisation considers antimicrobials to be threats to human health.[479] Poland, Spain and Italy, all large exporters of food to the UK, are in the top five antimicrobial users in the EU. If the EU had done such a good job, how come greenhouse gas emissions from agriculture in the EU overall have been rising since 2012? Official EU figures for 2017 showed emissions higher than they were in 2005. Globally, about a third all greenhouse gas emissions come from farming. Unless we get to grips with that, low or zero net carbon will remain a pipe dream. That means using all the tools at our disposal, including genetically modified (GM) crops. GM crops could significantly lower farming's carbon and greenhouse footprint. But irrational fears – and they are irrational, thirty years ago when GM was new, the fears were more understandable – have held up progress in applying GM technology.

The EU bans GM organisms but its ban is not evidence-based. In 2016 the WTO ruled against the ban. The EU then simply refused to comply with the WTO's ruling. Britain could follow the global scientific consensus and allow these products. Consumers would then be free to buy any of these products, or not, if they doubt their safety or object to the way they are produced. Outside Europe, GM crops have been widely planted over the last twenty years. They are used in about 12 per cent of the world's cropland. Billions of people have eaten GM crops, and scientists have conducted over 130,000 studies on GM technologies and there was no evidence of harm or of changes to our chromosomes from eating GM food. It was hard to see how there could be: every time you ate a banana, you ingested thousands of billions of genes, over half of which are completely foreign to humans.

The CAP kept food prices artificially high. OECD data suggested EU farm prices are around 5 per cent above world prices, so UK consumers paid around £2 billion per year in higher prices due to the CAP. Every year, the EU paid out $65 billion in farm subsidies supposedly as an essential safety net for hardworking farmers across the Continent to keep rural communities alive. The EU subsidised landowners by paying them for owning or using land. Just as long as they were not smallholders: you needed to own at least 5 hectares, about 12 acres. It had to be open land, so landowners got rid of ponds, wide hedges, trees big enough to form a canopy. As Monbiot wrote, it was 'a €55 billion incentive to destroy wildlife

257

habitats'. No wonder populations of Europe's farmland birds are in freefall, down 55 per cent in the past three decades and at their lowest since records began.[480]

Studies have repeatedly shown that four fifths of the money went to the biggest fifth of all recipient farms. Across Hungary and much of Central and Eastern Europe, most went to a connected and powerful few. A company formed by the Czech Prime Minister, Andrej Babis, collected at least $42 million in subsidies in 2019. Subsidies underwrote Mafia-style land grabs in Slovakia and Bulgaria. In Bulgaria, the subsidies became welfare for the biggest landowners. The Bulgarian Academy of Science found that three quarters of the main type of EU agricultural subsidy to the country ended up in the hands of about 100 organisations. A special report in the *New York Times* found that the EU's agricultural subsidies 'underwrite oligarchs, mobsters, and far-right populists' and that 'national leaders use the subsidies to enrich friends, political allies, and family members'.[481]

The European Parliament was complicit. It rejected a bill that would have banned politicians from benefiting from the subsidies they administered. They had dismissed a 2015 report that recommended tightening farm subsidy rules as a safeguard against Central and Eastern European land grabbing. They swatted away suggestions of fraud. "We have an almost watertight system," Rudolf Mögele, one of Europe's top agricultural officials, said in a 2019 interview. There was an overlap between the geographical payment of subsidies and environmental pollution, as EU officials knew full well. Non-EU countries in Western Europe like Switzerland, Norway and Iceland supported their farming communities and we should do so too. We did so after World War Two. The 1947 Agriculture Act protected farmers, particularly arable farmers, against the vagaries of the market in the form of minimum guaranteed payments for their produce.

Every country needs food security. The Cameron/Clegg government axed the previous government's 'Food 2030' strategy. Cameron closed the Royal Commission on Environmental Pollution and the Sustainable Development Commission and cut back the Food Standards Agency and the Environment Agency. 'Winging it' seems to have been his preferred way of operating. It failed him and it is bad for a country. A lack of self-reliance leads to loss of resilience. Some think that we get lots of food from lots of countries, so we do not need a food policy: other people will always feed us. A Cabinet Office official said, "we don't need farmers, we can buy on open markets." A senior economic advisor to the Treasury, Dr Tim Leunig, is reported as saying that Britain does not need its farming and fishing industries because Singapore manages to be 'rich without having its own agricultural sector'. We produce only 53 per cent of what we eat. We produce only 57 per cent of our vegetables, just 12 per cent of our fruit. We should produce far more, nearer to 80 per cent, a level to which we could resort in a crisis. Free trade means we rely on exploiting other countries' land, ecosystems, and cheap labour.

Fishing

Under the United Nations Convention on the Law of the Sea, our fishing waters are British sovereign territory, just as much part of the UK as the land mass. The 2019 Conservative manifesto promised to 'Ensure we are in full control of our fishing waters': "we will leave the Common Fisheries Policy, become an independent coastal state, and take back control of our waters in December 2020." Restoring control over our fishing waters would increase the value of our fish catch by up to £800 million a year. Johnson said in February 2020, "We are

259

ready to consider an agreement on fisheries, but it must reflect the fact that the UK will be an independent coastal state at the end of this year 2020, controlling our own waters. And under such an agreement, there would be annual negotiations with the EU, using the latest scientific data, ensuring that British fishing grounds are first and foremost for British boats."

We have made an agreement with Norway, with mutual respect for sovereignty. We could have similar agreements with Ireland, Iceland, Denmark and Greenland. As an independent coastal state outside the EU, we have complete control of our coastal waters. We can if we wish, make independence-compliant annual reciprocal deals with the EU on access to our fishing waters, as Norway, Iceland, Faroe and Greenland do. We can allow access to our waters only for surplus resources, granted only when we receive reciprocal value of fishing opportunities in return.

Yet the EU is demanding joint sovereignty over our fishing waters, a clear attack on our sovereignty. The French agriculture minister, Didier Guillaume, said in August 2019, "There is no scenario in which French fishermen should be prevented, could be prevented, would be prevented, by Boris Johnson from fishing in British waters. So I will keep telling Britain our fishermen must be allowed to keep fishing in its waters." We will keep telling the EU that our fishermen will have the first call on our fishing waters.

Pollution

We needed stronger regulations on the disposal of hazardous wastes, air and water pollution, the spread of potential carcinogens and toxic substances, and better safeguards of workers' health and safety. FoE Scotland stated, "It is largely thanks to 45 years of European laws on industrial pollution, water quality, nature protection and clean air that the environment we live in has improved." Not so. *The Times* conducted a study and found that "Dangerous pollutants in England's waterways have reached their highest levels since modern testing began [...] with no river in the country now certified as safe for swimmers."[482] An important part of the problem was that the EU only fines companies that break its laws. These garnered headlines and gave the illusion that it was doing something about pollution. Not so. Companies treated the fines, like the record £126 million fine that Ofwat imposed on Southern Water in June 2019 for dumping sewage into beaches, rivers and streams, as part of their business costs and passed the costs on to the consumers. Instead, we should make pollution or Volkswagen-style environmental cheating by a company a criminal offence. Lock up boards of directors.

Nuclear power

The catastrophists play fast and loose with risk in other areas, especially nuclear power. Pushker Kharecha and James Hansen published a study on nuclear power in the peer-reviewed journal *Environmental Science and Technology* in 2013. Hansen is famous for kick-starting US awareness about global warming in a landmark presentation to a Congressional committee in 1988, so he is no climate change denier. They found that, assuming quite reasonably that fossil fuels would have been used instead, between 1970 and 2009 the use of nuclear power around the world prevented around 1.8 million human deaths.[483] They noted that if Germany had never used nuclear power, pollution from other power sources would have killed 117,000 Germans up to 2009. According to the European Commission's 2019 report, in 2017 Germany alone was responsible for 26.4 per cent of the EU's entire energy-related greenhouse gas emissions. France, with its nuclear stations, 4.2 per cent. Yet in response to the Fukushima disaster in 2011, Germany stopped all nuclear development, closed 8 of its 17 nuclear power stations and was set to close all of them by the end of 2022. It opened another coal plant in 2020, ignoring the UN request that no more be opened.

The Fukushima disaster was an underwater earthquake, whose resulting tsunami killed an estimated 15,000 people. Poor practice at the Fukushima Daiichi power plant led to an exposed core and the worst nuclear accident since Chernobyl in 1988. It was a serious nuclear incident, not a massive nuclear disaster. By 2015, according to the World Health Organization, an estimated 574 people who had been living near the plant or working at the plant had died. 573 of them died from stress and privation caused by botched evacuations. Three days after the tsunami, 800 hospital patients were put on buses without medical care, water or food. For some the bus ride lasted 48 hours. Patients died of hypothermia, deterioration of existing conditions and dehydration. Radiation caused only 1 of the 574 deaths. (A further radiation death of a worker was reported in 2018. More workers at the plant might still die prematurely, but in 2020 there was no evidence of elevated radiation-related mortality in the general population.)

How can we protect the environment? When it comes to energy, keep on with nuclear power, or the task will be impossible. Build more nuclear stations. Six of the UK's seven nuclear reactor sites are due to go offline by 2030 and the remaining one, Sizewell B, is due to be decommissioned in 2035. Together they account for about a fifth of the country's electricity. New nuclear is essential if the UK is to meet its target of reaching net zero emissions by 2050 - where any carbon released is balanced by an equivalent amount absorbed from the atmosphere. Put money behind the idea of small nuclear reactors, where Britain – Rolls-Royce in particular – is a pioneer. A consortium led by Rolls-Royce has announced plans to build up to 16 mini-nuclear plants in the UK. Each plant would produce 440 megawatts of electricity - roughly enough to power Sheffield. The government is to announce at least £200 million to support the project as part of a plan for economic recovery. The project will create 6,000 new jobs in the Midlands and the North of England in the years 2020-25.

There are many calls to decarbonise the UK economy, in other words, to become a net zero-emitter of carbon. Labour Party policy was to do this by 2030 and to do it without nuclear power. It did not say 'without nuclear', but since all Britain's reactors were set to close by 2030 and Labour opposed building a fleet of new ones, that was the intention. Full decarbonisation will not happen by 2050 without nuclear power. It could happen without nuclear power, only if we stopped driving anything at all, even electric cars, washed just once a week, banned all power showers, replaced all gas cookers with electric and stopped gas and oil central heating.

Suits you, sir

We know how not to decarbonise the economy: export the carbon footprint by getting goods made abroad. That was cheating the figures, looking good while adding hugely to the real carbon footprint. The BBC website had a story headlined 'Can an English suit be made in Cambodia?'[484] It told how the suits for the English football team at Euro 2016 were made. The suits were designed by M&S in England. The wool came from Australia, was sent to China for processing, to Italy to be dyed, to Romania or Poland to be spun into yarn. It came to Yorkshire to be woven into cloth. The cloth was then sent to Cambodia to be made into a suit, then shipped back to Britain where it was sold as a '100 per cent British cloth suit'. Yes, 100 per cent British cloth because the cloth was woven in Britain.

Why Cambodia? Because it was cheap. And because it was 1 of the poorest 48 countries in the world and so made the EU's list of countries that were allowed to export anything (except weapons) to the EU without tariffs and without any restriction on quantity. This policy let the EU pose as the friend of developing countries while making it uneconomic to make clothes in Europe. Most of these countries, including Cambodia, were among the most corrupt in the world, with the worst health and safety standards for workers.[485] And the companies there paid well below a living wage, even for Cambodia.[486]

Sustainability in one country

The pro-EU camp was right to stress the importance of worker's rights, social protections and high environmental standards, but wrong to believe that the EU defended them. We could not rely on the EU to protect our NHS, our workers' rights or our environmental protections. We did not have to be in the EU to work within the framework of the Kyoto Protocol. Lieven summed up, "on key issues, climate change first among them, the United States and the European Union failed to live up to their own self-assigned global missions and provide enlightened, disinterested, and courageous global leadership."[487] How do we protect the environment? Climate scientist Myles Allen said individualism was no solution: the world would never achieve net zero carbon by relying on changing the habits and attitudes of its eight billion inhabitants. It will take political action to force the energy companies, for example, to offset all their emissions and factor that into their prices and into lower profits. Nuclear power operators had to factor in disposal and storage of their waste products for thousands of years, so we should make the energy companies do the same for fossil fuels.

We need to make companies responsible for all the emissions (and water use) in their products. Make it illegal to sell a product where the carbon emitted in its manufacture had not been offset. We need to stop relying on carbon-heavy global supply chains, cut down the food miles, the clothing miles, the white goods miles. Make things here. Grow food here – especially crops that need a lot of water, because quite a lot of water literally drops from the skies over Britain. Use science to grow produce better, with fewer nitrate fertilisers and pesticides, which will be much easier away from the anti-GM, anti-science EU. We can protect our environment and use our resources wisely. We can cope with the threats of climate change, pollution and resource depletion. We need to use reason and science, to take control of our economy away from the kleptocrats and take control for ourselves.

Chapter 18
Scotland

The making of the Union

The 1689 Convention of the Estates of Scotland, a sister institution to Scotland's parliament, comprised the estates of bishops, barons and representatives of the Burghs. In its Claim of Right, it listed the offences committed by James VII of Scotland (James II of England). It resolved that he had violated 'the fundamental constitution of this kingdom and changed it from a legal limited monarchy to an arbitrary despotic power'. It ratified the 1688 revolution which replaced James in both Scotland and England with his daughter Mary and her husband William of Orange. Building on this, the Scottish parliament advanced towards the Acts of Union of 1707. This was a union of states without a union of churches, more progressive than the age's usual practice of 'cuius regio, eius religio'. ('Whose the region, his the religion'.) In the new United Kingdom, the religion of the ruler of a state did not determine the religion of all the people of that state. The different peoples kept their different religions. Britain became a single state, with two established churches.

The Act of Security for the Kirk established the Church of Scotland, quite independent of the sovereignty of the British parliament. This won Presbyterian support for the Union. The Union forbade the Church of England to establish Anglicanism in Scotland (as Charles I had tried) and forbade Presbyterians to establish Presbyterianism in England (as the Solemn League and Covenant had tried). It ended wars of religion in Britain. The Union guaranteed the independence of Scottish law and of its fine educational institutions. The Union was no one-sided dictation, no simple product of imperial expansion and

267

assimilation, no simple incorporation. The vigour of Scotland's institutions and traditions helped to shape the Union. The economic arguments for union were strong. The English commissioners conceded the Scots' request that they should have 'full freedom and intercourse of Trade and Navigation within the [...] United Kingdom and Plantations thereunto belonging'. In return, the Scots agreed to adopt a single British Parliament and to accept the Hanoverian succession.

Before the union, Scotland's manufacturing was weak, its agriculture backward and its trade scanty. By insisting that the union should work to the advantage of Scotland, the Scottish parliament gave Scotland's aristocrats and burgeoning entrepreneurs great new opportunities for personal and national advance. As Scottish MP William Seton wrote in 1700, "This nation being poor, and without force to protect its commerce, cannot reap great advantage by it, till it partake of the trade and protection of some powerful neighbour nation, that can communicate both these [...] By this Union, we will have access to all the advantages in commerce the English enjoy."[488] Between 1720 and 1770 Scotland's foreign trade more than tripled, its linen production grew tenfold, its cattle shipments to England grew sevenfold and its imports of raw tobacco grew eightfold. Union enabled greater investment in Scotland, government grants to develop woollens, linen and fisheries, investment in roads and bridges and Scottish ports' access to all this expanded trade.

There were other good reasons for union. Political freedom was at stake. Britain was at war with the absolutist monarchy of Catholic France from 1701 to 1713. Presbyterians in Scotland urged their countrymen to support the Union to unite Britain against France and France's ally the deposed Stuart dynasty. An English MP warned that without union, "You will always find a Popish Pretender intriguing amongst you [...]

Embarrassing your Affairs [...] Jumbling you into Confusion [to] open a door to his own designes upon you." King Louis XIV of France had sent funds to Scotland "to bribe our Parliament [...] as to hinder the two nations from being united." Pope Innocent XII prayed for a Stuart restoration. In 1708, the Royal Navy foiled a French invasion force of 6,000 troops. After the 1713 Treaty of Utrecht, the pretender James Stuart (son of James II and VII) signed a secret treaty with Philip V of Spain in which he agreed to restore the Catholic Church in Britain. English people and Scottish people were united against 'Popish Bigotry and French Tyranny'.

Over the next 300 years, the British economy advanced as a single united economy. There was no separate English economy, or Scottish economy, or Welsh economy. People worked together, pooling their inventiveness to produce world-changing innovations. The engines of Matthew Boulton (English) and James Watt (Scottish) powered the industrial revolution, developing the earlier engines of Thomas Newcomen (Devonian, working in Cornwall). Britain's astounding industrial advance demanded coal, steel, engineering machines, trains and ships. Scotland's heavy industry – its mines, steel plants, engineering works, train-building and shipbuilding – all developed as part of the whole national economy. All this progress was due to Scotland's place within Britain. Scotland could not have achieved this on its own, nor could England have done it on its own. The Union created the market for all these products of industry throughout Britain and across the world.

Devolution and the 2014 referendum

The Union was a historic achievement. Then, in the late twentieth century, leading pro-EU politicians started to try to undermine this Union. It was not out of a wish for an independent Scotland but part of their effort to keep Britain inside the emerging European state. Breaking up our unity assisted their cause of ending our nation's sovereignty and independence. Under the EU enthusiast Edward Heath, the Conservatives became the first party to back devolution. In 1968 Heath abandoned his party's traditional opposition to Home Rule and pledged his support for a devolved Scottish assembly. In the 1979 referendum on establishing an elected assembly in Scotland 52 per cent voted for, just 33 per cent of the electorate. The SNP construed this as, "The longing of the people of Scotland for their own Parliament rings clear and true every time opinion is sounded." When Thatcher in 1989 used Scotland as a testbed for the poll tax, she did more to weaken the Union than any other politician in the previous hundred years. The Labour Party then was the first to play the nationalist card when it complained that England voted for Thatcher but Scotland voted for Labour. This sentiment assisted the SNP's rise and Labour's fall in Scotland.

In 1995 George Robertson, Labour's Shadow Secretary of State for Scotland, said, "Devolution will kill nationalism stone dead." More accurately, the SNP called devolution a stepping-stone on the way to full independence. Every act of devolution boosted secessionism. Devolution is secession on the instalment plan. Power devolved is power transferred, not retained. Devolution fuels separatism. The separatists swallow every concession and use it to demand more powers. This was the ratchet effect of devolution. In 2015 Robertson admitted, "I did feel that we made a mistake on devolution." Gordon Brown agreed, "It was naïve not to anticipate that devolution could create a megaphone for intensifying resentment." The SNP has often promised to deliver a referendum on secession and failed every time. In September 1991 it set itself the target of achieving 'independence within Europe' within fifteen months. In June 1992 it launched preparations for an unofficial referendum on Scotland's future. In September 1998 it declared it would hold a referendum within the first four-year term of the new parliament.

In the 1997 referendum, in a turnout of 60.4 per cent voted for, 74.3 per cent of those voting agreed that there should be a Scottish Parliament, which equalled 44.87 per cent of the electorate. In the Welsh referendum, in a turnout of 50 per cent voted for, 50.3 per cent of those voting agreed that there should be a Welsh Assembly, which equalled 25.15 per cent of the electorate. Devolution certainly did not kill Scottish nationalism, or secessionism (not the same thing), but it did not do its sponsor much good. Labour's fall speeded up as the Blair government adopted devolution as its policy. It introduced the Scottish parliament in 1999. Then it lost almost all its MPs in Scotland – from 56 out of 72 in 2001 to just one out of 59 in 2015. Successive UK governments worked on the basis that everything was devolved unless it was specifically reserved to the UK government. Since the 1997 referendum, the SNP has seized ever more powers, none of them powers that anybody voted to devolve in the referendum. These included the devolution of railways in 2005, of conservation, fishing, wind and wave energy in 2008, of borrowing, spending, and a host of taxation powers through the Scotland Act 2012, and of the Crown Estate, welfare, road signs and gas extraction through the Scotland Act 2016.

The SNP wanted more and called for a referendum on secession. Alex Salmond stated in January 2012, in his foreword to 'Your Scotland – Your Referendum - A Consultation Document', "We will decide our future in a vote which is beyond challenge or doubt." In the Edinburgh Agreement of 15 October 2012, the coalition government led by Cameron

271

accepted the SNP's call for a referendum in Scotland. Cameron signed an agreement with Alex Salmond and Nicola Sturgeon that the referendum should "have a clear legal base, be legislated for by the Scottish Parliament, be conducted so as to command the confidence of parliaments, government and people, and deliver a fair test and decisive expression of the views of people in Scotland and a result that everyone will respect." Cameron could have insisted that the future of the UK was a matter for the whole people of the UK to decide and he could have kept control of the wording of the question. Repeating Labour's error of 1997, he let the SNP have its way on both counts. His approach was to give the SNP half what it wanted in order to prevent them asking for all it wanted. It did not work.

The SNP wanted to be sure it could stay in the EU if the vote was to leave the UK. On 10 March 2014, the Convener of the European and External Relations Committee of the Scottish Parliament, Christina McElvie, SNP MSP, wrote to the EU Commission to ask whether Scotland would stay in the EU if it left the UK. The Vice-President of the EU Commission, Viviane Reding, replied on 20 March, "The Commission's position on the issue that you raise has been stated on a number of occasions since 2004. The Treaties apply to the Member States. When part of the territory of a Member State ceases to be a part of that State, e.g. because that territory becomes an independent state, the treaties will no longer apply to that territory. In other words, a new independent region would, by the fact of its independence, become a third country with respect to the Union and the Treaties would, from the day of its independence, not apply anymore on its territory." McElvie was not happy with this answer, so she wrote again on 11 April. Ms Reding replied on 3 June, "I have taken good note of the views and concerns you express. The Commission would like to refer to its previous reply on the upcoming referendum in Scotland and their possible implications."

This left the SNP with the prospect of leaving both the UK and the EU, without a deal. Yet Sturgeon claimed in July 2014 that her party had proposed 'a robust and common sense' position on why an independent Scotland would automatically inherit EU membership. The SNP may have proposed a position, but the Commission had already dismissed it. Nonetheless, the SNP campaigned in 2014 to take Scotland out of the UK, having been told this would mean leaving the EU. On 7 September 2017, Antonio Tajani, the President of the European Parliament, reaffirmed that if a territory seceded from an EU member state, it would become a third country with respect to the EU and the EU treaties would no longer apply there. Yet the SNP continues to claim that if Scotland voted to leave the UK it would stay in the EU. SNP MP Ian Blackford told BBC *Newsnight* in November 2019 that Scots had a choice between 'Brexit Britain or an independent Scotland in the EU'. The 2014 referendum question was 'Should Scotland be an independent country?' This question was not balanced. It ignored the central nation state at issue – the United Kingdom. There was no mention of the UK, as if it were not involved. Contrast this with the ballot paper's question in the EU referendum of 2016, which mentioned the UK twice, and the EU, which was at issue, five times.

In 2015 Cameron had proposed in his EU Referendum Bill that the question should be, "Should the United Kingdom remain a member of the European Union?" The Electoral Commission said this was unbalanced because it presented only one of the options. The Commission proposed instead that the question should be, "Should the United Kingdom remain a member of the European Union or leave the European Union?" The Commission view about the 2016 referendum question means that the 2014 question was unbalanced. Spelling out both options explicitly makes it clear that voting for one option means voting against the other, that, for example, to vote for secession is to vote not to stay within the UK. The campaign before the 2014 referendum was a fascinating exercise in democracy. The debate was both rational and impassioned. It was all about the people, it was of, for and by the people. The political parties and the campaigns played a secondary role. The Conservative party was for the Union, the SNP and the Greens were for secession. The Labour party's stance aided the cause of separatism that it was nominally opposing. Its anti-Tory focus strengthened the SNP. It talked up two threats – Toryism and separatism - instead of focusing on the one threat – separatism.

During the second TV debate in the 2014 campaign, Salmond challenged Labour's Alistair Darling about his working with the Tory Party in the Better Together alliance. Salmond wanted to say to the Scottish people, "The Tories are the enemy, this man is working with them, and you can only get rid of them, and him, by voting for independence." Had Darling replied that he would work with anybody and everybody to defeat separatism, that would have focused attention on the real threat. Instead, Darling left viewers with the impression that Toryism was as much a danger to Scotland as separatism. The logical conclusion for the viewer was, "If we want rid of the Tories, we'd better vote for separation." Darling's tactics boosted Salmond's case. Labour's Gordon Brown was no clearer. He spoke of supporting the Union and supporting secession as 'opposing extremes'. But maintaining the Union was not an extreme position. Calling it extreme boosted the SNP's claim to occupy the middle ground, to represent mainstream opinion.

Calls for a federal state were another tactic used by the EU and its supporters to break up the UK. Brown claimed that a 'federalist UK with maximum autonomy for Scotland' was 'a middle way' between the SNP's demand for full independence and what he claimed was the Conservative Party's belief in maintaining the 'status quo'. By supporting the SNP's federalist demand for ever more powers, Brown aided its drive for secession and paved the way for yet more concessions to the SNP. Some claimed that Scotland voted in 2014 to stay in the UK in the belief that this would mean staying in the EU. The SNP claimed that the 'no' campaign guaranteed that a pro-Union vote would keep Scotland in the EU in perpetuity. That was not true. In January 2013 Cameron had promised there would be an EU referendum, so everyone knew that voting against secession could mean leaving the EU. The SNP document *Scotland's Future* had mentioned in 2013 the possibility of a referendum that would take the whole UK out of the EU.

The issue in the 2014 referendum was the UK not the EU. There was no evidence that Scottish people voted as they did in 2014 because they believed that their votes would affect the later vote about the EU. Scottish people knew enough about the referendum question to know that they were rejecting secession in order to stay in the UK not in order to stay in the EU. On 18 September 2014 the Scottish people voted in a fair and free referendum by a majority democratic decision to uphold our national unity, 2,001,926 to 1,617,989 votes, 55.3 per cent to 44.7 per cent. Turnout was 84.6 per cent, the highest for any election or referendum in the UK since the January 1910 general election, which was held before universal suffrage. This compared to the average turnout of 53 per cent at the five Scotland-only elections for Holyrood since 1999. The Scottish people voted for a united Britain. They decided, democratically, one-person-one-vote, to stay in the UK. By voting in the referendum, whichever way they voted, the people of Scotland legitimised that decision-making process. The unprecedentedly high turnout added yet more weight to the validity of the process.

The SNP said over and over that Scotland had no say and that it should have the right to determine its own future. In 2014 the people of Scotland had the decisive say in whether Britain stayed as a united country. They determined their own future. Scottish people, alone, decided that our country would stay united: decisions did not come much bigger. The referendum was held according to the legal rules and was 'conducted so as to command the confidence of parliaments, government and people'. It did indeed 'deliver a fair test and decisive expression of the views of people in Scotland'. Not everyone respected the result. The SNP did not respect its signed pledge to respect the result. It did not respect the expressed will of the people in Scotland. It acted like Jean-Claude Juncker before the 2005 French vote on the EU Constitution, "If it's a Yes vote we will say on we go, and if it's a No vote we will say we continue." The UK government, supposedly so indifferent to the interests, rights and wishes of the people of Scotland, trusted them with the decision. How did the SNP's leaders repay that trust? By reneging on their signed commitment to respect the expressed will of the Scottish people. They tried to annul the Scottish people's decision by demanding another referendum. That was not respecting the result; this was breaking their signed word.

Martin Rogan from Ayr asked (letters, *Morning Star*, 24 December 2019) why we should 'accept a government based in London which can totally ignore our wishes'. The SNP's leaders, not the British government, totally ignored - and continued to ignore - the wishes of most Scottish people. The SNP's leaders used Holyrood as a platform from which to try to overturn the Scottish people's majority democratic decision to stay in the UK, just as pro-EU forces at Westminster used the state machine to try to overturn the British people's majority democratic decision to leave the EU. Salmond had told viewers of the BBC's Andrew Marr Show on 14 September 2014 that if the majority of Scottish people voted No to independence there would be no second referendum on the subject in this 'political generation'. He said, "If you remember that previous constitutional referendum in Scotland - there was one in 1979 and then the next one was 1997. That's what I mean by a political generation." It was not just Salmond's personal view. The phrase 'a once in a generation opportunity' appeared three times in the Scottish administration's own 2013 White Paper entitled *Scotland's Future*.[489] The pro-Union camp also stressed that the referendum was a once-in-a-generation chance to settle the matter. The decision to stay in the UK meant that the people of Scotland would participate as equals, one person one vote, in future UK-wide decisions in elections and referendums.

The 2016 referendum

The SNP's 2015 manifesto said, "If an in/out EU referendum does go ahead, we will seek to amend the legislation to ensure that no constituent part of the UK can be taken out of the EU against its will. We will propose a 'double majority' rule - meaning that unless England, Scotland, Wales and Northern Ireland each vote to leave the EU, the UK would remain a member state." This 'double majority' was really a quadruple minority lock. It would have meant that if any one of Northern Ireland, Scotland, Wales, or England had voted to stay in the EU, this vote would veto pro-leave majorities in the other three. A minority could have overruled the majority. The lock only applied one way. A pro-EU minority could veto a pro-Leave majority. But a pro-Leave minority could not veto a pro-EU majority. It was an attempt to claim an unequal right. Even Salmond said that Sturgeon had no veto over leaving. The SNP believes that it should have a permanent minority veto on policies it opposes, like British unity and leaving the EU.

A doctrine of minority veto power over democracy was proposed in the USA in the 1850s by Senator John C. Calhoun, to defend slavery. He believed that the Southern states should have veto power over the actions of the national government, claiming that this was a defence of minority rights against the possible tyranny of the majority. Ian Smith in Rhodesia and South Africa's National Party apartheid governments made similar claims. The SNP sought to legitimise the same principle, that majority votes were not binding, that a righteous minority was entitled to overrule the majority. US President James Madison rejected this 'right', saying that to give 'such power, to such a minority, over such a majority, would overturn the first principle of free government, and in practice necessarily overturn the government itself.' No minority, however it defines itself, has the right to veto the decision of the majority in a nation-wide vote. In a democracy, the majority has more rights than the minority. Only opponents of democracy could want the minority to overrule the majority. In a democracy, there is no moral right for a minority vote to prevail over the majority vote.

The SNP's 2015 manifesto said, "We will oppose a referendum on membership of the EU." It sought to deny the whole British people, including the people of Scotland, even having a vote on whether we stayed in the EU. Scottish people voted by a majority to stay in the UK, so when they voted in the 2016 referendum, they were voting as part of the British collective, not as a Scottish collective. They voted knowing that the question was, "Should the United Kingdom remain a member of the European Union or leave the European Union?"

The question was not, "Should Scotland remain a member of the European Union or leave the European Union? Everyone who voted did so knowing that the question was not whether Scotland should leave or remain, but whether the United Kingdom should leave or remain. It was a British referendum, not a Scottish referendum. There were not separate referendums, just the one. Everyone knew that the overall British vote would count, not the separate counts in the separate areas. Scottish people voted as part of the UK electorate and so as democrats were bound by the decision that the majority decided to make. When we all voted in 2016, we voted as one UK and we voted by a majority, in a free and fair referendum, to leave the EU.

In the 2016 referendum. Scotland's turnout was 67.18 per cent, as against the overall UK turnout of 72.2 per cent. (Scotland's turnout was far higher than the 55.6 per cent turnout in the May 2016 election to Holyrood.) 1,661,191 Scottish people voted for Britain to stay in the EU, 41.66 per cent of the Scottish electorate. 41.66 per cent was hardly the 'overwhelming' majority that Sturgeon ritually claimed. 1,018,322 Scottish people voted for Britain to leave the EU, 25.5 per cent of the Scottish electorate, nearly 40 per cent of those Scottish people who actually voted. More Scottish people voted to leave the EU than voted SNP in the 2017 election (977,569). 349,442 people in Northern Ireland voted to leave. So the total leave votes from Scotland and Northern Ireland were 1,367,764, which was more than the margin between leave and stay – 1,269,501. The people who voted leave in Scotland and Northern Ireland made the difference. By contrast, the people of Wales voted to leave the EU by 854,572 votes to 772,347, which was 52.53 per cent to 47.47. The 854,572 Welsh people who voted leave outnumbered those voting 'Yes' to devolution in the referendums of 1979, 1997 and 2011 and outnumbered those voting for anything in any Welsh election since 1997.

Chapter 19
For British unity

Mandate

When the SNP challenged the UK government's right to leave the EU, the UK Supreme Court upheld the UK government's right to do so. On 24 January 2017 the Court's President Lord Neuberger stated that, "On devolution issues, the court unanimously rules that UK ministers are not legally compelled to consult the devolved administrations before triggering Article 50. The devolution statutes were enacted on the assumption that the UK be a member of the European Union, but do not require it. Relations with the EU are a matter for the UK Government."[490] In 2019, the SNP ran an election campaign which shifted from being pro-secession to being pro-EU. 'STOP BREXIT' was the message emblazoned across the SNP campaign bus, its podium and its leaflets. It was dishonest of the SNP to claim that votes cast on this basis gave it a mandate for another unnecessary, divisive referendum. The SNP got 1,242,380 votes, 45 per cent, the same percentage as in 2014, when they failed in their bid to split our country. The majority of those who voted in Scotland, 54 per cent, voted for pro-union parties.

The Conservative Party stood on a manifesto that ruled out another referendum: page 45 of the manifesto - 'we are opposed to a second independence referendum' - and won an 80-seat majority, so it had a clear democratic mandate for opposing any second referendum. Yet Sturgeon demanded that the British government 'respect' the vote for the SNP! When will she respect the Scottish people's 2014 vote to stay in the UK? When will she respect the British people's 2016 vote to leave the EU? Those who called for a second EU referendum assisted the

SNP's demand for a second referendum on secession and boosted the SNP's rise in the polls. Labour's Keir Starmer worked to set a second referendum about the EU 'on the table'. He was the first member of the Shadow Cabinet to press for this, in his October 2018 Labour Party Conference speech. He declared that going back on Brexit altogether should be an option in that second referendum.

On 30 March 2017 and again on 19 December 2019, Sturgeon formally requested a second referendum, breaking her self-imposed promise that she would not do so until separation had been winning 60 per cent support in opinion polls for at least a year. Twice she set out a timetable for holding a new referendum and twice she failed to deliver the vote she promised. The SNP was split on how to achieve separation. Some supporters of separatism like Joanna Cherry wanted to hold an 'unofficial' referendum. Sturgeon has repeatedly rejected this idea. Speaking at a Women for Independence conference in November 2018, she said, "The beauty of 2014 was that it was an agreed process." On the Andrew Marr show on 15 December 2019, she denied that the SNP would hold an unauthorised referendum. Some SNP members even wanted a unilateral declaration of independence, like the white supremacist Ian Smith's UDI of Rhodesia. A Holyrood-held referendum would have no significance in law, as Sturgeon realised. The UK government would not and would not need to, prevent the holding of a legally meaningless referendum. An attempt to hold such a referendum in an attempt to embarrass the UK government would instead split the SNP.

Sturgeon's approach is to claim endlessly that a majority for the SNP in any Holyrood election would be a mandate for another referendum. But no Scottish election could give the SNP the legal authority to hold another referendum. Paragraph 1(b) of schedule 5 of the Scotland Act 1998 stated that 'the

Union of the Kingdoms of Scotland and England' was a matter reserved to the UK Parliament. No Act of the Scottish Parliament may relate to reserved matters. A devolved administration only has a mandate for devolved matters. Sturgeon knows that Holyrood does not have the power to hold a legal referendum, which is why she refuses to back calls to try legal action to test Holyrood's power in this matter. She rightly said that "it could set us back." In January 2021 a separatist campaigner, Martin Keatings, jumped the gun and tried to get the Court of Session to rule on whether Holyrood has the power to hold a referendum without the permission of the UK government. A week later the SNP published a draft referendum bill in which it committed to calling its own referendum if the UK government refused its consent. Aidan O'Neill, Mr Keatings' advocate, said that voters were entitled "to know whether that claim can actually be carried out or whether it's just bluff and bluster." In February 2021 the Court declined to rule that Holyrood had the right to call a referendum without the UK government's consent.

Johnson stood firm against holding another 'once-in-a-generation' referendum. He will not repeat Cameron's concession to the SNP. A government that faced down the entire EU is not going to bend to an SNP that won the votes of only 45 per cent of the people of Scotland in the 2019 general election (down from 46.5 per cent in the 2016 Holyrood election). His stand against separatism will strengthen the forces of Unionism. It is an SNP-sponsored myth that opposing them strengthens them. Sturgeon's 'strategy' of hoping that the UK government will change its mind is hapless and hopeless. The separatist party in Wales also did poorly in the 2019 election. Plaid Cymru's vote went down in the valleys of South Wales and plunged in Rhondda and Blaenau Gwent. It did not come second in a single seat, coming fourth in many, behind

Labour, the Conservatives and the Brexit Party. It got 9.9 per cent of the votes in Wales, down from 10.4 per cent in 2017. The UK government has the sole democratic mandate in our country, and its mandate, as reaffirmed in every general election, is of one united nation. By standing in British general elections and by taking up the seats they won, the Scottish Nationalists gave the UK Parliament – and the governments it formed – the authority to forbid a second referendum. Their MPs acknowledged this simply by taking part in its proceedings. Yet SNP MP Tommy Sheppard tweeted on 16 December 2019 that Prime Minister Johnson's 'mandate doesn't run in Scotland' - as if Scotland had seceded.

In November 2020, the SNP claimed that Prime Minister Johnson's pledge to block a new referendum was 'undemocratic' and 'straight out of the Trump playbook'. Presumably that was a reference to Trump's refusing to accept the result of the free and fair vote in the 2020 US election. But the SNP is following Trump; it has always refused to accept the result of the free and fair referendum of 2014. What is democratic about trying to overturn the result of a majority vote, a vote that the SNP's leaders had pledged in writing to respect? The rest of the people of the UK do not want our country destroyed by an SNP which refuses to accept any vote in which it is defeated - 2014, which it pledged to respect and then reneged and 2016, when it voted as part of the UK and so is bound by our majority vote to leave. The SNP cannot get a legal referendum and an illegal one would be futile and foolish. Both its options are bankrupt. It is in a cul-de-sac, a dead end and has nowhere to go politically. The secessionist movement, ironically, is splintering. The Cherry/Sturgeon split is growing. The Salmond/Sturgeon split is spreading through the party, setting activists against the bureaucrats. While this political posturing and infighting goes on, the SNP is not doing the day-to-day administrative jobs it was elected to do.

Secession illegal

The SNP has no right in either national law or international law to declare independence unilaterally. Stéphane Dion, Canada's minister of Intergovernmental Affairs from 1996 to 2003, pointed out, "A unilateral declaration of independence would fly in the face of democracy and the rule of law."[491] And, "There is no right at international law for constituent parts of a state to secede without the consent of that state."[492] Without the support of the British government, the international community would not recognise a unilateral declaration of Scotland's independence. Dion wrote, "Secession is defined as a break in solidarity among fellow citizens. That is why, in its wisdom, international law extends to peoples the right of self-determination in its extreme form, that is the right to secession, only in situations where a break in solidarity is evident, such as in cases of military occupation or colonial exploitation. The secessions that have taken place to date have always arisen out of decolonization or the troubled times that follow the end of authoritarian regimes. It is not simply a matter of chance that no well-established democracy that has experienced ten years of universal suffrage has ever faced secession. Such a break in solidarity appears very hard to justify in a democracy."[493]

The Canadian Supreme Court decided in 1998 that "[...] a right to secession only arises under the principle of self-determination of peoples at international law where 'a people' is governed as part of a colonial empire; where 'a people' is subject to alien subjugation, domination or exploitation; and possible where 'a people' is denied any meaningful exercise of its right to self-determination within the state of which it forms a part. In other circumstances, peoples are expected to achieve

285

self-determination within the framework of their existing state. A state whose government represents the whole of the people or peoples resident within its territory, on a basis of equality and without discrimination, and respects the principle of self-determination in its internal arrangements, is entitled to maintain its territorial integrity under international law and to have that territorial integrity recognized by other states."[494] 290 members of the Spanish Association of Professors in International Law and International Relations stated in relation to the illegal referendum called in Catalonia in 2017: "1. According to the United Nations doctrine as well as international jurisprudence, the International Law related to the self-determination of peoples only allows the right to independence to those peoples under colonial rule or subject to foreign subjugation, domination or exploitation."[495]

James Crawford, now a Judge of the International Court of Justice, formerly Whewell Professor of International Law at Cambridge University, stated, "The unwillingness of the international community to accept unilateral secession from an independent state can be illustrated by reference to the so-called 'safeguard' clause to the Friendly Relations Declaration, which, in elaborating the Charter principle of self-determination specifies that: 'Nothing in the foregoing paragraphs shall be construed as authorizing or encouraging any action which would dismember or impair, totally or in part, the territorial integrity or political unity of sovereign and independent States conducting themselves in compliance with the principle of equal rights and self-determination of peoples as described above and thus possessed of a government representing the whole people belonging to the territory without distinction as to race, creed or colour.'"[496]

The 1993 United Nations World Conference on Human Rights held in Vienna reaffirmed the 'safeguard' clause. The

Vienna Declaration stated: "In accordance with the Declaration on Principles of International Law concerning Friendly Relations and Cooperation Among States in accordance with the Charter of the United Nations, this [the right of self-determination] shall not be construed as authorizing or encouraging any action which would dismember or impair, totally or in part, the territorial integrity or political unity of sovereign and independent States conducting themselves in compliance with the principle of equal rights and self-determination of peoples and thus possessed of a Government representing the whole people belonging to the territory without distinction of any kind."[497]

Professor Crawford concluded, "In accordance with this formula, a state whose government represents the whole people of its territory without distinction of any kind, that is to say, on a basis of equality, and in particular without discrimination on grounds of race, creed or colour, complies with the principle of self-determination in respect of all of its people and is entitled to the protection of its territorial integrity. To put it another way, the people of such a state exercise the right of self-determination through their participation in the government of the state on a basis of equality."[498] In his edition of the definitive book on international law, Professor Crawford concluded, "The international system remains opposed to secession [...]."[499]

For a successful all-Britain economy

On 25 November 2019, Ian Blackford, the SNP's Westminster leader since 2017, claimed that "Scotland has subsidised the rest of the UK for most of the last 40 year period." Scotland was indeed a net contributor for the ten years from 1981, thanks to the North Sea oil boom. But the boom ended. Scotland was a net beneficiary in every year since 1990/91, except for2008/2009. Eleven years out of forty was not 'most'. In any case, it is divisive and false to pose the question of one part of the country subsidising another part. We were all members one of another. It was like saying that the lungs subsidised the heart. We talk of and value partnership between nations, but we do not talk of partnership within a nation. It was like saying that the heart was a partner of the lungs. Scotland's public spending in 2019-20 was 12.4 per cent higher per head than the UK average.

The General Expenditure and Revenue Scotland figures for 2019/20 showed that each person in Scotland received £1,633 more than the UK average in public spending and paid £308 less tax, leading to a 'Union dividend' of £1,941 each. If Scotland chose to leave the UK, it would lose this money. The Barnett-based funding paid by the UK government to Scotland in 2021-22 was £38 billion. A separate Scotland would lose this too.

The same report showed an estimated net fiscal balance (including a geographical share of North Sea oil) in Scotland of minus £15.1 billion or minus 8.6 per cent of Scottish GDP for 2019-20. This compares with a UK net fiscal balance of minus 2.5 per cent of UK GDP.[500] The SNP's Sustainable Growth Commission accepted the UK Office for Budget Responsibility's estimated deficit of 7.1 per cent in 2021-22, way above the EU's 3 per cent limit. Scotland would fail to qualify for euro membership, so it would not qualify for EU membership. The only way to meet the EU's target would be to impose austerity, the EU's standard remedy for what it judges to be excessive deficits. The Institute for Fiscal Studies (IFS) warned that implementing the SNP's 2019 election manifesto would push a separate Scotland into more austerity than the Conservative Party had ever done. Taxes would have to rise, or cuts made. The IFS noted that the SNP had not published detailed costings of its plans.

David Phillips, associate director of the IFS, said the SNP's promise to reduce Scotland's deficit would mean austerity and that this was 'inconsistent' with the party's criticism of 'Tory cuts'. He wrote, "Pursuing the types of policies suggested in the SNP manifesto in an independent Scotland would mean either those cuts would have to be even bigger, or other taxes would have to be increased to pay for the proposed net giveaways. [...] in the short-term at least, independence would likely necessitate more not less austerity."

When Andrew Neil interviewed Nicola Sturgeon, whose SNP has always said it opposed austerity, she admitted that a separate Scotland would have to impose more austerity to meet EU deficit rules. In 2014, the SNP campaign portrayed separation as needing very little change and as not being disruptive or threatening to people's finances. The SNP said that the currency would stay the same, the border would stay open, and Scotland and England would share regulation of finance and much else besides. But these SNP claims did not convince the people of Scotland. The 2014 Scottish Social Attitudes survey found 43 per cent believed the economy would do worse if Scotland seceded, only 26 per cent thought it would do better.[501]

That could not be argued since 2016. The SNP's new policy on the currency was two-pronged but unachievable on either count. First, ask Westminster if it could please use the pound, but without Scotland having any control over it. This would not work. After Czechoslovakia split into two countries, the Czech Republic and Slovakia, the two countries shared a currency. Within days it became clear that this was unstable. Each had to create a new currency within weeks. Second, if and when this shared currency did not work, see if the EU was going to force

Scotland to join the euro. The EU would most likely insist that Scotland had to join the euro, as it has done with all new member states in the twenty-first century. Philippe Lamberts, Co-President of the Greens in the European Parliament, confirmed in December 2020 that "any new member has to adopt the euro." (The SNP continued to deny this: Blackford said in 2019 that Scotland would not 'necessarily' have to adopt the euro. Sturgeon said in 2020, "No, I don't think it would […] No, we wouldn't […].")

Scotland would be bound by the pro-austerity Fiscal Compact and by the deflationary monetary union. All this would be hard to sell to voters, particularly to those with a salary, mortgage, bank account, savings and pension all denominated in sterling. Having a central bank is another condition for EU membership. In 2008, the Halifax Bank of Scotland and the Royal Bank of Scotland both collapsed in disgrace, the largest crash in British banking history. It would have ruined Scotland if it were not in the United Kingdom. But it was and the taxpayers of the whole UK could save it. But with two failed banks, both bailed out by the British taxpayer, Scotland would be unable to found a central bank. A separate Scotland would have no single market and no banking union with the rest of Britain. It would have a huge deficit, with no control of the currency in which it issued its debt. As the SNP admits, it would suffer ten years of austerity. It would have little revenue, no rebate and no veto.

The separatist movement in Scotland is committed not to independence but to EU membership. There is no independence within the EU. Within the EU, Scotland would be bound to accept the EU's four freedoms – free movement of capital, of labour, of services and of goods. There is no pro-growth policy available within the EU. There is only the treaty-bound policy of Thatcherism. To rejoin the EU would be to rejoin its Thatcherite policies, imposed inescapably by treaty, not by changeable votes. Scotland needed economic union with the UK far more than it needed economic union with the EU. Sturgeon has refused to rule out imposing a hard border between Scotland and England. An unnecessary new international border where none has existed for centuries would make the rest of the UK a foreign country to Scotland.

Between 2002 and 2017, the value of Scottish trade with the rest of the UK grew from £28.6 billion to £49.8 billion. Scotland's trade with the EU grew from £11.4 billion to £12.3 billion. When Scotland exported roughly four times as much to the UK single market as to the EU's single market, which single market should Scotland seek to remain part of? In 2017, the rest of the UK accounted for 61 per cent of Scottish exports and 67 per cent of Scottish imports. A 2021 study conclude that leaving the UK would cost Scotland £11 billion a year, cutting income per person by between £2000 and £2800 a year. This is "primarily because Scottish trade with the rest of the UK is four times larger than its trade with the EU."[502] The authors note that "[...] rejoining the EU would do little to mitigate the costs of Scottish independence."[503] The authors sum up, "[...] our analysis shows that, at least from a trade perspective, independence would leave Scotland considerably poorer than staying in the United Kingdom."[504]

The SNP fails the people of Scotland

The SNP has failed as an administration. Scotland's economy lags further behind the UK average than when the Sturgeon took over. The SNP has refused to support workers in threatened industries, citing EU regulations on state aid. The Burntisland Fabrication (BiFab) offshore wind project was a key part of Scotland's wind farm revolution. The trade unions there have long demanded that contracts should include a requirement of local content within the supply chain. Instead, contracts have gone to yards in China, the United Arab Emirates, Spain and Indonesia. The agreement for BiFab to manufacture eight wind turbine jackets for the Neart Na Gaoithe (NnG) development of a £2 billion offshore wind farm collapsed in October 2020 when the SNP pulled financial support from the three BiFab fabrication yards in Fife and on the Isle of Lewis.[505] The collapse lost the taxpayer over £50 million. Gary Smith, GMB Scotland secretary, and Pat Rafferty, Unite Scotland secretary, said the plight of the firm 'exposes the myth of Scotland's renewables revolution' and shines a light on 'a decade of political hypocrisy and failure'.

Smith said, "It's a scandalous end to a decade which started with promises of a 'Saudi Arabia of renewables' supporting 28,000 full-time jobs in offshore wind and now finishes in mothballed fabrication yards and no prospect of any contracts or jobs on the horizon." The SNP administration's response was to fall back on doing 'everything possible to support the business while recognising the need for us to remain in line with state-aid regulations'. Ageing ferry ships that have provided life-line services to dozens of islands around the coasts of Scotland should have been replaced in 2018, but the wait for them has been extended until at least 2023.[506] The costs of the new ships have risen dramatically by three times the original estimates to over £300 million, with a delay in construction of over five years. The cross-party Rural Economy and Connectivity Committee of the Scottish Parliament looking into the construction and procurement of ferries in Scotland published its report in December 2020. The report condemns the 'complete lack of transparency' on loans of £45 million made to the winner of the original £97 million contract, Ferguson Marine Engineering. The report concludes that the

SNP's management of the process was a 'catastrophic failure'. Mick Cash, RMT General Secretary, commented: "This saga reinforces RMT's position that vessel procurement and design will only succeed under full public ownership of Scotland's public ferry contracts."

In the 2020 Index of Social and Economic Well-being study of the 32 OECD countries, Scotland has fallen from 16th to joint 21st since 2006. Scotland experienced the joint biggest fall, along with Wales.[507] The report's author John McLaren sums up: "3 countries experienced falls in their overall Index scores: Greece, Scotland and Finland. Within the UK, the ranking of England did not change, remaining a little above mid-table (i.e. second quartile); Scotland fell into the third quartile of countries, due to a decline in its education and income performances, the latter associated with the decline in North Sea related activity. Despite this, Scotland's very poor life expectancy performance remains its weakest area of performance; Wales and Northern Ireland both fell into the bottom quartile of countries, principally due to poor GDP performances. The relatively poor Scottish performance, in terms of education and health, suggests that changes may be needed to the, still young, devolved political system. [...] Looking across the UK as a whole, the results highlight the fact that greater political devolution alone does not easily lead to an improving performance in key areas of wellbeing."[508] Life expectancy growth had stalled since 2012-14.

Scotland's education service has fallen in the rankings since the SNP took over the administration of education. In 2000, Scotland was near the top for English, maths and literacy. By 2016 it had fallen into the second quartile. The bi-annual Scottish Survey of Literacy and Numeracy, set up by the SNP administration, showed a fall from 2012 to 2014 and another fall from 2014 to 2016. The SNP's response? It closed down the

293

Survey. Under the SNP, the poorest young people in Scotland are half as likely to get to university as the poorest young people in England. The chance of getting to university for people from the poorest backgrounds was rising twice as fast in England as in Scotland. Far from responding better to the Covid crisis, the SNP did no better than the UK government and in some ways worse. In November 2020, official figures covering the second wave of the virus found that Scotland had a higher Covid death rate than England in each of the previous four weeks. A Stirling University report found 47 per cent of Scotland's Covid deaths in the first wave were in care homes, compared to 30 per cent in England.

In the summer of 2020 Sturgeon repeatedly claimed that Covid-19 was five times more prevalent in England than in Scotland. The Office for Statistics Regulation rebuked her, explaining that "it is important to recognize that a comparison of COVID-19 prevalence rates is not straightforward [...] if it is to be undertaken, the results and the uncertainties should be communicated transparently," and that the sources Sturgeon used did not "allow for a quantified and un-caveated comparison of the kind that was made." In December 2020 the Office for Statistics Regulation rebuked her again, saying that her claim in September, when she said at Holyrood that 'around 40 per cent' of Scottish care homes 'now allow and enable' indoor visits, was 'a very loose approximation based on incomplete data'. In December 2020 Sturgeon admitted her government's record on drugs was 'indefensible' after the National Records of Scotland reported that Scotland's drug deaths had reached a new record high and Scotland still had by far the worst record in Europe. The report calculated Scotland's drug-related death rate as 231 per million people and estimated the rate for the whole of the UK to be 64. There was a 6 per cent rise to 1,264 drug-related deaths in 2019, more than double the total a decade ago.

The SNP had cut drug rehabilitation facilities. Dr Roy Robertson, an Edinburgh-based GP and professor of addiction medicine at the University of Edinburgh, said, "Frontline services have been cut back mercilessly by the Scottish Government." Annemarie Ward, CEO of the addiction charity Favor Scotland, accused SNP ministers of 'posturing rhetoric and farce' and 'largely ignoring' the charity's recommendations. David Liddell, chief executive officer of the Scottish Drugs Forum, said that "nobody should regard these preventable deaths as acceptable" or "anything other than a national tragedy and disgrace." The SNP wanted to re-join the detested Common Fisheries Policy. It wanted to allow EU member nations' fishing vessels to fish in Scotland's waters. Its 2019 election manifesto said, "The SNP is clear that access to Scotland's waters must not be traded away permanently by the UK Government, nor should our waters be closed off to our international neighbours and partners."

Britain one nation

On 14 March 2020 Starmer said, "There is obviously the question of whether people want Scotland to be torn apart and independent from the United Kingdom - I don't. I think we are stronger if the whole United Kingdom stays together. I don't want more borders." When he was asked "would you support Nicola Sturgeon's call for another referendum?" he replied, "No, I think we should go into the 2021 election making the argument for the United Kingdom." It appeared that he had realised that Labour cannot compete with the Nationalists on nationalist territory, that you cannot outNat the Nats. But when he was asked on 20 September 2020 if there should be another referendum if the SNP won in May 2021, he told Sky News'

295

Sophy Ridge, "This is a question for Scotland, people of Scotland. [...] If there's a majority it's got to be looked at in Westminster, but the Labour party will be campaigning into May on the basis that what we don't want is another divisive referendum." This was no commitment to oppose holding that referendum. On 23 September he gave a boost to the SNP policy of calling a second referendum by conceding that the SNP would have a mandate for such a referendum if it won a Holyrood majority in 2021.

Starmer would do what any Labour leader would do - head into a general election stating there is no chance of a deal with the SNP, and that Labour stands firm for the Union. Then, when opinion polls show that Labour will not win a majority, he says we will 'open discussions' with the SNP after the election, knowing quite well the SNP's price for supporting a coalition government - that he allow another referendum.[509] Labour is untrustworthy on the issue of whether there should be another referendum in Scotland on secession. Indeed, it could be said that they were doing exactly what the SNP wanted. Some pro-EU people accused the people who voted to leave the EU of endangering the Union, but the secessionist pro-EU SNP and the Labour Party, not the people who voted to leave, threatened the Union. Some who accused Leave voters of threatening the Union spent their time praising the SNP and lambasting the Johnson government, doing the separatists' work for them.

The SNP was ever ready to call for more powers for the EU and for more EU interference. SNP MP Pete Wishart wanted to ask the EU to publicly support another referendum on secession. The SNP would wreck the UK to serve the EU. International relations are a matter reserved to the UK government, but the SNP administration has been running a separate foreign office costing an unnecessary £27 million a year, with expensive properties around the world. It had set up a Scottish Affairs Office in the USA and more than 30 Scottish Development International offices around the world. These should cease with Brexit. Scotland had 9 per cent of MPs in the UK Parliament (59 out of 650) but only 0.7 per cent of Members of the European Parliament (6 out of 766). In which union did Scotland have more influence? John Lloyd noted, in the best recent book on Scotland's options, "At the same time as the EU and the more integrationist-leaning national leaders proclaim their commitment to making it more democratic, its most important moves are closed-door events. It is to this Union that the Scots nationalists, strongly sensitive to anything which smacks of undemocratic behaviour on the part of the Westminster government, propose to commit Scotland."[510]

Lloyd observed, "An irony of Scots nationalism in this context is that they seek, enthusiastically, to join a Union, most of whose members also ban secession or attempts to secede. In Spain's case, the state put leaders of the movement in jail, then hand down vicious sentences for peaceful political protest. In the United Kingdom, organization in favour of secession is protected."[511] Another irony for the SNP - the EU backed the Spanish government when it sentenced the Catalonian secessionist leaders to up to thirteen years in jail. What would Scotland 'win' by seceding? A decade of austerity, at best. Far less influence in the European parliament than it has at Westminster. Loss of its fishing industry, given back to Brussels. In 2014, the people of Scotland were far too sensible to choose to be weaker and poorer for no other gain. Nothing has changed since then.

Unity is strength

Some separatists have argued that it was hypocritical of the British government to deny Scotland the right to leave the UK when that government exercised the right to leave the EU. The two situations were quite different. The EU is an international organisation comprising twenty-seven member states. The UK is a single nation-state. The EU aspired to be a single nation-state, but it is not one now and never will be. There is no legal oppression or subjection of Scotland. There is equal protection for all under the law. As Salmond acknowledged in 2012 in his Foreword to 'Your Scotland – Your Referendum - A Consultation Document', "Scotland is not oppressed and we have no need to be liberated." The average turnout at the five Scotland-only elections for Holyrood since 1999 was 53.24 per cent. The average turnout in Scotland for the five all-UK general elections since 2001 was 64.7 per cent. Measured by turnout, Westminster had more democratic legitimacy in Scotland than did Holyrood. The SNP averaged 35.46 per cent of the votes cast in the Holyrood elections and 31.6 per cent in the general elections. 35.46 per cent of 53.24 per cent is 18.87 per cent. 31.6 per cent of 64.7 per cent is 20.45 per cent. Even when it peaked in the 2015 general election with 50 per cent of the vote, on a turnout of 71.1 per cent, this was only 35.5 per cent of the electorate. Hardly the 'unstoppable mass movement' some SNP members claimed.

Some Scottish nationalists falsely accused 'England' of being still in thrall to the empire, trapping it into reactionary views of its present and future. Some claimed that this nostalgia for empire fully explained why the majority did not want Scotland to leave the Union.[512] This accusation added an unnecessary level of explanation. Why not accept that people wanted to keep the country united because they preferred unity to division? It is never a good idea to hold a referendum on secession unless it is to confirm a clear national consensus for such a radical political change. In the world's thirteen cases of secession, outside the colonial context, in which a referendum has been held since 1945, the average majority for secession was 92 per cent. There is no such consensus in Scotland. The Savanta ComRes online poll of 1,008 Scottish adults aged over 16 of 6-13 August 2020 asked, "Should Scotland be an independent country?" It found support for secession at 49 per cent, 42 per cent were against and 9 per cent were undecided. A YouGov/*The Times* poll of 6-10 August 2020, of 1,142 Scottish adults aged over 16, asked, "Should Scotland be an independent country?" It found support for secession at 45 per cent, 40 per cent were against, and 9 per cent were undecided. 4 per cent said they would not vote and 1 per cent refused to answer.

As in the 1975 referendum on the UK staying in the EEC, the question in all these polls was loaded because it spelt out only one of the two options, contrary to the Electoral Commission's guidance. The SNP won the votes of only 45 per cent of the people of Scotland in the 2019 general election. The Survation survey of 1,008 Scottish people, conducted between 10 and 12 September 2020, found that 63 per cent said that "a second independence referendum is not a priority at this time." Asked about May 2021's Scottish election, 72 per cent said the election debate 'should be primarily focused on the economy and public services ahead of other issues such as Scottish independence'. Asked to choose the most important issues facing Scotland, only 11 per cent said constitutional affairs and independence. The majority oppose another secession referendum. The majority think that secession is not a priority. Crucially, the survey asked people how they would vote in a referendum with the question "should Scotland remain in the United

Kingdom or leave the United Kingdom?" The question rightly offered both options. When the undecided were excluded, 56 per cent said they would vote to remain in the UK, 44 per cent would vote to leave. All these polls showed less than 50 per cent support for secession.

Every time the SNP has fought a referendum on an issue of UK-wide import, it has lost – 2011, 2014 and 2016. It is less effective at delivering a vote than opinion polls suggested it would be. Secession could only be achieved by breaking down our bonds of solidarity and mutual respect. The SNP traded on divisiveness and disrespect. Even the prospect of secession brought political and economic uncertainty and social division and intolerance. Far better to turn to a far more noble independence cause, that of building an independent Britain. The world's multinational corporations cared little for solidarity, nations' rights to self-determination and democracy. These corporations preferred to deal with many small states rather than a few larger ones, because this increased their bargaining power.[513] Secession, devolution, federalism, regionalisation, privatisation, deregulation and selling off national assets all let multinational corporations operate more freely. Strong united nation-states like Britain are our best defence against predatory global capital.

By contrast, the people of Britain are very attached to the unity of our country. A poll in *The Times* of 26 May 1995 found that only a fifth of the British public backed the call for Scotland to be independent. The 2018 British Social Attitudes survey found that 85 per cent of people in England want Scotland to remain part of the UK.[514] The Savanta ComRes survey of British public opinion for the *Daily Telegraph*, reported on 14 November 2019, found that 41 per cent opposed holding a second referendum in Scotland, 24 per cent were for it. An online poll of 1,384 adults was undertaken between 17 and 18

June 2020.[515] The report in the pro-SNP paper *The National* said, "The independent YouGov poll organised by YesCymru, the non-party campaign for an independent Wales, found that more than a third of people in England do not want the Union of the United Kingdom to continue. With don't knows and those who refused to answer removed, the polling has shown 35% of people in England now favour English independence – in line with several surveys of English opinion in recent years." It could perhaps have emphasised that the majority – 65 per cent - supported the unity of Britain!

The question in the poll was, 'Should England be an independent country?' This is the kind of one-sided question that the Electoral Commission says should not be asked. 51 per cent said No, 27 said Yes, 18 were Don't knows, and 4 refused to answer. Only 27 per cent of those asked, not 35 per cent, responded that England should be independent. The question was vague. Some respondents may have been answering the question, should England be independent of the EU? Our union is a success, and we should improve it even more now that we have decided to stay united and to become independent of the EU. Britain is our place, our home. All who live here and see their future here are members of the nation of Britain. We share a single British citizenship. We hold what everybody calls a British passport, even though it is issued by the United Kingdom.

The people of Scotland are members of the proud and historic nation of Scotland, and the people of Wales are members of the proud and historic nation of Wales. A nation does not have to have its own state to be respected as a nation. Britain is one nation, a nation composed of three nations: England, Scotland and Wales, a family of nations gathered into one. We can be British and English, British and Scottish, British and Welsh. Our common nationality of being British unites us.

As one might expect with Britain, this arrangement is most unusual, if not unique. Far more unites us than divides us. Some secessionists claimed that the English people had a conservative culture incompatible with Scottish values of social justice and compassion. But polls found that Scottish, Welsh, and English people were united in support of the values of tolerance, solidarity, and justice. Scottish Social Attitudes surveys found that Scottish people were no more left-wing than English people.[516] "Scotland is more social democratic than England – but the difference is only modest" and "Scotland has become less – not more – social democratic since the advent of devolution."[517]

Attitudes to the EU were also far less different than the SNP claimed. Ian Montagu observed, "the proportion of those in Scotland who favour a *looser* relationship with the EU has not differed dramatically in recent years from the rest of Britain. According to comparable data from the high-quality British and Scottish Social Attitudes surveys, levels of Euroscepticism in both Scotland and Britain as a whole were well above 50% in each of the three years prior to the referendum, with the most recent available reading suggesting that by 2016, Euroscepticism in Scotland had increased to 66% (compared with 76% across Britain as a whole). [...] as amongst voters elsewhere in Britain, the majority of voters in Scotland wish to end freedom of movement whilst maintaining free trade with the EU. The most recent wave of fieldwork undertaken on both sides of the border (in October 2017) suggests that support for retaining free trade stands at 90% in Scotland compared with 88% across Britain as a whole, while the equivalent figures for ending freedom of movement are 59% and 64% respectively."[518]

The 2019 Scottish Social Attitudes survey found that 19 per cent of Scots wanted to leave the EU. 34 per cent wanted to stay in but reduce its powers. So, 53 per cent took a broadly Eurosceptic position. Curtice and Montagu summed up, "In the period since 2013, at least, over half of people in Scotland have consistently backed one or other form of Euroscepticism."[519] 34 per cent wanted to stay in and keep its powers the same. 5 per cent wanted to stay in and increase the EU's powers, 4 per cent wanted to work to form a single European government. 43 per cent took a pro-EU position.[520] MSP Neil Findlay in an article calling for 'Redeveloping the Scotland United campaign' (*Morning Star*, 2 February 2021) recounted how Scotland United was formed in 1992 to campaign for a multi-option referendum on Scotland's future. It failed. Findlay urged a re-run of that failed campaign, to unite 'people who support constitutional change, be it independence or devo-max, in a drive for a multi-option referendum'. This drew the line of division in the wrong place. Why should we unite with people who want to tear our country apart? Why should we unite against people who want to maintain our Union as it is? Whatever people thought about devolution, if they opposed secession, they were allies.

We have an overarching national working class culture that unites us all. We live and work as one class, one nation. Now we need to reach a higher level of national unity, respecting and enjoying our various social and cultural achievements, yet committed to union. We can appreciate that people have passionate commitments to their local cultural and historical traditions while recognising that this can happily consort with commitment to political and economic union. We need more great transport, energy and infrastructure, projects to unite the whole country. Concrete achievements strengthen our unity. Constitutional tinkering does not. It has been encouraging to see the Johnson government advocating that UK government-funded projects in Scotland will be branded as such, and that UK national policies that benefit those living in Scotland will be clearly seen as being British ones. Too often the SNP has taken credit for developments for which they have not been responsible.

To demand that Wales, or Scotland, or the North-East, all be treated as separate economic units would destroy the chances of success that a united country can achieve. We need to plan for the future, treating the whole of Britain as one economic union. This will enable the economies of scale and the interconnectedness that a successful economy needs. To succeed, this plan must give due weight to advancing the interests of all parts of the country. The UK-EU Trade and Cooperation Agreement of December 2020 exposed the feebleness of SNP claims that Scotland must depend on the EU. As part of an independent Britain, Scotland will thrive (despite the SNP's poor performance). Sturgeon said an Agreement could never be achieved, and if it was, it would be so bad that it would put wind in the SNP's sails. The Agreement burst the SNP's hot air balloon.

In March 2019, Humza Yousaf, SNP Justice Minister, tweeted, "Not voting against No Deal is simply unforgivable, the chaos it would unleash would be catastrophic." Yet during 2019, SNP MPs – under instruction from SNP HQ – repeatedly voted against the deals that May proposed. Blackford said in October 2019, "If Scotland is dragged out of the EU against its will with no-deal it will be economically catastrophic for Scotland and will cost 100,000 Scottish jobs." In December 2020 the SNP voted for no-deal by voting against the Trade and Cooperation Agreement. All trade unions are gearing up to fight looming unemployment, especially among younger age groups. The backbone for this comes from Britain-wide solidarity, as must the fight to keep the country together in the face of the attempts to tear it apart. As John Lloyd concluded, "Scotland, in the twenty-first century, is both as free and secure a nation as the world of the early twenty-first century allows. It would be worse than a mistake, a crime, to hazard that for an independence which can bring nothing better."[521] A continued and renewed Union is better both for the people of Scotland and for their fellow British citizens. Our unity enriched us all, economically, culturally, and morally. Scotland's essential interests will be secure in the Union, far more than they ever were in the EU.

Chapter 20
Exchange of mind

Some thoughts about thought[522]

We should always look for the positive in everything. Too many people, especially in the 'left', look for the negative in everything. As the philosopher Hegel wrote, "The learner always begins by finding fault, but the scholar sees the positive merit in everything." Everything, everybody, has a weakness, but to focus on finding and exploiting that weakness is immoral and one-sided. 'Critical theory' is a caricature of Marxism, and the 'critical practice' carried out by some on the left involves jumping to wrong conclusions, making false accusations and dividing the working class. It is not a good argument against a law or a statement that it could be used in a bad cause. Even a good law can be abused. That it can be abused says nothing about its truth or falsity. Censorship of the most extreme and vile hate speech does not lead inevitably to censorship of all dissent. Banning anti-vaccination lies does not mean the end of free speech. Shouting 'fire' in a crowded theatre, when there is no fire, is not an exercise of free speech but an act endangering, not saving, people's lives.

This is the 'thin end of the wedge' argument, 'the slippery slope', whereby any curtailment of freedom, even in a good cause, is seen as the harbinger of fascism. When the House of Commons in 1976 debated the introduction of seat belts in cars, Enoch Powell and Michael Foot successfully objected that this would infringe our civil liberties. The Act was finally passed in 1981. There was no 'slippery slope' to the destruction of all our civil liberties. Blackout rules in WW2 infringed our civil liberties. Anyone who broke the rules endangered themselves, their families and neighbours. Having to wear hard hats on building sites infringed the civil liberties of building workers. Making it compulsory to wear seatbelts in cars is called the end of all freedom, mass vaccination against Covid-19 is called totalitarianism run mad. Any extension of democracy leads straight to the guillotine or the gulag. But there was no slippery slope from the Enlightenment to Auschwitz. There is no 'is' from a 'could'.

Slippery slope arguments are like 'lumping together' claims. Some people who voted to leave are racists, so they all are, so there is something intrinsically racist about Brexit. But some does not equal all. Some lump together Bolsanaro, Trump and Johnson, stressing superficial similarities, ignoring the vast political, historical and cultural differences between the three nations that elected these leaders. To say that an act is understandable says nothing about the act. To say that an act is understandable is not to justify it. To say we understand the causes of a war is not to justify that war, just as to understand the causes of a disease is not to justify the disease. A statement of fact is ethically neutral. A fact does not justify anything. To describe is not to defend. To explain is not to advocate. There is no 'ought' from an 'is', as the Enlightenment philosopher David Hume observed. There is no 'is' from an 'ought'.

Generalisations about other people usually say more about the person making the judgement than about the people being judged. Premature generalisation is the sign of pop psychology and cod sociology. The poet Alexander Pope wrote, "whatever is, is right."[523] Some seem to think that 'whatever is, is wrong'. Both statements are too simple to be true. One swallow does not make a summer. 'For example' is not an argument. An anecdote is not a case. Someone who insults a whole people is more likely to be speaking accurately about herself than about the whole people. Belittlers of Britain reveal their limits not Britain's. That patriotism is the last refuge of the scoundrel does not prove that every patriot is a scoundrel. It is a statement about the scoundrel not about patriotism. Some discounted evidence about other people's attitudes, claiming that they knew better than people themselves what they 'really' thought. This revealed the prejudice of the claimant, not the prejudice of the people. When people guessed at other people's motives, they usually revealed only their own motives. The greedy think everybody is greedy, the lustful think everybody is lustful, the corrupt think everybody is corrupt.

Misanthropy says all too much about the misanthrope. Dystopias are misanthropic and therefore reactionary, reactionary and therefore misanthropic. The genre of horror fiction is basically dystopian, as in the works of the Marquis de Sade and Edgar Allan Poe. Horror story writers seem more than half in love with not very easeful forms of death, visited on other people. As the historian Peter Linebaugh pointed out, "the Gothic is the attitude of overwhelming forces of death, famine, war, pestilence." Seeing death as overwhelming is a germ of fascism, witness the Spanish Falangists' slogan of 'Long live death!' All too many writers of fantasy and science fiction were reactionaries. Jules Verne was a lifelong Catholic. He rejected one of the most important scientific achievements of his time, saying he was 'entirely opposed to the theories of Darwin'. He supported Louis Napoleon's regime and opposed the socialist Paris Commune of 1871. In the 1890s he sided with the anti-Semites in the Dreyfus Affair. H. G. Wells was a eugenicist. In The Time Machine he portrayed a working class of sub-human Morlocks. H. P. Lovecraft was a thoroughly reactionary anti-Semite.

C. S. Lewis opposed Darwin, science and democracy, writing, "democracy always in the end destroys education." Aldous Huxley's Brave New World was another dystopia: Huxley always supported the Eugenics Society. Like so many other reactionaries, he called for 'an aristocracy of the intellect' and wrote of 'the irreconcilable differences between human beings'. J. R. R. Tolkien supported Franco's fascist regime. Eric Blair (George Orwell) grassed colleagues to MI5 and wrote two anti-communist dystopias which have ever since been compulsory reading in secondary schools. '1984' contains scenes of torture porn, which should not be forced on any child. More recent fantasy writers have given us their opinions on the real world. Philip Pullman campaigned against Brexit and concluded, "We're done for really as a nation." Margaret Atwood said, "It is another predictable mess that people have got drawn into because a big honking pack of lies was told about it." She said that if she could wave her magic wand she would "cause us to go back in time and maybe avoid this rash, unconsidered and badly informed moment. I think lies were told and I don't think people thought through the consequences, because the people who did this didn't think it was going to pass." She was commenting on what she had read about the campaign, not addressing the issues at stake.

We need to analyse each new situation, not take a single slice through it and then subordinate all other considerations to that slice. We should discuss the merits of issues, not leap to premature accusations of bad faith or bad motive. A fact cannot be racist. If somebody says that 13 of the 18 people she saw not wearing a mask on public transport were young black men, this is not a racist remark. It states a fact about the people she saw. A statement about a fact is not at the same time a statement about the state of mind of the person making the statement. It is not a statement about the person making the remark, not a giveaway by that person. It is not about what the person thinks about the fact. To confuse the two is subjective idealism. Some have accused people who voted leave of 'borderline racism', a charge impossible to disprove. If it is impossible to refute, it is unfalsifiable and therefore unscientific. The accusation fails. Some ultra-lefts said, "Britain is a racist nation." Wouldn't that mean that all black Britons are racists? Or aren't these ultra-lefts counting black people as part of the nation?

That someone makes a racist remark does not prove that the person is – irredeemably – a racist. Such an absolutist accusation is worthy of a witchfinder. That a person is right on one issue does not mean they are right on any other. "Put not your trust in princes." To act in order to be an example to others is vainglorious. We should not slavishly chant 'Tories bad, Labour good'. MSP Neil Findlay wrote of 'the real enemy, the Tories' in an article in *Morning Star* of 2 February 2021. Marx and Engels in The Communist Manifesto focused on capitalism as the enemy, never mentioning any political party. Karl Popper accused Marxism of being unfalsifiable. Yet there have been the workers' revolutions that Marx foresaw. If there had never been any workers' revolution anywhere, then the prediction would have been falsified. So the forecast was falsifiable and proved not to be false. Almost everything Marx wrote was falsifiable, and has been found to be true not false: the dangers of recurring slumps, the increasing concentration of capital, the growth of monopolies, the growing dominance of finance capital, the globalisation of capital (in 1848!), the development of imperialism, that the reserve army of labour holds down wages, etc.

Some people, when you criticise something they back, like the EU, then imagine it as reformed and think they have rebuffed the criticism when they have only evaded it. Analogy is not identity. One can compare anything to anything. We should ask, does this comparison assist understanding? Most analogies are a lazy substitute for analysing the unique situation before us. So are hypothetical statements. Alternative history really is bunk. "'If' doesn't exist", as the tennis champion Rafael Nadal - clearly a materialist philosopher - said. If it were true that we live in a 'post-truth' world, then we do not. The slogan contradicts itself. We should take relativism at its word – it cannot be true. Similarly with postmodernism. One of its advocates, Ryszard Kapuscinski, wrote, "The past does not exist."[524] Postmodernism is now, thankfully, part of the past, so on its own word it does not exist now. It is a matter of opinion that turquoise is a beautiful colour. It is not a matter of opinion that turquoise is a colour. It is part of what we understand when we use the words turquoise and colour. Some call Britain a 'post-imperial' society. To define a society in terms of its past is as useful as calling Britain a 'post-feudal' society or calling a novel 'post-modern'.

Key is independence of mind, achieved by social interaction, including debate.[525] As William Blake wrote, "without contraries is no progression." Thomas Jefferson wrote, "Difference of opinion leads to inquiry, and inquiry to the truth." Good policy, good science and good laws all developed in, not apart from, controversy. Explicitly presenting both options is one of the good features of Britain's adversarial political and legal systems. One has to imagine the best case that the opposition can make. One has to put oneself in the opposition's shoes. Thus, the adversarial approach, paradoxically, encourages empathy and mutual understanding. We progress through dialogue. Engaging with other thinkers and writers, past and contemporary, sharpens the wits. We should encourage workers' independence of mind, through exchange of thought. This is a mental discipline, a refusal to be swayed by fashion or dogma, primarily an internal discipline, backed by external discipline by union or Party when necessary.

Workers are thinking beings, so we do not make excuses for them. All workers think. All acts are conscious; there was no such thing as a spontaneous, thoughtless action, born out of just emotion - that would be to say that the class was mindless. Workers are responsible for what they think and do. We treat the working class with respect. The CPGB's approach was that it had 'the task of guiding the unthinking masses'.[526] Everybody who was not a communist was deemed to be unthinking. Communists were supposed to lead this unthinking mass, by whatever means. This 'vanguard' concept of a party was corrupting, undemocratic and of course ineffective. Workers did not like being told they were stupid, backward and needed to have their consciousness (if any) raised. Thought and language are social, not private. Isolation stultifies, notwithstanding the myths of Robinson Crusoe, the scholar in an ivory tower and the lonely genius. Claiming to be above society – the self-regarding myth of 'the outsider' – is anti-social. So are the slogans 'Not my president', 'not in my name', 'still European'. All are refusals to recognise legitimate majority democratic decisions. All express independence from society and are declarations not of independence but of irresponsibility. Similarly, those who decry 'the idiotic electorate' presumably are not including themselves in this insulting description.

We can appreciate art inspired by religion, just as we can love France without wanting to stay in the EU. We should avoid false apologies of the form 'I'm sorry you feel that way'. This states my attitude to your feeling. It implies that you should not feel that way, that the problem is the way you feel. It is a refusal to take responsibility for whatever action of mine caused that feeling. It is not an apology. An apology is a regretful acknowledgement of one's own offence or failure. We need to focus on changing the present state of society, not on speculating about the origins of human society, or about human nature. Such studies usually start and end in idealist

313

abstractions. We are indeed material beings and part of that material reality is our biological sex. This is not a social construction; it is an objective reality. Our sex is not determined by our 'self-report'. It is philosophical idealism to believe that what people say about themselves has to be true. It is philosophical idealism to believe that somebody's making a statement makes it true. A hate crime is not created by somebody stating that one has been committed.

Unmoored political opinions, either for the government or against the government, were often disabling rather than enabling, a waste of energy and time. We have all met people who have opinions about everything, who seem to have no time left ever to do anything. Some talk a lot because they do not want to listen to other people's views and ideas. Those who do nothing but criticise the government are as much in thrall to the government as its diehard supporters. Both think, wrongly, that politics begins and ends with the government's actions. Treating the government as the sole focus of politics boosts the government. All too much criticism in politics is just captious – they're damned if they do, damned if they don't. When whatever someone does is criticised, the criticism becomes banal and trivial. This kind of criticism cancels itself out, damning the critic not the criticised.

One cannot self-identify as a communist. Communism is not an opinion; it is a commitment. A communist is someone who works as a member of their country's communist party. One can call oneself what one likes, but the test is practice – are you working as a member of the communist party? Words without deeds, theory without practice, are nothing. Shakespeare has Iago complain about Cassio, "Mere prattle without practice is all his soldiership."[527] Of course, Iago was slandering Cassio. We know from Desdemona that Cassio had 'shar'd dangers' with Othello.[528] Later in the same play, Roderigo justly charges

314

Iago, "Faith, I have heard too much, for your words and performances are no kin together."[529] More recently, the author Patrick Ness wrote, "You do not write your life with words ... You write it with actions. What you think is not important. It is only important what you *do*."

In praise of tolerance

The zero-tolerance policy towards crime that the liberal President Clinton imposed – 'three strikes and you're out' - caused massive injustices, with overly severe punishments for minor crimes. Cancel-culture is all too similar: purist in theory, intolerant and bullying in practice. Ideological purity is very like racial purity, idealist in theory, vicious in practice. Purity is nullity. Utpal Dholakia wrote, "A core characteristic of canceling (relative to other rejections) is that to many (but not all) observers, the canceler's punitive actions appear disproportionate to the magnitude of the transgression. Relatedly, when canceling someone, the canceler bypasses the legal due process. There is no complaint, no trial, no prosecution, no conviction, and no presumption of 'innocent until proven guilty'. The canceler's judgment that the transgressor is at fault is sufficient to trigger punitive action. "Social canceling is not based on a balanced assessment of the transgression or any absolute criterion of wrongdoing. Because it's a visceral response and relies on one particular shared understanding of the transgression (through the lens of a political or a social ideology), one side of the story so to speak, every canceling campaign is necessarily grounded in bias. However, the lack of tolerance for opposing views, the restriction of free speech by coercion or censorship, and the disproportionate punishment given to the canceled entity are separate processes, marshaled in support of punitive action."[530]

In November 2020, Cambridge University's Council proposed a new rule requiring dons to be 'respectful of the diverse identities of others'. The Campaign for Cambridge Freedoms, a group of academics, succeeded in opposing the proposed change. These dons wrote, "The bottom line is that in future we might face disciplinary charges and even dismissal for mockery of ideas and individuals with which we disagree. The University has no right to demand that we be respectful towards all beliefs and practices: on the contrary, we have a right, in some cases practically a duty, to satirize and to mock them. [...] We should not be expected to respect patently false opinions concerning vaccination or climate change [...] Nor should the University demand respect for all political or religious identities, from white nationalism to Islamic fundamentalism. But we must permit them to exist. That is exactly what 'tolerance' means."

Dr Arif Ahmed, a fellow at Gonville and Caius and a Senior Lecturer in philosophy, told *Times Higher Education*, "The problem with requiring 'respect' of all opinions and 'identities' is that 'respect' is vague, subjective and restrictive. For instance, David Hume certainly wrote disrespectfully about the Christian religion. Am I being disrespectful to that opinion or identity if I teach or endorse his views? Who gets to decide?" Tolerance means 'willingness to accept behaviour and beliefs that are different from your own, although you might not agree with or approve of them'.[531] The verb tolerate means "allow the existence or occurrence of without authoritative interference, leave unmolested, not be harmed by, find or treat as endurable."[532] Tolerance of one's opponents means not acting to ban the expression of views, it means not punishing people for their beliefs. It means allowing the free expression of beliefs. But free expression in turn means there is the freedom to debate, to challenge, with whatever words– not actions - people

316

choose.

There is no obligation to respect any ideas. The noun respect is defined as 'deferential esteem felt or shown towards person or quality'. The verb respect means "regard with deference, esteem, or honour; avoid degrading or insulting or injuring or interfering with or interrupting, treat with consideration, refrain from offending or corrupting or tempting."[533] Saying that we should respect every view and every identity does not mean that every view and identity is worthy of respect. The first statement is about how we should behave; the second is about the view. Asking for respect for opinions or persons is demanding a higher standard of behaviour, but paradoxically this accompanies demands for social sanctioning, shaming and even banning – precisely the kind of 'authoritative interference' that tolerance forbids. To insist on respect is to move beyond verbal disagreement to trying to enforce certain behaviours. Trying to achieve respectful behaviour by imposing it breaches the laws of toleration. This striving for more moral exchanges erodes the walls of civility and fails to reach even the minimum standards of toleration. The effort to achieve higher standards by recourse to administrative measures breaches the rules of debate. Oxford University maintains the distinction between tolerance and respect, and tells its students and academics that the University cannot uphold 'respect', because "not all theories deserve equal respect."

Black Lives Matter

The police killing of a black man, George Floyd, in the US city of Minneapolis on 25 May 2020 provoked a huge response of anger and revulsion across the world.[534] In this country, it triggered lively debate and demands to address the issues for black people, especially young black people, of police

317

harassment (a daily experience for many), and widespread injustice – open or tacit – in employment and elsewhere. We need to end inequity in policing, employment, conditions of work, everywhere. Capitalism has always thrived on setting one group of workers against another, on whatever specious grounds it can find. Workers must always resist the employer's attempts to divide us. A good starting point for fighting racism is to grasp that there is only one race: the human race. Unity, not division, must be our watchword. 'Race' was a socially constructed idea that can have devastating effects on people's lives.

Every worker in Britain, regardless of ethnicity, is part of the British working class. An injury to one is an injury to all. People who lived and worked in Britain were British. Some people had an Asian, African, or other background, but when you lived and worked in Britain and had British citizenship, you were British. Having an Asian or Afro-Caribbean background did not make you Asian or African or Caribbean. (If you go back far enough, we all have an African background.) Many people were also Scottish or Welsh but when you had British citizenship, you were British. Identity was not arbitrary or self-chosen, it was material, based on where you lived and worked. In Britain, we are for equal rights for all people - black people and white people, men and women, gay people and straight people, disabled people and non-disabled people and transgender people and cisgender people. We have passed the 1995 Disability Rights Act and the 2010 Equality Act.

Black Lives Matter was a mass movement against the unjust treatment of people on grounds of race. Its positive aspects outweighed the negative. Focusing on the misstatements of some of its spokespersons was not fair. We must not take the part for the whole. Very few BLM supporters wanted to tear down Churchill's statue. Young people, all people, were right

318

to condemn racism in all its forms in theory and in practice. We must not let the ultra-left or the openly racist ultra-right divide us. Instead, we as a class must work in unity and take responsibility for the way Britain is run and where it is heading. Together we must take control of our country, get involved and shape a future for the needs of us all. The ultra-left agreed with the League of Empire Loyalists that the British people gained from the Empire. Only the capitalist class gained from empire. The empire created no wealth, only redistributed it by stealing the wealth that other peoples produced.

Some leftists pushed ideas of 'white privilege', looking to the history of empire to claim that the (mostly) white working class of Britain benefited from crumbs dropped from the tables of imperialists, particularly from the vast profits of the vile and criminal slave trade. What benefits? After centuries of supposedly receiving the loot from empire, as late as 1911, of every thousand children born in the five major boroughs of South Wales, 380 died.[535] Gwydion Williams observed, "Maybe one-twentieth of British society had a serious involvement with the non-white portions of the British Empire. For most of the society, it was something distant and exotic and they never missed it once it was gone. It may have helped Britain's industrial revolution, although other European nations industrialised with few colonies or no colonies."[536]

This crumbs theory was a variant of the discredited trickle-down notion, that the wealth of the rich would – eventually - somehow reach the poor. The notion of 'white privilege' is a variant of this idea. The claim that every white worker enjoys a privileged position over every black colleague divides the working class. Poverty is less in Britain than in non-industrialised countries because the more highly industrialised a country is, the more productive is its labour power and the greater the value that its working class produces. Workers can

319

through struggle make some inroads into the value they create. The employing class never gives workers anything; workers have to fight for everything – wages, conditions, the weekend, the welfare state, the NHS, etc. Welfare measures are no gifts but are paid for by taxes on workers' wages.

Nation

Nationalism has been defined as "a cultural movement that includes prominently a program whose goal is a sovereign state giving expression to core collective values."[537] The British working class uses its creative and intellectual powers to develop its skills, arts, culture (including values and language) within the nation to improve life physically and mentally. Stalin defined a nation as "a historically constituted, stable community of people, formed on the basis of a common language, territory, economic life, and psychological make-up manifested in a common culture." By this definition, Britain is clearly a nation. Note, Stalin did not write that a nation had to have a state to be defined as a nation, so Scotland, England and Wales could all be nations. A novel contribution to Marxist thinking on the national question is to identify the British working class with the nation of Britain, they are the same, they are synonymous – a national working class, a working class nation. The Communist Manifesto said, "the struggle of the proletariat with the bourgeoisie is at first a national struggle. The proletariat of each country must, of course, first of all settle accounts with its own bourgeoisie."

Britain has developed as a working class nation. In Britain, the end of feudalism meant the end of the peasantry as a class. Workers on the land became a part of the wider working class, defined as all those who worked, with hand and brain, to make a living. Workers owned only their labour power, which they had to sell to survive, as against the tiny minority employing class, who owned the means of production. All who go to work in Britain are working class: our two-class line leads directly to our concept of a working class nation. The British working class has for around two centuries comprised the vast majority of the population. Historian David Rollison explained: the working class is "a class of individuals without capital, dependent on wages earned by working for others. [...] this is the condition of us all. We grow up knowing we have to work, get a job, hopefully a long-term, 'regular' one. Success in pursuit of wages makes us independent, i.e. not 'dependent' on hand-outs from others."538

Workers' nationalism is based on a renewal of skills and industry - because the working class is industry and industry is the basis of independence. The working class must take responsibility for industry and for our independence as a nation. In so doing, we take responsibility for democracy. Only nation states uphold and advance democracy. Democracy is imperilled outside the nation state. The Irish trade unionist, patriot and socialist James Connolly said, 'I deem that to be patriotic which is in the interest of the working class!' It is about national self-respect, not about dominating other nations, just as respecting oneself as a person does not mean disrespecting anybody else. A YouGov poll of June 2020 found that 67 per cent of British people – both white and ethnic minority - were proud of being British. Being proud of your country does not mean being proud of everything that every one of its governments has ever done over the centuries.

This workers' nationalism is a precondition of internationalism, which is based on the equality of nations. This is a policy for all nations, all workers, to assert themselves and challenge the international power of capital. An accusation endlessly repeated was that 'nationalism caused two world

321

wars'. Nationalism is an idea, or a set of ideas. Ideas do not start wars. Governments start wars. World War One was a war between rival empires, whose governments exploited ideas of nationalism to persuade their peoples to fight 'for King and country'. Another all too familiar claim was that all nationalism is bad because Hitler was a nationalist. Hitler advocated domination not nationalism. He wanted to enforce a Reich - Reich means empire - a resurrection of the German Holy Roman Empire, to end all other countries' independence. He aimed to destroy the nation-state system and impose an imperial order. As Goebbels said in 1943, "the Reich will one day rule all Europe, [...] and, from then on, the road to world domination is practically spread out before us." The Nazi drive to enforce a fascist version of imperialism, not nationalism, caused the Second World War.

The EU promotes the belief that nationalism is stupid and backward. EU Commission President Jean-Claude Juncker insulted patriotic people across Europe when he said on 23 May 2019, "These populists, nationalist, stupid nationalists, they are in love with their own country." Some saw Brexit not as a mass movement based on genuine national self-respect and a sense of national interest, but as a mass delusional ignorance created by wicked leaders. This is a repeat of the old imperialist claim that national liberation movements were not based on a people's demands but derived only from cynical manipulation by corrupt demagogues. Yet, paradoxically, the EU wanted to break down the nationalism that people already had, to replace it with a love of Europe. Why was a Europe-wide nationalism so much better than a country-wide nationalism?

The arguments against Brexit were very often the same as the arguments against working class movements, trade unions and socialist and communist parties. These were allegedly not created by workers seeking to advance their own interests but were created by self-seeking elites ('trade union bosses', conspiratorial extremists). The common theme is that ordinary people, other people, cannot think for themselves, indeed cannot really think at all. They, we, are supposedly driven by emotion, not governed by reason. 'Bolshevik', the Russian word for majority, was twisted into meaning emotional, irrational. In some private schools, the phrase 'in a bolsh' meant 'in a very bad mood'. EU leaders from the start called for a single European state. Konrad Adenauer said, "My dream is that one day we might be able to applaud a United States of Europe." Pierre Moscovici said, "It is essential for the EU to become a political power and not just a group of nation states." In his farewell speech on 19 January 1994 Jacques Delors said that the euro 'cannot exist without the counterpart of a European Government'. Guy Verhofstadt said, "The Constitution is the capstone of a European Federal State."

This state was no partnership of equals. Germany and France dominated all the other member states. They made the rules, they used the euro to advantage their economies, they enforced austerity on the other states. The northern states dominated the southern states. A single state demands a single citizenship. According to Article 9 of the 1992 Treaty on European Union, "Every national of a Member State shall be a citizen of the Union. Citizenship of the Union shall be additional to national citizenship and shall not replace it." But in the 2001 Grzelczyk case, the European Court of Justice declared that "Union citizenship is destined to be the fundamental status of nationals of the Member States." In December 2017 YouGov asked the citizens of seven countries this question: "Martin Schulz, head of the Social Democratic Party in Germany (SPD), spoke at the SPD party conference about his vision to transform the EU into the United States of Europe by 2025 - with a common constitutional treaty. EU

323

members who do not agree with this federal constitution would then have to leave the EU. Do you support or reject this vision of the United States of Europe?" Britain had the lowest support for Schulz's vision of a United States of Europe, at just 10 per cent, with 43 per cent against. In Germany 30 per cent of people approved, 33 per cent disapproved. In Finland and Sweden 13 per cent of people backed the idea, in Denmark and Norway 12 per cent. Only in France did more people back the proposal than opposed it, by 28 to 26 per cent. In the September 2017 German federal election, Schulz's party recorded its worst-ever performance and he resigned as its leader.

Chapter 21
Building for independence

The UK at last left the economic institutions and jurisdiction of the EU at the end of 2020, with the Trade and Cooperation Agreement that the establishment had said was impossible. With independence, our future is in our hands. We can rebuild industry; we can restore the economy after the virus. We need industry, apprenticeships, a good public health system, better infrastructure, and national unity. We must run the economy in the interests of manufacturing industry and the whole country, instead of in the interests of international finance capital and parts of London. We need to stop relying on finance to save us. Prioritising finance led to the 2008 crash and to the loss of self-reliance and resilience that has cost us so dear. Outside the EU we were free to use 'state aid' - forbidden by the EU – to remedy our over-reliance on finance capital.

Nationalising the railways, water, and energy; building council houses; a national investment fund; a national investment bank; linking public sector procurement to a regionally balanced industrial strategy; these were all good policies. When we were inside the EU, we could not implement these policies. EU treaties bound us into not nationalising; bound us into not investing the necessary sums into building more homes; stopped us creating a national investment fund or a national investment bank; stopped us backing public sector procurement; and stopped us developing a regionally balanced industrial strategy. Only outside the EU are we free to carry out these policies.

We should implement an industrial strategy, a programme of national industrial recovery. We need to take control of the economy - that is, people's livelihoods – and produce the values – goods and services – that we need. We needed to develop

325

industry, to plan the development of Britain as a coherent and balanced whole. The 1945 Distribution of Industry Act had given the government powers to direct firms to areas where they were needed. The 1947 Town and Country Planning Act used Industrial Development Certificates to get investment into areas that needed industry. We needed to demand of capitalists, if you want to sell goods here, you must make them here. The Conservative government of the early 1950s made Pfizer produce its drugs here if it wanted to sell them here.

A country should produce all the goods and services needed to maintain the health and security of the nation. That means curtailing the market-led globalisation of international finance capital. We should immediately expand and accelerate all public construction and procurement projects – infrastructure, social housing, schools, hospitals – taking the opportunity to make them energy-efficient, with a public sector job and training guarantee. It should be part of a permanent system for ending the unemployment that has scarred all economies since the Industrial Revolution. Every person of working age able and willing to work who cannot find work in the private sector at the minimum wage should be offered a public-sector job or training at the minimum wage. Such a scheme, by guaranteeing work for all those able and willing to work, would fulfil the old trade union demand of 'work or maintenance'.

Invest to rebuild

To recover we needed to increase our manufacturing from 10 per cent of GDP to more like 15 per cent. Christopher Nieper, the chief executive of over-50s fashion brand David Nieper, said in November 2020, "Manufacturing in Britain makes business accountable and allows control over each step of the production process. Offshoring manufacturing is essentially offshoring responsibility and indeed pollution. Currently two-thirds of emissions from UK clothing occur overseas. It's not acceptable to shift the problem to where it's out of sight and out of mind." We need to reshore as much manufacturing as possible. To make things here, we need to invest here. Our investment has been far too low for far too long. Gross investment from 2005 to 2016 was 17 per cent of GDP per year, our social rate of return was 8 per cent and our growth rate just 1.4 per cent. The world average for the same years was investment 26 per cent, social rate of return 14 per cent, and growth rate 3.5 per cent. Only 2.7 per cent of our GDP (down from 3.6 per cent in 2008) has gone into the most productive forms of investment, in machinery and equipment.

Public sector net investment was planned to rise by 23 per cent in 2020-21, 20 per cent in 2021-22, 9 per cent in 2022-23, 5 per cent in 2023-24 and 5 per cent in 2024-25. This was the biggest public sector investment programme for 40 years. For years the *Guardian*, quite rightly, denounced successive governments' austerity policies and their obsession with cutting the deficit as the top priority. But when Johnson pledged to increase public spending on education and infrastructure, the *Guardian* urged prioritising cutting the deficit. Government debt does not impose a 'burden' on our grandchildren. Government debt does not have to be repaid like household debt or company debt. A country's central bank can convert government bonds into central bank money, which does not have to be repaid any more than a five-pound note must be repaid. Government bonds shift purchasing power over time. Some think that we get lots of goods from lots of countries, so we do not need an industrial policy: other people will always supply us. But world markets are uncertain and volatile. Relying on long supply chains and distant supply sources is risky. Other buyers might have deeper pockets.

Paying for imports puts a burden on the rest of the economy.

Economist John Mills wrote, "Since 2000, the cumulative value of the UK's balance deficit has been close to £1 trillion. To finance this very substantial sum, which is equal to about half our annual GDP, not only have we had to borrow large sums from abroad, we have also sold off huge swathes of our national assets. These include most of our ports and airports, our football clubs, our power and utility companies, billions of pounds worth of commercial and residential properties, and much else. An ONS report produced in 2014 showed that by then as much as 29% of UK annual gross value added was generated by foreign owned companies."[539] It was essential to our recovery to rebuild our manufacturing skills. No industrial economy can grow sustainably without investment in human skills. We needed to invest in education and training but spending on these fell from 4.9 per cent of GDP in 2012/13 to 4.1 per cent in 2017/18. We need to be educating and training more young British people to higher standards. We need to invest in our young people. They have every right to quality apprenticeships, affordable education, decent well-paid jobs, affordable homes, a better life. We need to have universal full fibre (one gigabyte a second), fibre optic cables from local exchanges direct to all premises. South Korea has 99 per cent coverage, we have only 6 per cent. The government has made only £200 million available to increase access to less than half of all premises by 2025. It should be in all new-build homes.

As Mills put it, to make sure that "a competitive environment actually delivers the investment and export-led recovery, we need to ensure that manufacturing industry has access on favourable and plentiful terms to the finance needed to make it happen. There is ample evidence in the UK that banks are reluctant to lend to manufacturing industry. [...]Lending decisions which may be prudent case by case for banks do not, however, necessarily add up to a strategy which makes sense for the economy as a whole. This is because the total returns to the wider economy, especially on the most productive forms of investment, vastly exceed the private returns to banks. Bank lending to industry therefore needs to be firmly guided and possibly underwritten by the state, as has indeed been done to support companies generally during the current coronavirus pandemic. Concentration should not, however, be on propping up existing companies which are short of liquidity but should be primarily targeted at encouraging manufacturing investment across the board."[540]

Money

Since the Covid-19 lockdown the amount of cash used to purchase goods and services has dropped.[541] There has been a corresponding increase in electronic transactions. Both trends were already happening, quite rapidly, but accelerated dramatically with 2020's events. The buying of goods and services is becoming easier to administer. With this change, the ability of the Bank of England – which is after all a socially owned institution – to plan expenditure and investment should increase. This could make control over the financial system far easier to attain, to sap the power of finance capital. The Bank of England – along with other central banks – has been looking at the changed methods of payment for goods and services. This has prompted the Bank to start a series of talks on the 'future of money' in which the Bank consulted nationally and internationally on how to introduce a digital pound for commercial and retail purposes. The offering would be known as a Central Bank Digital Currency (CBDC). In October 2020, the world's top state banks (including the Bank of England and the US Federal Reserve) issued a major report on CBDC. The message is clear: during the past few years CBDC has moved from the world of economic theory to active development. It is on its way.

The Bank has tacitly accepted that CBDC will be far easier to introduce now that Britain is out of the EU and its financial control mechanisms. Others have seen this too. *Cointelegraph* noted in July 2020, "England could realise such an undertaking relatively soon [...] Following Brexit, the country does not have to deal with European Union bureaucracy, nor is it a part of the Eurozone, giving it a certain amount of flexibility in its monetary policy and development." Companies and people looking for credit receive additional finance when the commercial banks (those in the high street, such as HSBC and Barclays) issue agreed loans. This loan activity is tantamount to creating money. There is no existing money held in a credit card account before the user begins to spend. Instead of using money already in circulation the card user generates new credit, acquiring extra purchasing power. This means the card user – whether a company or an individual – can pay for products many times more than the actual amount of money they could access hitherto. Commercial banks by facilitating credit loans increase the amount of circulating currency far more than the Bank of England does.

The commercial banks – not the Bank of England – determine the amount of currency in circulation by creating credits as a means of payment, limited only indirectly by interest rates and by the dangers of making unwise loans. Credit at present is therefore a deregulated system of money creation. By contrast, CBDC would enable the Bank of England to determine the amount of circulating currency and credit, taking that role away from the commercial sector. We would have one big bank using technology to facilitate real-time settlements and to clear deposits between commercial entities and directly with individuals. Who then would need commercial banks as they are? The ancient and still current activity of banks clearing cheques and creating unregulated credits would end. Compare this approach to what led to the 2008 banking collapse. It was estimated that British commercial banks had created credit five times greater than Britain's GDP, which at the time stood at around £1,600 billion. The amount of currency in circulation bore no resemblance to the annual productive value in the British economy – hence the eventual collapse.

The Bank of England is still trying to conceal this failure. That is evident in its 2020 consultation paper.[542] It seeks ways of supporting the commercial banks through 'open competition'. Later in the paper the Bank concedes that under CBDC workers and companies will want their digital bank accounts moved to the Bank of England, away from the insecure commercial banking sector – not surprising given the financial shambles that the commercial banks have created. Of course, credit does not in itself constitute a danger to the currency, as long as an increase in credit is accompanied by a commensurate increase in production. Imagine a Britain where each bundle of short-term circulating credit is tied to a known quantity of newly produced British goods available for circulation, where credit is granted when it enables a transfer of goods from one hand to another within the production and consumption process. The circulation of currency and the circulation of goods stay in equilibrium. That is – or should be – a basic principle of currency policy, however it is managed. Many workers and their representatives shy away from developing an understanding of banking and finance. They need to grasp the nettle. The people of Britain will never be able to take control of the country without taking democratic control of our national finances.

One of the fundamental opportunities – and challenges – of becoming free of EU hindrance is to fund productive work in the regions where people live. One approach could be to draw up an annual credit plan. Each manufacturing and commercial sector would compile its anticipated credit requirements for the coming year. As each year unfolds, the plan for each sector would be further refined to allow for unexpected day-to-day production occurrences or emergencies – including pandemics. Another part of a coordinated approach would be to ensure that credit was available between manufacturer and retailer so that the manufacturer was always able to embark on further production before the retailer has sold the first batch of manufactured products. Overall, this arrangement would take care of shorter-term working capital requirements within the national economy. As part of an overall planning process, British commercial banks could be given a new role as specialist investment banks with detailed knowledge of a particular sector: agriculture and horticulture for one bank, chemicals and pharmaceuticals for another and so on. The task for each bank, according to the plan, would be to administer the longer-term grants and subsidies (fixed capital for investment in plant and machinery) to be allotted to each sector every year. This long-term fixed capital investment could be sourced from the annual increase in value created in the economy during the previous year.

A further innovation would be to anticipate the future increase in the value of production projected over say the next four years. The projected value could then be immediately released as credit for fixed capital investment. This would further help to accelerate production while mitigating the risk of inflation. It would avoid the dead hand of a long-term plan projected well into the future that would only serve to paralyse immediate action. Is this all too much to ask? Workers and their organisations have not always been blind to the need to transform the financial system. The National Executive of the Labour Party said in 1944, "[…] finance must be the servant and the intelligent servant of the community and productive industry, not their stupid master." We have yet to achieve that. Such thinking deserves to be the main trend in financing the country. After all, that is what Take Control demands.

Transport

Another key demand is to improve transport outside London. Trade between Northern towns was hampered by poor inter-city links. Services from London travelled at average speeds of 65-93 mph, compared with 20-60 mph elsewhere. That included Liverpool Central to Chester, which took 41 minutes for a 14-mile journey. Another need: Leeds was the largest city in Western Europe without a light rail or metro system. The building of HS2 is moving from preparatory work to full-scale construction works, bringing around 22,000 skilled jobs and over 2,000 high-quality apprenticeships.[543] It will support the creation of many other jobs and will play a key part in supporting Britain's post-Covid-19 recovery. Britain will eventually have a 21st-century railway that connects its main cities, helping to unite the whole country. By transferring inter-city fast trains off the existing railway, much-needed extra capacity will be freed for commuter services and for many more freight trains. This is a welcome development that begins the process of building a better future, especially for Britain's young people when the Covid-19 pandemic has caused a massive contraction in the economy and large-scale redundancies.

HS2 itself is recruiting 500 new staff. The first phase of HS2 construction from London to the West Midlands will see 7,000 new construction jobs with main works contractor Balfour Beatty VINCI. The contractor has stated that it will focus on recruiting young people under 25. A separate contract to build the new HS2 terminal in London at Euston will need another 3,000 workers. The management of HS2 estimates that there will be 400,000 supply chain contracts providing opportunities for British businesses in the first phase alone. General union GMB's National Secretary, Jude Brimble, said, "The UK urgently needs to deliver investment in infrastructure, and the start of main works is a critical step in the construction of HS2." HS2 can make a difference to Britain's capacity to rebuild its industries in a way that is sustainable and modern, and which could benefit the environment by removing the necessity for thousands of freight lorries which thunder through our towns and countryside.[544] We are often told that the money spent on HS2 should be spent on upgrades to the existing railway network. But building HS2 *is* an upgrade of the existing railway network. The segregation of high-speed trains onto their own line untangles the complex mixture of slow and fast services that constrains capacity and this allows the remaining services to bunch up more closely together.

This allows at least a doubling of capacity for the remaining services into Birmingham, Manchester and Leeds. The speed of travel on the HS2 lines allows the freeing up of space on the existing lines and scope to improve passenger services on those lines too. Even more importantly, it holds the key to expanding the movement of freight by rail. On 11 November 2020, Logistics UK – formerly the Freight Transport Association– published a report stressing that HS2 is 'the only opportunity this century' to grow rail freight. The association believes that the opportunity for freight to use released capacity from HS2 is substantial, creating paths for up to 144 extra freight trains per day, potentially removing 10,944 heavy lorries daily from the road network. We hear about HS2 harming the environment. Inevitably, a major project of this nature will impact on the environment but that must be set against the damage done by moving freight by road. Road traffic, particularly heavy road freight traffic, is running over wildlife, shaking our homes and impacting on the natural environment. No one involved with HS2 denies there will be some environmental impact, but even one of the House of Lords committees scrutinising the project has praised the engineers for choosing a route which minimises the impact on ancient woodland. The 470 miles of HS2 impact on little more ancient woodland than the 14 miles of the proposed Lower Thames Crossing motorway.

NHS

Richard Tuck noted, "the creation of the National Health Service [...] would have been impossible in a country with strong constitutional constraints on the legislature, since it required large-scale expropriation of private property in the shape of the old endowed hospitals. That is a major reason why so few countries have adopted the NHS model: in most of them it would have been illegal, just as similar proposals would be illegal in the EU today."[545] EU rules forbade nationalisation without compensation. Nationalisation is no panacea, but it does give workers opportunities to take control. Between 2011 and 2020 the EU issued 63 separate demands on its member states to cut health spending and to privatise or outsource health services. Some pro-EU people told us that leaving the EU would threaten our NHS, but they wanted to trap us in an EU that constantly promotes privatising health services.

The EU's Public Procurement Directive stated that any public tender over a certain amount must be open to any company with a subsidiary in the EU and that any contract for a service not delivered 'in-house' must go to tender. This included services for hospitals, materials, or drugs used in the NHS, and the work of chemists, opticians, and dentists, who provide their services in the NHS. Under EU procurement law, European companies can bid for NHS contracts. EU procurement law forced an Oxford NHS trust to farm out its PET-CT imaging for cancer to a sub-contractor, over the doctors' protests. Private firms already get 70 per cent of NHS clinical contracts. They already run some hospitals. Labour and Conservative governments alike have encouraged US and other foreign private companies to get involved in the NHS. Blair's obsession with 'testing the market' and Gordon Brown's Private Finance Initiative compromised the NHS's integrity. The Labour government enabled this through its 1998 Competition Act and its 2002 Enterprise Act. From 2006, the Hospital Corporation of America (HCA) formed several NHS-HCA Ventures: public-private partnerships that provided NHS facilities only to private patients. The HCA's UK subsidiary was part of the Private Hospitals Alliance, a lobbying firm that called for greater private sector involvement in the NHS.

US firms have acquired UK healthcare companies. In 2015, the US firm Tenet Healthcare acquired Aspen Healthcare, which operated private hospitals in the UK. On taking over Aspen, Tenet talked about privatising our entire health service. 7.3 per cent of funding for clinical services is in private hands. Imaging, pharmacy, commissioning, and business planning are increasingly in private hands. Virgin holds 400 contracts. Optum, Capita and the like run referral management systems and data management. Poorly regulated, privately-owned health apps proliferate. The Labour Party always scaremongered about the threat to the NHS from US corporations. The 2019 Labour manifesto said that a

Conservative government "would leave our NHS at the mercy of a trade deal with Donald Trump." Full Facts said that for the Labour Party to call it 'certain' that Johnson would do a dodgy deal with President Trump, sending £500 million a week of NHS money to US drug companies, was 'misleading and unjustified'. They cited the Nuffield Trust: "If you look at other countries that have concluded a trade deal with the USA containing provisions on medicines, they have not experienced increases in pharmaceutical spending to the same level per person. In fact the gap with Australia has not closed at all."

The National Institute for Health and Care Excellence guidelines kept the prices of drugs and medical devices under some control, so pharma companies objected that they pulled down prices. In previous trade deals the USA did not demand an end to price controls. Johnson said 'under no circumstances' would he do a free trade deal with the USA that would put the NHS on the table. It was 'not for sale'. As soon as Johnson was able to do so, he made every effort to redeem his pledge to spend more on the NHS. In his government's first budget, in March 2020, the Chancellor pledged £5 billion extra to the NHS and pledged to boost spending on the NHS by £33.9 billion a year by 2023-24 and he put that pledge into law. Outside the EU, our NHS is no longer at the mercy of the EU and its Public Procurement Directive. Outside the EU, the government and the NHS can insist that providers of services must be based in this country.

Chapter 22
Taking control

2017-2019

The Conservative party's 2017 election manifesto made several pledges about Brexit. It pledged that a Conservative government would respect the referendum result: "Following the historic referendum on 23rd June 2016, the United Kingdom is leaving the European Union." It ruled out continued membership of the single market and the customs union: "As we leave the European Union, we will no longer be members of the single market or customs union but we will seek a deep and special partnership including a comprehensive free trade and customs agreement." In the 8 June 2017 election, the Conservative party won more votes than any party had done for 25 years. The people voted to make the Conservative party the largest party in the House of Commons. Labour's manifesto pledged, "Labour accepts the referendum result." Both parties defined Brexit as leaving the Single Market, the Customs Union, and the remit of the European Court of Justice. Between them, they won 85 per cent of the votes cast. The LibDems, unequivocally against Brexit, saw their vote fall by 0.5 per cent, and their former leader Nick Clegg lost his seat.

In July 2017 Johnson, the new Foreign Secretary, appointed David Frost his special Brexit adviser. Johnson spelt out to Prime Minister Theresa May his red lines for an agreement with the EU – get out of the single market, no more compulsory payments into EU budgets, an Australian-style points-based system of controlled immigration, end the jurisdiction of the European Court of Justice, and stop any EU legislation applying to Britain. But May's Withdrawal Agreement was a withdrawal agreement in name only. Professor Mervyn King, formerly governor of the Bank of England, said, "There are arguments for remaining in the EU and arguments for leaving. But there is no case whatever for giving up the benefits of remaining without obtaining the benefits of leaving. Yet that is exactly what the government is now proposing [...]."

On 6 July 2018 May tried her Chequers ambush of the Cabinet, to try to get them to back her (Non) Withdrawal Agreement, after which Johnson resigned. He rejected May's pleas to back her Agreement. He voted against it in January and March 2019. On 29 March the European Research Group of Conservative MPs voted against May's third attempt to get her Agreement passed. It was defeated by 58 votes. The Labour party and the SNP could have got most of what they wanted if they had voted for May's Bill. Instead they kept voting to defeat it. In 2019 the prospect of Brexit was leading to a rise in wages. LinkedIn's survey, released on 13 May 2019, indicated that conditions of work were improving too. It found that three-quarters of recruitment companies had seen a rise in the number of businesses looking to find staff from within Britain. The trend coincided with a fall in the number of jobseekers in the EU looking for work in Britain. Between 2016, when the referendum took place, and 2019, 30 per cent fewer LinkedIn members moved from mainland Europe to Britain.

When the pro-EU Lord Heseltine was reminded that our economy was doing better than EU countries like Italy and Germany, he said, "This country's economy is doing significantly better than you might hope." He was admitting that he wanted our economy to be doing worse. Some pro-EU people had falsely accused people who voted to leave of voting to make themselves poor, or proclaimed that nobody voted to make themselves poorer. Lord Heseltine openly wished that people become poorer. He was admitting that the doom-laden forecasts of some EU enthusiasts had not come to pass.[546]

340

Heseltine had once told *The Spectator* that Britain would one day be so seamlessly woven into the EU that the very name of Britain would be forgotten. Being in the EU had corrupted our institutions and our constitution. The quality of government fell, constituencies were increasingly estranged from parliament, people were increasingly estranged from their representatives, the judiciary encroached on the legislature and the executive and the executive encroached on the rights of the people.

People knew about all this and were deeply concerned about corrupt politicians, rapacious banks, corporate greed, economic inequality and social injustice. It was not surprising that people did not trust MPs and members of the House of Lords after the scandals over lobbying, the cash in brown envelopes, the abuse of parliamentary expenses, the absurdly well-paid speech circuit for retired politicians, and the 'revolving door' through which they and retired top civil servants moved into well-paid directorships and consultancies and exploited their contacts to finance private deals. A scathing verdict on Westminster politicians under the May government came on 17 January 2019 in the ComRes poll of over 2,000 voters commissioned by *The Daily Express*. Andrew Hawkins, executive chairman of ComRes, said, "Parliamentarians will be alarmed to see the extent to which the Brexit stalemate has damaged the reputation of politics and politicians and is triggering significant support for constitutional change. [...] Whatever other impact Brexit may have, it is already pitching Parliament against the will of the voting public and the staggeringly low levels of positive sentiment towards politicians should give enormous cause for concern."

Three-quarters of voters said the Brexit process had shown that today's MPs were 'not up to the job'. Three quarters agreed that the Brexit process had shown that politicians were not in touch with the mood of the country. Only 13 per cent thought the political system 'allows my voice to be heard', 67 per cent disagreed. 79 per cent agreed that Parliament was not emerging from the Brexit process in a good light. 72 per cent of people wanted a root-and-branch overhaul of the country's entire political system. In the EU elections held on 23 May 2019, 31.6 per cent of the people who voted cast their votes for the Brexit Party. The Conservatives came fifth, with 9.1 per cent, their worst election result for 200 years. May announced that she would resign on 7 June. Johnson at once pledged to take Britain out of the EU on 31 October, 'deal or no deal'. On 23 July 2019, he was elected party leader by 66.4 per cent of his party members.

Boris Johnson

Some of Johnson's political opponents tried to portray him as hard-right, far-right. But their accusations were false. He was the first senior Conservative to back equal marriage, back in 2004. He has championed an amnesty for illegal immigrants in the UK. In 2009 Johnson, at the Conservative Party Conference, had called for an in/out referendum, three years before it became Cameron's policy. In 2014 Johnson backed a report by his economic adviser Gerard Lyons which showed that leaving the EU would be better for Britain than staying in on the existing terms. In 2015 Johnson read Business for Britain's *'Change, or go'*, which was serialised in *The Telegraph* from 21 June 2015. He said that before the referendum he wrote two articles, one for staying in the EU and one for leaving and then compared them. Some called this indecision; others see it as a good way to come to a decision.

Nimco Ali wrote in *The Daily Telegraph* of 8 June 2019 that she first met Johnson in 2011 when he was campaigning in

Putney High Street and she asked him to help to end female genital mutilation (FGM). "He and his team at City Hall went on to work with me over several years to inform people about FGM and help protect girls in London. I will never forget his kindness, dedication and commitment to helping me. [...] Boris gave me the confidence to speak up. He listened. He not only helped me find my voice, but has also continued to support my work over the years. Since that chance meeting, ending FGM has become an 'electoral issue' – but it was Boris who got it first. "I also worked with him in the Foreign Office where one of his priorities was girls' education. As foreign secretary he used every platform available to advance the cause of female education around the world, specifically campaigning to make sure that every girl gets 12 years of full-time quality education." He wrote in 2001, "Female emancipation has been the biggest social revolution since print. [...] Female education is the answer to the global population problem. It is the ultimate answer to the problem of Islamic fundamentalist terrorism."[547]

His biographer Tom Bower observed that when Johnson was Mayor of London, "the so-called 'lazy buffoon' got up at 5:30 AM to read the briefs and documents for that day's meetings, to set off before 7:30 AM to speak at one or two breakfast meetings on most days and arrive by 9:00 AM in City Hall."[548] Some of his critics called him an Islamophobe because he wrote that women wearing burqas resembled 'letterboxes' in an article in which he defended women's right to wear the burqa and criticised the Danish government's ban on wearing it.[549] Some called him a racist because he wrote the word 'piccaninny', when he used the word mockingly to criticise Blair's colonial treatment of Africa.[550] Johnson's government was more ethnically diverse than all its predecessors put together, but some critics called this 'tokenism' and singled out the non-white ministers as 'race traitors'.[551] His three leading

343

cabinet colleagues were Dominic Raab, Priti Patel and Rishi Sunak, not the most Anglo-Saxon names. Some on the 'left' called him a liar, while lying that he was a racist.

At first he was leading a minority government unable to pass the law for Britain to leave the EU and his party was not united behind him. He had a nominal Commons majority of just two, but many Conservative MPs opposed Brexit. At once, he took a number of key decisions. He fired seventeen of May's ministers. He made the no-deal threat to walk out of negotiations, the only way to defeat the EU's inflexible stance. On 3 August he pledged an extra £20 billion for the NHS. On 4 August, 25 pro-EU Conservative MPs led by Philip Hammond threatened to bring down the government if it tried to leave without a deal. Johnson pledged not to resign even if he lost a vote of no confidence. On 2 September, fifteen senior pro-EU Conservative MPs came to Downing Street and threatened to support Labour to bring down the government. The next day, twenty-one Conservative MPs voted against the government, in favour of Labour's Bill. MPs defeated a motion to approve a snap election. Johnson then expelled the twenty-one pro-EU rebels, including Hammond, from the Conservative party.

On 22 October MPs defeated the government's timetable to legalise Brexit, as pledged, on 31 October. Johnson asked Corbyn to agree to an election on 12 December. On the 29th, Corbyn agreed - another mistake that assisted the pro-Brexit camp. Some likened our time to the 1930s. This facile analogy pictured Trump as Hitler and Johnson as Mussolini. Trump has left the White House, after inciting a criminal but unsuccessful assault on the Capitol and after much pathetic and futile bluster against the election result. Trump started no new wars, unlike Hitler in his first four years, when he sent huge armed forces to Spain. Britain has not launched any new wars either, and far from attacking anyone or becoming an autarchic state has

344

signed a Trade and Cooperation Agreement with the EU. Yet some people attacked Johnson's government in the name of fighting fascism and felt obliged to try to overthrow our democratic vote to leave. Social democrats and liberals have often sided with reaction, thinking that by doing so they were preventing an even more right-wing takeover. Their stance was classic conservatism – the belief that it is right to uphold an actual injustice in order – supposedly - to prevent some possible future injustice. Their allying with May to overthrow Brexit was like Clegg allying with Cameron supposedly to prevent a harder-right government.

Many still underestimate the extent to which Johnson changed both government policy and the Conservative party. He has gone far further than many – both friends and enemies – thought he could. Johnson decisively broke with Thatcherism. Thatcher and her pro-EU Chancellor Geoffrey Howe started the destructive policy of austerity. Cameron and May and their pro-EU Chancellors George Osborne and Philip Hammond continued it. Thatcher signed the Single European Act in 1986, 15 years before Johnson even became an MP. Johnson took us out of that Act. Johnson rejected the austerity economic policies approved by the EU and sacked the austerity-enforcers. He ditched the pro-EU, pro-austerity wing of the Conservative party (Cameron, May, Osborne).

'Get Brexit done'

In the May 2019 EU election, the Brexit Party topped the poll with 30.5 per cent of the votes, winning every region in England and Wales except London. The Conservatives got just 8.8 per cent of the votes, their worst ever result in a national election, down from 24 per cent. Labour got 13.6 per cent, the LibDems 19.6 per cent and the Greens 11.8 per cent. In Scotland the SNP got 38 per cent, the Brexit Party 15 per cent, the Conservatives 12 per cent and Labour 9 per cent. The election showed that leave would win again and with an even greater majority. The Conservatives, Labour, the Brexit Party, the DUP and UKIP added together got 58.1 per cent of the vote. The anti-EU camp – the LibDems, Greens, Plaid Cymru, the SNP and ChangeUK - got 40.4 per cent. Before the December 2019 general election, Conservative peer Daniel Finkelstein wrote, "there is a very good chance that Jeremy Corbyn will be prime minister." Psephologist John Curtice prophesied that the Conservatives would lose at least 20 seats to the LibDems and the SNP. Ex-Conservative MP Matthew Parris said he would vote LibDem because 'a reckless cult' had taken over the Conservative party. The establishment's pundits were as accurate as usual. The more that they, the BBC and much of the rest of the media vilified Johnson, the more popular he became.

In the election, the Conservative party, the party that most clearly backed the popular and democratic demand to get Brexit done, won 365 seats, an overall majority of 80. It gained 47 seats. 13,966,565 people voted for it, 43.6 per cent of those voting, the highest percentage for any party since 1979. 'Get Brexit done' was a winning policy. It united the Conservative Party, split the Labour Party, pulverised the LibDems and marginalised the Brexit Party. The Labour party was pledged to call two unnecessary referendums, trying to overturn two majority democratic decisions. This would have fostered fresh separatist feeling in Scotland, revived divisions between people across the country and renewed uncertainty. 10,269,076 people, 32.2 per cent of those voting, voted for the pro-EU Labour Party. It won 203 seats, its worst result since 1935. It lost 59 seats. There was a 7.9 per cent swing away from Labour since the 2017 election, largely because of its more openly pro-EU posture. In strong Leave seats, the Conservatives' vote share went up by 6.1 per cent and Labour's fell by 10.4 per cent. The Conservatives won in every single socio-economic category, winning the votes of 48 per cent of people in social strata C2DEs, where Labour won just 33 per cent. Labour lost in the 2017 and 2019 elections because so many people did not trust it to defend our independence and unity.

The 2019 election was the 'get Brexit done' election. As Labour's deputy leader John McDonnell acknowledged, "people did want to get Brexit done." Verhofstadt said, "Brexit will happen. The British people have confirmed their referendum decision." Lord Heseltine said, "We've lost. Brexit is going to happen and we have to live with it." The EU campaign to annul our democratic referendum vote was defeated. The British working class refused to be bullied into submission. Labour peer Lord Glasman wrote, "The working class, the Nation-State and democracy are key features of the new era. Far from being losers, the post-industrial working class has decided the two most significant votes of our time."[552] The election victory confirmed our majority democratic decision of 2016. The 2019 election elected a Brexit government, which carried out its pledge to get Brexit done.

Downing Street stated on 8 January 2020, "The PM was clear that the UK would not extend the Implementation Period beyond 31st December 2020; and that any future partnership must not involve any kind of alignment or ECJ jurisdiction. He said the UK would also maintain control of UK fishing waters and our immigration system." All who want Britain to be truly independent will have to do what we can to ensure that the government honours these undertakings. Johnson said on 25 July 2020, "Brexit was a fundamental decision by the British people that they wanted their laws made by people that they can elect and they can remove from office and we must now respect that decision and create a new partnership with our

European friends – as warm and as close and as affectionate as possible."

We the people cannot leave it to Johnson to deliver independence. To win the independence we voted for, we must assert our own sovereignty, our own control. We voted to take control, to take responsibility. This demand has a logic of its own that goes far beyond the 2016 referendum. We needed to go forward to working together as a whole nation, a united community, a team, reaching across any lines of division to find common ground. The people must take control of Britain, not let the market take control. Some in the Leave camp had promoted the slogan 'take back control'. This implied restoring the previous state of affairs before we joined the EEC. But people did not want to go back to the 1960s. Nor were the people the same as they were in the 1960s. We had a better understanding of our country and its prospects, based on our decades of experience of the EU and the austerity that it had imposed on us. We had a better understanding of politics, based on our experience of the pro-EU camp's four-year effort to overturn our 2016 decision. We had become tactically astute, flexible enough to use UKIP, the Brexit Party and the Conservative Party to get what we wanted.

31 December 2020 we leave the EU

The UK Major Ports Group, which handles three quarters of UK seaborne trade, confirmed that it had "the capacity and infrastructure to handle large volumes of both EU and non-EU trade today without 'logjam'." The Mayor of Calais said delays would be 'economic suicide'. The BBC reported accurately that "French officials dismiss UK fears of Calais 'go-slow'."[553] Early in 2019 the BBC reported on its news programmes that people would not be able to book tickets on Brittany Ferries after 26

March because of Brexit. Brittany Ferries at once responded that the report was 'nonsense', that people could of course still book their tickets and that the company had recently expanded its fleet so there were even more tickets available. There will be no shortages of medicines. The WTO's Pharmaceutical Tariff Elimination Agreement means that tariffs do not apply to finished medicines. This Agreement covers 10,000 medicinal products across the EU, Canada, the USA, Japan and Norway. It covers almost nine tenths of the world's pharmaceutical trade. Most of the UK's insulin comes from one Danish company. It said it had six months' supplies, that it was prepared for all eventualities, and that no patient would go without insulin.

Planes continued to fly to and from the EU. The EU announced on 13 November 2018 that it would allow UK airlines to fly over, land in and return from EU airports even if there were no Withdrawal Agreement. This was barely reported, allowing the 'planes won't fly' scare to run and run. Eurostar pledged to maintain its services, saying "we plan and expect to maintain services on the existing basis and timetable following Brexit." In the end we did indeed leave on 31 December 2020. The Trade and Cooperation Agreement did not tie us to EU rules, policies, procedures and jurisdiction. We have a new relationship, based on mutual respect for sovereignty. There may well be bad deals to come, but we have more sovereignty, more control over our own affairs, than we have done since we signed up to the EEC. The Agreement was achieved by brilliant tactics, including the bluff on no-deal that surprised and trumped the EU – and fooled all too many EU enthusiasts. The Act proved wrong all those doomsters who had wailed that we would end up Billy-no-mates, isolated, unloved, scorned by all.

Johnson held the line on Brexit, against those who wanted to surrender to the EU. He is holding the line on national unity, against those who want to break up our country. He is refusing to let the pro-EU SNP split our country to the benefit of the EU. Just as in World War Two, it was right to back Churchill and afterwards right to kick him out after he had done the job he was put there to do, so we must press Johnson to do the job we have given him to do, and then, and only then, will we kick him out. Some say that they do not trust Johnson. That is a statement about how they feel and says nothing useful about his performance.

The Johnson government has got us out of the EU, but we need to move on from that. It has failed to control migration, as it was pledged to do. It does not want to cut migration because it wants to use migration to cut wages. We have not gone through all the turmoil of leaving the EU only to put up with the same sort of conditions and policies that made us vote to leave the EU. Outside the EU, the UK needs its freedom to protect itself from arrangements in which it will have no say. While inside, the UK could not question the uneven playing field created by the Eurozone's legal structure, the effects of which included the dumping of financial risk on the UK, the dumping of goods through a structurally undervalued euro currency and unfair trade subsidies under the Eurozone's internal fiscal arrangements.

Chapter 23
Take charge, take over

EU hostility

Unfortunately, EU leaders still showed hostility to our independence. To deter other member states from leaving, we must be shown not to benefit from leaving. Manfred Weber, leader of the European People's Party in the European Parliament, said, "a country outside the EU cannot have a better deal than an EU member state." Michel Barnier said he wanted to prevent Britain becoming a 'manufacturing hub' on the EU's doorstep. The EU pushed the Irish 'backstop' provision in the Withdrawal Agreement to punish Britain. A senior German MEP, Hans Olaf Henkel, said in 2017, "They would seek to make sure that Brexit was such a catastrophe that no country dares to take the step of leaving the EU again." This was very like the British government's response to the USA's winning its independence in 1776. After America's War of Independence, the British government was slow to honour the treaty that ended the war. It obstructed American commerce, retained its customs posts near the Great Lakes and accorded the United States little of the respect due to the independent nation that America had become.

The Withdrawal Agreement, as revised by the Johnson government, still limits our sovereignty. These would have damaging economic and strategic consequences if they were not dealt with. Under the European Union (Withdrawal Agreement) Act of 2020 we can override the Withdrawal Agreement by a later Act. We should terminate the Agreement and the Political Declaration. The clearest evidence of the EU's hostility was its interference in Ireland. There is not a problem with the Irish border. The UK government, the Irish government and the EU have all stated that there is no need to introduce infrastructure or checks on the border between Ireland and Northern Ireland.[554] Jon Thompson, CEO of HM Revenue & Customs, said, "Our consistent advice to ministers has been, we do not [...] require any infrastructure at the border between Northern Ireland and Ireland under any circumstances." His Irish counterpart Niall Cody said in 2017 that he was 'almost 100 per cent certain' of the same. Lars Karlsson, former head of the world customs association and Hans Maessen, head of the Dutch Association of Customs Brokers, both told the Northern Ireland Select Committee that no border infrastructure was needed to operate an effective customs operation. The Freight Trade Association agreed. WTO rules do not require a hard border. WTO representatives who visited Ireland confirmed that no new border infrastructure was needed.

Tony Smith, a former director general of the UK Border Force, explained: "What [the EU] have missed is (a) that borders generally globally are going through a paradigm shift [with the] introduction of digital technology and systems, and processes. So the days in which I operated, when you are sitting out in a kiosk, checking papers on a border post, are disappearing anyway, globally. Regardless of what's happening in Ireland I think they need to give due weight to that and look a lot more closely - you know, you can actually have an invisible border. There are other ways of doing checks now because of technology. It's not just technology, it needs regulation as well and cooperation and goodwill. I think that's what's been lacking." We could introduce the same technological solutions for dealing with customs clearances away from the border that work well everywhere else in the world. The border can stay as it is, virtual, invisible.

Britain is Northern Ireland's chief market. In 2018 Northern

Ireland's imports from Britain were £13.4 billion, from the Irish Republic £2.8 billion, from the EU £2.6 billion, from the rest of the world combined £2.4 billion. Sales to Britain were £10.6 billion, to the Republic £4.2 billion, to the EU £2.5 billion, to the rest of the world £4.5 billion. The Withdrawal Agreement's Northern Ireland Protocol's Irish Sea border splits Northern Ireland from Britain, crippling this trade. The Withdrawal Agreement clearly damages the integrity and sovereignty of the UK. It is legitimate for a state to amend or end a treaty when the terms of the treaty become a danger to the state's sovereignty and integrity. We have every right to amend it or end it. The Good Friday Agreement, which is an international treaty between the British government, the Irish government and representatives of the communities in Northern Ireland, has itself been updated many times with further amendments. The 2006 St Andrews Agreement, for instance, made a number of revisions to the Agreement, on the basis of the foundations which had been laid in 1998.[555] The EU was not even a party to the Agreement, which did not stop Guy Verhofstadt from claiming that the EU had brought peace to Northern Ireland.

Naturally, the forces for division – the EU, the SNP, Plaid Cymru – back the Withdrawal Agreement. The Protocol must be replaced by a new arrangement for an invisible border on the island of Ireland which would respect our sovereignty and ensure that there was no application of EU law to Northern Ireland. The people of Ireland, not the EU, should take all decisions about the future of Ireland. Under international law we are not obliged to pay the EU any of the monies it wants from us. Nor are we obliged to pay for any lingering liabilities of the European Investment Bank, which we should leave at once. The House of Lords' (heavily pro-Remain) EU Financial Affairs Sub-Committee concluded that "Article 50 allows the UK to leave the EU without being liable for outstanding financial obligations under the EU budget." We must be positive and ambitious, this is a chance to recast our country, to turn the threat into an opportunity. We need to unite as many people as possible, especially those who wanted us to stay in the EU because they genuinely wanted the best for Britain. Most of the people of Britain believe in Britain and want us to have a better future. We should all work together to do what is best for Britain in our new circumstances.

Covid-19

Independence is the best way to solve the problems we face, including Covid-19. Companies are switching production to personal protective equipment. The logic of independence, the way it must work in practice, pushes government towards self-reliance, towards our becoming a manufacturing country producing mainly for home consumption. That does not mean that independence determines what choices people make, the people will have to make this practical independence happen. The pandemic tested all our institutions. It forced a revaluation of our values. We can see that many people are doing a great job. NHS workers have been magnificent. The emergency services have performed valiantly. We have found that binmen, postmen, delivery workers, bus drivers, train drivers are all essential workers. The army has shown its value as another emergency service. The people have responded with discipline and determination to minimise the impact of this pandemic.

The response of British workers to the pandemic shows the potential of collective and people-led organisation. Faced with a threat unprecedented in recent history, Britain's workers got on with the job. The results became clear with the successful roll-out of the vaccines. By 12 February 2021, England had given the first dose of a vaccine to 86 per cent of those over 70,

Scotland 64 per cent, Wales 73 per cent and Northern Ireland 61 per cent. By 24 February, 18.2 million in all. The achievements of creating the Oxford vaccine are immense. By late 2020 tens of millions of doses of the Oxford University/AstraZeneca vaccine were being produced by Oxford Biomedica in a 'virtual' partnership with a far better funded Vaccines Manufacturing and Innovation Centre. Almost at a stroke, large-scale vaccine manufacturing has been restored to Britain. It shows what can be done: Britain can be rebuilt. All that is needed is the will and the ambition – and for the working class to take control.

Vaccine development is not the only success area. Dexamethasone is a widely used and relatively cheap anti-inflammatory drug, at just £5 per treatment. British researchers found that it reduces deaths of Covid-19 patients on ventilators by up to a third – a life saver on an epic scale. This was an 'investigator-initiated trial'. No big funder, no government department, no company had the bright idea of starting it. Researchers themselves began it, rapidly finding time and money from several sources (which is where the government agencies and the other funders came in). Researchers – workers – took responsibility. 176 hospitals – all NHS – were involved in the trial, the length and breadth of the country: from Cardiff to Glasgow, from the Isle of Wight to the Western Isles. The coordinated, national initiative makes a mockery of the petty regionalism that has marred the public health response to the crisis. It is no accident that this research was carried out here, in Britain. Where else in the world would you have had such a massive study carried out in record time and yielding such powerful results? Where else in the (capitalist) world do you have an NHS?

Early in the crisis, when Britain was desperately short of testing facilities and PPE, many scientists not researching

Covid-19 organised themselves, with no urging from above, to provide backup support. The Crick Institute in London, the largest single workplace of biomedical researchers in Europe, turned over its laboratories for testing. Chemists at Imperial College London started making their own hand sanitiser for distribution locally. By December 2020 Britain was on course to make 70 per cent of its PPE. This was a far cry from the earlier farcical goings on that saw the RAF fly in a planeload of PPE from Turkey, only for many of the gowns to be ditched as being of too low quality. As of 26 January 2021 the UK had administered 10.3 doses per 100 of our population. Germany has managed 2.1 doses per 100, France 1.7, Denmark, the EU's best-performing member, 3.6. The EU average was 1.9. The European Commission threatened to block exports of vaccines made in the bloc, including to Britain, in breach of commercial contracts. The Commission answered the question Kate Hoey asked in parliament on 22 October 2018, "The EU does not want a hard border and will not put one up. We will not put one up. The Republic of Ireland will not be putting one up. Who is going to put this hard border up?"

The UK invested earlier and to a greater extent in the production, clinical trials and procurement of vaccines than did the EU. Von der Leyen admitted on 4 February 2021 that "I am aware that alone a country can be a speedboat, while the EU is more like a tanker." The Office for Budget Responsibility's November 2020 Fiscal and Economic Outlook presented alternative scenarios. In its more optimistic scenario, envisaging keeping the Covid-19 infection rate in check and an effective vaccine becoming available in Spring 2021, output returns to pre-Covid levels by the end of 2021 and the debt ratio returns to the 90 per cent level with no need for any spending cuts or tax increases: "the medium term impact of the pandemic in this scenario is negligible." On 1 January 2021 Britain left the

EU's regulatory systems. Now workers will have to harness their collective experience and knowledge and apply their collective energy to the task of taking control of the direction of the country. Nobody says now, 'the market will provide', especially after Covid. People are far more aware of the need for a strong, competent nation-state. There should be no self-doubt: our response to Covid-19 has shown that workers truly can change the world.

Common ground

The authors of an October 2020 survey reported, "We find common ground in Britain on many issues, with large majorities which: – share a sense of national pride in many similar things – such as the NHS, our countryside, and our volunteer tradition – feel proud of Britain's progress on gender equality and becoming a more tolerant and diverse nation – are committed to gender equality and racial equity – believe that as a society we need to focus on responsibilities as much as rights – believe in closing the unfair gap between the haves and have-nots, and making sure that the hard work of key workers and others is better rewarded – want Britain to protect our countryside and lead on climate change – believe we should strike a balance on difficult issues such as immigration – feel decision making is too centralised in London – want political leaders to compromise rather than just sticking to their positions and fighting."[556]

It went on: "73 per cent of Britons believe inequality is a serious problem in the UK today. 2 in 3 people believe that 'in the UK, the system is rigged to serve the rich and influential.' Only 13 per cent believe that ordinary working people get a fair share of the nation's wealth. Almost 3 in 4 Britons believe that there is one law for the rich and one for the poor. 58 per cent of people say that the pandemic made them more aware of the living conditions of other people in the country. Over 90 per cent of Britons support the idea that if businesses receive government support, they should have a responsibility to society. This includes paying their taxes in full and not using offshore tax havens to avoid paying tax, paying fair wages, onshoring jobs, and reducing carbon emissions."[557] The report concluded, "The Covid-19 pandemic has strengthened our belief that this is a moment for change. There is a rare opportunity to bring people in Britain together around new agendas for the 2020s in which we fix what we know is broken in our society, while also preserving those things that we most highly value. We cannot find another major western democracy where the appetite for change is stronger than it is in the UK. Britain has remarkable potential. Now is a moment for leaders at every level of society and for local communities to step up."[558]

Whether people voted for or against Brexit does not matter any longer. What matters is how we face the future. We do not want to be ruled by the giant multinational corporations through free trade agreements.[559] We should position the UK to benefit and prepare for the prospect of trading freely. This is the only fair and sovereign outcome for Brexit and the only solution consistent with the right of self-determination exercised by the British people. Outside the EU we can trade in ways that are more internationalist than the EU's. The EU had a high average external tariff – 5.1 per cent compared to the US 3.5 per cent – and its tariff regime hurt poorer countries trying to add value to their primary commodities. Outside the EU's Customs Union, we could assist poorer countries to trade their way out of poverty and become less dependent on aid. The choice is between supporting Britain or supporting the multinational corporations. There is no middle ground.

Another task is to ensure that liberation from the EU's free movement of labour does not turn into reliance on importing workers from outside the EU. True internationalism is about maintaining skill and living standards through training and employment here. True internationalism is against poaching scarce skilled workers from countries that desperately need them.

A new democracy

We must work to build a self-reliant economy and a democratic socialist society. There is more support for this than usually understood: a *Daily Mail* headline of 17 October 2020 said, "Why the UK should have followed the example of Cuba." Eatwell and Goodwin wrote about the leave camp, "This challenge to the liberal mainstream is in general not anti-democratic. Rather, national populists are opposed to certain *aspects* of liberal democracy as it has evolved in the West. Contrary to some of the hysterical reactions that greeted Trump and Brexit, those who support these movements are not fascists who want to tear down our core political institutions. A small minority do, but most have understandable concerns that these institutions are not representative of society as a whole and, if anything, are becoming ever more cut adrift from the average citizen. […] most national-populist voters want *more* democracy – *more* referendums and *more* empathetic and listening politicians that give *more* power to the people and less power to established economic and political elites."[560] They explained, "contrary to the popular claim that it is a new form of fascism, national populism strives towards a new form of democracy in which the interests and voices of ordinary people feature far more prominently."[561]

Those who supported Britain's independence, far from

wanting to destroy representative democratic bodies, wanted our ruling bodies to be more representative and democratic. The prime case of an unrepresentative body was the House of Commons of 2016, with 480 MPs backing Remain and just 159 backing Leave. The 2016 referendum created a unique event in British history - the House of Commons would be tasked with carrying out a policy which most MPs opposed. It was no better by 3 September 2019, when it voted by 328 to 301 to try to pass a law designed to prevent a no-deal Brexit. Democracy consists not just in letting people have a say but in then acting on what they say. Votes should be enacted. We were told our 2016 majority decision would be enacted, but many MPs - despite being elected on pledges to do so - instead tried to enact the minority view. In the referendum, the working class exercised control over capitalism. But as we progress, we have to realise that in the end we cannot control capitalism, we have to get rid of it.

We needed a new democracy – what should be its content? We needed an annual reckoning, like the National Committee of the engineers' union used to have, based on its principles of democratic centralism. Democratic centralism is very like the British principle of cabinet responsibility. Free discussion results in an agreed decision, and then all agree to carry out that decision. How do we make elected representatives responsible to the people? We need to control the people we elect locally and nationally. Democratic societies need fair voting systems and strict controls on spending to prevent corporations or individuals 'buying' votes. There should be term limits for holders of public office. An agreed number of people should be able to force a by-election to recall representatives who let us down. There should be a renewal of local democracy to encourage participation, not mayoral oligarchies. There could be a specified right for an agreed number of people to have the right to call for a referendum. There should continue to be strict rules to ensure fair referendums. We could have a second chamber chosen the same way we chose juries - at random. The members could serve for two or three years and be paid a reasonable salary plus expenses. They could call on experts for advice.

A name and a party designation on the ballot paper and arguably a party manifesto, were what we voted for in a general election. People did not like it when political parties changed their policies after they were elected. We voted more for a party's manifesto than we did for an individual MP. We did not like it when MPs changed their political parties after they were elected, as one in ten did in the Theresa May parliament of 2017-19. The manifesto is a mandate not because of the intrinsic qualities of the policies, but because it is the way electors authorise a policy. Manifestos are supposed to control wayward MPs, but do not seem to work. Lord Salisbury, Conservative leader in the Lords in the 1940s and 1950s, developed the Salisbury Convention after 1945, when the Labour government, with a huge Commons majority, faced a huge Conservative majority in the Lords. This Convention was that the House of Lords does not stand in the way of a government delivering on the manifesto promises on which it won office. The Lords cannot introduce wrecking amendments and will not oppose measures carrying out manifesto promises on second reading. The Convention had force because it recognised a political reality – the power of a modern democratic vote – even though in strict law manifestos had no special significance.

The late Raymond Williams wrote eloquently, "Democracy, as in England we have interpreted it, is majority rule. The means to this, in representation and freedom of expression, are generally approved. But, with universal suffrage, majority rule will, if we believe in the existence of the masses, be mass-rule. Further, if the masses are, essentially the mob, democracy will be mob-rule. [...] I do not think of my relatives, friends, neighbours, colleagues, acquaintances, as masses; we none of us can or do. The masses are always the others, whom we don't know, and can't know. Yet now, in our kind of society, we see these others regularly, in their myriad variations; stand, physically, beside them. They are here, and we are here with them. And that we are with them is of course the whole point. To other people, we also are masses. Masses are other people. [...] we ourselves are all the time being massed by others. To the degree that we find the formula inadequate for ourselves, we can wish to extend to others the courtesy of acknowledging the unknown. [...] 'Democracy would be all right', we can come to say, 'it is indeed what we personally would prefer, if it were not for the actual people'."[562] Indeed, the masses are other people. We are the masses, we are the other people, we are the ordinary people.

Stefan Collini wrote, "Perhaps Williams's greatest achievement by 1961 was to have fashioned a form and idiom in which to combat the dominant cultural pessimism without ceding the moral high ground. What he identified as the 'long revolution' was a record of 'actual growth', of a liberation of human potential rather than a dilution of 'standards'. As he put it [...] 'Everything that I understand of the history of the long revolution leads me to the belief that we are still in its early stages.' That was an important thing to say in Britain at the end of the 1950s; it's still an important thing to say [...] he was right about this central matter, impressively and inspiringly right. Claims that everything is going to the dogs all too often rest on the hidden supports of parochialism, snobbery, class insouciance, and a wilful refusal of the intellectual effort to try to draw up a more realistic balance-sheet of gain and loss."[563]

Independence

Referendums go beyond parliament and parliamentary politics. The referendum was an assertion of people's sovereignty. To achieve independence, we will have to go yet further beyond parliament and parliamentary politics. The people will have to enact people's sovereignty, to take control, to take charge. The genie of British independence is out of the bottle and cannot be put back. Everyone needs to get involved. Whichever way people voted, we need to work together to achieve the improvements we all want. Brexit is the future, but we will have to build it ourselves. Independence brings change, change brings independence. Thomas Jefferson asked, "Who will govern the governors? There is only one force in the nation that can be depended upon to keep the government pure and the governors honest, and that is the people themselves. They alone, if well informed, are capable of preventing the corruption of power, and of restoring the nation to its rightful course if it should go astray. They alone are the safest depository of the ultimate powers of government."

The 2019 British Social Attitudes survey showed continuing staunch support for our independence. 51 per cent agreed that being in the EU "undermines Britain's right to be an independent country that makes its own laws." 28 per cent disagreed. People have staunchly upheld our nation's historic commitment to national sovereignty, majority rule, and the rule of law. Janice Turner wrote in *The Times* of 14 December 2019, "in much of the north, Leave or Remain, the majority belief is that a binding referendum result should be honoured. We should celebrate that in these chaotic times, our fellow citizens uphold the rule of law." We should never rely on others to solve our problems for us. It is bad politics and bad morals. We should not devolve our responsibilities outside ourselves. Only the people of a country can solve its problems. Let us build better! (Not 'build back better'. Like the slogan 'take back control', this harked back to the old days – we are looking forward, not back.)

No independence, no democracy. As an independent country, we can choose democratically how we run our country. When we elect a bunch of rascals, we can later kick them out. We can make our own decisions about policy, about how much the government should intervene in the economy. We can sell goods and services to those who want to buy them anywhere in the world, with no need for permission from politicians or the EU. We can unite our whole country behind a programme for progress. The national government, local authorities, our businesses and services must all plan to make a success of independence. People talk about the government running the country, but most of the time workers run the country. It is workers who run the NHS, day in and day out. Workers who keep the power lines humming. Workers who drive the buses, the trains and the vans and trucks. The crucial challenge facing the working class is how to take control in the interests of the people of Britain. The unavoidable conclusion for workers is that they must wrest control for themselves. We are so close to the levers of power already that we could reach out and grab them – if we choose to organise to do so.

Chapter 1

[1] Robin Griffith-Jones and Mark Hill, *Magna Carta, Religion and the Rule of Law* (Cambridge University Press, 2015), p. 18.

[2] Blandine Kriegel, *The State and the Rule of Law* (Princeton University Press, 1995), p. 74.

[3] Winston S. Churchill, *History of the English-Speaking Peoples, Volume 1: The Birth of Britain* (Bloomsbury Academic, 2015), p. 135. (Originally Cassell & Co., 1956).

[4] Winston S. Churchill, *History of the English-Speaking Peoples, Volume 1: The Birth of Britain* (Bloomsbury Academic, 2015), p. 138. (Originally Cassell & Co., 1956).

[5] Blandine Kriegel, *The State and the Rule of Law* (Princeton University Press, 1995), p. 74.

[6] Blandine Kriegel, *The State and the Rule of Law* (Princeton University Press, 1995), foreword by Donald R. Kelley, p. x.

[7] David Rollison, *A Commonwealth of the People: Popular Politics and England's Long Social Revolution, 1066-1649* (Cambridge University Press, 2010), p. 250.

[8] David Rollison, *A Commonwealth of the People: Popular Politics and England's Long Social Revolution, 1066-1649* (Cambridge University Press, 2010), p. 284.

[9] Peter Marshall, *Heretics and Believers: A History of the English Reformation* (Yale UP, 2017), p. xviii.

[10] Peter Marshall, *Heretics and Believers: A History of the English Reformation* (Yale UP, 2017), p. 414.

[11] Peter Marshall, *Heretics and Believers: A History of the English Reformation* (Yale UP, 2017), pp. 577-8.

[12] Steve Pincus, *1688: The First Modern Revolution* (Yale University Press, 2009), p. 7.

[13] Steve Pincus, *1688: The First Modern Revolution* (Yale University Press, 2009), p. 34.

[14] William Holdsworth, *A History of English Law, Volume VI* (Methuen & Co., 1924), p. 230.

[15] Sir D. L. Keir, *The Constitutional History of Modern Britain Since 1485* (Adam & Charles Black, 1969), p. 269.

[16] Steve Pincus, *1688: The First Modern Revolution* (Yale University Press, 2009), p. 247.

[17] Steve Pincus, *1688: The First Modern Revolution* (Yale University Press, 2009), pp. 309 and 349.

[18] Steve Pincus, *1688: The First Modern Revolution* (Yale University Press, 2009), p. 224.

[19] Steve Pincus, *1688: The First Modern Revolution* (Yale University Press, 2009), p. 485.

[20] Steve Pincus, *1688: The First Modern Revolution* (Yale University Press, 2009), p. 371.

[21] Steve Pincus, *1688: The First Modern Revolution* (Yale University Press, 2009), p. 383.

[22] John Locke, *Second Treatise of Government* (1689), paragraph 149.

[23] John Locke, *Second Treatise of Government* (1689), paragraph 132.

[24] John Locke, *Second Treatise of Government* (1689), paragraph 90.

[25] John Locke, *Second Treatise of Government* (1689), paragraphs 240 and 241, italics in original.

[26] Hugo Grotius, *De Iure Belli ac Pacis* (1625), p. 74, Richard Tuck, *The Sleeping Sovereign: The Invention of Modern Democracy* (Cambridge University Press, 2016).

[27] Thomas Hobbes, *De Cive* (1642), p. 97, Richard Tuck, *The Sleeping Sovereign: The Invention of Modern Democracy* (Cambridge University Press, 2016).

[28] Thomas Hobbes, *Leviathan* (1651), p. 104, Richard Tuck, *The Sleeping Sovereign: The Invention of Modern Democracy* (Cambridge University Press, 2016).

[29] Jean-Jacques Rousseau, *Social Contract* (1762), p. 129, Richard Tuck, *The Sleeping Sovereign: The Invention of Modern Democracy* (Cambridge University Press, 2016).

Chapter 2

[30] Richard Tuck, *The Sleeping Sovereign: The Invention of Modern Democracy* (Cambridge University Press, 2016), p. 229.

[31] Gordon S. Wood, *The Creation of the American Republic, 1776-87* (University of North Carolina Press, 1988), p. 377.

[32] Joseph Story, *Commentaries on the Constitution of the United States* (1833), p. 228, Richard Tuck, *The Sleeping Sovereign: the Invention of Modern Democracy* (Cambridge University Press, 2016).

[33] Michael Fry, *The Dundas Despotism* (John Donald Publishers, 2004), p. 59.

[34] Robert Tombs, *The English and Their History* (Penguin, 2015), pp. 587-8.

[35] Ben Wilson, *Empire of the Deep: The Rise and Fall of the British Navy* (Weidenfeld & Nicolson, 2014), pp. 471-2.

[36] Sian Rees, *Sweet Water and Bitter: The Ships that Stopped the Slave Trade* (Vintage Books, 2010), pp. 3-4.

[37] Sian Rees, *Sweet Water and Bitter: The Ships that Stopped the Slave Trade* (Vintage Books, 2010), p. 308.

[38] Ben Wilson, *Empire of the Deep: The Rise and Fall of the British Navy* (Weidenfeld & Nicolson, 2014), p. 471.

[39] Ben Wilson, *Empire of the Deep: The Rise and Fall of the British Navy* (Weidenfeld & Nicolson, 2014), p. 491.

[40] Sean Wilentz, *The Politicians and the Egalitarians: The Hidden History of American Politics* (Norton, 2017), p. 216.

[41] Sean Wilentz, *The Politicians and the Egalitarians: The Hidden History of American Politics* (Norton, 2017), pp. 94-5.

[42] Angela Saini, *Superior: The Return of Race Science* (Fourth Estate, 2020) and Angela Saini, *Inferior: The True Power of Women and the Science That Shows It* (Fourth Estate, 2017).

[43] Sean Wilentz, *The Politicians and the Egalitarians: The Hidden History of American Politics* (Norton, 2017), p. 222.

[44] Sean Wilentz, *The Politicians and the Egalitarians: The Hidden History of American Politics* (Norton, 2017), p. 49.

Chapter 3

[45] *State Duma (Russian Empire)* <https://en.wikipedia.org/wiki/State_Duma_(Russian_Empire)> [accessed 21 November 2020] and Orlando Figes, *A People's Tragedy: The Russian Revolution, 1891-1924* (Viking, 1997), p. 270.

[46] Michael Hughes, *Inside the Enigma: British officials in Russia, 1900-1939* (Hambledon Press, 1997), p. 106.

[47] Sir George Buchanan, *My Mission to Russia and Other Diplomatic Memoirs, Volume II* (Cassell & Co., 1923), p. 185.

[48] Giles Milton, *Russian Roulette: A Deadly Game: How British Spies Thwarted Lenin's Global Plot* (Sceptre, 2013), pp. 156-63.

[49] Ronald Suny, 'Revision and Retreat in the Historiography of 1917: Social History and Its Critics', *Russian Review*, Vol. 53 (1994), pp. 165-82 and Terence Emmons, *Unsacred History* (New Republic, 5 November 1990), p. 36.

[50] *The Structure of Soviet History: Essays and Documents*, ed. by Ronald Suny, 2nd edn (Oxford University Press, 2013), p. 21.

[51] Robert Gerwarth, *The Vanquished: Why the First World War Failed to End, 1917-1923* (Penguin, 2017), p. 35.

[52] Robert Gerwarth, *The Vanquished: Why the First World War Failed to End, 1917-1923* (Penguin, 2017), pp. 89-90.

[53] Robert Gerwarth, *The Vanquished: Why the First World War Failed to End, 1917-1923* (Penguin, 2017), p. 92.

[54] Jonathan Smele, *Civil war in Siberia: The Anti-Bolshevik Government of Admiral Kolchak, 1918-1920* (Cambridge University Press, 1996), p. 387.

[55] Frederick Schuman, *Soviet Policies at Home and Abroad* (Robert Hale Limited, 1948), p. 165.

[56] Clifford Kinvig, *Churchill's Crusade: The British Invasion of Russia, 1918-1920* (Hambledon Continuum, 2006), p. 318.

[57] Gabriel Gorodetsky, *Grand Delusion: Stalin and the German Invasion of Russia* (Yale University Press, 1999), p. 2.

[58] Stephen Dorril, *MI6: Fifty Years of Special Operations* (Fourth Estate, 2000), p. 402.

[59] Stephen Dorril, *MI6: Fifty Years of Special Operations* (Fourth Estate, 2000), p. 8.

[60] *Chips: The Diaries of Sir Henry Channon*, ed. by Robert Rhodes James (Weidenfeld & Nicolson, 1967), p. 182 and Lord Templewood (previously Samuel Hoare) *Nine Troubled Years* (Greenwood Press, 1976), p. 154.

[61] Lord Avon (previously Anthony Eden), *Facing the Dictators* (Cassell, 1962), p. 311.

[62] 'Ukraine under Bolshevist Rule', *Slavonic Review*, Vol. 12, (1933-34), p. 342.

[63] Frederick Schuman, *Russia Since 1917: Four Decades of Soviet Politics* (Alfred A. Knopf, 1957), pp. 151-2.

[64] Mark Tauger, 'The 1932 Harvest and The Famine of 1933', *Slavic Review*, Vol. 50, No.1, (1991), pp. 70-89.

[65] Mark B. Tauger, *What Caused Famine in Ukraine? A polemical response*, RFE/RL Poland, Belarus and Ukraine Report, Prague, Vol. 4, No. 25, (25 June 2002).

[66] Mark B. Tauger, '7. Grain Crisis or Famine? The Ukrainian State Commission for Aid to Crop-Failure Victims and the Ukraine famine of 1928-29', in *Provincial Landscapes: Local Dimensions of Soviet Power, 1917-1953*, ed. by Donald J. Raleigh (University of Pittsburgh Press, 2001), pp. 146-70.

[67] Adam Ulam, *Stalin: The Man and His Era* (Viking, 1973), p. 349.

[68] Matthew Klein and Michael Pettis, *Trade Wars Are Class Wars: How Rising Inequality Distorts the Global Economy and Threatens International Peace* (Yale University Press, 2020), p. 74.

[69] Richard Evans, *In Hitler's Shadow* (Tauris, 1989), p. 170.

[70] Richard Overy, *The Dictators: Hitler's Germany and Stalin's Russia* (Allen Lane, 2004), p. 194.

[71] William Shirer, *The Rise and Fall of the Third Reich* (Simon & Schuster, 2011), p. 192.

[72] 'Communism with the mask off', Nuremberg Rally speech (13 September 1935), in <https://research.calvin.edu/german-propaganda-archive/index.htm>.

[73] The National Archives, *Records of the Cabinet Office: Cabinet Papers, 21:38*, (29 July 1936).

[74] Hansard, *House of Commons Debates*, Columns 1493-1501, (26 March 1936).

[75] 'From Neurath to Ribbentrop', *DGFP*, Series D, Vol. 1, Doc. No. 228, (1 June 1937), pp. 427-8.

[76] Harold Nicolson, *Diaries and Letters, 1930-1939*, ed. by Nigel Nicolson (Harper Collins, 1966), p. 266.

[77] Lawrence R. Pratt, *East of Malta, West of Suez: Britain's Mediterranean Crisis, 1936-1939* (Cambridge University Press, 1975) p. 20.

[78] Sidney Aster, *1939: The Making of the Second World War* (Harper Collins, 1973), p. 85.

[79] For documentation of this; A. L. Rowse, *All Souls and Appeasement* (Macmillan, 1961), p. 28. L. S. Amery, *My Political Life, Volume 3. 1929-40* (Hutchinson, 1955), p. 74. Nicholas Bethell, *The War Hitler Won* (Allen Lane, 1972), p. 286. Keith Middlemas, *Diplomacy of Illusion: The British Government and Germany, 1937-39* (Littlehampton, 1972), p. 432. Gaetano Salvemini, *Prelude to World War Two* (Doubleday & Co, 1954), pp. 10-11. Douglas Little, *Malevolent Neutrality: The United States, Great Britain, and The Origins of the Spanish Civil War* (Cornell University Press, 1985), pp. 22-23. Lord Gladwyn, *The Memoirs of Lord Gladwyn* (Weidenfeld & Nicolson, 1972), p. 55. Mario Toscano, *Origins of the Pact of Steel* (Johns Hopkins University Press, 1968), p. 137.

[80] Clive Ponting, *Churchill* (Sinclair-Stevenson, 1994), p. 380.

[81] Maurice Cowling, *The Impact of Hitler: British politics and British Policy, 1933-1940* (Cambridge University Press, 1975), p. 148.

[82] For the best account of this incident and indeed of the whole war; Arthur Landis, *Spain: The Unfinished Revolution* (New York: International Publishers), 1972.

[83] Henry Channon, *Chips: The Diaries of Sir Henry Channon*, ed. by Robert Rhodes James (Weidenfeld & Nicolson, 1967), p. 73.

[84] For details of Hitler's invasion of Spain; Robert H. Whealey, *Hitler and Spain: The Nazi Role in the Spanish Civil War 1936-1939* (University Press of Kentucky, 1989), especially pp. 5-9.

[85] The National Archives, *General Correspondence, Political Foreign Office Papers*, 371, File 23, Reference 22414, (1938), p. 241: Annex 17 of R 8513.

[86] *Documents on German Foreign Policy, 1918-1945: Series D (1937-1945), Volume III: Germany and the Spanish Civil War, 1936-1939* (HMSO, 1951), pp. 932-3, in Editors' Note.

[87] Keith Feiling, *The Life of Neville Chamberlain* (Macmillan, 1946), p. 347.

[88] The National Archives, *General Correspondence, Political Foreign Office Papers, File 22407, R 3033/23/22, 18* (March 1938), p. 179 and *The Committee's Draft Telegram to Lord Perth*, p. 6 of Appendix II.

[89] Oliver Harvey, *The Diplomatic Diaries of Oliver Harvey, 1937-40*, ed. by John Harvey (Harper Collins, 1970), p. 148.

[90] The National Archives, *General Correspondence Political Foreign Office Papers, Ref. 22412. F. O. Memo R5387/23/22. F. O. Minute, file* p. 299.

[91] The National Archives, *Records of the Cabinet Office: Cabinet Minutes and Conclusions, March 1938 – September 1939: Cabinet Papers, 28 (38) 4,* (1 June 1938).

[92] J. Alvarez del Vayo, *Freedom's Battle* (William Heinemann, 1940), p. 252.

[93] Enrique Moradiellos, *La perfidia de Albión: El Gobierno británico y la guerra civil española, Siglo XXI de España Editores* (S. A., 1996), p. xvi.

[94] *New York Times* (23 January 1939).

Chapter 4

[95] Genevieve Tabouis, *They Called Me Cassandra* (Charles Scribner's Sons, 1942), p. 257.

[96] Winston S. Churchill, *The Second World War, Volume 1, The Gathering Storm* (Houghton Mifflin Harcourt, 1986), p. 258. For more on the Tukhachevsky plot; Geoffrey Bailey, *The Conspirators* (Harper & Brothers, 1960), pp. 135-40, 176-90 and 212-24. On Tukhachevsky's talks with the German High Command; p. 190. Also Grover Furr, Vladimir Bobrov and Sven-Eric Holmström *Trotsky and the Military Conspiracy: Soviet and Non-Soviet Evidence; with the Complete Transcript of the "Tukhachevsky Affair" Trial* (Erythros Press and Media, 2021).

[97] See Grover Furr, *Trotsky's Conspiracies of the 1930s, Volume 2, Leon Trotsky's Collaboration with Germany and Japan* (Erythros Press & Media, 2017) p. 294.

[98] Grover Furr, *The Moscow Trials as Evidence* (CreateSpace, 2018), pp. 149-50.

[99] Joseph Goebbels, *The Goebbels Diaries: 1942-1943,* ed. by Louis P. Lochner (Hamish Hamilton, 1948), p. 277.

[100] Grover Furr, *Trotsky's 'Amalgams': Trotsky's Lies, the Moscow Trials as Evidence, the Dewey Commission. Trotsky's Conspiracies of the 1930s, Volume One* (Erythros Press & Media, 2015), p. 45.

[101] Grover Furr, *Trotsky's 'Amalgams': Trotsky's Lies, the Moscow Trials as Evidence, the Dewey Commission. Trotsky's Conspiracies of the 1930s, Volume One* (Erythros Press & Media, 2015), p. 507.

[102] Grover Furr, *Trotsky's 'Amalgams': Trotsky's lies, the Moscow Trials as Evidence, the Dewey Commission. Trotsky's Conspiracies of the 1930s, Volume One* (Erythros Press & Media, 2015), pp. 104-5.

[103] Grover Furr, *Trotsky's Conspiracies of the 1930s, Volume 2, Leon Trotsky's Collaboration with Germany and Japan* (Erythros Press & Media, 2017), p. 104.

[104] Grover Furr, *The Moscow Trials as Evidence* (CreateSpace, 2018), p. 147.

[105] Grover Furr and Vladimir Bobrov, *Nikolai Bukharin's First Statement of Confession in the Lubianka* (Cultural Logic, 2007), pp. 16-7 and 37.

[106] *Moscow Trials. The Case of Bukharin: Interrogation of accused Bukharin - Evening Session March 5* <https://www.marxists.org/archive/bukharin/works/1938/trial/1.htm> [accessed 19 March 2013].

[107] Grover Furr, *Trotsky's Conspiracies of the 1930s, Volume 2, Leon Trotsky's Collaboration with Germany and Japan* (Erythros Press & Media, 2017,) pp. 293 and 297.

[108] Grover Furr, *Trotsky's 'Amalgams': Trotsky's Lies, the Moscow Trials as Evidence, the Dewey Commission. Trotsky's Conspiracies of the 1930s, Volume One* (Erythros Press & Media, 2015), p. 176.

[109] Stephen Cohen, 'Bukharin na Lubianke', *Svobodnaia Mysl'*, Vol. 22, No. 3, pp. 60-1.

[110] Grover Furr, *Trotsky's Conspiracies of the 1930s, Volume 2, Leon Trotsky's Collaboration with Germany and Japan* (Erythros Press & Media, 2017), p. 247.

[111] Sheila Fitzpatrick, *On Stalin's Team: The Years of Living Dangerously in Soviet Politics* (Princeton UP, 2015), p. 130.

[112] Grover Furr, *Trotsky's 'Amalgams': Trotsky's Lies, the Moscow Trials as Evidence, the Dewey Commission. Trotsky's Conspiracies of the 1930s, Volume One* (Erythros Press & Media, 2015), p. 29.

[113] Grover Furr, *Trotsky's Conspiracies of the 1930s, Volume 2, Leon Trotsky's Collaboration with Germany and Japan* (Erythros Press & Media, 2017), p. 208.

[114] Robert Thurston, *Life and Terror in Stalin's Russia, 1934-1941* (Yale University Press, 1996), p. 26.

[115] Sarah Davies and James Harris, *Stalin's World: Dictating the Soviet Order* (Yale University Press, 2015), p. 91.

[116] Leon Trotsky, *The Transitional Program (1938)* <https://www.marxists.org/archive/trotsky/1938/tp/transprogram.pdf>, p. 2.

[117] Grover Furr, *The Moscow Trials as Evidence* (CreateSpace, 2018), p. 154-5.

[118] *DGFP, Series D, Vol. 1, Doc. No. 136* (3 March 1938), p. 238. This account was confirmed by Weizsacker's memorandum on the Chamberlain-Grandi talks; *DGFP, Series D, Vol. 1, Doc. No. 130* (28 February 1938), p. 227.

[119] G. E. R. Gedye, *Fallen Bastions* (Left Book Club, 1939), pp. 400-4.

[120] *Documents on British Foreign Policy, 1919-39*, ed. by E.L. Woodward and R. Butler, Third Series, Vol. 2, Doc. No. 1140, pp. 571-3. Mark Arnold-Forster, *The World at War* (Collins, 1973), p. 21. *The Diaries of Sir Alexander Cadogan*, ed. by David Dilks (Cassell, 1971), p. 122.

[121] Charles L. Mowat, *Britain Between the Wars* (Methuen, 1955), p. 617. Sir John Wheeler-Bennett, *Munich: Prologue to Tragedy* (Macmillan, 1948), p. 106.

[122] *DBFP, Third Series, Vol. 3, 1938-9, Doc. No. 325* (24 November 1938), p. 306.

[123] *DBFP, Third Series, Vol. 3, 1938-9, Doc. No. 325* (24 November 1938), pp. 306-307.

[124] *DBFP, Third Series, Vol. 3, 1938-9, Doc. No. 500, 11-12* (January 1939), p. 525. The full report is on pp. 517-530.

[125] Robert Service, *Trotsky: A Biography* (Macmillan, 2009), pp. 459-60.

[126] Ronald Suny, *The Soviet Experiment: Russia, The USSR, and The Successor States* (Oxford University Press, 1998), p. 300.

[127] Leon Trotsky, *Problem of the Ukraine* (Socialist Appeal, 9 May 1939). Leon Trotsky, *The Independence of the Ukraine and Sectarian Muddleheads* (30 July 1939). Leon Trotsky, *Writings of Leon Trotsky 1939-40* (New York, 1977), pp. 44-54.

[128] As recorded in his later book, Neville Chamberlain, *The Struggle for Peace* (Hutchinson, 1939), p. 322.

[129] *DGFP, Series D, Vol. 4, Doc. No. 260*, p. 320.

[130] *DGFP, Series D, Vol. 4, Doc. No. 260*, p. 320.

[131] Orlando Figes, *Viewpoint: The Nazi-Soviet Pact* (BBC News, 21 August 2009).

[132] Paul Hanebrink, *A Specter Haunting Europe: The Myth of Judeo-Bolshevism* (Belknap Press, 2020), p. 129.

[133] *The Diaries of Sir Alexander Cadogan 1938-45*, ed. by David Dilks (Cassell, 1971), p. 182.

[134] *The Ironside Diaries 1937-1940* ed. by R. Macleod and Denis Kelly (Constable, 1962, entry for 10 July 1939), p. 78.

[135] Maurice Cowling, *The Impact of Hitler: British Politics and British Policy 1933-40* (Cambridge University Press, 1975), p. 300.

[136] L.B. Namier, *Diplomatic Prelude, 1938-1939* (Macmillan, 1948), p. 188. For a full account of the negotiations, see Chapter V, pp. 143-210.

[137] Alvin Finkel and Clement Leibovitz, *The Chamberlain-Hitler Collusion* (Merlin, 1997), p. 8.

[138] John Loftus and Mark Aarons, *The Secret War Against the Jews: How Western Espionage Betrayed the Jewish People* (New York: St Martin's Griffin, 1994), p. 495.

[139] Stephen F. Cohen, *Sovieticus: American Perceptions and Soviet Realities* (W. W. Norton, 1987), pp. 99-100.

[140] Brian I. Fugate and Lev Dvoretsky, *Thunder on the Dnepr: Zhukov-Stalin and the Defeat of Hitler's Blitzkrieg* (Presidio Press, California, 1997), pp. xi-xii.

[141] Evan Mawdsley, *World War II: A New History* (Cambridge University Press, 2009), p. 140.

[142] Richard Overy, *Russia's War* (Allen Lane 1998), p. 64.

[143] Albert Axell, *Stalin's War: Through the Eyes of his Commanders* (Arms & Armour Press, 1997), pp. 69-72, 121-3 and 189.

Chapter 5

[144] *The Irving Judgement: David Irving v. Penguin Books and Professor Deborah Lipstadt* (Penguin Books, 2000), p. 114.

[145] *The Irving Judgement: David Irving v. Penguin Books and Professor Deborah Lipstadt* (Penguin Books, 2000), p. 70.

[146] *The Irving Judgement: David Irving v. Penguin Books and Professor Deborah Lipstadt* (Penguin Books, 2000), p. 143.

[147] Mark Mazower, *Hitler's Empire: Nazi Rule in Occupied Europe* (Allen Lane, 2008), pp. 281-2.

[148] David Stahel, *Retreat From Moscow: A New History of Germany's Winter Campaign, 1941-1942* (Farrar, Straus & Giroux, 2019), p. 266.

[149] Mark Mazower, *Inside Hitler's Greece: The Experience of Occupation, 1941-44* (Yale University Press, 1993), p. 9.

[150] David Stahel, *Retreat From Moscow: A New History of Germany's Winter Campaign, 1941-1942* (Farrar, Straus & Giroux, 2019), p. 374.

[151] David Stahel, *Operation Typhoon: Hitler's March on Moscow, October 1941* (Cambridge University Press, 2015), pp. 2, 16 and 26.

[152] Prit Buttar, *Battleground Prussia: The Assault on Germany's Eastern Front 1944-1945* (Osprey, 2015), p. 10.

[153] Evan Mawdsley, *Thunder in The East: The Nazi-Soviet War 1941-1945* (Hodder Arnold, 2007), p. 11.

[154] David Stahel, *Retreat From Moscow: A New History of Germany's Winter Campaign, 1941-1942* (Farrar, Straus & Giroux, 2019), pp. 354-61.

[155] George Kassimeris, 'The Second World War: A Barbarous Conflict', in *The Barbarisation of Warfare*, ed. by George Kassimeris (Hurst & Company, 2006), pp. 39-57 and 42.

[156] Prit Buttar, *On a Knife's Edge: The Ukraine, November 1942 – March 1943* (Osprey Publishing, 2019), pp. 120-1.

[157] Prit Buttar, *On a Knife's Edge: The Ukraine, November 1942 – March 1943* (Osprey Publishing, 2019), p. 121.

[158] David Stahel, *Operation Typhoon: Hitler's March on Moscow, October 1941* (CUP, 2015), p. 121.

[159] Prit Buttar, 1943 *On a Knife's Edge: The Ukraine, November 1942 – March 1943* (Osprey Publishing, 2019), p. 123.

[160] Hew Strachan, 'Preface', in Evan Mawdsley, *Thunder in The East: The Nazi-Soviet War 1941-1945* (Hodder Arnold, 2007), pp. xvi-ii.

[161] Prit Buttar, *On a Knife's Edge: The Ukraine, November 1942 – March 1943* (Osprey Publishing, 2019), p. 121.

[162] Prit Buttar, *On a Knife's Edge: The Ukraine, November 1942 – March 1943* (Osprey Publishing, 2019), pp. 277-8.

[163] Prit Buttar, *On a Knife's Edge: The Ukraine, November 1942 – March 1943* (Osprey Publishing, 2019), p. 16.

[164] David Stahel, *Retreat from Moscow: A New History of Germany's Winter Campaign, 1941-1942* (Farrar, Straus & Giroux, 2019), p. 155.

[165] Winston Churchill, *Speech in the House of Commons* (October 1944).

[166] John L. Gaddis, *The United States and The Origins of the Cold War 1941-1947* (New York: Columbia University Press, 1972), p. 5.

[167] Winston Churchill, *War Situation*, Speech in the House of Commons (2 August 1944).

[168] *Memoirs of Field Marshal the Viscount Montgomery of Alamein* (London: Collins, 1958), p. 454.

[169] William Mandel, *A Guide to The Soviet Union* (New York: The Dial Press, 1946), p. 119.

[170] Anne Eliot Griesse and Richard Stites, 'Russia: Revolution and War', in *Female Soldiers – Combatants or Noncombatants? Historical and Contemporary Perspectives*, ed. by Nancy Goldman (Greenwood, 1982), p. 75.

[171] Roger R. Reese, *Why Stalin's Soldiers Fought: The Red Army's Military Effectiveness in World War II* (University Press of Kansas, 2011), p. 305.

[172] Roger R. Reese, *Why Stalin's Soldiers Fought: The Red Army's Military Effectiveness in World War II* (University Press of Kansas, 2011), p. 313.

[173] Philip M. H. Bell, 'British Government Views on the Importance of Public Opinion During the Second World War', *Mélanges de l'École française de Rome. Italie et Méditerranée*, Vol. 108, No. 1 (1996), pp. 33-8.

[174] Winston S. Churchill, *Complete speeches, 1897-1963, Volume III*, ed. by Robert Rhodes James (Macmillan, 1974), p. 2664.

[175] Chris Bellamy, *Absolute War: Soviet Russia in the Second World War: A Modern History* (Macmillan, 2007), p. 424.

[176] Stephen Dorril, *MI6: Fifty Years of Special Operations* (Fourth Estate, 2000), p. 12.

[177] Tom Bower, *Red Web: MI6 and the KGB Master Coup* (Mandarin Paperbacks, 1993), p. 41.

[178] Roger R. Reese, *Why Stalin's Soldiers Fought: the Red Army's Military Effectiveness in World War II* (University Press of Kansas, 2011), p. 175.

[179] Grover Furr, *The Mystery of The Katyn Massacre: The Evidence, The Solution* (Erythros Press and Media, 2018), pp. 41-2

[180] Mark Mazower, *Inside Hitler's Greece: The Experience of Occupation, 1941-44* (Yale University Press, 1993), pp. 328-9.

[181] Andrew Roberts, *The Storm of War: A New History of the Second World War* (Allen Lane, 2009), p. 534. Will Podmore, *The War Against the Working Class* (Xlibris, 2015), pp. 75-9.

[182] Robin Edmonds, *The Big Three: Churchill, Roosevelt and Stalin in Peace and War* (Hamish Hamilton, 1991), p. 385.

[183] Timothy Snyder, *Bloodlands: Europe Between Hitler and Stalin* (The Bodley Head, 2010), p. 306.

[184] Paul Hanebrink, *A Specter Haunting Europe: The Myth of Judeo-Bolshevism* (Belknap Press, 2020), p. 203.

[185] Paul Hanebrink, *A Specter Haunting Europe: The Myth of Judeo-Bolshevism* (Belknap Press, 2020), p. 203.

[186] Prit Buttar, *Battleground Prussia: The Assault on Germany's Eastern Front 1944-1945* (Osprey, 2015), pp. 21-2.

[187] Mao Tse-tung, *On Correcting Mistaken Ideas in the Party, Selected Works, Vol. I* (December 1929), p. 110.

[188] Hansard, *House of Commons Debates* (28 February 1945).

[189] Paul Hanebrink, *A Specter Haunting Europe: The Myth of Judeo-Bolshevism* (Belknap Press, 2020), p. 167.

[190] Paul N. Hehn, *A Low Dishonest Decade: The Great Powers, Eastern Europe, and The Economic Origins of World War Two, 1930-1941* (New York: Continuum, 2002), p. 394.

[191] J. W. Durcan and W. E. J. McCarthy, 'The State Subsidy Theory of Strikes: an Examination of Statistical Data for the Period 1956-70', *British Journal of Industrial Relations*, Volume 12, (1976), pp. 26-47.

[192] Justin Davis Smith, *The Attlee and Churchill Administrations and Industrial Unrest, 1945-55: A Study in Consensus* (Pinter, 1990), pp. 5 and 42.

[193] Thomas J. McCormick, *America's Half-Century: United States Foreign Policy in the Cold War and After*, 2nd edn, (Johns Hopkins University Press, 1995), pp. 55-6.

[194] Ben Pimlott, *Hugh Dalton* (Cape, 1985), p. 436.

[195] John Baylis, *Anglo-American Defence Relations, 1939-80* (Macmillan, 1981), p. 34.

[196] D. W. Pike, 'Franco and the Axis Stigma', *Journal of Contemporary History*, Volume 17, Number 3, (July 1982), pp. 369-408. Qasim Ahmad, *Britain, Franco Spain, and the Cold War, 1945-1950* (New York: Garland, 1992), Passim, but especially pp. 110 and 206.

[197] Anthony Verrier, *Through the Looking Glass: British Foreign Policy in an Age of Illusions* (Cape, 1983), p. 67.

[198] Ian Brownlie, *International Law and the Use of Force by States* (Oxford: Oxford University Press, 1963), pp. 282-9. Ian Brownlie, *Principles of Public International Law*, 3rd edn, (Oxford: Oxford University Press, 1979), pp. 282 and 442-4. D. W. Greig, *International Law*, 2nd edn, (Butterworth, 1976), p. 526.

[199] J. D. V. Allen, *The Malayan Union* (Yale University Press, 1967), p. 19.

[200] John Mills, *The Elephant In The Room* (Civitas, 2020), p. 133.

[201] Girsh Khanin, 'The 1950s – The Triumph of the Soviet Economy', *Europe-Asia Studies*, Vol. 55, No. 8, pp. 1187-212, (2003), pp. 1196-9.

[202] *The Challenge of Slums, Global Report on Human Settlements* (Earthscan Publications Ltd on behalf of the UN Human Settlements Programme, 2003), p. 30.

[203] Europe and Central Asia Region Human Development Sector Unit, *BELARUS: POVERTY ASSESSMENT. Can Poverty Reduction and Access to Services Be Sustained?*, <http://documents1.worldbank.org/curated/en/9618314680 12054036/pdf/274310BY0belarus1pa01PUBLIC1.pdf>, (November 2004), pp. vi, vii, vii, 11, 14 and 74.

[204] Vincent Bevins, *The Jakarta Method: Washington's Anti-Communist Crusade and The Mass Murder Program That Shaped Our World*, (Public Affairs, 2020), pp. 266-7.

[205] John Coatsworth, 'Chapter 10: The Cold War in Central America, 1979-1991', in *The Cambridge History of the Cold War, Volume 3: Endings*, ed. by Melvyn P. Leffler and Odd Arne Westad (Cambridge University Press, 2010), pp. 201-221.

Chapter 6

[206] Michael Schaller, *The U.S. Crusade in China, 1938-1945* (Columbia University Press, 1979), p. 274.

[207] On the huge scale of the US intervention, see Michael Schaller, *The U.S. Crusade In China, 1938-1945*, especially 'Chapter 11, SACO: The Counter-Revolution in Action', (Columbia University Press, 1979), pp. 231-50 and pp. 264-74.

[208] Jack Belden, *China Shakes the World (1949)* (Penguin Books, 1973), p. 602-3. On the crossing of the Yangtze, see pp. 596-606.

[209] Angus Maddison, *Chinese Economic Performance in The Long Run, Organisation for Economic Co-operation and Development* (1998), p. 15.

[210] Interview, *US News and Views* (13 August 1954). Ernie Trory, 'Chapter 11: The Invasion of North Korea', in *Peace and The Cold War. Part 1. Labour in Government: 1945-51* (Crabtree Press, 1996), pp. 225-34. William Blum, *Killing Hope: U. S. Military and CIA Interventions since World War II* (Black Rose Press, 1998), pp. 46-9. Bruce Cumings, *The Origins of the Korean War, Volume II The Roaring of The Cataract 1947-1950* (Princeton University Press, 1990), pp. 431-5, 599 and 617-9.

[211] Alex Carey, 'The Bureaucratic Passport War: Wilfred Burchett and The Australian Government', in *Burchett: Reporting the Other Side of The World 1939-1983*, ed. by Ben Kiernan (Quartet Books, 1986), p. 79.

[212] Editorial, *Toronto Globe and Mail* (22 February 1961).

[213] Paul Thomas Chamberlin, *The Cold War's Killing Fields: Rethinking The Long Peace* (Harper, 2018), p. 146.

[214] Curtis LeMay and MacKinlay Kantor, *Mission With LeMay: My Story* (Doubleday, 1960), p. 382.

[215] Robert Beisner, *Dean Acheson: A Life In The Cold War* (Oxford University Press, 2006), p. 438.

[216] Robert Beisner, *Dean Acheson: A Life In The Cold War* (Oxford University Press, 2006), p. 438.

[217] Christian Appy, *The Vietnam War: The Definitive Oral History, Told From All Sides* (Ebury Press, 2008), p. 405.

[218] Otto Kolbl, *The evolution of infant mortality in China since 1950*, <https://www.rainbowbuilders.org/china-development/infant-mortality-china-evolution>.

[219] Chun Lin, *China and Global Capitalism: Reflections on Marxism, History, and Contemporary Politics* (Palgrave, 2013), pp. 49-50.

[220] Robert Price, *International Trade of Communist China 1950-1965: An Economic Profile of Mainland China, Vol. II* (US Joint Economic Committee, 1975), pp. 600-1.

[221] Robert C. North, *Chinese Communism* (Weidenfeld & Nicolson, 1966), p. 191.

[222] Henry C. K. Liu, 'Mao and Lincoln Part 2: The Great Leap Forward Not All Bad', *Asia Times Online*, <http://rauschreading09.pbworks.com/f/Great+Leap+Forward+Not+All+Bad+-+Asia+Times+Online.pdf>.

[223] Felix Greene, *The Wall Has Two Sides: A Portrait of China Today* (Jonathan Cape, 1964), p. 402.

[224] Ed. by Mark Selden, *The People's Republic of China: A Documentary History of Revolutionary Change* (Monthly Review Press), 1979, Note p. 134.

[225] Barry Naughton, 'Chapter 11, Agriculture: Output, Inputs, and Technology', in *The Chinese Economy: Transitions and Growth* (MIT Press, 2007), pp. 251-70.

[226] Y. Y. Kueh, 'Mao and Agriculture in China's Industrialization: Three Antitheses In A 50-Year Perspective', *China Quarterly*, No. 187, (September 2006), pp. 700-23.

[227] The World Bank, *World Development Report*, <https://openknowledge.worldbank.org/bitstream/handle/10986/5964/WDR%201981%20-%20English.pdf?sequence=1&isAllowed=y>, (August 1981), p. 85.

[228] The World Bank, *China: Socialist Economic Development, Vol. I, Washington: World Bank, 1983*, I-94-5.

[229] Y. Y. Kueh, *China's New Industrialization Strategy: Was Chairman Mao Really Necessary?* (Edward Elgar, 2007), p. 32.

[230] Amartya Sen, *Development as Freedom* (Oxford University Press, 1999), p. 260.

[231] Maurice Meisner, 'The Significance of the Chinese Revolution in World History', (London: *LSE Asia Research Centre Working Papers 1*, 1999), pp. 1 and 12.

[232] Jean Drèze and Amartya Sen, *Hunger and Public Action* (Clarendon Press, 1989), pp. 214-5.

[233] Jean Drèze and Amartya Sen, *Hunger and Public Action* (Clarendon Press, 1989), pp. 204 and 205.

Chapter 7

[234] Joseph Buttinger, *A Dragon Defiant: A Short History of Vietnam* (Praeger, 1972), p. 79.

[235] Christian Appy, *American Reckoning: The Vietnam War and Our National Identity* (Viking, 2015), p. 20.

[236] John Spanier and Steven W. Hook, *American Foreign Policy Since World War II*, 13th edn., (Washington: Congressional Quarterly Inc., 1995), p. 130.

[237] Robert Buzzanco, *Vietnam and The Transformation of American Life* (Blackwell, 1999), p. 57.

[238] Marilyn Young, *The Vietnam Wars 1945-1990* (Harper, 1991), p. 53.

[239] John Marciano, *The American War in Vietnam: Crime or Commemoration?* (Monthly Review Press, 2016), p. 58.

[240] Christian Appy, *American Reckoning: The Vietnam War and Our National Identity* (Viking, 2015), p. 43.

[241] John Marciano, *The American War in Vietnam: Crime or Commemoration?* (Monthly Review Press, 2016), p. 60.

[242] John Marciano, *The American War in Vietnam: Crime or Commemoration?* (Monthly Review Press, 2016), p. 60.

[243] Joseph Buttinger, *Vietnam: The Unforgettable Tragedy* (Horizon Press, 1977), p. 48.

[244] Joseph Buttinger, *A Dragon Defiant: A Short History of Vietnam* (Praeger, 1972), both p. 100.

[245] Paul Thomas Chamberlin, *The Cold War's Killing Fields: Rethinking The Long Peace* (Harper, 2018), pp. 195-6.

[246] Christian Appy, *American Reckoning: The Vietnam War and Our National Identity* (Viking, 2015), p. 27.

[247] John Marciano, 'Civic Illiteracy and Education: The Battle For The Hearts and Minds of American Youth', *New York Times*, 28 July 1972, (Peter Lang Publishing, 1997), p. 119.

[248] Edwin Moïse, 'Land Reform and Land Reform Errors in North Vietnam', *Pacific Affairs*, Vol. 49, No. 1, (1976), pp. 70-92.

[249] Edwin Moïse, 'Land Reform and Land Reform Errors in North Vietnam', *Pacific Affairs*, Vol. 49, No. 1, (1976) pp. 70-92.

[250] John Marciano, *The American War in Vietnam: Crime or Commemoration?* (Monthly Review Press, 2016), p. 75.

[251] Paul Thomas Chamberlin, *The Cold War's Killing Fields: Rethinking The Long Peace* (Harper, 2018), p. 206.

[252] Edwin Moïse, *Tonkin Gulf and The Escalation of The Vietnam War* (Naval Institute Press, 2019), p. 249.

[253] Edwin Moïse, *Tonkin Gulf and The Escalation of The Vietnam War* (Naval Institute Press, 2019), p. 217.

[254] Edwin Moïse, *Tonkin Gulf and The Escalation of The Vietnam War* (Naval Institute Press, 2019), pp. 98-9 and 100-1.

[255] Christian Appy, *American Reckoning: The Vietnam War and Our National Identity* (Viking, 2015), p. 68.

[256] Christian Appy, *American Reckoning: The Vietnam War and Our National Identity* (Viking, 2015), p. 276.

[257] Nixon Presidential Materials Project, *Henry A. Kissinger Telephone Conversations Transcripts, Home File, Box 29, File 2, 106-10.*

[258] Mao Tse-Tung, *The Bankruptcy of The Idealist Conception of History, Selected Works, Volume IV* (Foreign Languages Press, Peking, 1969), pp. 451-9.

[259] David Maraniss, *They Marched Into Sunlight: War and Peace Vietnam and America October 1967* (Simon & Schuster, 2004), p. 130.

[260] David Maraniss, *They Marched Into Sunlight: War and Peace Vietnam and America October 1967* (Simon & Schuster, 2004), p. 200.

[261] Christian Appy, *American Reckoning: The Vietnam War and Our National Identity* (Viking, 2015), p. 217.

[262] Christian Appy, *American Reckoning: The Vietnam War and Our National Identity* (Viking, 2015), p. 335.

[263] John Marciano, *The American War in Vietnam: Crime or Commemoration?* (Monthly Review Press, 2016), p. 158.

Chapter 8

[264] John Mathews, Ford Strike: The Workers' Story (Panther Books, 1972), p. 66.

[265] Chris Wrigley, 'Chapter 2: Women in the Labour Market and In The Unions', in *British Trade Unions and Industrial Politics: Volume 2: The High Tide of Trade Unionism, 1964-79*, ed. by Alan Campbell, Nina Fishman and John McIlroy, (Ashgate, 1999), pp. 43-69.

[266] Sander Meredeen, *Managing Industrial Conflict: Seven Major Disputes* (Hutchinson, 1988), p. 33.

[267] Sally Groves and Vernon Merritt, *Trico: A Victory to Remember. The 1976 Equal Pay Strike at Trico Folberth, Brentford* (Lawrence & Wishart, 2018), pp. 141 and 143.

[268] Sally Groves and Vernon Merritt, *Trico: A Victory to Remember. The 1976 Equal Pay Strike at Trico Folberth, Brentford* (Lawrence & Wishart, 2018), p. 180.

[269] Sally Groves and Vernon Merritt, *Trico: A Victory to Remember. The 1976 Equal Pay Strike at Trico Folberth, Brentford* (Lawrence & Wishart, 2018), pp. 156-7.

[270] Sally Groves and Vernon Merritt, *Trico: A Victory to Remember. The 1976 Equal Pay Strike at Trico Folberth, Brentford* (Lawrence & Wishart, 2018), p. 173.

[271] Sally Groves and Vernon Merritt, *Trico: A Victory to Remember. The 1976 Equal Pay Strike at Trico Folberth, Brentford* (Lawrence & Wishart, 2018), p. 189.

[272] Sean Wilentz, *The Age of Reagan: A History, 1974-2008* (Harper Perennial, 2009), p. 437.

[273] Sidney Pollard, *The Development of The British Economy 1914-1990*, 4th edn, (Arnold, 1992), pp. 376-432.

[274] Joseph Stiglitz, *Rewriting the Rules of the European Economy: An Agenda For Growth and Shared Prosperity* (W.W. Norton, 2020), p. xvii.

[275] John Mills, *The Elephant in The Room* (Civitas, 2020), p. 189 and p. 264, footnote 413.

[276] Joseph Stiglitz, *Rewriting the Rules of the European Economy: An Agenda For Growth and Shared Prosperity* (W.W. Norton, 2020), p. 17.

[277] Robert Taylor, *The Trade Union Question in British Politics: Government and Unions Since 1945*, (Blackwell, 1993), p. 303.

[278] Michael Heseltine, 'Chapter 2: Creeping Federalism', in *The Challenge of Europe: Can Britain Win?* (Weidenfeld and Nicolson, 1989), pp. 15-37, especially p. 23.

[279] Kenneth Dyson and Kevin Featherstone, *The Road to Maastricht: Negotiating Economic and Monetary Union* (Oxford University Press, 1999), p. 710.

[280] Kenneth Armstrong and Simon Bulmer, *The Governance of the Single European Market* (Manchester University Press, 1998), p. 302.

[281] Charlotte Bretherton and John Vogler, *The European Union As A Global Actor* (Routledge, 1999), p. 58.

[282] Stephan Leibfried and Paul Pierson, 'Chapter 10 Social Policy: Left To Courts and Markets?', in *Policy-Making in The European Union*, ed. by Helen Wallace and William Wallace, 4th edn. (Oxford University Press, 2000), pp. 267-92, especially p. 268.

[283] John Turner, *The Tories and Europe* (Manchester University Press, 2000), p. 151.

[284] On the SEM's effects; Nicholas Costello, Jonathan Michie and Seumas Milne, *Beyond the Casino Economy: Planning For the 1990s* (Verso, 1989), pp. 28, 31, 36 and 44-5.

[285] John Turner, *The Tories and Europe* (Manchester University Press, 2000), p. 96.

[286] Richard Tuck, *The Left Case for Brexit: Reflections on The Current Crisis* (Polity Press, 2020), p. 75.

[287] Roger Bootle, *Making a Success of Brexit and Reforming the EU: The Brexit Edition of The Trouble With Europe* (Nicholas Brealey Publishing, 2017), p. 166.

Chapter 9

[288] Joseph Stiglitz, *Rewriting the Rules of The European Economy: An Agenda For Growth and Shared Prosperity* (W.W. Norton, 2020), p. 3.

[289] Bojan Bugarič, 'Europe Against the Left? On Legal Limits to Progressive Politics', *LEQS Paper* No. *61/2013* (May 2013), pp. 23 and 25.

[290] Joseph Stiglitz, *Rewriting the Rules of The European Economy: An Agenda For Growth and Shared Prosperity* (W.W. Norton, 2020), p. xix.

[291] Roger Eatwell and Matthew Goodwin, *National Populism: The Revolt Against Liberal Democracy* (Pelican, 2018), p. 46.

[292] Roger Bootle, *Making A Success of Brexit and Reforming The EU: The Brexit Edition of The Trouble With Europe* (Nicholas Brealey Publishing, 2017), pp. 162-3.

[293] National Centre for Social Research, *British Social Attitudes 2017*, p. 3.

[294] Ray Bassett, *Ireland and The EU Post Brexit* (Grangeland Ventures Ltd, 2020), p. 198.

[295] Richard Tuck, *The Left Case For Brexit: Reflections On The Current Crisis* (Polity Press, 2020), p. 50.

[296] Joseph Stiglitz, *Rewriting the Rules of The European Economy: An Agenda For Growth and Shared Prosperity* (W.W. Norton, 2020), p. 207.

[297] Anatol Lieven, *Climate Change and The Nation-State: The Realist Case* (Allen Lane, 2020), p. 94.

[298] Joseph Stiglitz, *Rewriting the Rules of The European Economy: An Agenda For Growth and Shared Prosperity* (W.W. Norton, 2020), p. 19.

[299] Joseph Stiglitz, *Rewriting the Rules of The European Economy: An Agenda For Growth and Shared Prosperity* (W.W. Norton, 2020), p. 15.

[300] John Mills, *The Elephant In The Room* (Civitas, 2020), p. 27.

[301] John Weeks, *Brexit: reflecting the EU's neoliberal shift* (2016) <https://www.primeeconomics.org/articles/brexit-reflecting-the-eus-neoliberal-shift/>.

[302] Joseph Stiglitz, *Rewriting the Rules of The European Economy: An Agenda For Growth and Shared Prosperity* (W.W. Norton, 2020), pp. 3 and 68.

[303] Paul Krugman, *Arguing With Zombies: Economics, Politics, and A Fight For A Better Future* (Norton, 2020), pp. 184-5.

[304] Dani Rodrik, *Straight Talk On Trade: Ideas For a Sane Economy* (Princeton University Press, 2017), p. 28.

[305] Joseph Stiglitz, *Rewriting the Rules of The European Economy: An Agenda For Growth and Shared Prosperity* (W.W. Norton, 2020), p. 263.

Chapter 10

[306] *The Report of the Iraq Inquiry*, <https://webarchive.nationalarchives.gov.uk/2017112312323 7/http://www.iraqinquiry.org.uk/> (2016).

[307] *Libya: Examination of Intervention and Collapse and The UK's Future Policy Options*, House of Commons Foreign Affairs Committee, Third Report of Session 2016–17, Report together with formal minutes relating to the report. Ordered by the House of Commons to be printed 6 September 2016.

[308] Ed. by James Crawford, *Brownlie's Principles of Public International Law*, 9th edn. (Oxford University Press, 2019), pp. 730-1.

[309] John Marciano, *The American War In Vietnam: Crime or Commemoration?* (Monthly Review Press, 2016), p. 129.

[310] Mark Danner, *Spiral: Trapped In The Forever War* (Simon & Schuster, 2016), p. 147.

[311] Derek Leebaert, *Magic and Mayhem: The Delusions of American Foreign Policy From Korea To Afghanistan* (Simon & Schuster, 2010), p. 299.

[312] Cullen Murphy, *God's Jury: The Inquisition and The Making Of The Modern World* (Allen Lane, 2012), p. 87.

[313] Mark Danner, *Spiral: Trapped In The Forever War* (Simon & Schuster, 2016), p. 71.

[314] Mark Danner, *Spiral: Trapped In The Forever War* (Simon & Schuster, 2016), pp. 17-8.

[315] *The Handling of Detainees by UK Intelligence Personnel in Afghanistan, Guantanamo Bay and Iraq (CM 6469).*

[316] House of Lords - *A (FC) and others (FC) (Appellants) v. Secretary of State for the Home Department (Respondent) (2004) A and others (Appellants) (FC) and others v. Secretary of State for the Home Department (Respondent) (Conjoined Appeals)*, <https://publications.parliament.uk/pa/ld200506/ldjudgmt/jd051208/aand-4.htm>

[317] Citing Lord Hoffmann in R v Sec of State for the Home Department, Ex p Simms [2000] 2 AC 115, 131.

[318] Tom Bingham, *The Rule Of Law* (Allen Lane, 2010), p. 154.

399

Chapter 11

[319] Keith Bolender, *Cuba Under Siege: American Policy, The Revolution, and Its People* (Palgrave Macmillan, 2012), p. 47.

[320] Arnold August, Cuba and its neighbours: democracy in motion, (Zed Books, 2013), p. 101.

[321] Lars Schoultz, *That Infernal Little Cuban Republic: The United States and The Cuban Revolution* (University of North Carolina Press, 2009), p. 61.

[322] *Department of State, Foreign Relations of the United States, 1958-1960, Volume VI, Cuba (1991)*, p. 885.

[323] Salim Lamrani, *The Economic War Against Cuba: A Historical and Legal Perspective on The U.S. Blockade* (Monthly Review Press, 2013), p. 13.

[324] Keith Bolender, *Cuba Under Siege: American Policy, The Revolution, and Its People* (Palgrave Macmillan, 2012), pp. 87-8.

[325] Aleksandr Fursenko and Timothy Naftali, *Khrushchev's Cold War: The Inside Story of An American Adversary* (W.W. Norton & Company, 2006), p. 314, pp. 318-9 and 321.

[326] Helen Yaffe, *We Are Cuba! How A Revolutionary People Have Survived In a Post-Soviet World* (Yale UP, 2019), pp. 176-7.

[327] Ed. by Sandor Halebsky and John M. Kirk, *Cuba: Twenty-Five Years of Revolution, 1959-1984* (Praeger, 1985), pp. 193-4.

[328] Sarah Marsh, *U.S. trade embargo has cost Cuba $130 billion, U.N. says*, <https://www.reuters.com/article/us-cuba-economy-un idUSKBN1IA00T#:~:text=U.S.%20trade%20embargo%20has%20cost%20Cuba%20%24130%20billion%2C,the%20same%20estimate%20as%20the%20island%E2%80%99s%20communist%20government.> (May 2018).

[329] Ed. by Philip Brenner, Marguerite Rose Jiménez, John M. Kirk and William M. LeoGrande, *A Contemporary Cuba Reader: Reinventing the Revolution* (Rowman & Littlefield, 2008), p. 21.

[330] Steve Ludlam, 'Cuban Labour at 50: What About the Workers?', *Bulletin of Latin American Research, Vol. 28, No. 4* (2009), pp. 542–57.

[331] On Cuba's Sustainable Development; Pamela Stricker, *Towards a Culture of Nature: Environmental Policy and Sustainable Development in Cuba* (Lexington Books, 2007), pp. 1-13. On its farming, see pp. 15-44. On its renewable energy sources – biomass, biogas, solar, hydroelectric and wind, see pp. 45-50 and 56-7. On its efforts to cut energy use, see pp. 50-2.

[332] John M. Kirk and H. Michael Erisman, *Cuban Medical Internationalism: Origins, Evolution, and Goals* (Palgrave Macmillan, 2009), pp. 13, 107-8, 137-9, 141-6 and 156.

[333] For more on CELAC; Arnold August, *Cuba and Its Neighbours: Democracy In Motion* (Zed Books, 2013), pp. 72-4.

[334] John M. Kirk and H. Michael Erisman, *Cuban Medical Internationalism: Origins, Evolution, and Goals* (Palgrave Macmillan, 2009), pp. 51-5, 57, 128, 132, 135-7, 139-42, 152, 169, 182 and 213.

[335] Duncan Green, *From Poverty To Power* (Oxfam, 2008), p. 251.

[336] Steve Brouwer, *Revolutionary Doctors: How Venezuela and Cuba Are Changing the World's Conception of Health Care* (Monthly Review Press, 2011), p. 38.

[337] Steve Ludlam, 'Cuban Labour at 50: What About the Workers?', *Bulletin of Latin American Research, Vol. 28, No. 4* (2009), pp. 542–57.

[338] Steve Ludlam, 'Cuban Labour at 50: What About the Workers?', *Bulletin of Latin American Research, Vol. 28, No. 4* (2009), pp. 542–57, especially 542.

[339] *Cuba Sí* (Autumn 2013), p. 24.

[340] For more on Cuba's system of local democracy; Peter Latham, *The State and Local Government: Towards a New Basis For 'Local Democracy' and The Defeat of Big Business Control*, (Manifesto Press, 2011), pp. 305-22. On People's Power; Arnold August, *Cuba and Its Neighbours: Democracy in Motion* (Zed Books, 2013), pp. 112-4. On the 1997-98 elections; *Democracy in Cuba and the 1997-98 Elections* (Editorial José Marti, 1999).

[341] On Cuba's elections; 'Chapter 7, Elections in Contemporary Cuba', in *Cuba and Its Neighbours: Democracy in Motion* (Zed Books, 2013), pp. 146-94.

[342] For more on the workings of the National Assembly; 'Chapter 8, The ANPP and The Municipality: Functioning Between Elections', in *Cuba and Its Neighbours: Democracy in Motion* (Zed Books, 2013), pp. 195-227.

[343] Sergio Díaz-Briquets and Jorge Pérez-López, *Corruption in Cuba: Castro and Beyond* (University of Texas Press, 2006).

[344] Lois M. Smith and Alfred Padula, *Sex and Revolution: Women in Socialist Cuba* (Oxford University Press, 1996), pp. 142 and 182.

[345] Edward W. Campion and Stephen Morrissey, 'A Different Model: Healthcare in Cuba', *New England Journal of Medicine*, 368, (2013), pp. 297-9. <https://www.nejm.org/doi/full/10.1056/NEJMp1215226>.

[346] Margo Kirk, 'Chapter 32: Early Childhood Education In Revolutionary Cuba During the Special Period', in *A Contemporary Cuba Reader: Reinventing the Revolution*, ed. by Philip Brenner, Marguerite Rose Jiménez, John M. Kirk and William M. LeoGrande (Rowman & Littlefield, 2008), pp. 302-8.

[347] Priscilla Lounds, 'Cuba declared "best place to be a mother"', *Liberation News*, <https://www.liberationnews.org/10-05-09-cuba-declared-best-place-to-be-html/>.

[348] Don Fitz, *Cuban Health Care: The Ongoing Revolution* (Monthly Review Press, 2020), p. 141.

[349] John M. Kirk and H. Michael Erisman, *Cuban Medical Internationalism: Origins, Evolution, and Goals* (Palgrave Macmillan, 2009), pp. 143, 160 and 177.

[350] Helen Yaffe, *We Are Cuba! How A Revolutionary People Have Survived In A Post-Soviet World* (Yale UP, 2019), p. 91.

[351] Monty Don, *Around The World In 80 Gardens* (Weidenfeld & Nicolson, 2008), p. 97. 'Accounts of Organopónico Vivero Alamar', pp. 90- 2, 'Huerto Alberto Rojas', pp. 93-4 and 'Huerto Angelito', pp. 95-7.

[352] Richard Wilkinson and Kate Pickett, *The Spirit Level: Why Equality Is Better For Everyone* (Penguin, 2010), p. 220.

[353] Helen Yaffe, *We Are Cuba! How A Revolutionary People Have Survived In A Post-Soviet World* (Yale UP, 2019), p. 64.

[354] Pamela Stricker, *Towards A Culture Of Nature: Environmental Policy and Sustainable Development In Cuba* (Lexington Books, 2007), pp. 95-104; on Cubans' understanding of sustainable development, pp. 105-19.

[355] Helen Yaffe, *We Are Cuba! How A Revolutionary People Have Survived In A Post-Soviet World* (Yale UP, 2019), p. 100.

[356] Helen Yaffe, *We Are Cuba! How A Revolutionary People Have Survived In A Post-Soviet World* (Yale UP, 2019), pp. 273 and 278.

Chapter 12

[357] Centre for Brexit Policy, *Replacing the Withdrawal Agreement: How To Ensure the UK Takes Back Control on Exiting the Transition Period* (2020), pp. 10 and 11.

[358] Roger Eatwell and Matthew Goodwin, *National Populism: The Revolt Against Liberal Democracy* (Pelican, 2018), pp. 98-9.

[359] *Report On Renegotiation* (Cmnd 6003), para 153.

[360] Both quotes from *Britain and the European Union: Lessons from History* (Mile End Institute, Queen Mary University of London, March 2016), p. 16.

[361] Adam Tomkins, *Public Law* (Oxford University Press, 2003), p. 10.

[362] Richard Tuck, *Brexit: A Prize In Reach For The Left* (17 July 2017).

[363] John Lloyd, *Should Auld Acquaintance Be Forgot: The Great Mistake of Scottish Independence* (Polity Press, 2020), p. 196.

[364] Richard Tuck, *The Left Case For Brexit: Reflections On The Current Crisis*, (Polity Press, 2020), p. 20.

[365] Ed. by Frank Keoghan, Ruan O'Donnell & Michael Quinn, *A Festschrift For Anthony Coughlan: Essays On Sovereignty and Democracy* (Iontas Press, 2018), p. 17.

[366] *House of Lords Hansard*, Vol. 137, Cols. 613 (31 October 1945).

[367] *Daily Telegraph* (27 June 2016).

368 A. V. Dicey, *Introduction To The Study Of The Law Of The Constitution*, 8th revised edn. (Liberty Fund Inc., 1982).

369 C. B. Macpherson, *Democratic Theory: Essays In Retrieval* (Clarendon Press, 1973), pp. 143-56, especially p. 146.

370 Milton Friedman, *Capitalism and Freedom* (University of Chicago Press, 1962), p. 14.

371 C. B. Macpherson, *Democratic Theory: Essays In Retrieval* (Clarendon Press, 1973), p. 146.

372 Adam Smith, *Wealth of Nations* (1776).

373 Karl Marx, *Capital, Volume 1* (Lawrence & Wishart, 1970), pp. 331-2.

374 Peter Linebaugh, *Stop Thief! The Commons, Enclosures, and Resistance* (Spectre, 2014), p. 226.

375 Tom Bingham, *The Rule Of Law* (Allen Lane, 2010), p. 78.

Chapter 13

376 Tim Shipman, *All Out War: The Full Story Of How Brexit Sank Britain's Political Class* (Collins, 2016), p. 50.

377 Tim Shipman, *All Out War: The Full Story Of How Brexit Sank Britain's Political Class* (Collins, 2016), p. 317.

[378] For evidence of the BBC's pro-EU bias, see the excellent series of publications by *News-Watch*. 'The BBC and Brexit: BBC Bias By Omission – Leave and the 'left' 2002-2017', *News-Watch* (2017), especially pp. 3, 4, 8, 14, 15, 21-2 and 30. 'The BBC and Brexit: Survey of Series 3 of BBC Radio 4's Brexit: A Guide for the Perplexed', *News-Watch* (19–23 February 2018), especially pp. 16 and 32. 'The BBC and Brexit: Survey of a day of special Radio 4 Programmes: 'Britain at the Crossroads', (29 March 2018), *News-Watch*, especially pp. 3 and 10-11. 'The BBC and Brexit: Survey of BBC Radio 4 'Brexit: A Love Story?', *News-Watch* (2018), especially pp. 15, 16 and 60-1. 'The BBC and Brexit: the BBC's coverage of Brexit and the EU', *News-Watch* (July 2020).

[379] Míriam Juan-Torres, Tim Dixon and Arisa Kimaram, *Britain's Choice: Common Ground and Division in 2020s Britain* (More in Common, 2020), p. 14.

[380] For example, Les K. Adler and Thomas G. Paterson, 'Red Fascism: The Merger of Nazi Germany and Soviet Russia In The American Image Of Totalitarianism, 1930's-1950's', *American Historical Review*, Vol. 75, No. 4, (1970), pp. 1046-64.

[381] *The Guardian* (14 April 2019).

[382] Richard Tuck, *The Left Case For Brexit: Reflections On The Current Crisis* (Polity Press, 2020), pp. 68-9.

[383] *The UK In A Changing Europe*, Brexit and Public Opinion (2019), p. 17.

[384] Sidney Webb and Beatrice Webb, *Industrial Democracy* (Longmans, Green, 1902), p. 8. 407

[385] 'Support for death penalty drops below 50% for the first time', *BBC News* (2015), <https://www.bbc.co.uk/news/uk-32061822>.

[386] *Spectator* (December 2018).

[387] Richard Bourke, *Empire and Revolution: The Political Life of Edmund Burke* (Princeton UP, 2015), p. 388.

[388] Wilson, Ors, R (On the Application Of) v The Prime Minister, <https://www.casemine.com/judgement/uk/5c7e03502c94e03890f0f6ce> (2019).

[389] Wilson v Prime Minister [2018] EWHC 3520 (Admin). See *"THE COURTS ARE NOT CONCERNED AT ALL WITH THE MERITS OF LEAVING OR REMAINING IN THE EU": JUDICIAL REVIEW OF DECISION TO TRIGGER ARTICLE 50 REJECTED* (2019) at <https://civilrightsuk.home.blog/2019/03/10/the-courts-are-not-concerned-at-all-with-the-merits-of-leaving-or-remaining-in-the-eu-judicial-review-of-decision-to-trigger-article-50-rejected/>.

[390] England and Wales Court of Appeal (Civil Division) Decisions, <https://www.bailii.org/ew/cases/EWCA/Civ/2019/304.html>, Paragraphs 37, 42, 43 and 49.

[391] Jim Waterson, *Saudi state part-owns Evening Standard and Independent, court told* <https://www.theguardian.com/media/2019/jul/23/evening-standard-and-independent-unable-to-rebut-concerns-over-saudi-ownership>, [accessed 27 October 2020].

[392] Alex Hern, 'Microtargeting, Bots and Hacking: Will Digital Meddling Really Swing This Election?', *The Guardian* (12 November 2019).

Chapter 14

[393] National Centre for Social Research, 'Chapter: Key Findings', in *British Social Attitudes 2017*, pp. 3 and 7.

[394] Akala, *Natives: Race and Class In The Ruins Of Empire* (Two Roads, 2019), p. 9.

[395] National Centre for Social Research, 'Chapter on the EU', *British Social Attitudes 2017*, p. 16.

[396] National Centre for Social Research, 'Chapter on the EU', *British Social Attitudes 2017*, p. 3.

[397] National Centre for Social Research, 'Chapter on the EU', *British Social Attitudes 2017*, p. 2.

[398] National Centre for Social Research, 'Chapter on the EU', *British Social Attitudes 2017*, p. 4.

399 Patrick Cockburn, *Brexit unleashed an English nationalism that has damaged the union with Scotland for good*, <https://www.independent.co.uk/voices/brexit-scottish-referendumenglish-nationalism-damaged-union-for-good-a7635796.html> (March 2017).

400 National Centre for Social Research, 'Chapter: Key Findings', *The British Social Attitudes Survey 2018*, p. 17.

401 Patrick Cockburn, Brexit unleashed an English nationalism that has damaged the union with Scotland for good, <https://www.independent.co.uk/voices/brexit-scottish-referendumenglish-nationalism-damaged-union-for-good-a7635796.html> (March 2017).

402 National Centre for Social Research, *The British Social Attitudes Survey of 2018*, p. 24.

403 National Centre for Social Research, 'EU Chapter', *The British Social Attitudes Survey 2018*, p. 7.

404 National Centre for Social Research, 'EU Chapter', *The British Social Attitudes Survey 2018*, p. 8.

405 National Centre for Social Research, 'EU Chapter', *The British Social Attitudes Survey 2018*, p. 13.

406 National Centre for Social Research, 'EU Chapter', *The British Social Attitudes Survey 2018*, p. 23.

410

Chapter 15

407 *Business for Britain* (Change or Go, 2015), p. 250.

408 Joseph Stiglitz, *Rewriting the Rules of the European Economy: An Agenda for Growth and Shared Prosperity* (W.W. Norton, 2020), pp. 23 and 24.

409 Dani Rodrik, *Straight Talk on Trade: Ideas for a Sane World Economy* (Princeton University Press, 2017), p. xi.

410 Richard Tuck, *The Left Case for Brexit: Reflections on the Current Crisis* (Polity Press, 2020), p. 16.

411 Richard Tuck, *The Left Case for Brexit: Reflections on the Current Crisis* (Polity Press, 2020), p. 50.

412 Joseph Stiglitz, *Rewriting the Rules of the European Economy: An Agenda for Growth and Shared Prosperity* (W.W. Norton, 2020), pp. 314-5.

413 Joseph Stiglitz, *Rewriting the Rules of the European Economy: An Agenda for Growth and Shared Prosperity* (W.W. Norton, 2020), pp. 288, 289 and 304.

414 Richard Aldous, *Reagan and Thatcher: The Difficult Relationship* (W. W. Norton & Company, 2013), p. 26.

415 Anatol Lieven, *Climate Change and the Nation-State: The Realist Case* (Allen Lane, 2020), p. 103.

[416] Dani Rodrik, 'Recasting Globalization's Narrative', *The Montréal Review*, (March 2012), <https://www.themontrealreview.com/2009/The-Globalization-Paradox-Democracy-and-the-Future-of-the-World-Economy-by-Dany-Rodrik.php>.

[417] Anatol Lieven, *Climate Change and the Nation-State: The Realist Case* (Allen Lane, 2020), pp. xxii-xxiii.

[418] Anatol Lieven, *Climate Change and the Nation-State: The Realist Case* (Allen Lane, 2020), p. 140.

Chapter 16

[419] National Centre for Social Research, *British Social Attitudes 2017 - 34*, Chapter on Immigration, p. 5.

[420] National Centre for Social Research, *British Social Attitudes 2017 - 34*, Key Findings Chapter, p. 9.

[421] British Social Attitudes 37, *How should Britain use its newly acquired sovereignty? Public attitudes towards post-Brexit public policy*, <https://www.bsa.natcen.ac.uk/media/39375/bsa37_post-brexit-public-policy.pdf>, p. 2.

[422] Max Fisher, 'A fascinating map of the world's most and least racially tolerant countries', *The Washington Post* (15 May 2013), <https://www.washingtonpost.com/news/worldviews/wp/2013/05/15/a-fascinating-map-of-the-worlds-most-and-least-racially-tolerant-countries/?noredirect=on>.

[423] Timur Moon, 'Britons are World's Most Racially Tolerant People', *International Business Times* (16 May 2013), <https://www.ibtimes.co.uk/world-values-survey-racial-tolerance-britain-468205>.

[424] *The Observer* (23 October 2016).

[425] Europeans remain welcoming to immigrants', *The Economist* (19 April 2018), <https://www.economist.com/graphic-detail/2018/04/19/europeans-remain-welcoming-to-immigrants>. See also Robert Ford, 'There's a remarkable change in the air – our hostility to migrants is on the retreat', *The Guardian* (19 May 2018), <https://www.theguardian.com/commentisfree/2018/may/19/is-brexit-britain-turning-liberal-as-hostility-to-migration-beings-to-collapse>.

[426] Special Eurobarometer 469, *Integration of immigrants in the European Union* (2018), pp. T2, T19.

[427] *Second European Union Minorities and Discrimination Survey: Being black in the EU* (2018), pp. 15 and 21.

[428] M. D. R. Evans and Jonathan Kelley, 'Prejudice against immigrants symptomizes a larger syndrome, is strongly diminished by socioeconomic development, and the UK is not an outlier: insights from the WVS, EVS, and EQLS Surveys,' in *Frontiers in Sociology* (2019), Volume 4, Number 12, pp. 1 and 14. Doi: 10.3389/fsoc.2019.00012.

[429] M. D. R. Evans and Jonathan Kelley, 'Prejudice against immigrants symptomizes a larger syndrome, is strongly diminished by socioeconomic development, and the UK is not an outlier: insights from the WVS, EVS, and EQLS surveys', in *Frontiers in Sociology*, 2019, Volume 4, Number 12, pp. 18-19. Doi: 10.3389/fsoc.2019.00012.

[430] Roger Eatwell and Matthew Goodwin, *National Populism: The Revolt Against Liberal Democracy* (Pelican, 2018), p. 162.

[431] Vince Cable, 'Why it's time to end EU free movement', *New Statesman* (4 January 2017).

[432] David Rollison, *A Commonwealth of the People: Popular Politics and England's Long Social Revolution, 1066-1649* (Cambridge University Press, 2010), p. 39.

[433] David Rollison, *A Commonwealth of the People: Popular Politics and England's Long Social Revolution, 1066-1649* (Cambridge University Press, 2010), pp. 38-9.

[434] David Rollison, *A Commonwealth of the People: Popular Politics and England's Long Social Revolution, 1066-1649* (Cambridge University Press, 2010), p. 34.

[435] Anatol Lieven, *Climate Change and The Nation-State: The Realist Case* (Allen Lane, 2020), both p. 141.

[436] Devesh Kapur and John McHale, Give Us Your Best and Brightest: The Global Hunt for Talent and Its Impact on the Developing World (Center for Global Development, 2005), p. 38.

[437] Richard Tuck, *The Left Case for Brexit: Reflections on the Current Crisis* (Polity Press, 2020), p. 30.

[438] Ed. by Amrita Narlinkar, Martin Daunton and Robert M. Stern, *The Oxford handbook on the World Trade Organization* (Oxford UP, 2012), p. 47.

[439] Anatol Lieven, *Climate Change and The Nation-State: The Realist Case* (Allen Lane, 2020), p. 53.

[440] Stephen Nickell and Jumana Saleheen, *The impact of immigration on occupational wages: evidence from Britain* (Bank of England, December 2015) <https://www.bankofengland.co.uk/-/media/boe/files/working-paper/2015/the-impact-of-immigration-on-occupational-wages-evidence-from-britain.pdf>.

[441] Anatol Lieven, *Climate Change and The Nation-State: The Realist Case* (Allen Lane, 2020), p. 40.

[442] Dan Bloom, 'Head of the NHS tears into Leave campaigners saying Brexit will be "very dangerous" for patients', *The Mirror* (22 May 2016) <https://www.mirror.co.uk/news/uk-news/head-nhs-tears-leave-campaigners-8024252>.

[443] Roger Bootle, *Making a Success of Brexit and Reforming the EU: The Brexit edition of The Trouble with Europe* (Nicholas Brealey Publishing, 2017), pp. 160-1.

[444] *5 Million Migrants Expected to be Deported From UK Post – Brexit*, <https://www.thestudentroom.co.uk/showthread.php?t=6285542>, [accessed 13/5/21].

[445] 'Continue to live in the UK if you're an EU, EEA or Swiss citizen', <https://www.gov.uk/staying-uk-eu-citizen>.

[446] Erasmus+, *The transition period* (18 January 2021), <https://www.erasmusplus.org.uk/the-transition-period>.

[447] Joseph Stiglitz, *Rewriting the Rules of the European Economy: An Agenda for Growth and Shared Prosperity* (W.W. Norton, 2020), p. 225.

[448] Joseph Stiglitz, *Rewriting the Rules of the European Economy: An Agenda for Growth and Shared Prosperity* (W.W. Norton, 2020), p. 342.

[449] Devesh Kapur and John McHale, *Give Us Your Best and Brightest: The Global Hunt for Talent and Its Impact on the Developing World* (Center for Global Development, 2005), p. 183.

[450] Devesh Kapur and John McHale, *Give Us Your Best and Brightest: The Global Hunt for Talent and Its Impact on the Developing World* (Center for Global Development, 2005), p. 8.

[451] N. U. Haque and S. J. Kim, 'Human Capital Flight: Impact of Migration on Income and Growth', *IMF Staff Papers* 42, No. 3, pp. 577-607.

[452] Devesh Kapur and John McHale, *Give Us Your Best and Brightest: The Global Hunt for Talent and Its Impact on the Developing World* (Center for Global Development, 2005), p. 207.

[453] Howard Catton, 'Fair pay: the only option that helps us keep the nurses we have', *Nursing Standard* (15 September 2020) <https://rcni.com/nursing-standard/opinion/comment/fair-pay-only-option-helps-us-keep-nurses-we-have-165431>.

Chapter 17

[454] United Nations, *General Assembly* (28 September 2019) <http://undocs.org/en/A/74/PV.11>.

[455] Helen Yaffe, *We Are Cuba! How a Revolutionary People Have Survived in a Post-Soviet World* (Yale UP, 2019), p. 99.

[456] Naomi Klein, *On Fire: The Burning Case for a Green New Deal* (W.F. Howes, 2019), pp. 158-9.

[457] Naomi Klein, *On Fire: The Burning Case for a Green New Deal* (W.F. Howes, 2019), p. 82.

458 Anatol Lieven, *Climate Change and The Nation-State: The Realist Case* (Allen Lane, 2020), p. 111.

459 Míriam Juan-Torres, Tim Dixon, and Arisa Kimaram, *Britain's Choice: Common Ground and Division in 2020s Britain* (More in Common, 2020), p. 22.

460 Anatol Lieven, *Climate Change and The Nation-State: The Realist Case* (Allen Lane, 2020), p. 143.

461 Anatol Lieven, *Climate Change and The Nation-State: The Realist Case* (Allen Lane, 2020), p. 18.

462 Bill McKibben, *Deep Economy* (Henry Holt, 2007), p. 73. Also World Wildlife Fund, Living Planet Report 2006, <http://awsassets.panda.org/downloads/living_planet_repo rt.pdf>, p. 19, [accessed 13/5/21].

463 Ben Pontin, *The Environmental Case for Brexit: A Socio-legal Perspective* (Hart Publishing, 2020), p. 6.

464 Ben Pontin, *The Environmental Case for Brexit: A Socio-legal Perspective* (Hart Publishing, 2020), p. 3.

465 Ben Pontin, *The Environmental Case for Brexit: A Socio-legal Perspective* (Hart Publishing, 2020), p. 13.

466 Ben Pontin, *The Environmental Case for Brexit: A Socio-legal Perspective* (Hart Publishing, 2020), p. 8.

467 Ben Pontin, *The Environmental Case for Brexit: A Socio-legal Perspective* (Hart Publishing, 2020), p. 8.

[468] Ben Pontin, *The Environmental Case for Brexit: A Socio-legal Perspective* (Hart Publishing, 2020), pp. 10 and 131.

[469] JNCC, *Ramsar Convention*, <https://jncc.gov.uk/our-work/ramsar-convention/>.

[470] Ben Pontin, *The Environmental Case for Brexit: A Socio-legal Perspective* (Hart Publishing, 2020), p. 135.

[471] Ben Pontin, *The Environmental Case for Brexit: A Socio-legal Perspective* (Hart Publishing, 2020), p. 10.

[472] Ben Pontin, *The Environmental Case for Brexit: A Socio-legal Perspective* (Hart Publishing, 2020), p. 11.

[473] Extinction Rebellion, *Our Demands*, <https://rebellion.earth/the-truth/demands/>.

[474] Green Party, *Policy - Industry and Jobs* (June 2019) <https://policy.greenparty.org.uk/in.html>.

[475] *News Nation*, 'Auto CO2 emissions 40% higher than claimed: report', <https://english.newsnationtv.com/auto/cars/auto-co2-emissions-40-higher-than-claimed-report-92395.html>.

[476] George Monbiot, 'The shocking waste of cash even leavers won't condemn', *The Guardian* (June 2016) <https://www.theguardian.com/commentisfree/2016/jun/21/waste-cash-leavers-in-out-land-subsidie>.

419

[477] George Monbiot, 'The one good thing about Brexit? Leaving the EU's disgraceful farming system', *The Guardian* (October 2018) <https://www.theguardian.com/commentisfree/2018/oct/10/brexit-leaving-eu-farming-agriculture>.

[478] Angling Trust & Fish Legal et al., *BREXIT, FISHERIES AND THE WATER ENVIRONMENT* (October 2016) <https://www.theriverstrust.org/media/2016/10/Joint_Brexit_Paper_Final-2.pdf>.

[479] World Health Organisation, *Food Safety - Antimicrobial resistance in the food chain* (November 2017) <https://www.who.int/foodsafety/areas_work/antimicrobial-resistance/amrfoodchain/en/>.

[480] Bird Life International, *The Vanishing: Europe's farmland birds* (February 2017) <https://www.birdlife.org/europe-and-central-asia/news/vanishing-europe's-farmland-birds>.

[481] *New York Times* (3 November 2019).

[482] *The Times*, 'Pollution: no river in England is safe for swimming' (2 August 2019) <https://www.thetimes.co.uk/article/pollution-no-river-in-england-is-safe-for-swimming-q8thdx678>.

[483] Pushker Kharecha and James E. Hansen, 'Prevented mortality and greenhouse gas emissions from historical and projected nuclear power', *Environmental Science and Technology* (2013), Volume 47, No. 9, pp. 4889-95.

[484] Robert Spencer, 'Can an English suit be made in Cambodia?', *BBC News*, (February 2016), <https://www.bbc.co.uk/news/magazine-35521559>.

[485] Human Rights Watch, *Cambodia: Labor Laws Fail to Protect Garment Workers*, (March 2015), <https://www.hrw.org/news/2015/03/11/cambodia-labor-laws-fail-protect-garment-workers>.

[486] Labour Behind The Label, *A Living Wage is a Human Right* <https://labourbehindthelabel.net/campaigns/living-wage/>.

[487] Anatol Lieven, *Climate Change and The Nation-State: The Realist Case* (Allen Lane, 2020), p. 139.

Chapter 18

[488] William Seton, *The Interest of Scotland in Three Essays* (London, 1700).

[489] *Scotland's Future: Your Guide to an Independent Scotland*, pp. i, viii and 556.

Chapter 19

[490] Ray Bassett, *Ireland and the EU Post Brexit* (Grangeland Ventures Ltd, 2020), p. 102.

[491] Stéphane Dion, *Straight Talk: Speeches and Writings on Canadian Unity* (McGill-Queen's University Press, 1999), p. 187.

[492] Stéphane Dion, *Straight Talk: Speeches and Writings on Canadian Unity* (McGill-Queen's University Press, 1999), p. 209.

[493] Stéphane Dion, *Straight Talk: Speeches and Writings on Canadian Unity* (McGill-Queen's University Press, 1999), p. 23.
[494] Ed. by James Crawford, *Brownlie's Principles of Public International Law*, 9th edn, (Oxford University Press, 2019), p. 131.

[495] Voices From Spain, *Statement On The Lack Of Foundation On International Law Of The Independence Referendum That Has Been Convened In Catalonia*, <https://voicesfromspain.com/2017/09/27/statement-on-the-lack-of-foundation-on-international-law-of-the-independence-referendum-been-convened-in-catalonia/>, (19 September 2017).

[496] James Crawford, *State Practice and International Law in Relation to Unilateral Secession* (19 February 1997), citing Declaration on Principles of International Law concerning Friendly Relations and Cooperation among States in accordance with the Charter of the United Nations, General Assembly Resolution 2625 (XXV) (24 October 1970), 'The principle of equal rights and self-determination of peoples', para. 7. <https://is.muni.cz/el/1422/jaro2006/MP803Z/um/1393966/INTERNATIONAL_LAW_AND_UNILATERAL_SECESSION.pdf#:~:text=There%20is%20only%20one%20clear%20example%20of%20successful,the%20United%20Nations%20against%20the%20declared%20wishes%20of>, p. 17.

[497] United Nations World Conference on Human Rights, *Vienna Declaration and Programme of Action* (25 June 1993), 32 ILM 1661, p. 1665.

[498] James Crawford, *State Practice and International Law in Relation to Unilateral Secession* (19 February 1997), <https://is.muni.cz/el/1422/jaro2006/MP803Z/um/1393966/INTERNATIONAL_LAW_AND_UNILATERAL_SECESSION.pdf#:~:text=There%20is%20only%20one%20clear%20example%20of%20successful,the%20United%20Nations%20against%20the%20declared%20wishes%20of>, p. 18.

[499] Ed. by James Crawford, *Brownlie's Principles of Public International Law*, 9th edn, (Oxford University Press, 2019), p. 133.

[500] Scottish Government, *Government Expenditure and Revenue Scotland (GERS) 2019-2020*, https://www.gov.scot/publications/government-expenditure-revenue-scotland-gers-2019-20/pages/6/>, (26 August 2020).

[501] John Curtice and Ian Montagu, *Is Brexit fuelling support for independence?* <https://whatscotlandthinks.org/wp-content/uploads/2020/11/SSA-2019-Scotland-paper-v5.pdf#:~:text=The%20latest%20Scottish%20Social%20Attitudes%20%28SSA%29%20survey%20was,general%20election%20that%20was%20called%20for%20December%2012.>, Table 6, p. 13.

[502] Hanwei Huang, Thomas Sampson and Patrick Schneider, *Disunited Kingdom? Brexit, trade and Scottish Independence,*

'Centre for Economic Performance', (3 February 2021), <https://cep.lse.ac.uk/pubs/download/brexit17.pdf>, p. 3.

503 Hanwei Huang, Thomas Sampson, and Patrick Schneider, *Disunited Kingdom? Brexit, trade and Scottish independence*, 'Centre for Economic Performance', (3 February 2021), <https://cep.lse.ac.uk/pubs/download/brexit17.pdf>, p. 4.

504 Hanwei Huang, Thomas Sampson, and Patrick Schneider, *Disunited Kingdom? Brexit, trade and Scottish independence*, 'Centre for Economic Performance, (3 February 2021), <https://cep.lse.ac.uk/pubs/download/brexit17.pdf>, p. 18.

505 Hamish Penman, *BiFab collapse into administration exposes 'myth of Scotland's renewables revolution'*, <https://www.energyvoice.com/renewables-energy-transition/283594/bifab-administration-unite-gmb/>, (03/12/2020).

506 Communist Party of Britain Marxist-Leninist, *SNP ferries fiasco*, <https://cpbml.org.uk/news/snp-ferries-fiasco>, (January/February 2021).

507 John McLaren, *An Index of Social and Economic Well-being (ISEW) across 32 OECD countries - 2006 to 2018 Scottish Trends*, 'Scottish Trends', <http://scottishtrends.co.uk/wp-content/uploads/2020/01/Index-of-Well-Being-Full-Report-2020-full.pdf>, (January 2020).

[508] John McLaren, An Index of Social and Economic Well-being (ISEW) across 32 OECD countries - 2006 to 2018 Scottish Trends, 'Scottish Trends', <http://scottishtrends.co.uk/wp-content/uploads/2020/01/Index-of-Well-Being-Full-Report-2020-full.pdf>, (January 2020), p. 2.

[509] Simon Johnson, *Jeremy Corbyn pledges to 'open discussions' with Nicola Sturgeon over second independence referendum*, 'The Telegraph', <https://www.telegraph.co.uk/news/2017/05/29/jeremy-corbyn-pledges-open-discussions-nicola-sturgeon-second/>, (May 2017).

[510] John Lloyd, *Should Auld Acquaintance Be Forgot: The Great Mistake of Scottish Independence*, (Polity Press, 2020), p. 21.

[511] John Lloyd, *Should Auld Acquaintance Be Forgot: The Great Mistake of Scottish Independence*, (Polity Press, 2020), pp. 35-6.

[512] John Lloyd, *Should Auld Acquaintance Be Forgot: The Great Mistake of Scottish Independence*, (Polity Press, 2020), pp. 52 and 53.

[513] Nancy McLean, *Democracy in Chains: The Deep History of the Radical Right's Stealth Plan for America*, (Viking, 2017), p. 294.

[514] National Centre for Social Research, *The British Social Attitudes survey of 2018*, p. 23.

515 *YouGov / Yes Cymru Survey Results,*
<https://docs.cdn.yougov.com/9ibhldbfuq/YesCymru_Resu
lts_200618_EnglandPoll_IndependenceW.pdf>.

516 John Curtice and Rachel Ormston, *Is Scotland more left-wing than England?,* 'Scottish Social Attitudes', <https://www.ssa.natcen.ac.uk/read-the-reports/scottish-social-attitudes-2011/scotland-more-left-wing-than-england.aspx> (2011).

517 ScotCen, *Is Scotland more left-wing than England?,* <https://www.scotcen.org.uk/media/176048/2011-is-scotland-more-left-wing-than-england.pdf>, (December 2011).

518 Ian Montagu, *What do Scots think about Brexit and the EU?,* LSE, (3 February 2018).

519 John Curtice and Ian Montagu, *Is Brexit fuelling support for independence?,* ScotCen, <https://whatscotlandthinks.org/wp-content/uploads/2020/11/SSA-2019-Scotland-paper-v5.pdf#:~:text=The%20latest%20Scottish%20Social%20Attitud es%20%28SSA%29%20survey%20was,general%20election%20t hat%20was%20called%20for%20December%2012.>, p. 9.

520 John Curtice and Ian Montagu, *Is Brexit fuelling support for independence?,* ScotCen, <https://whatscotlandthinks.org/wp-content/uploads/2020/11/SSA-2019-Scotland-paper-v5.pdf#:~:text=The%20latest%20Scottish%20Social%20Attitud es%20%28SSA%29%20survey%20was,general%20election%20t hat%20was%20called%20for%20December%2012.>, Table 3, p. 10.

[521] John Lloyd, *Should Auld Acquaintance Be Forgot: The Great Mistake of Scottish Independence*, (Polity Press, 2020), pp. 198-9.

Chapter 20

[522] Peter Hacker's magnificent Human Nature tetralogy: *Human Nature: The Categorial Framework* (Wiley-Blackwell, 2010), *The Intellectual Powers: A Study of Human Nature* (Wiley-Blackwell, 2013), *The Passions: A Study of Human Nature* (Wiley-Blackwell, 2018) and *The Moral Powers: A Study of Human Nature* (Wiley-Blackwell, 2021). Also *Language, Sense and Nonsense: A Critical Investigation Into Modern Theories of Language*, written with Gordon Baker (Blackwell, 1984) and *Philosophical Foundations of Neuroscience*, written with Maxwell Bennett (Wiley-Blackwell, 2003).

[523] Alexander Pope, *An essay on Man*, 'Epistle 1'.

[524] Ryszard Kapuscinski, *Travels with Herodotus* (Knopf, 2007), p. 262.

[525] Will Podmore, *Reg Birch: Engineer, Trade Unionist, Communist* (Bellman Books, 2004), pp. 75-7, 89, 91 and 213.

[526] *Communist* (14 October 1920).

[527] William Shakespeare, *Othello*, Act 1, scene 1, lines 26-7.

[528] William Shakespeare, *Othello*, Act 3, scene 4, line 96.

[529] William Shakespeare, *Othello*, Act 4, scene 2, lines 183-4.

530 Utpal M. Dholakia, *What Is Cancel Culture?*, < https://www.psychologytoday.com/us/blog/the-science-behind-behavior/202007/what-is-cancel-culture>, [Posted Jul 27, 2020].

531 Cambridge Dictionary, <https://dictionary.cambridge.org/dictionary/english/tolerance>.

532 Ed. by J. B. Sykes, *The Pocket Oxford Dictionary of Current English*, 6th edn, (Clarendon Press, 1978), p. 767.

533 Ed. By J. B. Sykes, *The Pocket Oxford Dictionary of Current English*, 6th edn, (Clarendon Press, 1978), p. 959.

534 Communist Party of Britain Marxist-Leninist, *United we stand*, (July/August 2020), <https://www.cpbml.org.uk/news/unity>.

535 Kenneth Morgan, *Rebirth of a Nation: A History of Modern Wales, 1880-1980* (OUP, 1987), p. 71.

536 Gwydion M. Williams, *Orwell on Spain and Britain*, <https://gwydionwilliams.com/44-fascism-and-world-war-2/45-1-more-on-fascism-the-world-wars/491-2/>.

537 Michael H. Hunt, 'Chapter 13 Nationalism as an umbrella ideology', p. 220, in *Explaining the History of American Foreign Relations*, ed. by Frank Costigliola and Michael J. Hogan, 3rd edn, (Cambridge University Press, 2016), pp. 217-31.

[538] David Rollison, *A Commonwealth of the People: Popular Politics and England's Long Social Revolution, 1066-1649*, (Cambridge University Press, 2010), p. 307.

Chapter 21

[539] John Mills, *Manufacturing a Recovery from Coronavirus*, (The John Mills Institute for Prosperity, 2020), p. 16.

[540] John Mills, *Manufacturing a Recovery from Coronavirus*, (The John Mills Institute for Prosperity, 2020), p. 33.

[541] 'The future of money', *Workers*, (November/December 2020), <http://www.cpbml.org.uk/news/future-money>.

[542] Bank of England, *Discussion Paper - Central Bank Digital Currency: Opportunities, challenges and design*, (March 2020), <https://www.bankofengland.co.uk/-/media/boe/files/paper/2020/central-bank-digital-currency-opportunities-challenges-and-design.pdf>.

[543] 'Jobs and apprenticeships as HS2 begins full-scale construction', *Workers*, (1 December 2020), <http://www.cpbml.org.uk/news/jobs-and-apprenticeships-hs2-begins-full-scale-construction>.

[544] 'HS2: Two projects in one', *Workers*, (20 September 2020), <http://www.cpbml.org.uk/news/hs2-two-projects-one>.

[545] Richard Tuck, *The Left Case for Brexit: Reflections on the Current Crisis*, (Polity Press, 2020), pp. 18-9.

Chapter 22

[546] *HESELTINE: UK "ECONOMY IS DOING SIGNIFICANTLY BETTER THAN YOU MIGHT HOPE"*, (20 May 2019), <https://order-order.com/2019/05/20/heseltine-uk-economy-significantly-better-might-hope/>.

[547] Boris Johnson, *Lend Me Your Ears: The Essential Boris Johnson*, (HarperCollins, 2002), pp. 355-6.

[548] Tom Bower, *Boris Johnson: The Gambler*, (W. H. Allen, 2020), p. 135.

[549] 'Denmark has got it wrong. Yes, the burka is oppressive and ridiculous – but that's still no reason to ban it', *Daily Telegraph*, (5 August 2018).

[550] 'If Blair's so good at running the Congo, let him stay there', *Daily Telegraph*, (10 January 2002).

[551] Kenan Malik, 'Johnson's cabinet may be diverse but it doesn't reflect modern Britain', *The Guardian*, (28 July 2019).

[552] The Full Brexit, *Analysis No. 45 - How Boris Johnson broke the Brexit interregnum*, (20 December 2019), <https://www.thefullbrexit.com/johnson-brexit-interregnum>.

[553] 'Brexit: French officials dismiss UK fears of Calais 'go-slow'', *BBC News*, (October 2018), <https://www.bbc.co.uk/news/uk-politics-45990243>.

Chapter 23

[554] European Parliament, *Smart Border 2.0 Avoiding a hard border on the island of Ireland for Customs control and the free movement of persons*,
<https://www.europarl.europa.eu/RegData/etudes/STUD/2017/596828/IPOL_STU(2017)596828_EN.pdf>.

[555] Colin Turpin and Adam Tomkins, *British Government and the Constitution*, 7th edn, (Cambridge University Press, 2012), p. 261.

[556] Míriam Juan-Torres, Tim Dixon, and Arisa Kimaram, *Britain's Choice: Common Ground and Division in 2020s Britain*, (More in Common, 2020), p. 18.

[557] Míriam Juan-Torres, Tim Dixon, and Arisa Kimaram, *Britain's Choice: Common Ground and Division in 2020s Britain*, (More in Common, 2020), p. 172.

[558] Míriam Juan-Torres, Tim Dixon, and Arisa Kimaram, *Britain's Choice: Common Ground and Division in 2020s Britain*, (More in Common, 2020), p. 270.

[559] The fight for a future, *Workers*, (January/February 2021), <https://www.cpbml.org.uk/news/fight-future>.

[560] Roger Eatwell and Matthew Goodwin, *National Populism: The Revolt Against Liberal Democracy*, (Pelican, 2018), pp. xi-xii.

[561] Roger Eatwell and Matthew Goodwin, *National Populism: The Revolt Against Liberal Democracy*, (Pelican, 2018), p. 39.

562 Raymond Williams, *Culture and Society, 1780-1950*, (Chatto & Windus 1958), (Vintage, 2017), pp. 391-2, 393-4 and 399.

563 Stefan Collini, *Common Writing: Essays on Literary Culture and Public Debate*, (OUP, 2018), p. 122.

Index

Kriegel, Blandine, 2
Krugman, Paul, 123
Kueh, Y. Y., 95
Kyoto Protocol 1997, 253, 264

455

Right-wing extremism, 232
Roberts, Andrew, 71
Roberts, Geoffrey, 54
Robertson, George, 270
Robinson, Tommy, 228, 229
Rodrik, Dani, 123-4, 218, 222
Rogan, Martin, 276
Rollison, David, 3
Rolls Royce, 263
Roman Catholic Church, 6
Roman empire, 1, 7-8
Roman law, 2-3
Romania, 30, 73, 82, 124, 263
Rome, Treaties of 1957, 114, 175
Roosevelt, President Franklin D., 50, 66
Rousseau, Jean-Jacques, 13
Royal Bank of Scotland, 291
Royal College of Nursing, 240
Royal Navy, 21-2, 268, 269
Rule of law, 1, 3, 13, 22, 178, 183, 238, 285, 363
Rumsfeld, Donald, 136-2
Rusk, Dean, 99
Russia, 11, 25-30, 33, 34, 37-8, 51, 53-4, 56, 61, 62, 66-71, 81, 82,
86, 92, 88, 94, 182, 202, 205, 206-8, 216, 221-2, 323
Russian revolution 1917, 11, 25-30, 202
Russia Today, 206

Salazar, António, 31
Salisbury Convention, 361
Salmond, Alex, 206, 271-2, 274, 277-8, 284-5, 299
Salud International, 145-6, 149
San Domingo, 19

Bibliography

Abrams, A. B., *Immovable Object: North Korea's 70 Years at War with American Power*, (Clarity Press, 2020).

Abrams, A. B., *Power and Primacy: A History of Western Intervention in the Asia-Pacific*, (Peter Lang, 2019).

Abrams, A. B., *World War in Syria: Global Conflict on Middle Eastern Battlefields*, (Clarity Press, 2021).

Anon, *The Irving Judgement: David Irving v. Penguin Books and Professor Deborah Lipstadt*, (Penguin Books, 2000).

Baker, Gordon, and Hacker, Peter, *Language, Sense and Nonsense: A Critical Investigation Into Modern Theories of Language*, (Blackwell, 1984).

Bassett, Ray, *Ireland and the EU Post Brexit*, (Grangeland Ventures Ltd, 2020).

Bennett, Maxwell, and Hacker, Peter, *Philosophical Foundations of Neuroscience*, (Wiley-Blackwell, 2003).

Brownlie, Ian, *International Law and the Use of Force by States*, (Oxford: Clarendon Press, 1963).

Buttar, Prit, *On a Knife's Edge: The Ukraine, November 1942 – March 1943*, (Osprey Publishing, 2019).

Centre for Brexit Policy, *Replacing the Withdrawal Agreement: How to ensure the UK takes back control on exiting the transition period*, (2020).

Clarke, Harold D., Goodwin, Matthew, and Whiteley, Paul, *Brexit: Why Britain Voted to Leave the European Union*, (Cambridge University Press, 2017).

Cumings, Bruce, *The Origins of the Korean War, Vol. II: The Roaring of the Cataract 1947-1950*, (Princeton University Press, 1990).

Dion, Stéphane, *Straight Talk: Speeches and Writings on Canadian Unity*, (McGill-Queen's University Press, 1999).

Eatwell, Roger and Goodwin, Matthew, *National Populism: The Revolt Against Liberal Democracy*, (Pelican, 2018).

Fritz, Stephen G., *Ostkrieg: Hitler's War of Extermination in the East*, (University Press of Kentucky, 2011).

Furr, Grover, *Blood Lies: The Evidence that Every Accusation against Joseph Stalin and the Soviet Union in Timothy Snyder's "Bloodlands is false"*, (Red Star Publishers, 2014).

Furr, Grover, *Khrushchev Lied: The Evidence That Every 'Revelation' of Stalin's (and Beria's) 'Crimes' in Nikita Khrushchev's Infamous 'Secret Speech' to the 20th Party Congress of the Communist Party of the Soviet Union on February 25, 1956, is Provably False*, (Erythrós Press & Media, 2011.)

Furr, Grover, *Leon Trotsky's Collaboration with Germany and Japan:* Trotsky's Conspiracies of the 1930s, Volume Two, (Erythros Press & Media, 2017).

Furr, Grover, *The Mystery of the Katyn Massacre: The Evidence, The Solution,* (Erythros Press and Media, 2018).

Furr, Grover, *New Evidence of Trotsky's Conspiracy,* (Erythros Press and Media, 2020).

Furr, Grover, *Stalin: Waiting For ... The Truth! Exposing the Falsehoods in Stephen Kotkin's Stalin: Waiting for Hitler, 1929-1941,* (Red Star Publishers, 2019).

Furr, Grover, *Trotsky's 'Amalgams': Trotsky's Lies, the Moscow Trials as Evidence, the Dewey Commission. Trotsky's conspiracies of the 1930s, Volume One,* (Erythros Press & Media, 2015).

Groves, Sally, and Merritt, Vernon, *Trico: A Victory to Remember. The 1976 Equal Pay Strike at Trico Folberth, Brentford,* (Lawrence & Wishart, 2018).

Hacker, Peter, *Human Nature: The Categorial Framework,* (Wiley-Blackwell, 2010.

Hacker, Peter, *Intellectual Entertainments: Eight Dialogues on Mind, Consciousness and Thought,* (Anthem Press, 2020).

Hacker, Peter, *The Intellectual Powers: A Study of Human Nature,* (Wiley-Blackwell, 2013).

Hacker, Peter, *The Moral Powers: A Study of Human Nature,* (Wiley-Blackwell, 2021).

Hacker, Peter, *The Passions: A Study of Human Nature*, (Wiley-Blackwell, 2018).

Halligan, Liam and Lyons, Gerard, *Clean Brexit: how to make a success of leaving the European Union*, (Biteback, 2017).

Handley, Seb, *Brexit: How the Nobodies Beat the Somebodies*, (i2i Publishing, 2017).

Hanebrink, Paul, *A Specter Haunting Europe: The Myth of Judeo-Bolshevism*, (Belknap Press, 2020).

Hehn, Paul N., *A Low Dishonest Decade: The Great Powers, Eastern Europe, and the Economic Origins of World War Two, 1930-1941*, (New York: Continuum, 2002).

Jaffa, Harry, *Crisis of the House Divided: An Interpretation of the Issues in the Lincoln-Douglas debates*, (Doubleday, 1959).

Kassimeris, George, editor, *The Barbarisation of Warfare*, (Hurst & Company, 2006).

Keoghan, Frank, O'Donnell, Ruan, and Quinn, Michael, editors, *A Festschrift for Anthony Coughlan: Essays on Sovereignty and Democracy*, (Iontas Press, 2018).

Kulikoff, Allan, *Abraham Lincoln and Karl Marx in Dialogue*, (Oxford University Press, 2018).

Landis, Arthur, *Spain! The Unfinished Revolution*, (Camelot Publishing Company, New York, 1972).

Lieven, Anatol, *Climate Change and the Nation-State: the Realist Case*, (Allen Lane, 2020).

Lloyd, John, *Should Auld Acquaintance Be Forgot: The Great Mistake of Scottish Independence*, (Polity Press, 2020).

Macpherson, C. B., *Democratic Theory: Essays in Retrieval*, (Clarendon Press, 1973).

Mathews, John, *Ford Strike: The Workers' Story*, (Panther Books, 1972).

Meredeen, Sander, *Managing Industrial Conflict: Seven Major Disputes*, (Hutchinson, 1988).

Mills, John, *Manufacturing a recovery from Coronavirus*, (The John Mills Institute for Prosperity, 2020).

Moradiellos, Enrique, *Neutralidad benévola: el Gobierno británico y la insurrección militar española de 1936,* (Pentalfa, 1990).

Moradiellos, Enrique, *La perfidia de Albión: El Gobierno británico y la guerra civil española, Siglo XXI de España Editores*, (S. A., 1996).

National Centre for Social Research, *The British Social Attitudes survey 2017 – 34.*

National Centre for Social Research, *The British Social Attitudes survey 2018 – 35.*

National Centre for Social Research, *The British Social Attitudes survey 2019 - 36.*

Pincus, Steve, *1688: The First Modern Revolution*, (Yale University Press, 2009).

Podmore, Will, *Brexit: The Road to Freedom*, (i2i Publishing, 2018).

Podmore, Will, *British Foreign Policy Since 1870*, (XLibris, 2008).

Podmore, Will, *The European Union – Bad for Britain – A Trade Union View*, (Bread Books, 2005).

Podmore, Will, *Reg Birch: Engineer, Trade Unionist, Communist*, (Bellman Books, 2004).

Podmore, Will, *The War Against the Working Class*, (XLibris, 2015).

Pontin, Ben, *The Environmental Case for Brexit: A Socio-legal Perspective*, (Hart Publishing, 2020).

Rees, Sian, *Sweet Water and Bitter: The Ships That Stopped the Slave Trade*, (Vintage Books, 2010).

Rodrik, Dani, *Straight Talk on Trade: Ideas for a Sane World Economy*, (Princeton University Press, 2017).

Shipman, Tim, *All Out War: The Full Story of How Brexit Sank Britain's Political Class*, (Collins, 2016).

Stiglitz, Joseph, *Rewriting the Rules of the European Economy: An Agenda for Growth and Shared Prosperity*, (W.W. Norton, 2020).

Taylor, Frederick, *Dresden 13 February 1945*, (Bloomsbury, 2005).

Titmuss, Richard, *The Gift Relationship: From Human Blood to Social Policy*, (The New Press, 1997).

Tombs, Robert, *The English and Their history*, (Penguin, 2015).

Tuck, Richard, *The Left Case for Brexit: Reflections on the Current Crisis*, (Polity Press, 2020).

Tuck, Richard, *The Sleeping Sovereign: The Invention of Modern Democracy*, (Cambridge University Press, 2016).

Tyreman, Stephen, 'Evidence, Alternative Facts and Narrative: A Personal Reflection on Person-Centred Care and The Role of Stories in Healthcare', *International Journal of Osteopathic Medicine*, Vol. 28, pp. 1-3, (2018).

Van Ree, Erik, *The Political Thought of Joseph Stalin: A Study in Twentieth Century Revolutionary Patriotism*, (Routledge, 2002).

Williams, Raymond, *Culture and Society, 1780-1950*, (Chatto & Windus 1958; Vintage, 2017).

Wilson, Ben, *Empire of the Deep: The Rise and Fall of The British Navy*, (Weidenfeld & Nicolson, 2014).

Wolf, Lucien, *The Myth of the Jewish Menace in World Affairs; or, the Truth About the Forged Protocols of the Elders of Zion*, (Macmillan, 1921; Hardpress, 2019).